Names We Call Home

Names We Call Home:

AUTOBIOGRAPHY ON RACIAL IDENTITY

EDITED BY BECKY THOMPSON AND SANGEETA TYAGI

Routledge

New York • London

Published in 1996 by

Routledge
29 West 35th Street
New York, NY 10001-2299

Published in Great Britain by

Routledge
11 New Fetter Lane
London EC4P 4EE

Angela Davis's essay first appeared in the anthology *Picturing Us: African American Identity in Photography* (New York: The New Press, 1994), edited by Deborah Willie. June Jordan's essay was adapted from "Beyond Gender, Race, and Class," a speech delivered by the author at the Eighth Annual Gender Studies Symposium, "Visions and Voices for Change," at Lewis and Clark College, Portland, Oregon, in April 1989. It was published in *The Progressive*, June 1989 and in June Jordan, 1992. *Technical Difficulties: African-American Notes on the State of the Union*. New York: Pantheon. pp. 161–68. Cherríe Moraga's essay originally appeared in *The Last Generation* by Cherríe Moraga (Boston: South End Press, 1993), and is reprinted here courtesy of the author and publisher.

Library of Congress Cataloging-in-Publication Data

Names we call home : autobiography on racial identity / edited by
   Becky Thompson and Sangeeta Tyagi.
            p.   cm.
         Includes bibliographical references and index.
         ISBN 0-415-91161-3 (hb).— ISBN 0-415-91162-1 (pbk.)
         1. Ethnicity—United States. 2. Group identity—United States.
   3. United States—Race relations. I. Thompson, Becky W.
   II. Tyagi, Sangeeta.
   E184.A1N285 1995
   305.8' 00973—dc20

Contents

Acknowledgments

At a time in United States racial history that threatens to repeat the "nadir" at the turn of the 20th century, this book is meant as a political salvo, a psychic antidote, and a communal "laying on of hands," as the authors seek to claim racial identities that are not based on conquest or defacement. As this book goes to press, we give thanks first and foremost to the authors whose stories have dazzled and sustained us. As the activist writer Margaret Randall aptly notes, "as happens with all authentic projects, the material uncovered dictates the book to be written."[1] For the authors' unearthing of rich stories and fertile political thought, we are grateful. Although *Names We Call Home* is technically an edited volume, the authors' generosity throughout makes "collaboration" a more accurate term.

We are especially grateful to Gloria Anzaldúa whose writing on mestiza consciousness inspired the idea for this volume. Thanks as well to Becky's grandparents, Beth and Jim Fillmore, whose knowledge of Hopi and Navajo art led us to Dan Namingha's brilliant artistry and the painting that graces the cover of this book. We have also received able and creative support from the editors and production coordinators at Routledge, Jayne Fargnoli, Anne Sanow, and Kimberly Herald, and invaluable guidance from Sally and Edward Abood, Elly Bulkin, Atreya Chakraborty, Peter Erickson, Ruth Frankenberg, Lisa Freeman, Susan Kosoff, Gayle Pemberton, and Niko Pfund. We are grateful to Earl Jackson and Lisa Hall who gave of themselves in extraordinary ways throughout this project. We also give thanks to Vanetta Aaron, Duncan Thomas, Dave and Bill Wangsgaard, and Irving Zola—who have passed on during the time the editors and contributors worked on this volume, but whose spirits remain close to us. Finally, we give thanks for having the chance to work together again as editors. In *Sisters of the Yam*, bell hooks writes, "work makes life sweet."[2] We agree, and would add to this adage: "Working *together* makes life sweet."

1 Margaret Randall. 1994. *Sandino's Daughters Revisited: Feminism in Nicaragua*. New Brunswick, NJ: Rutgers. p. xiii.

2 bell hooks. 1993. *Sisters of the Yam: Black Women and Self-Recovery*. Boston, MA: South End Press, p. 41.

Storytelling as Social Conscience
The Power of Autobiography
Becky Thompson and Sangeeta Tyagi

Trying to understand race in the United States is like putting together a three-dimensional 1000-piece jigsaw puzzle in dim light.[1] Given the vicissitudes of historical amnesia and the elusive quality of communal memory, it is unclear if we even have all the pieces to begin with. Race is about *everything*—historical, political, personal—and race is about *nothing*—a construct, an invention that has changed dramatically over time and historical circumstance. From the smallest of gestures—what is packed in a child's lunch box or passed on in a smile or a frown—to the largest of historical statements—Brown vs. Board of Education, the Vietnam War, the Hyde Amendment—race has been, and continues to be, encoded in all of our lives. And yet, the fact that race operates on so many different levels is partly what makes talking about peoples' racial identities so difficult. This paradox, when coupled with race's plasticity when gender, sexuality, nationality, age, and religion are accounted for, makes for a conundrum—a puzzle admitting no easy or singular solution. This anthology offers courageous and innovative assessments of this conundrum, with twenty-seven appraisals of the everyday details and historical events that continue to inform and transform people's racial identifications.

The decision to call together these contributors for this joint project was born out of our interest in how progressive writers and activists in the 1990s carve out the creative spaces we need to maintain antiracist stances in our work and lives. As friends and intellectual partners for many years, we have grappled with, argued about, and marveled over how often we—as a heterosexual woman raised middle class and Hindu in India and as a white, mixed-class lesbian of Mormon extraction who grew up in the United States—experience the world similarly and differently in the same breath.

The very different ways we have needed to negotiate in the world have figured prominently in our vision for the anthology. The most pivotal component of Sangeeta's racial identity in the United States has centered on her experiences as an immigrant woman and the racialized process of getting a green card.[2] For Sangeeta, what "home" has meant has been inextricably linked to a politics of exclusion based on race and nationality. While Sangeeta has fought to establish her right to a home in the States, Becky has been working to create a safe one in a country where that is rarely guaranteed for women—across lines of race, class and sexuality. As we have been trying to create safe space amid very different threats to such security, we have been "home" to each other—as friends, intellectual partners, and political allies. These realities—and our discussions about them—have underscored our desire to know more about people whose multidimensional struggles and identities have required new names and the creation of new homes.

We both grew up intellectually and politically in the late 1970s and early 1980s on the writings of women of color, many of them lesbians—Gloria Anzaldúa, Toni Cade Bambara, Beth Brant, Angela Davis, Audre Lorde, bell hooks, Cherríe Moraga, Barbara Smith, Mitsuye Yamada, and others.[3] Their work challenged us to understand how rigorous political analysis can be fed through passionate accounts of one's personal and public life. These texts interrupted white feminist writing that focused on sexism at the exclusion of racism, heterosexism and poverty. The writing also scrutinized relations between women—women of color and white women, mothers and daughters, Jewish and gentile women, lesbians and heterosexual women.

In combination with the small but increasing body of contemporary writing by antiracist white women and Black gay men, this writing by women of color opened crucial narrative space to examine race and activism.[4] For Sangeeta, these books have been models of truth-telling about what it means to live as a colored woman in a profoundly racist society. The writing by women of color has put human faces to Third World, post-colonial theory and has provided company in college settings where Sangeeta has been the only faculty member of color. For Becky, *This Bridge Called My Back* and other autobiographically-grounded theory by people of color and antiracist white women taught her why feminism is bankrupt without examining race, and how antiracism for white people begins at home. This writing also helped her to keep her narrative voice in her scholarly writing as academic convention was requiring its absence. Given our shared indebtedness to this scholarship and our belief in the passion and intellectual promise of narrative writing, we knew that, first and foremost, we wanted this anthology to be autobiographical.

Because of our desire to know what racial identity *means*—politically, intellectually, and emotionally—we asked the contributors for the stories behind their antiracist politics. Over the years, we have often found ourselves searching through biographical sketches and acknowledgments in books for clues about what nurtures and motivates progressive race-conscious writing and living. By asking the contributors to this book to grapple with the turning points and specific, contextualized stories that most informed their identities and work, we were looking for road maps of how they came to understand the fight against racism as central to their lives.

In answer to our questions, the contributors examine key components of racial identity—what names they use to define themselves; what they were taught about race as children and teenagers; how various social movements have shaped their intellectual and artistic work; how they talk about and negotiate amid multiple identifications; what keeps them going in conservative political times, including those we currently face. In addition, the contributors offer ideas about what a future might look like when identity is not predicated on denial, dismissal, or making others alien.

Since we were keenly interested in how racial identity is shaped by other identities, history, activism, and geography, we sought a range of authors who could speak to these varying influences. They are a multiracial, multiethnic group—Mohawk, African American, Japanese American, Cherokee, Indian, Italian American, Native Hawaiian, Chicana, Scandinavian/ Nigerian, Anglo-American, Jewish, Vietnamese American, Brazilian-Puerto Rican, and Yamasee. We included white people who have stood against racial oppression, as well as Black, Latino, Asian American and Native American people, in order to counter the notion that people of color have a race while white people do not.

The contributors' age range—from their twenties to their sixties—shows how racial identifications and political alliances were forever and dramatically changed by key historical events and social movements from the 1930s to the present—the Jim Crow era in the South; the

Holocaust; imprisonment of Japanese Americans during World War II; the Birmingham bombings in 1963; the repression of the Black Panthers and other Black leaders; the assassinations of Malcolm X, Martin Luther King, Jr. and the Kennedys; the Intifada; the execution of the Rosenbergs; the McCarthy period; the Stonewall uprising. These historical events shape people's writing styles, self-representation, and understanding of what constitutes "identity." Though outlining the contributors' range of identities—in terms of race, class, sexuality, religion, age, and nationality—is a helpful start, not surprisingly, their own descriptions of themselves are much more useful and nuanced than perpetually imprecise generic religious, racial, or sexual labels. Racial identity formation occurs at the intersections of individual psychological development and community affiliation. Sarah Willie, for example, describes herself as "a multiracial person with Black African ancestry who has "spent a great deal of time and energy either defending my right to identify with the category Black or my right not to identify with the category Black." Pam Mitchell, a white, working-class, Californian lesbian who descended from Jewish immigrants from Eastern Europe and white Christian people from West Virginia, writes, "I'm the hyphenation between two mutually exclusive, antipathic cultures, each of which has been despised by mainstream U.S. culture."

By including writers who grew up in England, India, Brazil, the Caribbean, and the United States, the volume grapples with what "border crossing" means for diasporic communities as well as for those born in the United States.[5] Differentiating between these communities situates racial identity, since geography and language shape people's investments in racial politics in the United States. For Sangeeta Tyagi, who was born and raised in India, living in the United States has meant rarely being able to hear Hindi being spoken. Being bilingual in a putatively monolingual society diminishes her ease with and ability to think in Hindi—a loss not only of specific words, but also of a connection to the rituals, festivities, and childhood friendships that she had sustained through language. Being part of bilingual communities in the United States is Tyagi's protest against the fragmentation of memory and its accompanied disconnection. Ramon Torrecilha's national/racial identity was also freighted in the United States. Because officials at the American Consulate would not recognize him as a citizen, despite his Puerto Rican father, the Brazilian-born Torrecilha had to enter the United States first as an "illegal" migrant worker who was often identified as "Mexican" by employers.

In addition to immigrants, those people who have been treated as "internal outsiders" in the United States as a consequence of imperialism also struggle to name themselves racially. Andrew Spieldenner refers to himself as "a child of an unnamed war"—a product of a white man from Ohio and a Vietnamese woman—who grew up in a family where "Vietnamese is not yet legal tender." His adult community includes "other colored girls like me"—other gay men of color who "like glass, can reflect similar scars . . . and can crack into a multitude of jagged slivers." Lisa Kahaleole Chang Hall writes of her genealogy:

> We are a multiracial clan from way way back—our mixtures begin over a hundred years ago in
> Hawai'i alone. This is why "biracial" rhetoric has always left me cold . . . In Hawai'i the centuries of
> racial mixture are like the Caribbean, there is both language and a finely-honed recognition of racial
> features. In the United States I am a constant question.

Within the United States, people's multiple identifications defy neat racial divisions and unidimensional political alliances. The contributors include lesbians, gay men, bisexuals and heterosexuals who tease out how profoundly gender and sexuality influence racial identity. The inclusion of Jews, Christians, atheists, Hindus and people whose spirituality is rooted in their Native American heritage foregrounds the impact of religious identity, anti-Semitism, and Christian dominance on race relations in this country. The inclusion of people from working-class, middle-class and mixed-class families and neighborhoods illuminates how class informs people's racial politics.

As they grapple with their multiple identities, the contributors link their identifications clearly to their roots and political affiliations. For David Wellman, who was raised by white, working-class Communist parents in Detroit in the 1950s, being "red" meant his community was with black, not white, people—an identification based on politics, not race. During the 1960s, however, when Black activists asserted their right to organize on their own terms and pushed white people to do so as well, Wellman briefly saw being white and antiracist as an oxymoron; he then realized he could use his white skin as a means of getting places and hearing things he could use against white domination. For Herb Green, being a young Afro-Caribbean, gay writer means "feeling like I am trapped in a cell block of racial stereotypes struggling to find some way of escaping the racial difference that eroticizes and exoticizes my body." Yet, his activism, writing, and sexual desire require his embodiment and his ability to "turn the myths of Black masculinity inside/out." Echoing the complexity of being mixed-race in a racially stratified country, Cherríe Moraga, the daughter of a Chicana mother and a father of French and British-Canadian ancestry, explains, "We light-skinned breeds are like chameleons, those lagartijas with the capacity to change the color of their skins. We change not for lack of conviction, but lack of definite shade and shape. My lovers have always been the environment that defined my color." These and other contributors show the futility of simple equations between skin color and politics.

Telling Secrets: Trauma, Memory, and Resistance

The politics of self-definition become clear in these personal narratives, especially since the contributors account for how "secrets" correspond to the larger pressures of cultural amnesia. Memory is both produced and shaped by family dynamics and destructions, as it is contoured by legacies of injustice. Autobiography illustrates why racial identity formation occurs at the intersection of a person's subjective memory of trauma and collective remembrance of histories of domination. For Harry Kitano, gaps and silences within his own story mark his own understanding of injustice. While nowadays he speaks openly of his confinement in Japanese internment camps during World War II, when asked to write an autobiography in graduate school, he was too ashamed and afraid to include his life "behind barbed wire." His rage was turned inward into shame, as the single biggest influence on his racial identity—living in a closed environment with other Japanese Americans—had been driven underground. For Faith Adiele—born in the Northwestern United States to a white woman of Scandinavian descent and an Igbo Nigerian man—understanding her familial and community history means recognizing her parents' silences as "strategies of love." Her mother tried to shield her from racism, while her father saw no purpose in revealing the torture he experienced during the Biafran War. Having grown up in the "shadow of unspoken words," Adiele had to travel to Nigeria herself as an adult to "piece together history." For Evelyn C. White, racial identity as a Black woman has been shaped by the "genetic memory of her ancestors who were hunted down and preyed upon in rural settings." Coming to terms with her terror of the wilderness—and the outrage of knowing how much her life has been restricted by this fear—required facing it head on. For these and other contributors, remembering one's history and heritage serves a twin imperative: it enables them to explore individual life history while tapping communal memory and experience.

The contributors' stories about their childhoods reveal that, even in the most supportive families, growing up means facing great contradictions about race. Living through childhood amid these contradictions is, in effect, how people *become* raced, since children's exposure to contradictions—and their strategies for dealing with them—has everything to do with racial formation. Raised by her single mother in Boston in the 1930s, Gloria Johnson-Powell was taught that Boston was the "cradle of liberty and that race didn't matter in that city," although the city was starkly segregated (and still is). While she faced devastating racial exclusions at school, her mother said nothing for fear that she might frighten or discourage her daughter. For Calvin

Hernton, living amid racial contradictions was inevitable for a Black child growing up under Jim Crow in Tennessee in the 1930s and 1940s. As Black singers performed in white churches Black people could not attend, Hernton and other Black people "stood outside on the Sunday afternoon sidewalk, degraded, yet proud because the singers were superb." For Hernton, trying to remember how he was raced is like "trying to remember when you first learned your name."

Many children are raised by relatives whose own ethnic, racial, or religious identifications are themselves full of contradictions. In her essay about growing up Jewish and middle class in New York, Melanie Kaye/Kantrowitz writes that her father "loved all things Jewish, loved the sound of Yiddish but would not speak it." Kantrowitz's mother never went to shul and "spent her life-time hating her nose, her Jewish nose." Kantrowitz's mother tried to distance herself from many Jews even as she felt the threat of anti-Semitism. Gayle Pemberton's parents tried to protect her from racism through their sheltering and silences, while carefully negotiating where they travelled, whom they befriended, and what they allowed their children to do. Meanwhile, as they protected her from racism from without, within the family, color politics reigned, as light skinned relatives, including Pemberton's mother, were privileged.

Children who face racism while growing up often do not risk telling secrets about childhood lessons about race out of fear of betraying their family and community—the very places where they receive at least some shelter from racial storms. As a consequence, revealing painful or confusing messages about race can feel like they were being ungrateful, a traitor, a family snitch. When Lisa Kahaleole Chang Hall writes about the vexed lessons about race she got when she was growing up, she experienced "intense bursts of insomnia" and the sense of generations "smothering my voice," saying "Be quiet, you. Make no shame." Hall chronicles several early racial memories as she repeats a haunting refrain: "There are no stories in my family, nothing ever happened to anyone, and if anything ever did there would be no reason to discuss it." In this instance, what is revealing is how racial identity can be both taught and repressed, in the same moment, with lasting effect.

Growing up in violent families can also impede people's abilities to piece together their racial identities because of the effect of trauma on memory. Typically, children's memories about racial identity were driven underground *because* they were attached to family trauma that was too painful to be kept on the conscious family story circuit. Children's memories of violence are often partial precisely *because* of the power of forgetting as a method of coping.[6] Pam Mitchell, for example, writes about how trauma can "act as an eraser. When we numb out and forget details about our lives which have been unbearable, some of the other details fade with them. In the process, context and ethnic heritage can lose their shape, grow fuzzy, and indistinct." As a result of sexual abuse, Mitchell repressed a positive Jewish identity which she has struggled to reclaim as an adult.

By retelling childhood trauma, people often uncovered profound lessons about their racial identities. Many of the contributors' most complex and startling insights were ones they didn't actually "know" until they wrote them. The daughter of a Castilian mother and a Tsalagi (Cherokee) father, Vickie Sears was taken at age four from her family and placed by state authorities in various foster homes where she and her brother were vulnerable to sexual abuse and spiritual persecution. The coping mechanisms Sears developed to protect herself as a child left her with a complicated sense of her racial self. In stark contrast, Donald Grinde writes about how his entire sense of self as an American Indian child was nurtured by his connections to "place and kinship." In the face of health problems and numerous assaults—being knifed in grade school and the murder of his own son—he has always known that his family and the natural world would guide him.

The difficulty of sorting through lessons about racial identity also relates to the ways in which messages about race, as well as sexuality, class, and gender are signaled to children in countless, everyday ways—the furniture in their homes, their verbal expressions and accents, the ways they hold their bodies in public settings, the children with whom they are allowed to play. Often, these lessons are stated indirectly through lessons about manners, taste, and rituals. For example, Earl

Jackson was admonished by his Seventh Day Adventist parents for choosing flamboyant, colorful clothing as a teenager. His parents claimed that people would think Jackson was "colored" which, in their minds, meant armed and dangerous. It took years for Jackson to unpack all that his parents were communicating through their apparent aesthetic preferences. Although racial stratification surrounded Ruth Frankenberg in Wales and England when she was growing up—in segregated housing and schools, on television, and in movies—the privileges of "whiteness seemed not to be named, as far as my memory tells me." Rather than hearing explicit expectations of her as a white girl, racial superiority was taught in everyday ways—the Catholic uniforms she wore, the school she attended, the accent she learned. Only retrospectively has Frankenberg uncovered how she and other white children and adults came to see themselves as superior racially.

By tracing racial identity back to childhood lessons, the contributors offer crucial information about how and why they consider antiracism central to their work as adults. Many were raised by progressive relatives—card-carrying Communists, Civil Rights leaders, union organizers, leaders of post-colonial independence movements. As adults, several of the contributors are extending the work their relatives began. Beth Brant considers the spirit that nurtures her writing as "the collective consciousness of those Native writers who have passed on." Pam Mitchell, whose union-organizing grandparents helped build a multiracial labor movement in the 1930s and 1940s, is a member of a worker-owned print shop in San Francisco and writes about class, race, and Jewish identity. As a professor of African American Studies and a creative writer, Gayle Pemberton is, in many ways, continuing her father's work in the Urban League. Their stories are powerful reminders of how movement culture can be passed down and embellished upon in subsequent generations. Their experiences are also antidotes to the mainstream messages that political activism is dead and that children of progressive activists grow up to be reactionaries.

Still other essays reveal how—in the absence of progressive, race-conscious politics in one's own family of origin—people can still question and rebel against racist custom and convention. Raised in a family where there was great violence and violation, Earl Jackson eventually realized that "there was something fundamentally wrong with the people who had absolute authority over me." He learned not only to question their ideas about *his* life but to scrutinize their beliefs about others as well—Black people, poor people, educated people, and gay people.

For many of the contributors, a sense of justice developed out of their experiences of exclusion during childhood.[7] Angela Giudice ties her early questioning about racial ordering to feeling out of place as a passionate, bright, fat, Italian American girl in a WASP community. Her rebellion against this homogeneous and rigid community included a midnight ritual of turning over a neighbor's lawn chairs and refusing to stay within racial boundaries at school and in her neighborhood. Ruth Frankenberg partly ties her skepticism about racial messages to being raised by a single mother in an era when divorce was uncommon. As a teenager, Frankenberg joined a nationwide effort to unionize school students in Devon, England. Becky Thompson writes about how crossing regional and class borders and facing childhood trauma contributed to her opposition to racism as an adult. In these and other instances, the contributors offer multilayered accounts of the emotional and political work involved in developing racial consciousness.

Where Is the Way Home

The contributors to this volume are writing about "home" in the fluid and expansive sense of the word—people's physical, political, and spiritual homes—and the homes where they do the work that sustains them and their communities.[8] This way of seeing home links the public with the private and ties the emotional to the political. By writing about their multiple homes, the contributors refuse to relegate issues of safety and camaraderie, shared goals and a sense of community, to the private sphere. At the same time, they neither romanticize nor trivialize their homes of origins. In their political understanding of "home," the contributors oppose the exclusionary and nostalgic notions of home that the political and religious right has pushed in the 1980s and 1990s. In so doing, the contributors treat the search for and belief in "home" as a key challenge for creating a just future.

For all of the contributors, writing about racial identity required revisiting our homes of origin—our families, neighborhoods, and childhood communities. For many people, family is where a positive sense of one's racial identity is first introduced: where relatives cradled children if they were teased or ostracized at school; where children were both expected to and praised for learning English as well as their parents' or grandparents' first language—Italian, Yiddish, Mohawk, Spanish, Cherokee; and where family holidays were filled with smells, tastes, and touches that give texture to racial and ethnic identity throughout adulthood. Home is also the place where people learn some of the most debilitating lessons about race—where silences about race were stultifying; where the need for racial solidarity left little room for sexual explorations; where lessons about assimilation and racial superiority were taught and enforced.

The continuum among the writers in terms of what constitutes "home" for them as adults reveals much about identity, belonging, meaning, and activism. For Donald Grinde, home and identity are one and the same. Growing up among Native people in Georgia, who believe that one's place of birth magically and indelibly bestows an identity, Grinde now lives when he is not working, in keeping with matrifocal traditions—with his Navajo wife and children on the Navajo reservation in Arizona. On the other end of the continuum are contributors whose current homes are largely imagined, metaphorical and forever changing. Ramon Torrecilha has found home, in Matthew Arnold's words, "wandering between two worlds: the one dead, the other powerless to be born." With home an imagined space between Brazilian and Anglo cultures, Torrecilha finds it possible to be tied to neither and informed by both. And Lisa Hall writes, "I am a woman who wants to go home but never figured out where it is or why to go there . . . I have lost the words to chant my bloodline." The words of the contributors whose losses have denied them homes speak to the profound costs and vulnerability that result from homelessness. Their writing also highlights the political work ahead of us to insure people the means to find their way to homes that nurture them politically, spiritually, and physically.

By posing the question "Where is the way home?" Ruth Frankenberg treats the homes people create—the choices we make about where to live, who to share our lives with, and how we see community—as what ultimately sustains us. For Frankenberg, white people's ability to find the way home depends upon getting out of the master's house—learning ways to live that are not based on injury, insult and exclusion. For Becky Thompson, whiteness was taught through indirection and negation—not Native, not Chicano, not Black. After being taught to associate being white with condescension, guilt, fear, and appropriation, Thompson learned to see the search for home as partly involving political alliances and friendships with people whose white identities are positive and subversive.

Many of the contributors consider writing a way of finding home. For Sangeeta Tyagi, this means of survival and creativity situates her among post-colonial writers who have scrutinized the classical autobiographical dichotomy drawn between self and community.[9] Andrew Spieldenner writes, "I search so as to create a place a home a family a movement I never knew. I write to remake the world. I write to preserve the unremembered . . . to utter the intimacy rendered mute. To birth a nation." For Beth Brant, writing has been "home" as it draws her close to herself and other Native women.

In the poem that opens the volume, Kate Rushin asks, "What time can we call it home?"—a question she directs to people whose fast-paced lives and tenuous connection to the past leave us passing each other in the night. For Rushin "this body is home," a boundary she marks and celebrates by listening to Nina Simone, John Coltrane, and Abby Lincoln as she lights a candle and incense—all rituals of remembrance. In their remembrances, the contributors mark the past, wrestle with present-day conundrums, and point us toward a future as it unfolds.

Contours of the Volume

The poetry, interview, and essays are organized into four themes: how family, community, and inequality shape racial identity formation; how people piece together and make sense of our individual, family, and communal histories; how love and conversation weave in and out of the stories about racial identity; and how risk and vulnerability shape the contours of racial consciousness. The six essays in Part One, "Blood Ties, Communal Relations" trace early memories of racial identity. Part Two, "Piecing Together History" offers multilayered accounts of the emotional, political and intellectual work required to fasten memory in place and time, despite attempts to bury it. The four essays and the interview in Part Three, "Love Letters and Conversations" offer political readings of love and ritual in the 1990s. Part Four, "Acts of Creation: Sweat, Blood, Bone," chronicles the ways people learn to create themselves and their communities and why embodiment is integral to this task.[10]

The writing ranges widely in style and approach. The volume includes poetry and interviews that read like stories, stories that read like prayers, and political testimonials that read like poetry. The contributors border cross in their writing as urgently as they do in their lives. While Harry Kitano and Gloria Johnson-Powell, for example, offer methodical and chronological sketches of their lives, the essays by Andrew Spieldenner and Lisa Hall are anything but linear as they weave dreams, conversations, poetry and political speeches into their narratives. Radically different in terms of generation, tone, and approach, these writers underscore why and how racial identities must be understood within specific historical contexts.[11]

Taken as a whole, the volume chronicles the complexities of racial identity at the same time as it seeks historically sensitive and responsible ways to create a future. The contributors' acts of naming are not singular events or assertions of a univocal truth. They are not "staking a claim"— a territorial act—but rather "claiming a stake" in remembering, reliving, and retelling their lives, their histories and the processes that make this possible.[12] Through this journey, their words reveal the motivation behind their activism and the many forms it takes. By using personal narratives to connect key historical moments in the United States and internationally, the contributors rally against what Angela Davis refers to as a "nostalgic surrogate for historical memory." They explain how they grew up rebelling, why being a rebel can be a fight for survival, and what rebellion continues to look like in adulthood. In the process, the contributors offer us moral and political direction for this decade and beyond.

Notes

1   We are especially grateful to several people—Elly Bulkin, Jayne Fargnoli, Earl Jackson, Gayle Pemberton, and Jessica Shubow—who, with great generosity and patience, made major conceptual contributions to this introduction.

2   A green card signifies "resident alien" or "permanent resident" status which means a person without U.S. citizenship can live and work in the United States legally. Having a green card generally allows people more civilized treatment from the Immigration and Naturalization Service (INS) and differentiates them from people who are on student, tourist, work, or business visas.

3   Cherríe Moraga and Gloria Anzaldúa, eds. 1983. *This Bridge Called My Back: Writings by Radical Women of Color*. Lantham, NY: Kitchen Table: Women of Color Press; Toni Cade Bambara. 1970. *The Black Woman: An Anthology*. NY: New American Library; Beth Brant, ed. 1984. *A Gathering of Spirit: Writing and Art by North American Indian Women*. San Francisco: Sinister Wisdom; Angela Davis. 1974. *Angela Davis: An Autobiography*. NY: Random House; Audre Lorde. 1982. *Zami: A New Spelling of My Name*. Freedom, CA: Crossing Press; bell hooks. 1984. *Feminist Theory: Thinking Feminist, Thinking Black*. Boston:

South End Press; Cherrié Moraga. 1983. *Loving in the War Years: Lo Que Nunca Pasó Por Sus Labios*. Boston: South End Press; Barbara Smith, ed. 1983. *Home Girls: A Black Feminist Anthology*. Lantham, NY: Kitchen Table: Women of Color Press; Mitsuye Yamada. 1988. *Desert Run*. Lantham, NY: Kitchen Table: Women of Color Press.

4   Contemporary writing by anti-racist white women includes: Elly Bulkin. 1980. "Racism and Writing: Some Implications for White Lesbian Critics," *Sinister Wisdom* 13 Spring; Mab Segrest. 1985. *My Mama's Dead Squirrel: Lesbian Essays on Southern Culture*. Ithaca, New York: Firebrand Books; Elly Bulkin, Minnie Bruce Pratt, and Barbara Smith. 1984. *Yours in Struggle: Three Feminist Perspectives on Anti-Semitism and Racism*. Ithaca, NY: Firebrand Books. Writings by Black gay men include: Joseph Beam, ed. 1986. *In the Life: A Black Gay Anthology*. Boston: Alyson Publications; Essex Hemphill. 1992. *Brother to Brother: New Writings by Black Gay Men*. Boston: Alyson Publications.

5   For pioneering work on "border crossing" see, Gloria Anzaldúa. 1987. *Borderlands/La Frontera: The New Mestiza*. San Francisco: Spinsters/Aunt Lute; Gloria Anzaldúa, ed. 1990. *Making Face, Making Soul: Haciendo Caras*. San Francisco: Aunt Lute. For literary and historical criticism about borderland writing see Hector Calderon and Jose David Saldivar, eds. 1991. *Criticisms in the Borderlands: Studies in Chicano Literature, Culture, and Ideology*. Durham, North Carolina: Duke University Press.

6   Forgetting not only filters past trauma, it also traps healing energies that propel people forward. Psychologists Rosenwald and Ochberg (1992) explain, the "self-formative power of personal narrative may be constrained or stunted. As psychoanalytic experience suggests, the misfortunes of childhood may censor both memory and desire, impoverishing both the narrative past and how that narrative might seize the future." George Rosenwald and Richard Ochberg, eds. 1992. *Storied Lives: The Cultural Politics of Self-Understanding*. New Haven: Yale University Press, p. 1. See also, Judith Herman. 1992. *Trauma and Recovery*. NY: Basic Books.

7   For essays that trace connections between childhood rebellions and race-consciousness see: bell hooks. 1989. *Talking Back: Thinking Feminist, Thinking Black*. Boston: South End Press; June Jordan. 1985. *On Call: Political Essays*. Boston: South End Press; Joan Nestle. 1987. *A Restricted Country*. Ithaca, NY: Firebrand Books. Gayle Pemberton. 1993. *The Hottest Water in Chicago: Notes of a Native Daughter*. NY: Anchor. Minnie Bruce Pratt. 1991. *Rebellion: Essays 1980-1991*. Ithaca, NY: Firebrand Books.

8   For feminist writing that offers crucial analyses of "home" see: Ruth Hubbard and Margaret Randall. 1988. *The Shape of Red: Insider/Outsider Relations*. San Francisco: Cleis Press; Biddy Martin and Chandra Talpade Mohanty. 1986. "Feminist Politics: What's Home Got to Do With It?" in *Feminist Studies, Critical Studies*, edited by Teresa de Lauretis. Bloomington, Indiana: University of Indiana Press; Minnie Bruce Pratt. 1984. "Identity: Skin Blood Heart", in *Yours in Struggle: Three Feminist Perspectives on Anti-Semitism and Racism*. Ithaca, NY: Firebrand Books; Barbara Smith, ed. 1983. *Home Girls: A Black Feminist Anthology*. Lantham, NY: Kitchen Table: Women of Color Press.

9   For works relevant to these issues see: Francoise Lionnet. 1989. *Autobiographical Voices: Race, Gender, Self-Portraiture*. Cornell; Valerie Smith. 1987. *Self Discovery and Authority in Afro-American Narratives*. Cambridge: Harvard University Press.

10   The title of this section comes from Lisa Hall's essay in this volume.

11   This is one reason why models of racial identity that map transformations outside of history run the risk of reducing identity to developmental phases that are, by implication, devoid of political content. This volume may be useful to social scientists and educators in constructing racial identity models that account for gender, sexuality, and nationality as well as age, social movements, and family dynamics.

12   Thank you to Earl Jackson for making this crucial point.

Word Problems

Kate Rushin

If a train departs at 10:20 pm
traveling south and another train
departs at 10:10 pm headed north,
what time will it be when we finally
take haven in an indulgent bed
marooned in a multi-national hotel room
overlooking Central Park?

How many hours will it be before the edges
soften and we walk through the park, smile at
strangers we wrongly assume to be
New Yorkers, sit in overpriced cafes,
sip international coffee drinks and cognac,
regard male nude portraits executed by
Sigmund Freud's grandson hanging in the
Metropolitan Museum of Art? What time shall we
return to room service remote and bourgeois bed
the dubious privilege of somebody else compelled
to make it? The next morning, exposed in our 1970s
campus-style Afro-Am cultural nationalism,
we'll overtip the Third-World-Woman cleaning staff
then see each other off at Amtrak
just in time to make it back to our good jobs.

Yet, somewhere between the maxed-out credit cards,
mini-bar and starched linens, two grown colored women
inscribe a story. It's a story some brother with an agenda
declared couldn't exist due to inauthenticity. Some sister with
self-induced amnesia pretended she couldn't read between the lines,
had no idea what we were talking about. Some white woman
insisted the story was interchangeable with hers
and some white man reported it was not in evidence because
we'd never crossed his mind.

We are the last generation
raised by 19th-century women, the link between
our great-grandmothers in bondage and our
daughters in cyberspace. No wonder
we're standing here wondering; inhabitants of a land
everybody wants to occupy, but nobody wants to imagine.
As our daughters and sons set out on the
MTV artificial intelligence information superhighway
we haunt the crossroads. We're on the watch to pass them

a few books, a few photos, a few stories, a few words;
a broach, a piece of cloth, a song, a prayer,
a pressed flower; a feather, a shell and a bone.
We maintain that the elite have nothing going for them
except money technology and gall, all the while we fake
faith, hedge our bets: *Got to learn those computers.*
You'll go to that private school if I have my say.
We just can't risk stranding our children in that
so-called underclass we used to call home.

But like I said, there's nothing disembodied,
not what I'm talking about. Sign your name.
Turn off that television.
This ain't one of those nihilistic scenes lit by the despairing
blue light of the tube.
Find ourselves? Lose ourselves?
I don't claim to know the difference.
There's nothing to lose I haven't lost more times
than I thought possible. I won't hesitate or wait.
If we're lucky we'll get a corner room high enough to
catch a glimpse of the moon to remind us of other shores.
Put on some Nina or Coltrane,
Find Abby Lincoln on the FM stereo.
Incense, candle flame, papaya and cowry shell
mark the boundaries.
This body is home.
Look here.
This is the lush life
only for a minute.

Your train is traveling
south at 73 miles per hour.
Mine is headed north doing 68.
How long will it take us to arrive at
our separate definitions?
What time shall we begin, for real?
What time can we call it home?

Part I

BLOOD TIES,
Communal Relations

1

"When We Are Capable of Stopping, We Begin to See"
Being White, Seeing Whiteness

Ruth Frankenberg

Prologue

1. i was born, i will die, the end.[1]
2. ego loves to talk about itself.
3. but where is the way home?

"i" have been remade several times. Feminism remade "me." Recognition of the profound level of my coimplication with racism and imperialism remade "me." Migrations, across the UK and across the Atlantic, remade "me." Self-identification as lesbian remade "me." And a small yet infinite awakening to the vastness within which all these "me's" exist, is just now not only remaking "me" once again, but also asking *who* that "me" actually is.

i was born, i will die, ego loves to talk. And yet, the way home must be found. Increasingly, from a new (to me) vantage point that sharpens and reframes prior convictions, the unreality of "race" is evident. Of course it always was, and many people, among them a good number of race theorists, have asserted and clarified this point. Yet the challenge has remained that of how to, in Audre Lorde's terms, "dismantle the master's house" while, not only do we live in it but *it*, by some architectural trick, lives in *us*.[2] How to enter more deeply and self-consciously into one's racial identity in order to challenge it while making sure, in Gayatri Chakravorty Spivak's terms, that any moves toward essentialism remain "strategic."[3] Not, in other words beyond a point of *identifying* with one's (small "i") identity. Indeed it may be that a spiritual path of disidentification from what *appears* to be, is in reality the way home.

Finding the way home, then, entails finding the way out—out of the master's house. This essay will ask, though, how I got *in*—into the master's house—in the first place. For asking how we got in—into this mess called racism—is, I believe, an important step toward getting *out*. Toward getting home.

Placing the "i" in quotes, changing its casing? Changing its garb, remembering its provisionality, non-sovereignty. Not "i"dentifying means knowing there is an infinity beyond history. And yet. We live in our version of reality, its conventions, its violence. So I plunge back into the "I," in order to examine the conditions of its making.

I

I have been performing whiteness, and having whiteness performed upon me, since—or actually before—the moment I was born. But the question is, what does that mean?

While the subjective meanings of my racial identity have changed considerably over time, the objective meanings of my being white have changed little or not at all from the moment of my birth until now. Here, I mean to underscore the material bedrock of race and class structuring, which have served to anchor race privilege in my existence in the two countries in which I have lived. Coming to consciousness about one's racial identity and/or race privilege as white is not, then, by any means the same as transforming it. Racial positioning and self-naming are contextual and thus their transformation must always entail collective processes, ones that take place, so to speak, within history, rather than as individual journeys. Racial identity is also relational, made through the claiming and the imposition of samenesses and othernesses: I realized early in the work for this essay that writing it would by no means entail speaking only about myself. This relationality also means that I cannot discuss racialization without also talking about racism and antiracism.

However, let me suppose that I am concerned here, at least in part, with my sense of self. And let me also suggest that, in living out a sense of self, I enact—or better, I act from within and/or against—an assemblage of elements, drawn in turn from diverse histories, all the way from the familial, to the local, to the national, to the global, and translated into (self-)expectations, (self-)images, forms of (self-)disciplining, desires, and so on. Let me then suggest that my identity is all of this, and that it is also usefully understood as practice or as an ongoing process of practic-ing, rather as an entity or thing, whether stable or changing. Racial identity can, in short, be understood as the situated practicing of a multifariously marked self.

Let me begin with some basic socio-data: I was born in Cardiff, Wales, in 1957. I spent my childhood in the outskirts (as we say over there) of Manchester, England, one of two daughters in a single-parent household. Before my sixteenth birthday I left the nest by moving to a wild boarding school in Devon and then to a staid university in Cambridge. (Actually, however, certain conventionalisms—including unquestioned homophobia and a patronizing approach to class—sat alongside the liberatory pedagogy of the former; by the same token some of my early lessons in radicalism took place in context of the latter.) Finally, through what my dear friend Emma memorably described as "a whim that got out of hand," I found myself, in 1979, turning twenty-one years of age in Santa Cruz, California. Since 1984, I have lived mainly in Oakland, California, although with a three-year sojourn further up the west coast in Seattle, Washington.

Notice that I have been able to say all of the above without mentioning race, whether as defining feature, as impediment, or as benefit. And that, in fact, is part of the trick of whiteness, in this historical moment and in those parts of the world wherein I have been white. As I have frequently said to students in the past five or so years, race privilege is the (non)experience of not being slapped in the face. As expressed far more eloquently by a woman whom I unfortunately cannot name here, for us whiteness is "a privilege enjoyed but not acknowledged, a reality lived in but unknown."[4]

So, let me run that through again. I was born in Cardiff in what was, if my memory serves me correctly (and it should, for I continued to return to my grandmother's house there up into my teens), an entirely white part of that city. I now know that because of its status as a port, Cardiff has one of the longest-standing black communities in Britain as well as one of the longest histories of interracial marriage. But the black community was in the docklands area, very far from our home. Of course, being under three, I did not ponder this question at the time. However, I obviously knew about blackness somehow, because I actually remember startling my great-aunt by pointing to the (white) man delivering coal to our house, who, as a result of his line of work was completely covered in soot, and asking whether "that man was black." Both he and my aunt laughed, and told me no, it was just the coal.

How did blackness enter my consciousness (if only to reappear as misrecognition) in an apparently all-white world? Perhaps from my favorite children's story character of the time. In a series of books, which I would beg to have read to me again and again, the main character was Epaminondas, a "picaninny" who was constantly in trouble and who, as his mother would tell him at the end of each story, "didn't have the sense he was born with." Epaminondas and his mother lived on a plantation, somewhere in a mythified Africa. She wore bright dresses and bandanas, and smiled all the time, despite the endless trouble Epaminondas gave her. I was, then, at less than three years old, already a child of the British Empire, already taught through no malice aforethought on my mother's part, the beginnings of racist love. *Racist* love. Racist *love.*

It is interesting that one can, in fact (re)tell a white life through a racial lens. One can begin showing how, in fact, the white subject's formation is marked in myriad ways by her positioning in the racial order, spatially and discursively. Note too that my *racialization was displaced onto a putative Other. Seeing blackness was not seeing whiteness, although logically, it must, at some level, have also been just that.*

At three, I moved with my parents to the north of England. We lived on a brand new housing development (housing "estate" in British parlance)—so new in fact that our street was mud rather than pavement for quite some time. To my clear memory, no one of color (or to use British English, no one Black, no one of African, Caribbean, or South Asian descent) lived on the housing estate. When I went to preschool, all the children were white except for one girl of Caribbean descent. I can still picture the two thick braids worn around her head, framing her dark brown face. Although I have no other memories of her as a person (and indeed this is true of all the other kids at my preschool, too), I do remember some kind of solidarity between my mother and her father, since, like my mother by that time, he was a single parent.

When I saw blackness, this must have meant that I had already computed whiteness, or that I did so in that same instant. But whiteness seemed not to be named, as far as memory tells me. Odd really, since there was so much of it about . . . Also, notice that racialness did not totally define my mother's sense of this child's father—other contingencies were also in play.

Although the suburbs were all white in Manchester, this was not true of the city as a whole. I remember clearly driving into the city center with my mother, and passing neighborhoods that were poorer, and differently colored, from our own. The cracked paving-stones, the second-hand furniture stores, the men on the streets with loose flowing shirts and trousers (now I'd say kurta-pajamas), the women with saris and ill-matched cardigans, made an impact on my consciousness: fear of the unknown, fear of the dishevelled, of the seeming disorder which I can now more easily name as poverty.

About whom am I speaking? "Them," or me? How did I become white? Here, we may note that my whiteness and their Asianness were in part marked by class. I was positioned, historically, to drive through this neighborhood and find it Other, through the culmination of an imperial history that began long before my birth, through a process that in fact invented race and "classed" it. That history positioned this small child, me, as a spectator behind the glass of a car window. And these are, indeed, components of my whiteness. But another component of my whiteness is, in fact, my seeming neutrality, my seeming unmarkedness. For why do we not, apparently, need to know what I was wearing, whether my clothes were in my view matched or ill-matched, whether my family's trousers were tight, or whether they flowed. One can name only a part of one's racialization by making a spectacle of an Other.

At elementary (or primary) school, the children were again white except for the three children of one Indian family. The middle child in that family, Shalini, was in my class. I remember at least some of our classmates making hostile comments, mostly behind Shalini's back, and also leaving notes on her desk, with comments about her dark skin. Shalini and I had a friend in common (another classmate, also white), and the two of us were invited to tea. I was perhaps nine years old. Her family's house, just two doors from the Catholic church, smelled of spices unfamiliar to my nostrils (clichéd, but true). Her mother, when we went to tea, gave us snacks that at the time smelt and tasted completely different from anything I'd ever encountered—strange and therefore a little frightening, but not unpleasant. Now, of course, I'd recognize them, and be pleased to eat what I now know to be vegetable pakoras at anyone's house. Moreover, Britain is a different place now from how it was in the 1960s, and some version of Indian food has entered the white mainstream: white mothers are probably routinely picking up frozen pakoras at the supermarket and bringing them home to give to their white kids after school.

My connection with Shalini was such that she told me things—like her father's job; where her father was from; what her own middle name was, and what her sister's name meant (I still remember); what her father's full name was (long, complicated to my ears, and I forgot it immediately); how to pronounce her last name correctly, as opposed to how it was pronounced in England. I don't recall ever going back to Shalini's house, although I would play with her often in our other friend's backyard. Unlike most of our elementary school peers, Shalini and I ended up at the same high school (the selective one, for the supposedly "brainiest" kids), and we used to walk home together, braving the jeers of the kids coming out of the other school—what was at that time called a "secondary modern" or non-college preparatory school, on the way past.

In writing of Shalini, I was telling the truth (that is, I did not lie). But one may note that the burden of my narrative was one of redemption of my white self. I did not leave those racist notes. I did like the pakoras. I got to like them even better as an adult. I grew to love (the food of) the Other. In short, the narrative implies, I am a good *person, racially. I am, it claims, not racist. Shalini and I were united by class (or more precisely, by an educational stratification system that is generally class-marked). Therefore we were not divided. We were united. History made me, and had I been a few years younger, my story would have been different. I am telling what James Clifford, speaking of ethnographic practice, calls a "fable of rapport."[5] And as is true in general of fables of rapport, my narrative protests my own "innocence:" my innocence as in "not guilty," and my innocence as in "youthful, naive."*

Thus, this seemingly benign story, or rather, this story in which I appeared to myself *as benign—and here is the solipsism of racism—turned out to be rather less straightforward than it first appeared. It turned out, in fact, to have some quite sickening aspects. We are frequently complicit with racism even when we are absolutely confident that we are not. Why am I drawing attention to all of this? I could, after all, have simply re-edited my own story. But the way "out of the master's house," the way home, requires, I think, as great an honesty and clarity as the ego can muster in any given moment. I feel compelled, at* this *moment, to offer as much detail about my route "home" as ego will permit, as much of what is required of us as ego can, at any point, recognize and name. And I am drawing attention to this particular move, that of a narrative deployment of Others in such a way as to secure one's own "redemption," because it is a common one, a "wrong turn," taken frequently by antiracists and self-analysts of whiteness.*

As I said, I went to a new school. I was eleven. At this new school, out of about a thousand students, there were in addition to Shalini and her brother three others who were not white. It speaks to what Elizabeth Alexander has described as the "neon footsteps" effect of being a person of color in a primarily white environment that I can picture the three, and even remember two of their names.[6] But it is important to note that, while memorable as signs, by their sheer presence, this did not mean that there was a recognition of them, on my part, in terms of their personhood. For I did not know their personalities, their ethnicities, how they ended up in this school. It is true that there was perhaps no reason why I should remember or ever have known details about students who were not my age and therefore never my friends nor in classes with me. But in fact it was the unevenness of my recognition which makes it worth comment. For I cannot call to mind even the faces of any—truly—of the other perhaps three hundred white students who between them would have made up the cohorts of each of these black young people. As I said, then, these students were signs from my white standpoint, simultaneously over- and under-visible. Nor, I think, did their presence disturb the whiteness of this space, so much as it underscored it. For this was not an environment whose center of gravity was amenable to being moved away from its particular brand of northern English, middle-class, white conventionalism to accommodate even other varieties of whiteness, let alone any manner of non-whiteness.

Again, is the examination of my own racialization, my own whiteness, only to be achieved by this minute cataloguing of "Others I have encountered?" Indeed is it to be achieved at all by that means? What is whiteness? It is in part, I would suggest, a mere mirroring of a mirroring, a "not" of a "not." Whiteness comes to self-name, invents itself, by means of its declaration that it is <u>not</u> that which it projects as Other. And there is thus a level at which whiteness has its own inbuilt complacency, a self-naming that functions simply through a triumphant "I am not that." But beyond a point, I fail to name my whiteness if all I do is shout "not that," point to those who occupied the space of "almost," (that is to say, almost nonexistent from a white purview) in my "<u>almost</u> all-white" school.

To mark out whiteness beyond the "not," as an effect of its context-specific and historically formed disciplinary and cultural practices, is challenging since I write in one country, but about another. Whiteness, then, has both local and global resonances. Some of the terms and relationships through which *this* whiteness was articulated may be less than meaningful beyond their own context: that of a particular lower-to-middle middle class, northern English, Tory-voting, largely suburban, Cheshire-accented social conservatism. Although not a church-run school, the Church of England was much in evidence in it, with a religious assembly every day, and one religious knowledge class per week taught, as a matter of fact, by a master who was usually drunk. We called the teachers "Sir," if they were male, of course, or Mrs. So-and-So if they were female. They called the boys by their last names—"Thompson!" "Yes, Sir?"—and the girls by their first. We girls would be told off by the senior mistress for pushing the sleeves of our sweaters up to our elbows—"You're not a washer woman!" "Yes, Miss Greystone." We were told once by an angry Latin master to "Go home and dig potatoes! That's all you're good for!" One can, of course, note rather easily the class-coding of both insults, as well as the anti-Irish prejudice encoded in the latter.

We wore uniforms, which lagged stylistically about seven or ten years behind the world beyond. But we made them our own, turning school skirts into minis, school coats into midis or even maxis. We wore as many bangles as we could get away with on each arm (note that these were imported from India, and coincided with the "hippie trail" of our older white counterparts) and slouched around in a particular kind of shoe called "desert boots." Class, via the educational stratification system mentioned earlier, marked our bodies since all of Manchester, Stockport, and parts of Cheshire could tell, by uniform, which child went to which school, what that suggested about where she or he came from, and what it portended for her or his future. We were thus policed formally, and policed one another also, reading accent, musical taste, appearance, and translating all of these into the terms of class.

Is this, then, how I was taught to be white? Yes and no. No, since I was not born in the school, nor adopted into it from a childhood in the forest with wolves. I was, in other words, already thoroughly white before I arrived in that school. But what I <u>can</u> point to is the imposition, in context of that school, of a particular form of whiteness marked, as I have said, by region, class and political orientation.

There were clear markings of alterity within whiteness itself, and I learned these well. There was only one skinhead, for example, in the school. She dressed differently from the rest of us, and listened to soul and Motown music. All of this tagged her for the rest of us, and for herself, as working class. (Interestingly, though as no particular surprise, her taste in music did not connote any kind of connectedness to blackness, whether of the US or Britain.) There were, as I've said, only five students "of color" in the school.[7] There were also only three students with Germanic names (myself and my sister amongst them). And this too signalled Otherness or at least accrued a status of suspectness on our part, given both simple ethnocentrism, and the sense that in the minds of those around us, World War II had ended only last week. (Were we spies? Or just foreigners?) It seemed that, endlessly, people would say, "Are you German?" And I'd say, "No. My father's family are Polish Jews." (Choosing between alterities? Partly. But also telling the truth as I knew it.) Coming from a Labor-voting family was a mark of outsiderness (we scored there, too). Coming from a one-parent family was unspeakable. Our first term, we were taught how to correctly address the envelopes in which we would take home our school reports: make sure that the flap of the envelope is on the right, not the left side, and address it to your parents, "Mr. and Mrs. Andrew Smith . . . " Mortified, I addressed mine to both parents, and then tried, unsuccessfully, to erase the traces of my father from the envelope on the way home, so as not to hurt my mother.

What I gained from four years at this institution: a schooling in English, French and Latin grammar, from which I continue to benefit daily, and a feeling, while I was there, of laboring under a burden of not-fitting—yes, of difference. At that school I was most at home as one among a rather sad tribe of rebels, most of whom lived in the run-down "boarding" wing of the school rather than just attending on a daily basis. From them I gained a sense that there was strength in oppositionality, and came out of the closet as the child of a single-parent home. (One source of shame ditched for good.) I also joined at that time a nationwide movement by school students to unionize ourselves and seek to have some impact on the conditions of our education, inspired by the National Union of [university] Students. At a certain point, when the only impact I seemed likely to have on my own education was that of expulsion, my father spent most of what he had inherited after the death of his mother, and sent me to what was known in educational circles as a "progressive" boarding school.

How does this naming of whiteness link to the marking of it by its "not not-ness." The two are, of course, simultaneous operations. Crudely, the two taken together say, "We are not that, and within being 'not that,' we are this." To be 'that,' versus failing at one's designated task of being 'this,' were offences of a different order, of course. The Other without was largely, one might say, kept out. Or "happened" not to be there, having been already kept out by means of disciplinary practices external to the space of the school itself (immigration control, employment stratified by race, class-stratified education). The Other within, by contrast, was kept down, by punishment and/or by ridicule, and/or by the expectation of these. At times, the Other without was a resource for the Other within: bangles from India, music from black America.

This way of naming whiteness is much harder work, for it entails the specification and historicization of an almost infinite number of cultural and disciplinary practices. For I have not even begun to name the content of our education, the literature we studied, the history. Nor have I spoken of TV watched after school, novels read.

How was I racialized? How was I made white? I was made white, in the same moment that the effort was made to teach me to be English (not British), to be of the north, of the suburbs, to be lower-middle-class, to be Church of England, to be politically conservative, to be (of course) heterosexual. To be white. Without ever naming it, to be white. To be English. There is at least one "not that" as counterpart to each of these characteristics. And each has a set of histories and practices embedded in it.

II

Memory, and one's sense of self, are continually (re)formed. Chains of events in a life are such that each moment seems both to lead to or even make the next, and to be remade by the moments that follow it. My childhood was then, if not literally relived, certainly reconceived in context of my adult life. In this way, we can say my memories, my self, are (re)formed. Thus in order to say how it was that my first steps towards self-consciousness about the racialization of my own childhood happened, not in Britain but in Santa Cruz, California, I need to say how I came to realize myself as answerable to a set of questions about racism, imperialism and my own history and identity. And in order to explain how that happened, I need to explain how I got to Santa Cruz at all.

I came to Santa Cruz and, more exactly, to graduate study in the History of Consciousness Program at the University of California, fresh from completion of a BA at Cambridge, fresh from three years of intense political activism, and in love with socialist feminism (or as it was named in Britain at that moment, Marxist feminism). I had come to the US against the better judgment of my peers, all of whom viewed this place as the "belly of the beast," and therefore best avoided. For myself, I was pulled by the rumor that in the United States there was something called "women's studies," and pushed by a lack of inspiration about what to do next in Britain, for the trajectories I saw before me seemed either unmanageable or uninviting.

I landed in New York, was dazzled by street names and locations thus far encountered only on TV—Broadway, Central Park—and, rather than flying westward, took a hippie version of the Greyhound bus across the country, so as to know where I was. Cultural difference began to hit as, standing shoulder-deep in the hot water of a mineral spring near Cheyenne, Wyoming (you know, that place from the cowboy movies), an elderly gentleman standing next to his wife and dressed only in a stetson hat, drawled, "Welcome to our country." Back on the Grey Rabbit my new friend Laura commented wryly, "He wouldn't have said that if you were Mexican." I had no idea what to make of this, and didn't ask.

Thus, Ms. English Marxist Feminist arrived in Santa Cruz. In my mind, I'd figured I wouldn't have a problem settling in—we all spoke English, there'd be a left community and a feminist community, and once I found both I'd be all set. But somehow the codes seemed entirely scrambled. Early on a woman told me she was impressed that anyone heterosexual could be a feminist—not the inverse, mind you. She said it was noble of me to take on the feminist struggle as a straight woman (which I was at that time). I found her comment both mystifying and insulting. I had come from a strong network of women who were heterosexual, leftist and feminist: none of them seemed to find that a contradiction, but rather were committed to reframing heterosexuality and their relations with men.

I was taken, in my first week, to hear Meg Christian who was dressed in a Fair Isle sweater and sensible shoes, and who performed to a room full of women of whom one or more would burst out weeping every five minutes, overcome by I knew not what. A far cry from the Patti Smith, Marianne Faithful, Bob Dylan, and Bob Marley who had structured my own and my friends' listening pleasure. "Wholesome" was *not* my middle name. Honesty forces me to admit that I too burst into tears at the Meg Christian show, overcome, finally, by homesickness and the enormity of being in a strange land. Looking back it strikes me now that all of this destabilization had its benefits, beginning to shake open a cultural solipsism and presumed universalism that I had, entirely unconsciously, been carrying with me unexamined, along with the rest of my luggage.

But I still had my political lines intact. At first. In this regard, a key moment for me—although I confess that others to whom I have tried to tell this story have been left puzzled and unmoved by it—had to do with my very strong commitment to campaigning for the provision of workplace daycare for working mothers. I'm not sure, looking back, why working fathers were not also in my mind, but at that point I viewed the provision of "daycare" for children as a key aspect of women's liberation. Some of my earliest experience of political organizing had taken place in context of a struggle with Cambridge University to provide childcare for the children of faculty, staff, and students. At this point I can't remember why and how the question of public- and corporate-funded childcare came up in a seminar room early in my time at UCSC. But I do remember being blown away when two older women, June and Estée, both mothers, both working-class, the former white and the latter a Puertorriqueña from the east coast, told me firmly and pointedly that, not only were they not convinced of the benefits of workplace childcare for women, they had serious concerns in general about placing childcare in the hands of the state or of corporations.

Ms. English Marxist Feminist was stunned, not so much from a feeling that my position was questionable, but from a sense of unreality, of perceiving an impossibility in hearing these two women challenging the position I held. How could it be wrong? How could they believe themselves to be right? Where I came from, the pressure against childcare that I had encountered came from the right wing. It entailed the kind of back-to-the-home patriarchy that had served, since the end of World War II, to justify ideologically women's unequal access to paid work. My point of view, in other words, was embedded in a particular (and I would now say, a partial) reading of history, and my sense of its "rightness" came out of that narrative.

With the hubris of youth, I told Estée I'd like to discuss this some more, and with a generosity of spirit plus, perhaps, some curiosity, she invited me over to her apartment the next morning. At her house, two things happened.

The first of these was that she explained to me her criticisms of the "daycare" idea. First, she said, she distrusted the content of childcare programs, given the role, historically, of state- and corporate-funded education and childcare in the "cultural genocide" of Native, African American, and Latino people in the US. (Although she did not say this, we can also add working-class European immigrants to this list.) Second, in her view, this notion of childcare tied it to wage labor. Thus, while ostensibly a kind of support for women as mothers, it in fact served to make women more effective cogs in a capitalist machine. And this in turn reinforced the imposition of a double shift on mothers. By contrast, in Estée's view, poor and working women needed support as parents in general, rather than as *wage-laboring* parents in particular.

Fifteen years' distance means that I can clarify further what was going on here. Crucially, our two sets of conclusions were rooted in different appropriations of history, mine lacking any knowledge of the blatantly enforced practices of cultural assimilation or domination so significant in US history. And in thinking it all over once again, I am also struck by the realization that our thinking and activism in Cambridge had also side-stepped key questions about culture, class and the care of children. Looking back, I remember clearly our analytical focus: to debunk, from the standpoint of a gender-focused feminism, the arguments of developmental psychologists who (in context of pushing women out of wage labor after World War II) had asserted the necessity of an exclusive mother-child bond as the guarantor of successful early childhood socialization. But we did not think to scrutinize the class and cultural politics of the content of childcare. And we could have done so. For, before and during our activism, discussions were underway in Britain about how working-class identities and communities had been reshaped as the result of state education.[8]

Second, our position was, I think, class-marked in another way—for, although we viewed women's wage labor as both a right and an economic necessity, women's *right* to work was the matter for emphasis. That in turn was unconsciously linked to a kind of "room-of-one's-own-ish" notion of skilled or professional labor perhaps more pleasurable in itself than the kinds of work that sprang to mind as Estée pondered poor women forced, for example, off AFDC and into unskilled, low-paid work through the hypothesized creation of childcare facilities, thus finding themselves doing twice the work for (if they were lucky) the same pay.

The point of this story is not, however, to determine who was right and who was wrong—June and Estée, or me. Nor is it to relativize. Rather, I want to use this story to talk about how knowledge is, indeed, situated, and theory- and strategy-building similarly so. What it makes clear is that one *cannot* think creatively much beyond one's own backyard without detailed information from the backyards of one's neighbors; that second-guessing what is going on someplace else, or simply presuming that what's going on there is the same as what's going on for oneself, will, quite simply, miss the mark. What I learned that morning was one instance of what white feminists have been learning repeatedly (and all too slowly) since the early 1980s, that theorizing and strategizing from narrow but putatively universal subject positions will be at best irrelevant, and at worst more damaging than doing nothing at all. What I was offered that morning, to put it another way, was my first lesson about my own boundaries: the boundaries of my experience; the boundaries of my acquired knowledge; the boundaries of my imagination.

The second thing that happened that morning was this: when I arrived at Estée's, two other women were already there, each about Estée's age, both African Americans. All three were engaged in animated discussion about a younger woman, mother of two preschoolers, in a precarious process of recovery from heavy use of drugs and clearly in no place to take full care of her children. Over tears, coffee, and much discussion, a detailed plan was created whereby the young woman and her children would be helped through this difficult period. At no point did any possibility of recourse to the state come into the older women's plans except in the negative, for part of the concern of the women was to avoid these children being taken into the foster care system. I sat quietly through this discussion—what else, after all would have been appropriate? I was mesmerized, as I remember, as much by the newness to me of what the women had to say, as by the manner in which it was said, the triple-layered eloquences generated out of idiom, cadence, and emotional expression (remember, I was new to the US and even newer to Black English). As the women took their leave and headed downstairs to the door of the apartment, Estée turned to me and with a smile whose meaning my memory cannot quite interpret, said, "That's daycare." I took the point.

It is worth underscoring here that, with a very few exceptions, this was also the first time I had been in private space with women of color. Ever. In my life. This is, of course, not unexpected given the social segregation in play in all of the places I had lived to that date, including, I might add, these United States in which I had recently arrived. But, it took me some time, several months, to realize that something extraordinary had happened in my somehow being invited into that space and that conversation, if not as active participant then certainly as witness or observer.

III

I am not much of a journal writer. Rather, I am of the kind whose flurries of such activity signal periods of intense introspection, heightened emotionality, or a sense that something new is happening to me. The early eighties were a period unusually well documented by my standards.

Two journal entries, however, speak volumes by their very brevity and unfinished quality. The first, undated, but from its context somewhere in 1982 says, "The specific emotional work of being white is"—The rest of the page is blank, but for a single word, pencilled in parentheses at the end of the sentence, presumably at a later date: "(hard)." The second, from around the same time and equally telling, simply says, "I've been trying to write about racism all summer."

That period—1980, 1981, 1982, 1983—was both of the things expressed in the first statement, difficult to specify in the moment, and hard. *In preparation for writing this essay, I read and winced my way through a tortuous period, spotting the moments of insight and of eloquent unknowing, amid the youthful pain, the angst of two intermingled comings-out—coming out as a lesbian, and coming awake as an inheritor of particular raced, classed and national histories. In fact the more deeply I became conscious of whiteness, the harder it got . . . .*

Suspended within the two statements is a set of experiences difficult to make coherent then, and perhaps surprisingly, equally difficult now. As I remember it, even at the time I was struck by the ludicrousness of statement number two: the way it signaled so nakedly the privilege of "choice" about racism so fundamental to whiteness, and also the (ostensibly) displaced relationship to racism that, as a white person, I was able to enjoy. As a white person I needed only to write about racism, rather than experiencing it in any other way. And even if I could not achieve that, I still would not die of that failure.

This was of course a process rather than a matter of instantaneous "enlightenment." I remember, as one key experience, a feminist theory seminar which I attended in 1980, around the time of the "daycare" incident. In it, Gloria, an African American fellow student, criticized the syllabus for its racism, in the sense of its exclusion both of writings by feminist women of color, and for its universalizing assumption that the "history of philosophy" might be fully covered by an examination of Western philosophy. My first thought, when this woman said that we ought, for instance, to examine African philosophy in addition to the more conventional canon, was "But there *isn't* any African philosophy!" My next thought, as Gloria continued to insist that feminism was racist, was that she'd obviously never heard of Marxist feminism, which *"certainly* wasn't racist." I spent the next several weeks trying, almost without conscious thought, to prove this woman "wrong" on any and every point she made in the seminar (about racism or anything else), hoping, I think, to undermine for myself more than for anyone else, the place from which she spoke.

The part that I cannot adequately account for is the next one: how it was that I did not stop there? How was it that I moved onward, so that certainties and firmly held political positions crumbled? Education made us ignorant, it seemed to me, by tying us more firmly into a mindset that seemed ever more compromised as the weeks went by. I remember walking into class one day and actually thinking "I don't know which is the floor, here, and which is the ceiling." I can say, and it would be true, that between the two locations of an untiring challenge and commentary in the seminar room from Gloria, and a deepening connection with Estée, the actuality of racism's impact, both in the feminism that I held so dear and in the world at large, was impressed upon me. But that simply displaces the question—how was it that I stayed friends with Estée (or she with me)? How was it that I didn't simply ignore Gloria until she and the seminar disappeared at the end of the quarter?[9]

I do not know, still, how Estée and I became friends and how it was, in fact, that I stuck to her like glue for the next several years. If that sounds passive on my part, it is not so much that I did not pursue a friendship but that it seems bizarre that she would have wanted one. I was twenty-one to her late thirties (which as I write looks hilariously young on paper—my age!—but which seemed *much* older then). I was childless in comparison with her parenthood of five kids, and middle-class and educated to the teeth in contrast with her poverty-raised, community-activist history of learning-through-surviving. Estée was now trying to make sense of another white institution, the university. As we explained it to one another at some point in an intense connection that lasted around four years, over time we developed a deal whereby I would teach her to write, and she would teach me about the United States. But actually, that was not even one tenth of it. To a degree I think that we were fascinated by our differentnesses, the racial ones made manageable by the national ones, since the latter meant that, in direct terms, we were not actors in one another's racial landscapes. I don't know for sure and I don't think it necessarily matters. It just *was*. I don't know at this point whether I *did* alter her relationship to writing. But what I do know is that, by going where Estée went, meeting who she met, part of the time living with whom she lived with and, I might add, raising all manner of questions from those around us— were we lovers? Was I brainwashed? What *were* we to each other?—my worldview, my sense of self and other, of history, identity, race, class, culture, were remade.

Is it wise to try to explain everything*? Can one really rationalize contingency? The point being that what happened to "me," "Ruth Frankenberg," in the context of that relationship radically transformed what I knew "Ruth Frankenberg" to be. "i" was remade, that's all. This was not a theoretical experience. Rather, it was visceral, though "i" and Estée theorized it at the time, and one may theorize again after the fact. Which as a matter of fact "i/I," am seeking to do right now. And let me say, it is still* hard*.*

Difference. The word has been so overused as to have become almost meaningless. What went on for me, what stunned me, often, into an outer silence and inner turmoil might, once again, be easiest to begin naming as a process of remapping. The ways my world was put together, and the ways Estée's was made, were different in a way that literally shattered the logics and certainties in which I had formerly, and unthinkingly, been ensconced. What I am struggling to express here might be more easily named through some examples. But, as preamble let me note that what at that time I named to myself as all about racism might be more properly understood as an amalgam of issues of race, class, parenthood, culture, sexuality, *and* the idiosyncratic responses of individuals to particular situations.

OK. Let's take the "house" of racism and examine it, brick by brick. But will each brick show us enough to recognize much about the overall design?

Recognitions:
- the realization that while I tended to view the university as a benign institution that was in general my friend, Estée and women I met through her engaged it rather as one in an array of state institutions with which they had to negotiate—the welfare system, the juvenile justice system, Medi-Cal, DMV, the police—any one of whom one might have to deal with, more often with difficulty than with ease, in a given day. Relatedly, while studying was for me the primary focus of my life, for others I met it was one among many tasks to be juggled in any given day or week.
- slowly noticing that if in conversation someone named their friend, relative, husband, child, as being in jail, my instinctive first question—"Oh, what did he (or she) do?"—not only missed the point, but was offensive. Some of the points I missed were that if someone is in jail, that does not necessarily mean that, one, they actually broke the law; two, the crime was one with a victim besides the jailed person him- or herself; or, three, the overall life context and struggle of the jailed person and his/her family should be subordinated in one's attention to the fact of the state's decision to intervene in it. Taking this further, one might say that my subject position, in asking the question, "What did s/he do?" exposes itself as more closely allied with the state, its disciplinary functions, and the histories embedded within them, than with my interlocutor. As a friend set out to visit her son in Juvenile Hall, for example, her concern was not only with "what he had done" (although that was indeed cause for frustration and despair on her part), but also with whether the counsellor assigned to him would be "the racist one," or "the other one, you remember, he dealt with X's boy."

Mundane, daily examples:
- going into cafés in town with friends of color and being treated shoddily;
- talking to an African American friend who had moved with her teenaged sons from a much larger city to Santa Cruz. In this new place, with relatively fewer black youth than where they had previously lived, these young men, both close to six feet tall, found as they walked downtown that crowds would part and sidewalks empty, as white Santa Cruzans crossed the street to avoid them;

Moments when unequal histories met in the same room:
- meeting a woman who said she really didn't want to hear me talk about what I was doing in graduate school, she had never finished high school but had always wished she could go to college;
- being told by a seventeen-year-old friend about her ex-boyfriend, who'd bang his head against the wall, weeping and crying out "whitefolks, whitefolks, whitefolks, whitefolks . . . "

Will each brick described help clarify how I began to recognize the overall design? Who will believe me? Who will think I'm lying?

Difference. As I have noted, racialization is relational. There is a way in which I can only begin speaking about *my differentness, historically and experientially, from women friends who were working class and/or of color, <u>by taking that same route through which I learned about it</u>, that is, by talking about <u>their</u> experiences as different from <u>mine</u>. But there's a risk here, of <u>still</u> not naming or specifying the self, seeming to act as though the center still holds. But it didn't.*

So what <u>was</u> the specific emotional work of being white for me, in that period?

My sense of the normalcy—the unmarkedness although I did not know that word—of my own life was destabilized by the relativizing of my experience on a daily and repeated basis. My life, for a range of reasons, had been different from these friends' lives and would continue to be so. Moreover those reasons were not just any old reasons, but rather, the ugliest of reasons. My racial and cultural privileges were made obvious again and again, not unkindly but as matters of fact, in context of what *wasn't* happening to me. I *had* finished high school. I *was* highly literate, *could* think easily of which word to put where, how to edit the sentence. My kid would probably not be in Juvenile Hall, nor (as it was once expressed to me in the most elegant euphemism) "stationed" at San Quentin. White people's racism was repeatedly made visible to me as daily, hourly, I heard talk that was effectively about the micropolitics of racism in individuals' behavior, about the micropractices of racism in institutions. And the micropolitics of privilege too ("I've been trying to write about racism all summer . . . .") It didn't take a rocket scientist . . . .

To recognize and continue looking rather than turn away. To see these as some of the violent outcomes of whiteness's assertion that "We are not that."

So . But what was the specific <u>emotional</u> work of being white for me, in that period?

Varied. Shame, pain. An inordinate, almost bodily discomfort, perhaps that of twisting and turning to try to get away from, to resist, what was. What is. (*And did not need to be. The injustice. The unnecessary injustice.*) What or who I was. (*And again, did not need to be. Yet, was, <u>is</u>.*)

I viewed my racial privilege as total. I remember months when I was terrified to speak in gatherings that were primarily of color, since I feared that anything I did say would be marked by my whiteness, my racial privilege (which in my mind meant the same). Example. People would be chatting about their mothers. I would not say a word, because by the time I was finished weighing up whether what I was about to say would expose me as race privileged, the conversation would have moved onto what people's favorite breakfast food was. And by the time I'd finished weighing up whether my favorite breakfast was a racist one, the topic would be somebody's new girlfriend.

The idea that to speak would expose me as race-privileged. Expose me as white. Joke! What did I think I was, invisible? That silence would protect me?

In that silence, I tried to "pass" (as what? as racially unmarked? as exceptional? as the one white girl who could "hang"?). One may note that, in this sense, I broke all the rules, written and unwritten, of feminist "unlearning racism" practice—"Speak! Make mistakes! That way you'll learn!" But I was a quick study, and could see plenty, learn plenty, from other white people's mistakes. (White people, that is, who were not trying to unlearn anything.) Why repeat others' offenses? If that sounds terrible, I'm sorry, that's just how it was. How I was. In my silence, I learned. I witnessed. And, as well, my silence was often broken, whether I wanted it to or not.

Acknowledging that racism exists is not so hard. Knowing what to do with it is the issue. I remember when I was sharing a house with Estée and two of her daughters, the youngest, perhaps ten, came into my bedroom as I was putting a new poster on my wall. My mother had sent it to me, a sepia design of the Albert Memorial, one of Manchester's prize landmarks. As this child asked me what it was, and I began to explain it, it dawned on me: the Albert Memorial, Prince Albert, consort to Queen Victoria, here represented atop a tall stone column, presided not only over Manchester but over the building of the British empire. Imperial reverence now remade as imperialist nostalgia. And here I was trying to explain to a brown-skinned child why this image made me homesick . . . .

I have been performing whiteness, and having whiteness performed upon me, since before the day I was born.

IV

The micropolitics of racial cross-traffic. I watched, through those years, as an entire way of seeing crumbled apart (mine), and a whole new one opened up (whose? mine too? mine now? I didn't know). A bit like a kaleidoscope picture changing. Truthfully, "watching" is not really the correct term, or rather, not adequate alone. Watching an edifice collapse, and simultaneously *being* that edifice collapsing and, at the same time as both, being a new building under construction.

How was I made white? Certainly, more ways than I have named here. I have left out, for example, five years of my life between the ages of sixteen and twenty-one. In that time I attended two more "almost all-white" institutions. I became involved in antiracist/antifascist activism in Cambridge, and still did not yet "get it" that racism was, among other things, about me. In Santa Cruz I have left undiscussed the writing, workshops, and discussions about "women's work in the capitalist state" undertaken by the multiracial collective of which June, Estée, and I were all a part. Let me state for the record, then, that this is an incomplete story.

So what has this all been about? The same imponderable relationships between structure and agency? What is *the way home?*

Being and seeing. There is something here that must be examined: being white, seeing whiteness. What are the mutual impacts of these upon each other? The focus of this essay has been on the particular articulations of whiteness that have come to be a part of "me" along with my inhabiting of this body—classed, gendered, nationally and sexually marked as well as raced—that which we might, in shorthand, call "my" whiteness.

This whiteness has emerged as static in some respects, changing in others, and always as contingent, not essential. I have shown that this whiteness, "my" whiteness, is a product of history. That history, here, means both the short and the long durée. That "my" whiteness is, in the forever invaluable phrasing of Antonio Gramsci, yet another case of history having "deposited in [me] an infinity of traces, without leaving an inventory."[10] The effort here has been, amongst other things, to recover parts of that inventory, to display their traces upon me, and also to lay open for reflection some of the circumstances in which that recovery process has taken place. This is, then, about my *seeing* whiteness. And simultaneously it is about documenting, passionately or dispassionately, what my *being*, as a white being, is like. It is about my performing whiteness, my having whiteness performed upon me.

The contingency of "my" whiteness (and by implication of course, of anyone else's) has been dramatized, in my life, by the ways its materiality has been reconstellated through my insertion into a national history—that of the US—different from the one into which I was born and raised. The contingency of my ways of seeing have been vastly more multiply refracted, as evidenced by the number of (re)viewing processes to which it has been possible for me to subject it, the number of reviewing processes to which I have been made subject. But these "seeings" have of course been shaped and limited by my "being," contingent as it is, by my ongoing performances of whiteness.

That which has motivated my political commitment for as long as I remember is the conviction that things do not need to be this way. *That conviction only deepens in me as time goes by. Contingency, and the gridlock of structure and subjecthood seem to have us in a stranglehold.* But it need not be this way.

I am, indeed, still white (surprise!). What *has* changed, then? What has changed is, in varying ways, my *relationships* to the items on the inventory. In some instances the change has entailed a refusal to go along with certain practices and expectations (performing whiteness). In other instances, the change is that of stepping back from an earlier way of seeing, so that it may be witnessed rather than practised unthinkingly (some of the certitudes of "Englishness" may serve as case in point here). However, other items are less malleable. For example, attitudes are one thing, but stepping back to witness my passport will not alter it, nor will it change the fact that a British passport gets one a long way towards entry into most countries in the world. (Is this fact an example of "having whiteness performed upon me?" Or is it that *and* an instance of being performed upon with which I will readily continue to cooperate?) Similarly, my class position has changed but slightly, and the circumstances of that stability are only minimally of my own making, and, of course, not unconnected with race.

If I have changed the meaning of my whiteness, it is inasmuch as I have refused, whenever possible, to perform certain versions of it. When does seeing tip over the edge into refusing to perform? And what are the circumstances wherein that refusal might be successfully achieved? And in what moments can this be an individual question, and in what moments must it be a collective one?

Alertness and compassion. Seeing what is. Asking how it came to be. Disidentifying and remaking self. "When we stop running away from what presents itself in each moment . . . ."[11]

Notes

1   "When we are capable of stopping, we begin to see," Thich Nhat Hanh, 1991. (Thich Nhat Hanh is a Zen master, and the author of numerous books including *Being Peace*, Berkeley, CA: Parallax Press, 1987 and *Peace is Every Step: The Path of Mindfulness in Everyday Life*, New York: Bantam Books, 1991).

Thanks to Saidiya Hartman and Carol Lopes for reading and commenting on the essay, and to Terry Berman for encouragement. Thanks to Lata Mani for contributing the title and other kinds of wisdom to this essay, as well as for over a decade of dialogue on all matters, including race, whiteness, healing and transformation.

2   Audre Lorde, "The Master's Tools Will Never Dismantle the Master's House," *Sister Outsider: Essays and Speeches*, Freedom, CA: The Crossing Press, 1984, 110-113.

3   Spivak has discussed this concept in a number of places, including Gayatri Chakravorty Spivak, "Introduction", "Subaltern Studies: Deconstructing Historiography," Ranajit Guha and Gayatri Chakravorty Spivak, *Selected Subaltern Studies*, Oxford: Oxford University Press, 1988, 13.

4   Here I quote a woman interviewed by me for my book, *White Women, Race Matters: The Social Construction of Whiteness*, Minneapolis: University of Minnesota Press, 1993. Since this quote also appears in the book, to identify the speaker by name here would in fact reveal her identity in the book, something which I do not wish to do since the book interviews were confidential. But I would like to take the opportunity, here, to thank this woman once again for her insight and eloquence.

5   James Clifford, "On Ethnographic Allegory," James Clifford and George Marcus, editors, *Writing Culture: The Poetics and Politics of Ethnography*, Berkeley: University of California Press, 1986, 98-121.

6   Elizabeth Alexander, "Memory, Community, Voice," *Callaloo*, vol. 17, #2, 1994, 409.

7   I place "of color" in quotation marks, for it is not a term in play in Britain. There, black, or a specific national, regional, or ethnic term might more commonly be used. In fact, since I do not remember, as noted, their ethnic or national identities, nor do I know whether Black would have been a term acceptable to them, "of color" may be the most respectful option open to me in this moment.

8   For a discussion of this history, see Simon During, "Introduction," Simon During, editor, *The Cultural Studies Reader*, New York: Routledge, 1993, 1-25

9   Gloria, as a matter of fact, would not in any case have disappeared from sight. Gloria Watkins, or bell hooks, was at the point of completing graduate study in Santa Cruz at the time I arrived there. This seminar took place one year before the publication of bell hooks' first book, *Ain't I a Woman? Black Women and Feminism*, Boston: South End Press, 1981; see bell hooks' comments on this seminar and our interactions in it, in *Feminist Theory: From Margin to Center*, Boston: South End Press, 1984, 13.

10   Antonio Gramsci, *Selections from the Prison Notebooks*, tr. Q.Hoare and G.N. Smith, London: Lawrence and Wishart, 1971, 324.

11   "When we stop running away from what presents itself in each moment, our loving care for ourselves and one another can flow unimpeded," Jack Kornfield, undated. Jack Kornfield, a reknowned teacher of vipassana or insight meditation, is the author of a number of books including, most recently, *A Path With Heart: Perils and Promises of Spiritual Life*, New York: Bantam Books 1993.

2

Mrs. Brent

Gayle Pemberton

My sister Carolyn and I found Papa's flashlight. In the broad, full sun of a late summer Los Angeles morning in 1956 we trained its beam on the side of the white stucco duplex on Fourth Avenue. Then we marched several times around this home, owned by our grandparents—with its red tile roof and carefully manicured lawn—pointing the beam everywhere and anywhere. There was no flash in the light until we moved to the very end of the backyard, where a screened-in playhouse stood. It was a large, lovely space, shaded by a quartet of evergreen trees and shrubs that identified property borderlines. It was cool and dark, with a high ceiling. Carolyn and I had never really learned to make good use of the playhouse, though. It demanded a kind of play that I assign to the nineteenth century—or to my idea of large, well-to-do English families: an open, unadorned space where the imagination created everything that was necessary for fun. Peter Pan could have appeared to the Lord children in this space; Alice's looking glass might well have been in its corner. Nana, Papa, and Mother encouraged us to spend our days there, but we had no toys or play things during our summers in California. More to the point, play for my sister and me always was grounded in some kind of reality, and the emptiness of the playhouse was simply too much for us.

On this day, we had been cast out of the house seconds after my mother had received a telephone call from my father in Chicago. We knew something was wrong. Long-distance calls were too expensive to make even at night, but we *never* made them during daylight hours. This call had to be weighty and the odds were heavily on the side of awful news. We were dispatched so quickly that I have no recollection of even seeing my mother after she put the receiver down. And there was no call for lunch that day, although meals were a formal part of our lives and we always ate three of them, on schedule.

The flashlight provided no information for our Holmes and Watson probe. The playhouse seemed extra cavernous that day, arrogantly rebuking our labored attempts at play. We were worried and afraid. And we knew we were being protected from something we did not want to be protected from—whatever it was. Carolyn, older than I—and too old for the playhouse—tried her best to keep us both calm despite the pall, despite the eerie brightness of the house and of the day as we looked out from the dark, behind the playhouse screens.

Our agitated boredom and concern were finally allayed hours into the afternoon when Nana came out to tell us that Mrs. Brent, my mother's best friend, had been killed in an automobile accident. For hours my mother had been inconsolable, and following conventional wisdom, my grandparents deemed it a sight children should not see. They could only shelter us from the knowledge for a short time, however. Any longer would have encouraged our own barely suppressed panic.

We learned some details: Mrs. Brent had been thrown from the car; her daughter and husband had been injured, but not gravely. Carolyn and I looked at each other with a mixture of embarrassment and distress. Our search for clues with a flashlight now appeared thoroughly without style, intelligence, or sensitivity. We knew how much our mother had treasured her friend. Carolyn knew Mrs. Brent's daughter, Sylvia, but not well. We could not imagine losing our mother; what must Sylvia have felt? And much as we had been screened all day from this awful news, we wished we could have protected our mother from it, just as Sylvia, broken and motherless in some Chicago hospital, would have given everything, I'm sure, to save her mother.

I was seven. Mrs. Brent was the first person I knew who had died. And I witnessed her last meeting with my mother. Carolyn, Mother, and I were set to leave the next day for the biennial California summer. Hair-washing routines in black families can be arduous. Having just done mine—which meant washing and pressing and braiding it—my mother went about doing her own, which took much less time, as hers is almost completely straight. She had just finished washing it in the bathroom upstairs, when Mrs. Brent appeared at the front door. It was a warm June morning, and the breeze through the screen was promising and comforting. Mrs. Brent stepped in the door and mother, wrapping a towel around her head, smiled and apologized for her state. I was standing there, too, as I chose never to be very far away from my mother. Mrs. Brent said she was only stopping by to say good-bye. She looked up at us and insisted that Mother go about her business. Mrs. Brent was a pretty, fair-skinned woman with black curly hair, whom I adored because she was easy to be around, and other adults weren't. She was pretty, as my mother was, and the two of them together seemed right to me. She said she would call later, and as quickly as she had appeared on the threshold, she was off and away.

For months after the sad day we learned of her death, I was haunted by the image of Mrs. Brent standing there. Why that image of her gaze planted itself in my memory in the first place confounded me. But, perhaps by seven I already knew melodrama, and all the scene lacked as it occurred was a soundtrack with appropriate foreboding music, to indicate that something significant, or tragic, was going to happen. Now, so many years later, the import of what came to be my last sight of Mrs. Brent is charged with emotions tied to my racial, sexual, and class identities.

How and when the specter of race penetrates the consciousness of a black American cannot be gauged, of course. Frequently, in literature, our heroes—at five or six—discover their blackness in one daunting moment at school, or in a crowd, or from an evil adult. The children, spurned, are never the same after these revelations. Their ingenuous children's songs are replaced by those of experience and sad wisdom—their black selves invariably assaulted by the implicit or explicit repugnance that has accompanied the news. Famous fictional and autobiographical moments like this abound—in James Weldon Johnson's *The Autobiography of an Ex-coloured Man;* in Zora Neale Hurston's *Their Eyes Were Watching God;* in the first chapter of W. E. B. Du Bois's *The Souls of Black Folk;* in Langston Hughes's short story, "One Christmas Eve"—and in many, many others. However, chances are these memories and fictional creations are only partially correct, and that for most black people, the elements that lead to a discovery of one's racial self are rarely bound into one portentous moment or crystallized into one dramatic scene. It is the repetition of the elements—so often all negative—that gives the illusion of one, titanic moment. And while I can recall any number of attacks on my blackness in childhood, my understanding of what being black meant, and of what my status in life would probably be was as much a result of unpleasant incidents as of more tender ones, like my memory of Mrs. Brent the few times I saw her.

My most basic—and problematic—understanding of my racial being involved color. Long before there were genetic counselors, there was folklore. A considerable amount of it had (and still has) to do with the outward manifestation of one's black blood, be it a smidgen or a full dose. Perhaps some black people have residual memories from cradle days, when sage adult relatives, family friends, or hospital nurses, bent down to their baby faces and looked carefully at the backs of their ears in order to pronounce, with stentorian assurance, what color they would grow up to be. This was a *eureka* moment, savored by no one save the folk detective. As the back of the ear is almost never lighter than the rest of the body, when it is darker than the newborn's face—given our culture's worship of the fair—the news is bad. Hair texture, eye color, size of lips and nose all come under great scrutiny. My mother still wonders where the point on my baby nose went. I say, "It filled out."

In our unfinished passage from slavery to freedom we American blacks have managed, collectively, to resist many things. That resistance caused us to develop music of supreme beauty, irony, anger, humor, and reverence. Our laughter cascades over a spectrum that begins with the deadly serious and ends there, but that includes the zany and ribald along the way. Our speech is endlessly inventive, understated, mocking. But inwardly, the resistance always has been harder. The weight of white supremacy has taken its toll, and legions of black Americans have learned to hate themselves with a zeal reserved, we thought, only for those who hated us.

The range of color in my family went from the very fair, "passable," to very, very dark. My mother's father was the lightest of the ten children in his family, as fair as all but the whitest white people. His older brother, Frank, was very dark, and I remember seeing him a few times during other California visits. He would take my hands and play with the skin over my knuckles. I often wondered what it all meant, but I was sure there was some color logic involved. I was more fascinated with the fact that in the heat of California he would wear a black suit, and long, white underwear, the legs of which would show when he sat down. It was all very confusing since the only long underwear I had ever seen was on cartoon clotheslines. Uncle Frank was a kind old man, though, a World War I veteran, who had survived syphilis to live well into his eighties. He had never married—probably because of the syphilis. And like half of his married brothers and sisters who remained childless, probably because of what blackness in the United States meant to them, he had no children.

Uncle Frank was a living presence to me for a brief time, but it was in photographs that the power of color politics exerted itself. It was quite clear that lighter skin was in predominance in the pictures. But, as I also noticed, color was gendered. In a 1938 photograph, taken at a formal Christmas dance of my father's social club, a line of fifty men stand behind their seated ladies, fewer than five of whom are brown-skinned, although a good three-quarters of the men are of darker skin. In other kinds of group photographs—of people at picnics and parties, high school clubs and college Greek societies—the message was that *successful* women, those with some kind of power, or with men on their arms, or who were queens of this or that, were always fair. When she was about eighteen, after hearing him go on about the qualities he and his friends sought in a woman, my sister reduced my father to an abashed silence by saying, "I guess I wouldn't have had much of a chance with your group." The number one quality was fair skin—which neither Carolyn nor I had.

I remembered relatives saying that it didn't really matter what a man looked like—white or black—to get ahead. They would commiserate with each other over their brown girl-children, sighing when they didn't "get the color" or at least "the hair." In the world of middle-class northern Negroes to which I was born, the message was loud and clear. For me, the photographs—these chronicles of fifty years of family life—constituted a photographic montage with the soundtrack of reprised adult conversations, all forecasting my place as a brown black woman. I might aspire to be great—and there were certainly great brown black women held up to me as epitomes of possibility, steely-eyed founders of institutions and teachers of enormous power and depth, artists of great range and skill—but I would never be a woman in the way the light-skinned ones were.

It took many years for me to learn to luxuriate in my circumstances, to recognize that I did not want to be seen, as light-skinned women so frequently were, as objects of class, family, and male competitiveness. But at seven, I loved Mrs. Brent precisely because she was what I could not be. And if I thought her easy to be around, it was as much attributable to her kindness as it was to my appreciation of light-skinned being. Quite simply, she was my first crush.

How and whether black people can protect each other and themselves from the physical, psychological and emotional effects of racism are matters of politics, opinion, and custom. By this I mean that in its largest sense, we have not been able to do it with much success at all. Black men and women have suffered and died trying to protect each other and their children from assaults by whites. Black children, too, have wondered how they might protect their parents from the tedium of underpaid and thankless work or from the insult of no work. The inequities of race continue. Not long ago, I wanted to protect a black maid from the practiced, supervisory gaze of her white six-year-old charge who rode in the grocery basket she was pushing in a Memphis supermarket. I wished I were in a time warp, but I was not; it was 1993. And small as our futile search for clues to life and death with a flashlight was in the great continuum, my grandparents wanted to protect Carolyn and me from my mother's agony, and her from our inquisitiveness when Mrs. Brent died.

It is difficult enough for adults to try to protect a child from all sorts of dangerous and paltry things, not to mention the rude realities of racism. Poverty, ignorance, habit, and hunger—and all that they spawn—make such protection impossible for a large proportion of black people. For the rest, the difficulties reside in technique and strategy. Time, circumstance, and the everlasting racism are the opponents. There are those parents who never have tried, who have been philosophically against postponing the lessons. Symbolically they throw their children into the pool of racism, and yell "sink or swim." They reason that it is better to do the tossing themselves, than leave it up to fate and strangers in a place—like at school or in a store—before their children have developed reflexes and resources for survival.

These parents are matched by their philosophical opposites, who try to rise above the racial vilification the world directs at their children. They put as good a face as they can on the meanness of the world and rightfully and righteously tell their children that racism is primarily a white problem. I suspect a few more black nationalists are created by the first technique, and optimists by the second, but in the grand scheme of things, the point is moot.

What I knew because my parents loved me very much was what many children know: all the love in the world cannot protect us from sadness or evil. My parents could not keep from me the reality of racism. What I also learned was that all the love in the world could not protect a black person from the inanities of chauvinism and bias within the group. And the zero-sum game I played with myself for years meant that the quality of affection I had for someone like Mrs. Brent would necessarily diminish the love I had for myself. I did not know how to like the fair-skinned others and affirm myself, too.

I became a dreamer, a blood sister of Walter Mitty, a watcher, a large, large-breasted adolescent girl whose fantasies were solo voyages both to faraway places and to the abyss of her own heart. Academic achievement became the ideal displacement. Smart, I could aspire to the genderless category the world creates for bright white women and powerful dark brown ones. Smart, I could be funny and make people laugh. Smart, I also could be a "drum majorette for justice," for myself and others, beating the odds and the racial stereotypes through academic glory.

The nineteen-sixties were an appropriate time for all of this, too. From the vantage points of my *de facto* segregated junior and senior high schools, the future to me actually seemed to hold promise—a far more palpable and buoyant promise than that implied in the canned optimism of "diamonds in the rough" graduation speeches. The election of John F. Kennedy to the White House was part of it. He looked different, he certainly sounded different—there was none of Ike's standard midwestern in that seemingly Kennedy-exclusive Massachusetts accent. We were going toward the future with a young man leading us.

In 1960, the roughest days of the Civil Rights Movement were still ahead. But, in Birmingham, Little Rock, New Orleans, Prince Edward County, Virginia, and a host of other places the foaming-at-the-mouth resistance of whites to desegregation exposed their counterfeit southern gentility for the whole world to see. What assurance we had when we sang the "God is on our side" line from *We Shall Overcome*, even though it hurt to be so constantly reminded that we were despised! What a time to be growing up.

There's something about adolescence that even shots heard round the world can't shake. Yell "Fire!" and a significant proportion of teenagers will make sure their hair is right before heading for the egress. None of my unsubstantiated optimism about the future could possibly alter my creed of self-loathing. I was frumpy. I hated my body. The clothes my family could afford did nothing for it, and my taste did less. I carried large black purses; I hid behind glasses. And after major surgery to reconstruct my left knee after a fall down steel and concrete stairs at school, I half-believed, half-wished that I might walk with a limp for the rest of my life. With such an attitude, I could finally have used the Los Angeles playhouse; I was a gold mine of bathetic scenarios. In this way, I must have been like at least fifty percent of all adolescents, and eighty percent of all adolescents who become academics.

In 1962 Nana and Papa came to live with us in Kansas City. My father, who had grown up without his father, showed no hesitation in welcoming them into our home—he liked my grandparents and they liked him. It would mean a little more food and mortgage money, and he believed in the sanctity of family. The idea of placing ambulatory and sound parents in a nursing home was obscene to him, plain and simple.

I had seen little of Nana and Papa since my little girl California summers, and I looked forward to being with them, too. But I could not know that by being complete my family would become generationally divided. My parents were closer in age to Nana and Papa than they were to their own, somewhat late, children. The dominant relationships in the house became those of people born in the 1880s and in the first decade of the 1900s. There was little these four adults—middle-class blacks with Victorian sensibilities—could say to guide their nuclear-age progeny through the turbulent sixties, other than to reiterate their own Victorian sensibilities. Sex meant disease or pregnancy (they held equal weight). Acceptable pleasure was food.

My parents, especially my father, encouraged my scholarly bent—as he had my sister's. By 1962 she was in college. For many years I thought he encouraged us because he wanted to make sure we would become financially independent through reliable careers—like teaching. His mother had been treated badly by her husband, and she divorced him, striking out into the world with two children, little education and only one marketable skill: to clean. I'll give her this: she made the most of it, becoming a high priestess of clean. Daddy did not want his daughters to meet with a similar fate. But now, I know it went further than that—to the marrow of race and gender. If all the desirable women were fair—or if brown, necessarily very cute—then our independence was important not as an immunity from worthless or dependent men: it was the key to our survival as women alone. My father never once asked me if I was lonely, if I felt bad about being at home every Friday and Saturday night, or, during my years in college, if I had ever gone out on a date. What's more, I would have been shocked if he had asked, so convinced was I of the legitimacy of his aesthetic of life and love. My mother once allowed that perhaps I was too forthright in my opinions to be thought desirable by men. I was about seventeen then, and convinced that if one had to play dumb to be a woman, I would rather be the genderless thing I was. Maybe she had played dumb, but she was fair, so what difference did it make?

My tenuous self-regard was enhanced when I spent a year as an exchange student in the United Kingdom. The relationship between race and gender did not disappear; it merely became defined differently. I could see—as writers and critics had seen for years—that England's social fabric depended upon various charades, paramount being the predominance and preponderance of single-sex schools. Coeducation was only very slowly coming about, and then in what they called "secondary modern" schools for those not destined for a university education. The grammar and boarding schools remained for either boys or girls exclusively.

I was a curiosity: an American, a black, at the day grammar school I attended. The school had only recently admitted the daughter of a Pakistani family to what we would call the third grade. This concession was deemed worthwhile and brave by the community, despite the fact that the population of Pakistanis was growing at an enormous clip in Bradford. Mocked by T. S. Eliot in *The Waste Land*, the "Bradford millionaires" were changing their hue. It only made sense that their children would attend the best schools.

We wore uniforms to school for half the year. It made such great sense not to worry over clothes every day. More important for the British—and another charade category—uniforms leveled the playing field a bit. The scholarship girls, who befriended me and who naturally were my friends, could not be distinguished immediately from their more affluent schoolmates. And unless one hung around the senior prefect's room, or watched the wealthier girls being picked up in Jaguars and Bentleys at the end of the day, there was no telling who was what. Some of the well-to-do even rode buses.

In England, the great lesson I learned was that while I wrestled with my female identity via its racial implications, I watched my white British girlfriends sort theirs out in terms of class. My blackness was classed, of course; the black bourgeois world that created my parents prided itself on being the opposite of the putatively sexually licentious black lower classes. What else is any middle class for? But the colonized are not colonizers, and class was as palpable a reality in England as color was among black people. On the other hand, rocket science is not required to explain the nonexistent difference between an upper-class black and a lower-class one in the minds of racist white Americans.

I watched my schoolmates act out scenarios as old as their fading empire. The rich ones, who smoked and who sought to have about them a smart and knowing air—like Diana Rigg as Mrs. Peel on the British television hit of that season, *The Avengers*—were relaxed about sex. They could afford to be. If their A-level examinations failed to guarantee them a spot in some university, they had alternatives. I envision them now, permanent denizens of some Merchant and Ivory film, traipsing regularly out to the guest cottage of a country home to have trysts with earnest and ardent, but clumsy, public school lovers.

The middle-class and scholarship girls ran the gamut from the cloistered, to the fast, to those whose boyfriends of several years, it was understood, would become their husbands in a few years more. Some of these girls were religious nonconformists as they were still called—non-Church of England Protestants. And while many of them were considered "outsiders," these more actively Christian girls were quite comfortable with their identities. As far as I could see, their transgressions never threatened their class identities, as when a good friend of mine left school and was next seen as a waitress in Keswick, in the Lake District. She had shattered her chances to go a university. The reason seemed clear to me and others, and her actions were consistent with her class and gender according to the adult custodians of the status quo: she feared she might not do well on her examinations. There might well have been panic among the mostly sympathetic had she run off with a hod-carrier or a lord.

I left England reluctantly; I had become comfortable in my genderless, foreigner role. The prospect of going home merely intensified my sense of being an outsider in the land where I was born—more of a witness than a participant in life.

World and campus politics of the late nineteen-sixties were enough to unravel even the most poised and self-confident young people. At the precise moment when white colleges and universities began to open their doors to significant numbers of young black men and women, the Black Power Movement appeared with its impromptu nationalistic idioms, railing against the liberal integrationist sensibility supporting the black students' admission. On campuses with more than ten black students, this group would create prescriptions about what constituted appropriate black identity. I understood it. Students now took the opportunity to vent publicly the rage, frustration and anger that had been suppressed for so many years. But I could only partially enter into the deal, as the Civil Rights and Black Power Movements had quite openly consigned women to roles of helpmates at best, sexual vessels at worst. Within the context of Black Power campus politics, there was little room for me to mature beyond my very real alienation or my sophomoric certainty that the alienation would last forever.

I was still smart, though, and funny. Late at night I would make popcorn with my friend Karen, who was of Italian and Irish extraction. I transferred after two years, but I will always remember her with fondness because she believed we both suffered from the same malady. "Ace," she would say—the only nickname I've ever had that I liked—"Men look at our faces and they see that we're serious." Somehow that made the moment fine, because we wanted to be serious as much as— or even more than—we wanted men. She was attractive, but she was also smart, funny and tough. The last I heard she had married a much older man.

I walked a campus tightrope, spending most of my time with white female friends, going to black campus meetings and helping plan programs. But I cloistered myself from the sexual identity politics of Black Power—and that may have been the first self-affirming thing I'd done in years. Living in England had taught me enough to know that racial reasoning alone was inadequate to the task of explaining oppression. It was an early lesson in the limits of identity politics. I was content not to be fair, or cute, if brown. I may have been a pariah to those who looked upon my association with white students as the cardinal sin. But I preferred my apostasy over their deprecation and shunning of my female being. Of the two kisses I received in all my college years, the one from a woman was the best, but I was sure—as she was—that we did it only because we were castoffs who coincidentally had a particular urge at the same time.

Boston, according to the attitudes of millions of white and black people, is supposed to be a lousy town for black people. Perhaps it is because Boston is so self-consciously white—in its Irish, Italian, and WASP forms. The Irish are routinely singled out for their racism. But, Boston is more than Irish. Boston's religious character, the diverse Roman Catholics, and the dominant Congregational and Unitarian Protestants also reinforce white ethnic identities. Driving to the North End to buy some of the truly splendid ricotta and mozzarella cheeses one can find there my friend Kathy—blue-eyed and fair—said she was made to feel decidedly out of place as she entered the Italian cheese store.

I moved to the Boston area in 1969, and discovered that I liked it. I always ask people "compared to what?" when they speak of its racial climate. Could one seriously say that Chicago, or Detroit, or New York, or Washington, or Los Angeles, or Houston, or the oft-cited Atlanta, are really better places to be black? Perhaps they are because there are more blacks in those cities. But, having lived in several of them, I don't think so. El Dorado for black people hasn't yet been found. However, most people inside and out of Boston believe the press about it and conform. I never made a habit of going to Fenway Park, at that. But Boston was a fine place for me. I was in graduate school at Harvard. I could see what centuries of white, patrician success had wrought. Some people—professors included—made it a point to suggest that the university had gone to exceptional lengths to bring me and other blacks there. I allowed as how that was very good; we were worth it. Those blacks who say affirmative action makes them feel inferior because they can never, ever *really* know if they're good enough have always appeared to me to be foolish. They should relax and look around them to see that pure merit is a very difficult category to define. Does a high grade on a law school entrance examination ensure a brilliant student and great future lawyer? No. Are these white peers so unremittingly, without exception, fabulous? No. One's worth is intangible and incalculable on a scale of caprice.

In graduate school, I realized that some of my professors and classmates would never accept me on equal terms, and that others would. There are many more interesting exercises in life than trying to change the attitudes of people hardened not against one's self—they can't *see* that—but against one's color. And graduate study had enough pre-existing hoops for me to jump through already without my creating more.

I navigated through Harvard's waters by staying well away from my fellow graduate students in English and the black graduate contingent on campus. My independence, no matter what had brought it about, was complete. My only group association was with students and co-resident advisors at Radcliffe's North House, where I spent the lion's share of my residential graduate years. I've been told by a male friend that people looked upon my role as house mother at the small dormitory at 60 Walker Street as that of mammy. The free three squares a day in the House cafeterias had stimulated my tendency toward fat—and mammies are supposed to be fat—but his observation merely reaffirmed why I was independent. From the outside people would never understand the affirming, non-stereotypical relationships a group of women can develop among themselves. My charges were all of two or three years younger than I, so in honor of that wide chasm in age, they called me "Mother." And because my life at Radcliffe provided the longest and most cohesive residential life I'd had since puberty, I looked upon it more as an undergraduate life than as a graduate one. I feel no attachment to my two true undergraduate institutions; I will forever be devoted to Radcliffe.

Moreover, my journey through graduate school at Radcliffe resembled an undergraduate's journey. I revelled in the lives of my housemates: a group of nine women perceived to be bluestockings because they insisted on a single-sex dorm when the Harvard and Radcliffe houses were becoming coeducational. And they supported me in my life. We all were thought to be apolitical in a time when one was as likely to see the North Vietnamese flag hanging out of a dormitory window as the Stars and Stripes. We spent large chunks of time in the house kitchen, making and eating sweets. There was a regular presence of various males—half of them enamored, futilely, with one house resident or another, the other half hanging on tenaciously and barely to sleep-over status. Their visibility kept another label, that of lesbian, away from the house, although the two of us living there had no idea we were.

"Ace, men look at our faces and they see that we're serious." The black men in my life were homosexuals who liked me because I was serious, and funny. Maurice was one of my oldest friends. We said hello in our seventh grade classroom and I said goodbye to him two weeks before he died of AIDS, at the age of forty-five. He was as important to me as anyone in my life. We loved each other very much; we laughed hard, fought often but not seriously, and found comfort in silence together. I did not ask him more than he would tell me about his private life. He followed in like fashion, all the while accepting as a given the reality of my sexual existence and passion, when I did not know how to express it. And, perhaps because he was gay, he understood very, very well that gender and sexuality are inextricable components of racial identity. Our last fight, which was serious, and fraught with unnamed and unexamined ire, was in part due to his indignation and fear that I had given up on life. Maurice was wrong about me and life, but the fight did nothing to alter him in my memory: he was, quite simply, grand.

Remembering a year abroad, graduate school life, and Maurice establishes the link between my childhood sense—inchoate, but still sound—that my racial identity was tied to my being a girl— and my young adult acceptance of myself as foremost an independent traveler on the slippery slopes of racial, gender, and sexual politics. Long since past the idea of playing dumb, I realized I wasn't particularly interested in men. From the outside it seemed that all heterosexual relations were ultimately predicated upon the management of his ego. There were exceptions, of course, but they were just exceptions to me. It was easy, then, to settle into a private life that revolved around family, and a few close friends.

As a black, female English professor—a rare bird in the academic landscape—I was what I had always been: the fulfillment or lack thereof of white expectations of what a black person is. I was simultaneously a stereotype and an original at any given moment. As a woman in the academy, I was like my interest in black writing or my white female colleagues, undervalued and rarely rewarded. And as a romantic without an object, I was in good company.

Nothing remains of the house my grandparents owned in Los Angeles except photographs. It was in the path of the Santa Monica Freeway. I am sure that if I could see the playhouse now, I would marvel at its small size—just as the vast football field behind our home in the Chicago projects somehow turned into a standard-sized alley when I visited it as an adult. I don't know what happened to Mrs. Brent's daughter or husband, or if this memory of her would resurrect in them feelings of happiness or dismay. I do know that the fitful attempt that Carolyn and I made to find the secret of our mother's sadness, with a flashlight, on white stucco, on a bright, smog-less Los Angeles day in 1956, stayed with me for almost forty years. Seeking knowledge in broad daylight, with a hand-carried light (Papa called it a *torch*) is an appropriate metaphor for my attempt—and I believe that of my sister, too—to find out what being black is supposed to mean.

We went to the playhouse and tried to improvise something, in spite of the fact that we had not satisfactorily done it before. Excluded from the main drama in the house, we tried to figure out how to star in our own, to choose ways of pleasing ourselves, if we couldn't please anyone else. In the tacit belief of our family that women should be light-skinned, being brown meant that we had already lost some race that we didn't even know was being run. Improvising the self, then, became both a necessity and a choice. Going through life holding a light up to all the surfaces revealed not only the flaws and pretenses, but the hidden beauty, too. Living in a society where surfaces stand for all, I quickly learned that I would be judged by mine. It made the urge to reach the heart of things urgent, and I learned to distrust all narrowly prescribed ways of being either black, or a woman, or both. Life literally became a quest, not for the Grail—how boring to find it—but for more days to improvise a self.

My memory of Mrs. Brent is significant to me because I understand that not being able to look like her, I was released to make myself. Throughout the years since her death, I rarely look anyone in the eye who is leaving for more than a short, local trip. I absolutely refuse to wave or look down from a set of stairs at anyone who is walking out of the door. For almost forty years, I have averted my eyes at partings at airports, train stations and curbs. For almost forty years I thought that was my only legacy from Mrs. Brent.

3

Red and Black in White America
Discovering Cross-Border Identities and Other Subversive Activities

David Wellman

"There is no pure culture. Itinerancy is the rule."
—Paul Gilroy

Until recently, my racial identity had no name I would answer to. Whiteness was never an unmarked category for me. I've not taken my whiteness for granted, or experienced it as normal, invisible. My self-conception has been in a permanent state of war with the socially constructed version of who I'm supposed to be.

My family was always on the outside. We stood out in my neighborhood. When we moved to Clairmount Street on the northwest side of Detroit in 1950 our block was already "in transition." That meant liberal Jewish people were fleeing to the suburbs. By 1953 we were one of the only white families on the block.

But people didn't talk about our whiteness. Neighbors didn't say much about race. They were, however, fascinated by my parents' communist politics. We were the Reds on my block.

My parents were openly and publicly Communists. And when the Cold War got hot, their faces were splashed prominently on the front pages of all three Detroit newspapers. In September, 1952, my father was arrested for violating the Smith Act. He was charged with conspiring to teach and advocate the violent overthrow of the government. Soon after, my mother was arrested under the Walter-McCarren Act. Accused of being an "undesirable alien," she was subsequently ordered deported to Canada.[1]

Because they were communists, my parents didn't identify themselves ethnically. Even though they were both children of immigrants (my father's family came from eastern Europe, my mother's from Canada), neither saw themselves as ethnic. Or religious. My father's people identified as Jewish; my mother's as Christian. But neither side practiced religion. Their identity was political. They were Communists. That was their ethnicity. The powerful categories in our lives were not ethnicity, religion, or race. The category that defined us was politics. We were seen as Red, not white.

Anyone who read a newspaper or watched television knew we were Reds. And for those who managed to ignore the mass media, FBI agents marked our redness. The government's eyes, always at least two sets of them, were visible twenty-four hours a day, inside the FBI cars parked outside our house. Periodically we were followed to school by agents who made no effort to disguise themselves. My sister and I were the only two kids at Brady Elementary regularly tailed by the police. Looking back, and using today's language, we were raced as red. We weren't treated like white people. We were the Reds.

Taking Sides

Being red meant white kids marginalized us. We were pariahs. Some of my white classmates were not allowed to play with us. If they did, it was an act of rebellion. When whites hung-out with us, it was an incipient form of protest.

Being red also meant that some black kids held my parents in high esteem. Not for their politics, but because they were public outlaws. "Your old man must be some kind of bad dude!", Maurice whispered the day after my father's bail had been set at a six-figure mark.

The white teachers treated me no differently than my black classmates: suspiciously, and sometimes with contempt. Whatever privileges whiteness conferred were cancelled by my redness. So I didn't have a particularly well-developed sense of self. I'd been taught I wasn't very smart. I couldn't do arithmetic or spell. I didn't know the difference between articles of speech and articles of war. And I certainly couldn't diagram sentences. I agreed with Mrs. Ross, my sixth grade homeroom teacher, when she told me I had been assigned to a "good" homeroom next fall in junior high school. "There must be some mistake," she said. I thought she was right.

The mothers of my black playmates looked out for us. If Vickie or I got locked out by mistake, they took us in. When I skipped school, they called my mother. Every time I left George's house bound for home, Mrs. Smith would call my mother to say I was on my way. Maurice's mother made a special effort to let my mother know we had a place to stay if things got worse. I felt comfortable and protected—safe—knowing there were adults looking out for me, people I could count on. I could not help but recognize that, except for the small circle of my parents' communist comrades, the few friendly faces in an otherwise hostile world were black.

I don't remember ever wishing I was black. But I do recall taking the "black side" when arguments erupted along racial faultlines. I'd like to think I did that because it was the right side. I'm not sure that's true though. More likely, I did it because my black friends supported me. How could I take the white side when they treated me like an outcast?

Solidarity Forever

Being red had some benefits. It meant growing up in a world of living color. The red community was "integrated." Today we would say it was diverse and multicultural. Communists were "antiracists" long before racism was a word in the American political vocabulary. I discovered that dramatically one afternoon. I was maybe six or seven, sitting in the back seat of the family car carelessly rhyming words. I don't remember the particular rhyme. But I'll never forget what happened when I used the word nigger. Before I could utter another word, my mother turned around and slapped me. "Don't you *EVER* use that word again!", she yelled. "If I hear it, I'll wash your mouth out with brown soap."

I never used the word again. At least not until years later, when a couple of my black friends used it in a manner they considered affectionate. But my mother insisted they not use that word in her presence.

My parents didn't use words like "antiracism." They talked about right and wrong. Discrimination against Negroes was wrong. Keeping Negro baseball players out of the big leagues was not right. One of my mother's lapel buttons from World War II says it best: "Score

Against Hitler. Lift the Ban on Negro Players." So when Jackie Robinson broke the color barrier I became a dedicated Brooklyn Dodger fan. That was making a political statement in Detroit because the Tigers refused to hire black players. And didn't until much later, holding out as one of the last all-white teams in the majors. But I was deeply conflicted a couple years later when Jackie Robinson denounced Paul Robeson before a congressional committee investigating communist activities in the black community.

There was no official Civil Rights Movement yet. Nevertheless, my parents and their friends were already doing work that would later be called antiracist politics. Annie Shore headed up an organization called the Civil Rights Congress. Coleman Young and Chris Alston worked with the National Negro Labor Council. We went to meetings where I heard slogans like "Save Willie McGee" (a young black man in the Deep South sentenced to die for allegedly raping a white woman. He was not saved). I saw banners that read "Free Haywood Patterson" (one of the original "Scottsboro Boys" who had escaped from an Alabama chain gang and was arrested in Michigan. He was freed, but re-arrested on another charge and eventually died in a Michigan prison). My sister and I loved the Paul Robeson concerts at Reverend Hill's church. But we didn't have much choice when W.E.B. Du Bois came to town. We *would* go listen to Doc lecture, my folks insisted. Whether we wanted to or not. People sang the "Negro national anthem" ("Lift Every Voice and Sing") at the beginning of meetings. Events ended with a rousing rendition of "Solidarity Forever." And everyone knew the words to both songs. All the words.

Blackness was never a devalued identity in our house. Quite the contrary. Black people—or to be true to the language of the 1950s, "Negroes"—were held in very high esteem. Langston Hughes was a family hero. We had a picture of him sitting with my father in Civil War Spain. My mother loved Billie Holiday records. Lena Horne was another favorite. She listened to Count Basie and Duke Ellington. Many of my parents' closest friends and dearest comrades were black people: Tom Dennis, one of my father's co-defendants in the Smith Act trial. Dennis and his wife Ellen lived with us during the trial. George Crockett, Jr., my mother's lawyer and his wife, Etheleyne Crockett, my mother's doctor. Revels Cayton, a leader of the West Coast longshoremen's union, was my mother's childhood buddy from Seattle. When Communist Party leaders came to town they often stayed with us. My sister and I were excited when Louis Burnham, James Jackson, Claudia Jones, Claude Lightfoot, or Henry Winston (black people who were nationally recognized leaders of the Communist Party) were house guests. Black people moved in and out of our lives routinely, everyday. An all-white gathering would have been noteworthy, an exceptional event provoking comment. Mixed company was normal, taken for granted. Homogeneity was not.

Being Cool

While we weren't treated as white, I was not comfortable with the red identity being constructed for me by the government and the media. I didn't identify "red." My heroes were not communists. Lenin and Stalin were not my role models. I thought the communist kids who identified with communists were conformists. "Squares," I called them. I identified with James Dean and Marlon Brando. I worked hard to affect the rebellious sneer both of them did so well. Brando's role in "The Wild One" was my favorite. He spoke for me when the locals asked him what he was rebelling against. "What d'ya got?", he grunted. Miles (Miles Davis), "Bird" (Charlie "Yardbird" Parker), and "Mr. B." (Billy Eckstine) were my models for being male and masculine. I found them more complicated, mysterious, and rebellious than most of the white male communists I knew. The white guys were so damn linear, predictable, and single-minded. They had very little sense of humor or irony. They didn't know how to move, much less dance. And they clapped on the wrong beat. They were square, like their kids. I, on the other hand, saw myself as "cool." I identified with the "cats" at my junior high school.

Cool was gendered. Today it would be called masculinist. Girls couldn't be "cats." We called them "chicks." Or worse. I got smacked in the mouth when my mother overheard me call my girlfriend a "broad."

Hutchins Intermediate occupied strategic sociological territory. From the east side, it drew working class and poor black students, many of them first generation migrants from the deep South. From the west and a little bit north, came the remnants of a working-class Jewish community along with upwardly mobile working-class blacks. Immediately north of the school, an emerging black bourgeoisie was moving next door to retreating white industrialists; and to the south, poor whites—called "hillbillies," sometimes "hitwillies"—lived alongside poor blacks.

Out of the Hutchins' experience blossomed an amazing set of cultural innovators—in Gramsci's terms, "organic intellectuals"—who eventually left a profound and distinctive impact on American popular culture. People like actress-comedienne-writer Lily Tomlin, poet-essayist-novelist-screenwriter Al Young, Motown stars Smokey Robinson, Diana Ross, and Martha Reeves, along with songwriter Barrett Strong, were all Hutchins students in the mid-1950s.

Hutchins enabled strangers to invent an inclusive common identity, language, and code, while simultaneously acknowledging and valorizing the important differences between them. Without relinquishing their class, racial, or ethnic identities, a portion of these kids fashioned a collective outlook. They transformed elements of the hip jazz world, southern black and white culture, American-Jewish traditions, and working-class activities into an identity they called "cool." The red kid fit in perfectly.

Being cool meant being conversant in a distinctive language; it meant being what today would be called multilingual, being able to talk a special kind of talk, what we called talking "that talk." That talk included its own vocabulary: music was "sounds," hairstyles were "dos," glasses were "peepers," and when all was well, things were "copacetic." Using today's language, we could switch codes as well as modes.[2] In addition to being able to talk that talk, we had to be able to "walk that walk." We had our own dress code: white shirts, collars turned up, Levis—neatly pressed—with a handkerchief carefully folded over the right rear pocket, and highly shined, pointed shoes, preferably "Stacies."

We had to be able to recognize and use important distinctions. Like the difference between being "hip" and being "jive"; between being "jive" and being "lame"; between what was "happening" and what was "not happening." Jewish kids learned to distinguish between talking "shit," talking "jive," and talking "smack." Black as well as hillbilly kids talked about the differences between schmucks vs. putzs, on the one hand, and schlemiels vs. schlemazels on the other. Being cool involved cultural sharing as well as cultural dexterity. Cool black and hillbilly teenagers ate kosher deli. Cool Jewish kids learned to like grits, black-eyed peas, greens, ham-hocks, and chitterlings (and how to pronounce that as well).

Being cool provided us with more than the veneer of hipsterism. It also gave us the opportunity to participate effectively in what would now be called a multicultural world. We learned how to be bicultural, not just bilingual. We learned how to operate as competent actors in more than one cultural world. We became knowledgeable about what was appropriate and what was inappropriate, what was acceptable and unacceptable behavior and talk in cultures that differed radically from our own.

While recognizing racial and ethnic differences, "being cool" did not refer to one's race. Rather, it referred to a way of being, a style, a language, a pose. Like the adult jazz world it transformed, being cool was an existential ethos, a complicated style of rebellion which contained the seeds of a new culture, and a new identity in which it was possible to both transcend and valorize racial, class, political, and ethnic differences. Being cool was a negotiated achievement produced by the dialogue between racial, ethnic, and class cultures. It was an accomplishment, a construction—not an ascribed, primordial birth-right. One was not born with this identity. It was both practice and practiced performance. The cool identity was inclusionary (at least among males), improvisational, participatory, and adaptable. The perfect combination for a red boy who was white, but not treated so, who found security in the black community and emulated hipster rebels.

By the time I graduated from high school, my folks had left the Communist Party. We were no longer "the Reds." Now we were the only white family on our block. And I was perfectly comfortable with the status. In fact, I took pride in it. I was proud that my parents hadn't capitulated to the fears and fantasies that drove our white neighbors to the suburbs. I felt reassured by the close connection between their principles and practice. I liked that kind of predictability and consistency.

I also felt special. Not very many white guys were comfortable on Clairmount. They didn't know how to act, how to survive. They didn't know the culture and couldn't speak the language. They didn't know what was appropriate and what was inappropriate; what was acceptable and what was unacceptable. They didn't know the rules: when to make eye contact and when not to; when to smile and when to be expressionless; when to be revealing and when to be opaque. They didn't know how to be in the minority. They only knew one world and I knew two. I took pride in being able to function effectively in contexts my white high school classmates had only read about, or seen on television. I was proud to know how to be "different" and feel comfortable about that; able to be an "insider" in one situation, and an "outsider" in another.

It felt good to be trusted by our black neighbors, to know I had proven I was dependable. I was proud to be accepted. And excepted. I took it as a compliment when my black buddies confided that "you're not like most white people." I liked that kind of differentiation. I didn't object to being that sort of exception. I feared the white police, not my black neighbors. The cops were suspicious. What was a white guy doing in this neighborhood? And they didn't believe me when I said I lived there. So they frisked me and insisted I produce some identification. In contrast, the black guys on my block protected me: "Don't fuck with him," an outsider would be told, "he's cool."

Other than that, there was no name for people like me. We didn't have a concept, a label, or a special identity. On my block, I was "cool." That meant being part of the scene, competent, supposed to be there. My presence didn't call for a theory or an explanation. I didn't need to invent a reason for being there. My identity was "he's cool."

Everyone knew I was "white." Including me. But that wasn't the relevant category. On Clairmount that didn't matter. The critical category was "he's cool." He belongs here. I know from today's vantage point that sounds extraordinary. But what is even more remarkable is how *normal* I felt.

Unfortunately, the experience was not symmetrical. My black male partners were never "cool" in all-white neighborhoods. They would be "out of place," and rousted by Detroit's virtually all-white and notoriously brutal police force.

I didn't consider myself a "white Negro." I did read the Mailer essay in college but it didn't resonate with my experience. In fact, it disturbed me. Too dichotomous, biological, and unnecessarily sexual, I thought. Because my racial identity had no name at the time, I identified more closely with the title of James Baldwin's book, "Nobody Knows My Name."

The farther I got from the neighborhood and the experience, the more exceptional and extraordinary the two became. And the more difficult it was to convince my white friends that I really did live on Clairmount near Linwood, and that I actually felt quite comfortable there. A couple of middle-class (white) Jewish students in college challenged my account. "Prove it!" insisted one of them. So I told him to drop me off at the corner of 12th Street and West Grand Boulevard.

(Four years later 12th Street would be one of the sparks that ignited a bloody rebellion that convulsed through Detroit for a week.) "Pick me up at Clairmount and 12th Street in an hour," I told him. "I'll walk there." And I did. I knew there'd be no problem. 12th Street was one of my stops on the way to Hutchins.

Introductions to Whiteness

When I entered graduate school, in the early 1960s, I was the only person in my class who had been raised in a predominantly black neighborhood. That was my introduction to whiteness as an unmarked category. It took place at the University of California in Berkeley. For the first time in my life, whiteness was normal. It was invisible.

And I was terribly uncomfortable.

Except for the color of my skin, I shared almost nothing with my classmates. I was completely unprepared for life in an exclusively white world. I didn't know the rules these people followed. We used the same words but spoke radically different languages. I didn't know how to act. I was as uncomfortable in this all-white environment as my white high school classmates were on Clairmount. I couldn't wait to go home.

I discovered the source of my alienation when college experiences were discussed. Except for two working-class European-American women, also from the Midwest, the bulk of my cohort were educated at elite private schools, Ivy League colleges, or prestigious state universities. Very few came from land grant colleges, much less commuter schools like Wayne State in Detroit.

An old category, one my parents talked about a lot, took on new significance for me. The category was "class." And now it was quite salient. To this point, the word had been a weapon in my parents' ideological vocabulary. It was a slogan, an outmoded idealization, I thought. It was part of their Marxist ideology, and I wasn't a Marxist. No longer a hipster either, I now fancied myself an existentialist. (Though I had difficulty explaining what that meant.) All of a sudden, class became a lived category. And it explained my alienation from people who only shared complexion.

The category was useful in another way. It contained a language of differentiation that enabled me to distinguish myself from people with whom I shared similar amounts of melanin, but who treated me like an other, and toward whom I felt enormous hostility. I didn't have to be one of them. I could be "working class."

Ironic.

In Detroit, being working-class was normal. Class was the unmarked category, the taken-for-granted. Race and ethnicity were the salient markers. But in Berkeley the situation was reversed. As a result, my class identity was not discovered in working-class Detroit. It was constructed in bourgeois, all-white Berkeley.

I didn't call myself "white" until 1966. That was when the Student Nonviolent Coordinating Committee (SNCC) put Black Power on the American political agenda. White SNCC supporters were encouraged to organize against racism in the white community. For the first time, I was no longer "cool" in the black community. And though that was a deep hurt for me personally, I thought the strategy was a wise one. But it did present me with a political problem: what community would I work with? Realizing I wouldn't be a very good organizer in the white community, I decided to follow another path. Using my recently discovered identity as an unmarked category—my whiteness—and my graduate training in sociology, I would spy on the white world. Passing for white, I would find out what liberal middle-class whites really thought about black people. I saw myself as an undercover agent for the Civil Rights Movement. Recording what white folks said when black people weren't around, I would expose them. And I did. My findings were published in a book I titled *Portraits of White Racism*.[3]

I called myself "white" when I wrote the book. That identification was political. It was done to make the invisible visible, to force white Americans to recognize the reality of race in American life. So I called myself white for tactical political reasons. But I couldn't identify with the category. Except for certain morphological features, it didn't really fit. Instead, it felt like an uncomfortable garment. And I didn't wear it very well.

Convergence, Transformation, and the
Discovery of Borderlands Consciousness

It didn't fit because this social-political construction was at odds with my self-conception. And my experience. On Clairmount, racial identity was never neatly and dichotomously packaged in black and white. Identity was not a binary category, automatically produced by the color of one's skin. Nor was it fixed and static, the result of rules, roles, and obligations one is born into. Rather, it was constructed, negotiated, fluid, and dialogic. People were evaluated by their behavior, not their pigmentation. Melanin didn't matter if one was cool. The Civil Rights Movement reinforced my Clairmount experience. People who organized demonstrations, got arrested, and did community organizing called themselves "movement people," "brother," and "sister." SNCC people thought of themselves as members of a "beloved community." While serious differences between races were recognized, and actively engaged, most of us actually believed that we would overcome.

When the Civil Rights Movement was defeated, there was no language that spoke to my experience, that gave voice to my self-conception. Usually I was exceptionalized, constructed as different from other white people by my black friends. No longer "cool," or a member of the beloved community, I knew who I was not: not-black and not-white. I didn't belong in either category. I was none-of-the-above. The one whose racial identity had no name.

While proud of it, I've never been completely comfortable with that identity. An identity that has no name is not an identity. Being defined negatively, or not-someone else, is not a useful sense of self. It does not convey the depth and complexity of my experience; the richness and diversity of the self I have constructed.

Fortunately, times are changing. Languages are emerging that catch up with the racial identities forming in America during the past-quarter century. And, though nobody calls me by it, my racial identity finally has a name I can answer to. I realize now that I am a "border" person. Clairmount was a "borderland." So was SNCC. Unlike the borders that divide two countries, these borders are produced, to paraphrase Gloria Anzaldúa, when the life blood of two worlds merge and a third country emerges: a "border culture." Borderlands are those unintentional, multicultural spaces—sometimes called "common ground"—where disparate cultures meet; where the people living on these peripheries discover cultural parallels, and construct new as well as variable identities, based on—although neither reducible nor limited to—the old ones. "From this racial, ideological, cultural and biological cross-pollenization," writes Anzaldúa, "an 'alien' consciousness is presently in the making . . . . It is the consciousness of the Borderlands."[4] "The border houses the power of the outrageous," adds Juan Flores, "the imagination needed to turn the historical and cultural tables."[5] The border is not difference, Ian Angus comments, "it allows difference to appear."[6] Ruben Blades calls these borders "convergence." "Let's meet half way," he says, "and then we can walk either way together."[7] The people occupying this space are, in Renato Rosaldo's words, "border crossers."[8]

As a kid, I thought the "border" was that imaginary line in the middle of the Detroit River that marked the end of the United States and the beginning of Canada. At the time, I didn't know that Clairmount was another kind of border. I didn't realize that being cool was an "alien consciousness," part of a "border culture." Looking back, Clairmount (as well as many other Detroit neighborhoods) was a classic "borderland." Like Anzaldúa's intellectual mestizas, we learned to juggle cultures. We operated in a pluralistic world. We didn't use those words, of course. We said that was "getting down," and "making the scene," or "getting with it." Intellectuals today would say we practiced a "multicentric perspective." We called it being "hip." What Henry Giroux refers to as "new cartographies of identity and difference,"[9] we probably would have talked about as finding ways to be different and "together." I doubt that we would have described our talk as a "plurality of vernaculars." For us it was "street talk." But we would have understood what Juan Flores means when he writes that borderlands produce "multiple interminglings."

The new theoretical languages giving voice to the emerging visions of identity being invented and discovered on America's borderlands contain a number of concepts devised to explain the process of code switching, cultural mixing, and linguistic sharing that I experienced in Detroit. George Lipsitz calls the process cultural "bricolage."[10] Lynell George refers to it as "cultural fusion" and "recombinant culture."[11] In Marshall Berman's words, it is a "unity of disunity."[12] Stuart Hall's notion of "transformations," in my view, nicely captures border cultural exchanges and productions. Transformations, in Hall's words, are "the active work on existing traditions and activities."[13] Transformations actively rework traditions so that they come out a different way. They are historically specific cultural elements "that allow for the expression of collective popular memory and the reworking of tradition."[14] Hall's notion of transformations is useful for understanding the ways in which diverse groups create common ground, while continuing to acknowledge important differences. The idea of transformations means it is possible for diverse peoples to construct identities experienced as a common heritage.

I find the possibility attractive. It makes sense out of my experience. It names my identity. Sociologically speaking, it also makes my experience a lot less exceptional. It turns out I'm not alone, in a category of my own. I have a lot of company on the border. My experience is not an isolated instance of one individual who is out of place and therefore doesn't fit in. Rather, it is an example of a larger process: a process of transformations on American borders where inclusive, multidimensional identities have blossomed—unintentionally, fleetingly, and not always where expected.

That process continues. Thus, I was excited to recently discover that my experience in 1950s Detroit is being duplicated today. Traditions are being invented, new codes, languages, and collective memories are being created and identities constructed in contemporary border towns around Los Angeles, places like Culver City, Echo Park, and Carson. Describing an identity currently emerging at the edges of these neighborhood boundaries, one that seriously resembles mine, journalist Lynell George hears a language she calls New Age patois. She calls the young people in this world "cultural hybrids."[15] Cultural historian George Lipsitz notes that the mixing on these borders is not an exclusively class-based phenomenon. "When I see desegregated groups of graffiti writers," he reports, "one of the things that strikes me is that they're also mixed by class."[16] These class- and race-mixed groups do not, however, dilute the constituent cultures. They do not construct sameness. "There is a group of graffiti writers," Lipsitz points out, "who call themselves 'ALZA'—which stands for African, Latino, Zulu, and Anglo." ALZA, Lipsitz says, is Chicano slang for rise up. "They found each other," he reports. "Nobody set this up. Nobody put an ad in the paper. They look for spaces that are what we call 'multicultural.' I don't think that they ever think to look at it in those ways," he says, "but there's a sense of interest and excitement and delight in difference that makes them look for more complexity. It is their love of difference, danger and heterogeneity that brings them together."[17]

In Lynell George's estimation, this free-form amalgamation goes deeper than learning a handy salutation in Tagalog, being conversant in street slang, or sporting hip-hop-inspired styles. This sort of cultural exchange, she suggests, requires active participation and demands that one press past the superficial toward a more meaningful discourse and understanding. Instead of demanding that people reject their own identifiers, the mixing allows them to slip in and out of multiple identities. Like being cool on Detroit's West Side, this kind of mixing wreaks havoc with stereotypes and old-fashioned ideas about what it means to be African American, Latino, Asian American, or Anglo in a rapidly changing metropolitan area.

The idea of borders, and the cultural possibilities they contain, do more than articulate a vision for what might be. They also constitute a critique of current sociological theorizing about identity. Social analysts typically construct ethnic identity in "primordialist" terms. The primordialist approach views ethnicity as "genuine culture" rooted in similarities of physical appearance, a shared language, religion, a sense of common origin and history, and the perception of shared life chances. This approach, according to Clifford Geertz following Edward Shils, looks for "primordial attachments" which, he writes, has its origins in "the assumed givens of social existence . . . . [C]ongruities of blood, speech, custom and so on are seen to have ineffable and overpowering coerciveness in and of themselves."[18] So conceived, ethnicity refers to a set of rules, roles, and traditions passed on from generation to generation, essentially unchanged. The emphasis is on group differentiation. And in this construction, ethnicity is a matter of hyphenation. Ethnic identity, moreover, is assumed to be singular and static: only one ethnic identity is allowed per consumer. Assimilation, in this paradigm, is assumed to be a one-way street along which new arrivals "give up" one identity and "take on" another one. Old identities are "melted down" into "new" ones.

These constructions are useless when applied to America's borders. They inhibit understanding. In border cultures identities are not discrete and finite entities. They are plastic and open-ended; as much dynamic constructs as inherited facts, as much strategic responses to the present as an immutable series of practices and beliefs derived from the past. Border cultures produce identities that are neither singular nor static. In these locations, multiple cultural identities are invented, and people slip in and out of them without being called upon to renounce their initial identifiers. In this context, identity is achieved and inclusive. It is learned through the process of taking on and shedding the roles required to participate in complicated cultures. Border peoples trying on new and different identities learn that identities can be changed. They find out that one is not completely bound by bloodlines, nationality, or occupation. The roles they try on, the cultural practices they learn to perform, teach them how to be multicultural. They learn how to be culturally competent actors in multiple cultural contexts. Border cultures therefore contradict conventional sociological wisdom. They fracture received categories. The discovery of border cultures calls for a reformulation of sociological theories of cultural identity.

Michael Fischer's approach to ethnicity is a useful starting place for that project. Ethnicity, he writes, is "something dynamic, something that emerges in full . . . flower only through struggle . . . ."[19] "Ethnicity is a process of inter-reference between two or more cultural traditions . . . ."[20] Fischer's construction makes pluralism a fundamental feature of identity. In his words, ethnicity is "a matter of finding a voice or a style that does not violate one's several components of identity. In part, such a process of assuming an ethnic identity is an insistence on a pluralist, multidimensional, or multifaceted concept of self."[21] At the heart of borderlands consciousness is that pluralist, multidimensional, multifaceted concept of self—that voice which doesn't violate the many components of one's identity.

Practicing Borderlands Consciousness:
Dues, Blues, and Fears

I've spent the last 25 years constructing a voice that doesn't violate the many components of my identity. And when that voice is heard, I'm reminded that I still live on the border. That border is no longer in Detroit. It is now located at the intersection of class and race in the academy.

(And gender too. Although being a heterosexual male, I don't experience gender as border.) I was reminded of my border status many years ago when a senior "colleague" called me "you-people" in a drunken tirade directed at "aggressive working-class men" in the university. I discovered first-hand why my black classmates in Detroit bristled at the term. I am routinely reminded of my border status by the inner circle that runs my university. Members of this club make it quite clear that, even though we share melanin and gender, I don't belong. Even when I'm asked to sit on powerful committees, I'm not permitted to forget that I'm an outsider. I'm reminded when I don't laugh at their jokes. Not out of principle, but because I don't know they are "jokes." Or, thinking they *must be* kidding, I laugh when no one else does.

I know I am a border person when I realize university culture practices an etiquette that only certain people are taught. It is a class etiquette, gendered as well, and, as I discovered in graduate school, it is learned at the elite colleges where many university professors begin as undergraduates. The working knowledge of this culture is not shared with class outsiders. It is not discussed at career counseling meetings for junior faculty. Border academics glimpse it when they inadvertently violate these unwritten rules. Being too "passionate," we learn, is unacceptable. So is being committed to principles which university insiders call being "inflexible," or "unreasonable." We discover that survival in the academy depends upon learning that it is inappropriate to argue from the heart, or from a position of principle. The appropriate method is to invoke "empirical evidence," or remain silent until sufficient "data" have been collected. Border academics find out that direct talk, "telling it like it is"—or "speaking truth to power"—is counterproductive. The delicate language of euphemism and indirectness is the *lingua franca*. One learns that behavior which would be severely sanctioned on the mean streets of Detroit is acceptable in university settings where it is permissible to destroy someone's career so long as procedures are followed, and confidentiality is maintained. Outsiders soon discover that it is all right to impugn another's honor and integrity so long as it's done cleverly, with humor, and in "good taste."

While I find it comforting to now have a name for the identity I experience in the university, the identity does not permit me comfort. Being white, male, heterosexual *and* living on the academic border means being truly in-between, not belonging to any side, not fitting-in. There are no clearly identifiable borderlands where border crossers like me meet and share experiences. This kind of border crossing therefore demands heavy dues. It means never being completely accepted by any side; always being suspicious, and suspected. It means being on the outside, a potential traitor, always an exception. An outsider to insiders. An insider to outsiders.

Being a white, male, heterosexual border crosser also forces one to wonder whether the border category actually fits. I'm not entirely comfortable applying the concept to my experience. I worry that might be another version of cultural appropriation. Yvonne Yarbro-Bejarano is right: "It is one thing to choose to recognize the ways one inhabits the 'borderlands' and quite another to theorize a consciousness in the name of survival."[22]

The borders I live on are porous. My crossings are opportunities as well as options. I can choose to live on borders, or avoid them. That choice is privilege, even when experienced as pain. My colleagues of color don't choose border identities. They cannot refuse them either. And they can't move between them as easily as do I. The elements of choice and privilege in my life mean I cannot be otherized in the same way as people of color.

Still, the borders I cross are real ones. So are the consequences for crossing them. Thus, to borrow from Caren Kaplan, I don't consider myself a theoretical "tourist," a "boarder in the borderlands."[23] And I think the search for borderlands, the effort to generate common ground among border crossers, disrupts the core social order in a positive direction.

That is why the sociological tariff for border crossing is so personally expensive. Because it undermines conventional constructions, border crossing is a profoundly subversive activity. Border academics are troublesome to university culture because their crossings reveal borders that are otherwise invisible. Border crossers expose borders that universities refuse to recognize—borders the university denies guarding.

Border academics are double-trouble for the university. When we are not revealing borders, we expose the conflated character of other categories. White heterosexual male border academics are unique in this regard. Because we share melanin and gender with university insiders, our border status must be attributed to class. When we are on the border, whiteness is revealed to be as much about class as race. In addition to being constructed as not-black, university whiteness turns out to be not-working-class as well.

In racialized America, where the culture assigns people to either one racial category or another, border crossers are threatening because they refuse the assignment. By refusing the assignment and inventing a new identity, border crossers subvert the American construction of race. "White" border crossers are especially subversive. They undermine the construction of whiteness as "not-black." Because whiteness cannot be not-black when "whites" act "black," the defining feature of the category is subverted. The conventional definition of normal is disturbed. As a result, the norm of whiteness, to paraphrase Henry Giroux, cannot secure its dominance by appearing to be invisible. Plagiarizing a local bumper sticker, white border crossers "subvert the dominant paradigm." Maybe that explains why white Civil Rights workers were beaten so savagely in the south. Perhaps that's why white teenage border crossers are called "wiggers" in contemporary America.

But border crossing is subversive in a more profound sense. It radically disrupts key elements of American culture: conventional understandings of propriety, reason, rationality, and harmony are subverted by border crossers as they move between epistemological, cultural, political, and methodological boundaries. But the most important convention that gets disrupted is the American propensity to create dualisms, to manufacture dichotomies, to generate a zero-sum (you win-I lose) culture. Border crossing identities assault the racial dualisms in American culture. No surprise then, that racial border crossers are as threatening to white Americans as cross-dressers are to heterosexuals.

Because border crossing is so subversive, a cultural border patrol is being formed. Signs of it have been sighted in the university where border aliens are accused of practicing political correctness. While the border patrol doesn't yet come into classrooms (usually), it does carefully maintain borders. It also keeps the spaces between borders incredibly narrow and isolated. The border patrol isn't always obvious. Officers don't wear uniforms. Sometimes it is invisible, working undercover inside our minds.

The border patrol acts strategically. It protects America's cultural borders through a containment policy. Border consciousness is acceptable in its written form. At the university it is even rewarded when published. But it is also restricted, limited to specially designated territories like "cultural studies." And when border consciousness leads to subversive border practices, it is frowned upon. Sometimes it is punished.

I worry about the fate of border consciousness in the academy. Not that it will be silenced. But that it will flourish. And that the price for success will be the loss of practice. Especially in the academy, I fear that border consciousness stripped of border practice, will eventually undermine the multidimensional, subversive character of border identity. If that is allowed to happen, the border patrol will have succeeded. Diversity will be normalized and border crossing co-opted. Thus, like Marxism, border consciousness will have become just another academic discipline, another canon, another hegemony. A new academic territory will have been created: one with its own borders to patrol.

Notes

1   Two years later, my father was convicted and sentenced to four years and eight months in the penitentiary. While his conviction was eventually overturned by the Supreme Court, he spent nearly a year in jail as funds were being raised to cover his bail. My mother was spared deportation at the last minute. Her attorney discovered conditions under which Canadian officials would not be obligated to accept her. When a Canadian diplomat committed suicide after American officials insinuated he was a communist, the Canadian Minister of Immigration chose to exercise that option. Though permitted to remain in the U.S., she was placed on "supervisory parole." That meant she reported her activities and associations to the INS each month. As McCarthyism cooled, her monthly reporting was reduced to an annual event. But she was still on "supervisory parole" when she died in 1974.

2   An important qualification is in order: I am not suggesting that this language was generated at Hutchins. Some examples are partly Detroit and local. But anyone familiar with the period knows this language was standard talk in 1950s hip black culture throughout the U.S.

3   David Wellman, *Portraits of White Racism*, (2nd ed.). New York: Cambridge University Press, 1993.

4   Gloria Anzaldúa, *Borderlands/La Frontera: The New Mestiza*. San Francisco: Spinsters/Aunt Lute, 1987: 77.

5   Juan Flores, *Divided Borders: Essays on Puerto Rican Identity*. Houston: Arte Publico Press, 1993: 224.

6   Ian Angus, "Crossing the Border," *Massachusetts Review*. Spring-Summer 1990: 45.

7   Ruben Blades, *Chicago Sunday Times*. January 26, 1987. (Quoted in Flores, 216, 1993).

8   Renato Rosaldo, *Culture and Truth: The Remaking of Social Analysis*. Boston: Beacon Press, 1993.

9   Henry A. Giroux, "Post-Colonial Ruptures and Democratic Possibilities: Multiculturalism as Anti-Racist Pedagogy," *Cultural Critique*. (Spring, 1992): 23.

10   George Lipsitz, *Time Passages: Collective Memory and American Popular Culture*. Minneapolis: University of Minnesota Press, 1991.

11   Lynell George, "Gray Boys, Funky Aztecs and Honorary Homegirls," *The Los Angeles Times Magazine*. January 17, 1993: 14-19.

12   Marshall Berman, *All That Is Solid Melts into Air*. New York: Simon and Schuster, 1982: 15.

13   Stuart Hall, "Notes on Deconstructing 'the Popular,'" in Raphael Samuel, ed., *People's History and Socialist Theory*. London: Routledge and Kegan Paul. 1981: 228.

14   Ibid.

15   Lynell George, "Gray Boys, Funky Aztecs and Honorary Homegirls," *The Los Angeles Times Magazine*. January 17, 1993: 14–19.

16   Ibid., p. 17

17   Ibid., p. 17.

18   Clifford Geertz, "The Integrative Revolution: Primordial Sentiments and Civic Politics in New States," *The Interpretation of Cultures*. New York: Basic Books. 1973: 109–110.

19   Michael M.J. Fischer, "Ethnicity and the Post-Modern Arts," in James Clifford and George E. Marcus, eds., *Writing Culture: The Poetics and Politics of Ethnography*. Berkeley: University of California Press, 1986: 195–96.

20   Ibid., p. 201.

21   Ibid., p. 196.

22 Yvonne Yarbro-Bejarano, "Gloria Anzaldúa's Borderlands/La Frontera: Cultural Studies, 'Difference,' and the Non-Unitary Subject," *Cultural Critique* (Fall 1994): 8.

23 Caren Kaplan, "Deterritorializations: The Rewriting of Home and Exile in Western Feminist Discourse," in Abdul R. JanMohamed and David Lloyd, eds., *The Nature and Context of Minority Discourse.* New York: Oxford University Press. 1990: 367.

4

Writing in Search of a Home
Geography, Culture, and Language in the Creation of Racial Identity

Sangeeta Tyagi

In *Black Skin, White Masks,* Frantz Fanon states that, "To speak means to be in a position to use a certain syntax, to grasp the morphology of this or that language, but it means above all to assume a culture, to support the weight of a civilization."[1] For me these lines hold a special significance, as I have attempted to grapple with questions that have been with me for a good part of my adult life and that have only become more, rather than less complicated, with time and geographical movements. What has it meant for me to be bilingual within a post-colonial culture where the English language is a product of a colonial history? Or phrased differently, what has it meant for me to have, in Fanon's words, assumed a culture, supported the weight of a civilization that has been an imperializing presence within Indian history and present society? In what ways has my bilingual identity anchored me in multiple contexts at the same time as it irrevocably distanced me from others? What is the meaning of such words as "belonging" and "home" for an Indian woman educated by Irish nuns in a Christian school, more familiar with English literature than with Indian, with a Ph.D. from an American university, working and teaching within the U.S.? And since identity is also about how I am perceived by others, how do these aspects of my identity meld together under the searing heat of western racism—the orientalist understandings of an exotic, but essentially backward and traditional Indian-ness?

Let me begin here with the last of these questions and work my way backwards in terms of time and place. As an Indian woman, I come to this society with little history and consequently a different, less pernicious racial baggage than the one that shapes the lives of African-American people, for instance. Certainly, the experiences of Indians in Britain are very different as they continue to struggle against a colonial history and ongoing racism. In the absence of such a history within the U.S., however, there are other insidious ways in which racial meanings continue to shape the identities of Indians living here. While on the one hand, Indian culture, cuisine, and art have become instantly consumable commodities within this society, there exists little if any understanding of Indian politics, history or current global positioning. It is in the absence of the latter, that the former is rendered ahistorical and then exotic.

My first few months in this country were marked by the constant comment that I spoke fluent English with a "beautiful," "interesting," or "refreshing" accent. This comment almost always made me curious but it was only after the first few weeks that I fully understood it. On this occasion, the comment about my fluency was followed by the question about how long I had been in the U.S. I answered that it had been a few weeks, when the person exclaimed, "You have learned to speak English so well, so quickly."

I struggled with the desire to start a discussion on Indian history and the influence of British colonialism; on the fact that English was the state language for over a century; or perhaps on the creation and continuing existence of a system of education to train a cadre of English-speaking Indians who would assist in the colonizing project. I wanted to suggest that structures of colonialism do not disintegrate with the formal transfer of political power. I wanted to highlight the vexed and complicated history of the English language as a tool for cultural control across the globe, but decided against all these possibilities with the knowledge that I could not make this education my responsibility.

The flip side of this image was the equally common *lack* of surprise as I heard over and over again that Indian students were uniformly bright, spoke and wrote fluent English, and performed much better than their American counterparts within the U.S. academy. While on the one hand, I lost a possible teaching assistant position because of the professor's fear that I might not be able to communicate with the students in "clear English," I was given a job as a writing consultant without so much as an interview because of the assumption that Indian graduate students had a complete command of the language and hence would do well at the job. While this perception may certainly have been more flattering and useful, it was still part of the preconstituted identity that I stepped into within the U.S. A class issue comes to be represented as a race issue, as upper-middle-class Indian students with years of excellent education and the privilege of traveling to U.S. universities stand in as symbols for all Indian students.

When I was asked if I would pose in traditional Indian silk sari for the cover of a student catalogue, it was once again the exotic orient that was being summoned, as nothing in my life at the university indicated that I wished to wear or even possessed such attire. The travel catalogue's India of bright colors, luxuriant fabrics, and beautiful women was inextricably tied up here with the hot and spicy Indian food available at local restaurants, and the brass and sandalwood artifacts of Pier 1 stores across the country. As the Nature channel on television showcases India's lush tropical landscape populated by fascinating and fearsome tigers and lions, and public television does a series on train rides across the Indian deserts, a country of close to a billion people shrinks into a tourist's paradise of excitement and adventure halfway across the unknown globe. In fact, over the period that I have worked on this project, most of the news items on India in the *Boston Globe* have dealt with the plague, police brutality against the lower castes, conservation of the tiger population in India, and the release of a famous "bandit queen." Disease—unrest and violence—wild animals—bandits.

As the images circulate within the U.S., India becomes the quintessential Third-World "other"—the mythical place that provides, by contrast, a deep sense of well being with all things "modern," "rational," "efficient." It is in this way that cultures are created and re-created—their socio-cultural lives come to be caricatured as if in a hall full of distorting mirrors, while their political and economic realities are overlooked. Is it any wonder, then, that more people within the U.S. can talk about Indian women's "oppression" than they can about the role of U.S. corporations, the I.M.F., and World Bank in creating continuing economic dependence and its consequences for women's poverty within Indian society?

Not only am I an Indian woman in the U.S., however. I am an immigrant—a status rife with racial meaning and images. As a "non-resident alien" during the first few years of my life here, it was clear that even the possibility of home was to be denied in the language of classification. Not only was I "alien," I seemingly did not even reside here. As I completed my dissertation and accepted a job at a private college in Virginia, I applied for a change of status to what the Immigration and Naturalization Services of the United States, a.k.a. INS, calls a "resident alien." Still alien, I might at least now be allowed a residence within the bureaucratic imagination.

What appeared initially to be merely a maze of paperwork and forms quickly revealed its racialized underpinnings as ideas about "productive" and "unproductive" immigrants informed every step of the process. Not only were proofs of productive employment required, so were extensive health checks, finger prints, family histories, complete accounting of the past decade of my life, of marriage and relationships, as well as assurances of not belonging to the Communist Party, or having plotted to overthrow the U.S. government. While these, in themselves, may be brushed off as routine safeguards against possible abuses of the immigration system, it is the tenor and tone of these proceedings that highlight the racial assumptions built into the idea that "we" are letting "them" come in through the golden door of opportunity—notwithstanding that the door may be significantly tarnished by the historical excesses characteristic of immigration policy in the U.S.

As programs such as *60 Minutes, A Current Affair* and other similar examples of "investigative reporting" present unquestioned images of wealthy immigrants of color abusing the welfare and other support systems within this society, real people suffer the backlash of housing and job discrimination, anti-immigrant hysteria and racial violence. A rash of violence against the Indian community in Jersey City, New Jersey during the late 1980s stands as a vivid reminder of the consequences of such racialized images of immigrants of color. White extremists calling themselves "dot busters" not only reduced the Indian community to a cultural symbol—the red dot signifying married status worn by Indian women—they also decided to avenge themselves for the resources and jobs that these Indians had presumably wrongfully attained. What is insidious and dangerous about these images is the one-sidedness of the information that lies at the base of these perceptions. When immigrant scientists discover a new therapy or perform life saving surgery, news of those achievements does not come with information of their immigrant status in the same way that news of welfare fraud comes wrapped in stories of "illegal aliens."

While grappling with issues of race, ethnicity, and class in my sociology courses, my students tell me in no uncertain terms what they think of "these immigrants who are taking over our country and draining the welfare system." The collapsing of the term immigrant with the image of indigent cheats claiming welfare is so complete in their minds that they can barely make sense of my immigrant identity when I ask them who they think I am and what they make of the fact that I am gainfully employed at their college. These images are not merely food for discussion: they affect people's everyday interactions and shape their perceptions of their neighbors, the person sitting beside them on the train, and the owner of the newspaper stand at the corner of their street. For instance, at a recent conference, several African-American women professionals spoke of the harassment they faced as they crossed the borders following international travel—of the drug searches they had endured at the hands of immigration officials, as racist profiles of drug dealers implicated professional black men and women as well. These stories remind me vividly of my own apprehensions and tensions every time I enter this country—always fearful that I would be denied entry on the basis of some arbitrary charge that I will be unable to refute. "Denial of entry," "non-resident," "alien"—categories of classification that have become the pivot on which my notions of home and belonging have come to rest. Clearly, a place that carries an omnipresent potential of physical exclusion cannot be home and yet that is a logic that I must work to reject.

* * * * * *

I grew up in an upper-caste, middle-class professional home—and, as is typical of Indian families that fit this description, it was assumed that I would be bilingual in at least English and Hindi, and be able to function well in the worlds represented by those two languages. Indeed, the very cultural feature of being a modern professional was the ability to straddle these two milieus. The significance of these defining norms became clear to me only later as I began to understand that the association of "modernity" with the West was based on a binary opposition that associated "traditionality" with the ex-colonized Third World. To aspire to "modernity" within a post-colonial society, then, was a loaded concept—one that involved a choice of language, dress, cultural norms, gender expectations, indeed one's everyday cultural practices. Within my family, the context for these choices was established by my father's life.

My father grew up in the 1920s and 30s, and was educated in a traditional school with Sanskrit—the language of the old Indian texts and scriptures—as the medium of instruction. He went on to study medicine in Germany, practiced medicine for more than a decade in Indonesia, and finally settled down in India so my brothers and I would grow up amongst extended family. Fluent in five languages, he listened to the morning news on the radio in Sanskrit, and then went to work dressed in a suit and tie every day of his working life, speaking Hindi, English, and German within the course of a day. His daily movement between worlds seemed comfortable, even simple, with the desirability of multiple anchorings appearing to be self-evident.

Within this framework, I began my education in an all-girls Christian school run by Irish nuns. These were not only some of the better schools academically, but also the places where children of middle-class professionals learned their early lessons in the English language and culture— institutions that forever transformed one's relationships with oneself, with those who did not attend these schools, and subsequently with the very idea of one's own home and culture.

School was about learning and doing well, sports and extra-curricular activities, strict discipline, and rules. So all-encompassing was the experience that it took several years before I could even begin to analyze this period of my life. Each morning began with the Lord's Prayer, a selection of Christian hymns, and a class in "moral science" followed by the daily curriculum. The language of instruction and of conversation throughout the day was English with one class period a day devoted to the study of Hindi language and literature. In fact, students were punished for speaking in Hindi outside of this period. My memory of this time is a pleasant one—making it even more complicated to unravel the effects of this early socialization on my identity. My parents laid a high premium on doing well at school and I learned the rules of the game quickly. It was clear that the students who did consistently well were the ones who were most at ease with English—their abilities being rewarded with student leadership positions and increased teacher attention, which in turn helped them perform better. Not unlike the tracking system in U.S. public education, some of us were encouraged to read the classics of English and American literature while the others were written off as unable to enter the ranks of the professional middle classes except through marriage. After spending close to seven hours in school, we would return for evening sports and rehearsals, planning for activities, or just hanging out with friends—spending a total of ten to eleven hours within this environment and only half as many hours open to influence within the family.

These years fostered in me a love of reading, an appreciation for language spoken with grace and elegance, an admiration for a vast and imaginative vocabulary. I read voraciously—almost entirely in English, since the school library was well stocked with books in English and carried almost no Hindi books—and reveled in the worlds created by the stories. I related to the stories and the characters within them, believing for several years that schools such as Mallory Towers and St. Claire's described in Enid Blyton books actually existed. I wanted to attend these schools and found my own school boring compared to the exciting world of my story-book characters. Clearly, these years were both about learning to read and write as well as about becoming culturally literate. I participated in and accepted the implied logic and value system of these stories, allowing for a slow but definite cultural transformation.

There were other changes as well—our school uniforms of pinafores and neckties completely flouted the social norms for women's dress and subsequently of women's behaviors and roles. As young people fluent in English language, literature, history, and by then in western music and fashions, we stood across an ever-widening divide from cousins, family members, neighbors, and friends who had gone to local public schools, studied in Hindi, dressed in Indian clothes, and were more familiar and comfortable with Indian cultural norms. Socially, the messages were clear: that the English speakers were marked for a different social destiny from those who spoke Hindi. In the 1970s, three decades after India gained its independence from British colonial rule, most top-level managerial, professional, and civil service jobs were still held by people who had gone to private and English-medium schools. Indeed, we were the agents of the new westernized modernity for our generation.

Class was central in the shaping of these identities. Since ease with the English language was not merely a question of linguistic ease but also of cultural comfort—of English films, comic books, foreign travel, western cuisine, and imported clothes and toys—class became the single most important determinant of this ease. While the professional middle class is not necessarily the wealthiest strata of Indian society, exposure to westernization requires a certain class position. Moreover, this class possesses the legitimizing power that money alone can never establish. Not only did my education, then, create a specific cultural relationship with those who had gone through a different education system, it also laid the groundwork for different class relations.

As my brothers and I graduated from high school, it was taken for granted in our family that we would get admission into and attend certain colleges and professional schools—those that were considered elite and whose admission tests took familiarity with a certain body of knowledge and language for granted. These schools would, in turn, be the passports to more lucrative career options and choices. While our family, with my father as the only earner, did not have as much money as some others around us, we were solidly upper-middle-class and upwardly mobile in terms of the aspirations and expectations that my parents had of our careers. Failing in school work was never an option that any of us considered lightly, and not "making it" in the career world was not an idea that we spent any time on. Significantly for me, none of this was achieved through any overt pressure or sanctions—rather, the success of the message lay in my internalizing what "success" meant and in my simplistic refusal to imagine a life outside of those parameters.

What makes this combination of family expectations and school socialization particularly insidious is that it operates amidst vast poverty and enormous illiteracy. Not only were we agents in a deeply class-divided society, we had to believe that economic success was an inevitable factor in our lives even as we were surrounded by examples of the opposite. For instance, part of being middle-class in India, when I was growing up, also meant having the ability to hire domestic help. I grew up in a large home that was cleaned by two women: the gardener took care of the plants, the washerwoman went from home to home washing clothes, and somebody came in twice a day to wash the dishes. In the absence of dishwashers, vacuums cleaners, and washing machines, middle-class women in large homes supervised a retinue of domestic workers even as they themselves were beginning to enter the workforce in larger and larger numbers. While my parents and other adults around me were concerned about poverty—my father treated numerous tuberculosis and other patients free of charge if they were unable to pay, paid for the children of the domestic workers in our home to attend school, and made sure that they were taken care of medically—this concern took the structure of inequality for granted. While the equality of all human beings was a philosophical precept that children were taught, I knew with distinct clarity that our lives at home did not have that equality and could not support it.

In addition to class, region, religion, caste, and gender were all factors that shaped my sense of who I was in the world. As a Hindu and a North Indian, I could assume that the world would reflect my social milieu. While Hindus, Muslims, Parsis, Jains, Sikhs, Christians, and others mingled socially and their customs and cultural forms were commonly known and sometimes shared, Hindu dominance has been a fact of Indian social life. Despite the secular rhetoric espoused by the government and by social liberals, every level of political, social, and economic life has been controlled by Hindus. Nowhere do these liberal principles fall apart faster than in the case of intermarriage between a Hindu and somebody from another religion—providing grounds for intense family resistance and even violence. In most Hindu families, hierarchies of religious associations existed—intermarriage with Sikhs and Jains being considered more acceptable than alliances with Muslims or Christians. For me, this meant that even though my father was a nonbeliever in ritualistic Hinduism and the use of religious symbols and idols was kept to a minimum in our family, I grew up absorbing Hinduism from everything around me, even as I was learning about Christianity in school.

In the present day, religious and regional/linguistic dominance has become the grounds on which the most pitched political battles are being fought. Historically, north Indians have seen themselves as a "superior" race as compared to those from the southern states. Taller and bigger physically, and with lighter complexions, Northerners have considered themselves descendants of the Aryan race while Southerners have been believed to have descended from Dravidians. This color politics, combined with the consolidation of national political power within the north, has given rise to intense regional chauvinism. While children in southern schools learn Hindi as part of their curriculum, those in northern schools are not exposed to any southern language. Moreover, while people in the south may be able to talk about the different states in the north, many northerners are commonly heard referring to people from several southern states by the generic term "South Indian," or even the diminutive "Southie."

The color politics that was a factor in the regional chauvinism played itself out even more strongly in terms of gender. Beauty was completely collapsed with fair skin and those of us who did not have a "peach-and-pink" complexion could never aspire toward the label of attractiveness. What was supposed to be devastating about the dark skin was that nothing its bearer could do from there on would make her desirable as a wife to any man worth something. While I could not articulate the heterosexism within the assumption till I became an adult, the sexism made me bristle even as a child. I was not only a dark-skinned girl by north Indian standards, I was also a physically big girl—very tall for an Indian woman—and I knew very early that this was a race that I had to win by other means. Since I could never be the prettiest, most petite girl on the block, I would be the smartest—and if I was not considered attractive because of how I looked, then it would have to be my brightness and indifference that would shield me.

As a result, my reaction to these norms was to reject them to the extent that I disliked dressing in pretty, feminine clothes and preferred wearing my brothers' castoffs or even my father's baggy shirts and sweaters. I spent my time reading rather than learning to sew, knit, and embroider, and turned ballistic at the slightest hint from an unsuspecting adult that I use my time in a more gender-appropriate way. While my family had its own set of double-standards where men and women were concerned—my mother was a full-time homemaker and my father did little around the house—there was enough room within it for rebellion against these norms. I would refuse to attend celebrations and rituals at relatives' homes because it meant dressing up in feminine clothes; I was vocal and articulate in my opinions about my cousins' and friends' marriages to men they did not know; and I was simply not shy or demure enough to be slotted easily. Somewhere within me I knew that while I may not fit in with the crowd, it was a price I had to pay for any long-term ability to break out of these patterns.

While the message at home was that gender-appropriate behavior was a good thing to cultivate, there was also tacit encouragement for my choices. My parents made it a point to attend every school debate, drama, or other production that I participated in and encouraged me to do so even when that contradicted the norms of femininity. In fact, my parents' pride in these accomplishments and in my final decision to travel to the U.S. to complete my Ph.D. was often in direct contrast to the expected response. They would shake their heads in seeming despair at my irreverence even as they protected me against its consequences from the rest of our relatives and friends. Often I would hear my father or mother being chastised by an older relative for "allowing" me the freedoms that they did. They were accused of being irresponsible when they continued to finance my education rather than encouraging me to marry. And they were considered out of touch with reality when they encouraged my plans to do a Ph.D. in the U.S.

These contradictory messages about gender that I was receiving from my immediate family and extended family had as much to do with class as with my parents' own dreams and imaginations. As a professional who had his imagination expanded through travel, my father—patriarch though he was—had internalized a sense of boundless possibilities that clashed with the gender restrictions he was being asked to enforce. This sense of the world as a place for exploration had a distinctly upper-middle-class flavor to it, since the very idea required the existence of substantial financial resources. For my mother, the encouragement was in keeping with her own beliefs in women's education, and with the fact that she had begun her own career after 25 years of marriage and taking care of the family.

College life provided new arenas for excitement and discovery. I went away to college in nearby New Delhi—a city close enough for my parents to drive up to see me but sufficiently far for me to live in a college dorm. Once again the decision was met by skepticism from the wider circle of kin, but my parents prevailed. New Delhi was everything that my home town had not been. It was large, urban, and provided opportunities for social and academic growth that were thrilling to a seventeen-year-old. I remember these years as the period where I became a political being. Still cradled amongst elitism, I was now beginning to think about some of these things and question the contradictions that I had grown up with. I also realized with great satisfaction that there were others who had resisted gender norms and survived, that fair skin was not necessarily the only ticket to a possible relationship, and that male–female relationships were not the only ones that existed. A women's college provided particularly fertile terrain for such questioning and my years there were perhaps the most significant for my burgeoning feminist consciousness. Surrounded by women students and an all-female faculty, we learnt perhaps what no formal lesson in self confidence could have achieved. Feminism, however, was still a limited political category, as class and race were peripheral to our passionate discussions. It was not until my Master's degree work that I would first learn the tools to collapse these categories and think more comprehensively.

My Master's degree work was at an institution that prided itself in being "leftist" in its academic agenda. Here, for the first time in my privileged upbringing, I met people who combined activism and academic work, discussed politics all the time, and eschewed simple answers to social issues. It was within this environment that I developed the intellectual and political framework that would fuel my research in the U.S.

* * * * * *

As an adult, having lived in the U.S. for almost a third of my life, I face some curious contradictions in terms of my racial identity and my sense of home. While growing up, my social milieu provided a sense of being "at home" in more than one culture, while simultaneously making it difficult to be "at home" in either. My parents did what they could to provide roots within an Indian cultural heritage and yet there were certain deep contradictions with my other socializing influence, my schooling. Is it possible to support the weight of one civilization without, to some extent, letting go of another? How could I truly love English literature without participating in the sense of racial superiority embedded within its view of the rest of the world? And having sensed the devaluation of my culture at that level, did the privileges of class blunt the anger? Moreover, what of one's sensibilities and cultural tastes? No amount of cultural pride changes the fact that my deepest personal and intellectual expression continues to be in English—I cannot have a discussion about ideas and beliefs in Hindi, nor am I able to indulge in a passionate argument in anything except English. Even as I pride myself in being completely bilingual in both Hindi and English, I fear that I am losing my ease with Hindi, as I speak it less frequently than I speak English. Is all this merely about the difficulties of linguistic translation? Or is my consciousness so transformed that it is difficult to give voice to any sense of who I am, in Hindi?

Within such a set of contradictions, my decision to travel to the U.S. to attend graduate school was hardly an oddity. Rather, it may have been a logical continuation of a life lived off-center between two cultural systems. It is certainly no coincidence that the past decade has witnessed the most dramatic resurgence of western economic and cultural interest in India at the same time as the numbers of young Indians traveling to the U.S. for professional training has soared. It is not possible to separate the multinational interests of western capitalism through such agents as Benetton, McDonalds, and Walt Disney within the Third World from the increasing migrations of Third-World people to the United States. The reliance on a common cultural currency, after all, does not function along one-way streets.

As more and more of us try to make sense of our multiple anchorings, we unearth histories and racial topographies that become increasingly complex within a world of growing global communication, continuing economic dependence, and intensifying cultural hegemonies. That my father seemed able to straddle different cultural territories with less angst had to do as much with gender as it did with the historical period within which he came of age. For him, growing up in the 1920s and 1930s, British colonialism was an everyday reality, and amidst the nationalism of the times, one's identity as an Indian was clearly demarcated in opposition to the West. The prevailing racial politics at the time was that one adopted those aspects of western culture and values that enabled one to confront the West on its own terms—protecting the sanctity of other parts of one's life from the corruption of western influence. The post-colonial realities of the 1960s and 70s, within which I grew up, were much more insidious, as easily identifiable political control gave way to a cultural, intellectual/psychic, and economic control. Struggling against the formal political control was expected and was part of the ideological tenor of the times, while familiarizing oneself with the later cultural influences was considered a valued social skill.

Moreover, as I read about the deeply regressive religious and cultural politics within present-day Indian society, I find myself less and less able to feel any simple pride in a racial heritage—especially one that is increasingly based on religious persecution, regional chauvinism, and gender oppression. As I struggle to make sense of my place within such an exclusive "home," I have to do the soul-searching work of understanding what home really means amidst all this. Now a "resident alien" within the U.S., I continue to assert my right to have a home here and struggle to create a home that provides sustenance and safety. As an anti-immigrant wave passes through the U.S., some of us are fearful that this will set into motion yet another series of exclusions, violence, and intimidation for those who are not white and middle-class. Back in India, where my class background, my married status, and my religious status ensure me a "home," I feel compelled to distance myself from the precepts on which that home's "safety" rests. As I meet and converse with Indians whose politics I find troubling and chauvinistic, I am forced to move away from any simplistic notion of community and belonging. As a woman, I have as little in common with them as I do as an Indian immigrant with white Americans who support racism.

Ultimately, then, it is how one opens up one's notions of community and the struggles that one invests in that define the kind of home one creates. With a foot in two worlds, my psychic survival requires that I engage both with the racial politics within the U.S. and with the communal, sexual politics in India. For those of us who move between such disparate worlds, perhaps the only way to make sense of who we are is by creating an inventory of our investments and reckoning with it, ambivalence and all. Anything less than that is insufficient.

Note

1   Frantz Fanon. 1952. *Black Skin, White Masks*. (New York: Grove Press). p. 11.

5

Alice's Little Sister
The Self Concealed Behind the Self
Gloria Johnson-Powell

Introduction

What a child thinks and feels about herself is largely determined by what she feels other people think or feel about her. Very early in a child's life, her self-concept is shaped by the significant others in her life through a process of "reflected appraisals"—a child is appraised by others and in time begins to appraise herself. A critical phase in this process of self-differentiation and development of self begins when a child asserts herself, opposes others, and compares herself with peers. Many scholars have rightly noted that the self-perception in all its aspects is a predominantly social self.[1]

In my study of the effects of school desegregation on the self-concepts of southern school children, I reviewed and critiqued the development of self-concept in children, and particularly black children, involved in this process.[2] Those early writings, which have become the hallmark of my career, had their beginnings in my exploration of existentialist philosophers in high school and in college. In *Black Monday's Children*, I write:

> The feeling quality of being black is an existential phenomenon. Indeed, identity and selfness tug
> at the very core of existentialism, the task of which is to make every person aware of what she is
> and to make the full responsibility of her existence rest on her. The searching into the black self
> brings awareness of the black self and the other internal selves (for blackness is not the totality of
> a black person's self).

I then go on to discuss the existential reality of the "angst" of the black experience—the anguish, the dread, and the despair:

> The existential dimensions of being black lead one through various stages—the despair at not being
> willing to be a black self, the wishing to be another than one's self, and sometimes not willing to be a
> self. Such despair, which for Kierkegaard is "the sickness unto death," was there for our black slave

ancestors, there for black grandparents and their black children, and is still present for black parents and their children today.

Gender identity is as critical as racial identity in the development of the young child and has its own "angst." But in America racial identity may supersede gender identity and indeed shape the course of the individual's gender identity.

In this essay, I try to explore the social and psychological milieu in which my childhood and adolescence occurred. The context itself was unusual because it occurred in New England, primarily in Boston, a city which has a schizophrenogenic history for African Americans. "The Damn Yankees," as I am fond of saying, had their own brand of racism and discrimination that was as subtle as it was blatant. If that sounds contradictory, it should, because it aptly describes the situation. In such an environment, you never knew who you were, or worse still, who you should or shouldn't be. At an early age I realized that it was best never to let any white person perceive the real person within me.

My early years were spent in Massachusetts and during this time—from 1940 to 1954—I was involved in the process of defining myself both in terms of my sex and race, in a complex white New England environment—a context that shaped my childhood and adolescent years in a profound and lasting way. Since my return to Boston five years ago, I have revisited my childhood haunts and recalled moments that I had forgotten. The most significant recollections of what was essentially a delightful time, also include moments of doubt, confusion, and even rebellion. It is the specific processes, thoughts, reflections, and ponderings of those early years of growing up in Boston that I will attempt to recapture.

One of my earliest recollections of my childhood is of one of my first-grade classmates with blond hair, freckles, and blue eyes—a virtual reproduction of Goldilocks—who asked me, "How does it feel to be colored?"[3] That inquisitive, innocent question had increasingly more significance for me as I progressed through school—one of "the only ones" or one of "the few"—all too often the object of stares. Although I was a very visible, curious, black object, I was, nonetheless, still very invisible as a thinking, feeling person to those New England whites who encountered me. I retreated to a closet world, content to bury myself in books to avoid the pangs of rejection from the exclusion from birthday parties, club meetings, and other after-school activities of my white classmates. Eventually, with the loving guidance and nurturance of my family, I learned to live in two worlds and to become a hybrid person. It is about that hybridization process so long ignored by child development specialists that I write now—a process so critical in the psychosocial development of all minority-group children and one fraught with a hazardous terrain of quicksand, steep mountains, treacherous rivers, and a few peaceful grassy knolls.

If my childhood memories are filled with the ringing taunt that "Girls can't be. . . ," they are further filled with the more devastating cry that "Colored people can't be. . . ." Hence, the message of defeat is given very early in childhood that colored girls can accomplish only the more menial and unstimulating chores. The major task, then, of becoming a woman for me, was to search for models of competent and feminine professional women. However, the most arduous part of that task was to find models and images of African American womanhood—soft, gentle and pretty—strong, courageous, and noble—but competent and successful as well as acclaimed by both worlds. That search for those dual images is vital in the process of growing up black and female for more than 9.5 million African American women.

Transformations, Passages, Transitions:
The First Process of Self-Actualization

Nobody ever remembered my name. They remembered who I was or rather to whom I belonged, or my family, but never my name. It was "Lizabeth's child", "that quiet thin one," "that bright girl of Mrs. Johnson," or, most frequently, "Alice's little sister." There was no animosity or disdain in what they called me or how they said it. Indeed, in most instances it was said with some regard, but also with a quizzical tone.

Now Alice was known as Alice. Everybody knew her, and well they should. She was vivacious, pretty, kind, and knew everybody—the butcher, the grocer, and the newest child in school. As a young child she was mischievous. As an adult, she developed into a lovely woman with a lovely soprano voice. Everyone said she sounded just like Marian Anderson. I thought she sounded better, but then I adored my sister Alice. I was not only very thin, but also very shy and timid and, worst of all, good in school, a real target for teasing and bullying.

Although there was a rule that the Johnson children did not fight, if someone looked at me cross-eyed or dared to taunt me, Alice's fist was swift and hard. I think that's when everyone began to call me "Alice's little sister." Of course, after the fight there would be Mrs. Johnson's consequences and Alice's friends knew that she could not come out because she'd been in a fight over "her little sister." Although we were only two years apart, her maturation was quicker even than our older sister Barbara's, so it seemed that she was much older than I. She certainly was more gregarious and after puberty began she was a real beauty—at least in my eyes and, I think, in the eyes of many young men.

I can remember that Alice's rites of passages from childhood to adolescence and even from adolescence to adulthood seemed to be clearly marked and took place in timely fashion. My transformations were always "betwixt and between". Indeed, as Turner[4] has noted, there are no recurrent events in human culture which give clearer evidence of the archetypical structure of the human psyche than the initiation rituals or ceremonies that accompany the transition from one social status to another. Turner focused particular attention on "the betwixt and between" of the transition period of initiation or ritual liminality otherwise known as the initiation of rites of passage with all the richness and coherence that make the transitional phase important.

The major rites of passages in my family varied somewhat for each of Mrs. Johnson's five children, but there were some that were consistent for all of us. Going to nursery school was a major event for me, but I'm not certain if all of my siblings had the exciting experience of going to St. Mark's Congregational Church on Townsend Street for nursery school. It was only a block away from our house on Elbert Street and, on some occasions, I was allowed to walk that block while my mother stood at the corner and watched.[5] I can remember feeling so grown-up, almost as big as the big kids—Barbara and Alice.

When I went to kindergarten at the Boardman School, I knew I had graduated from being one of the little kids with Joyce and Billy and would soon be anointed into the big kid's club. I never really did become one of the big kids; I was always either a little kid trying to become a big kid or the middle kid, betwixt and between. It was in kindergarten that I announced that I wanted to become a doctor and when William Strickland said that girls could not be doctors, I became determined to prove him wrong.[6]

My rites of passage were deliberately academic or intellectual. Despite my baptism at Ebenezer Baptist Church I would later question the tenets of my assigned religion, which was the biggest adolescent rebellion that I staged. I rejected a god in whose image we were supposed to be made; the bible became a book written by many historians whose sources were questionable. However, I still believed in doing "unto others as you would have others do unto you." If there was a god, it was a spirit of love and caring, as we sang in Sunday School:

> *Praise him, Praise him all ye little children*
> *God is love*
> *Praise him, Praise him all ye little children*
> *God is kind*

In spite of my religious rebellion, I never rejected the moral–ethical principles taught by my mother and reinforced by the church, Sunday school, and Baptist Youth Fellowship. Ebenezer Church was a world where I had unconditional acceptance. It was a very important part of my childhood and adolescence, a haven from the white world from which I concealed my real self behind a dark mask.

I can remember that as early as five years old I decided that I did not want to grow up. The glimpses into the adult world that I perceived were too complex and troubling for me. As a child I had minimal responsibilities. I could think what I pleased without any contention, and was free to play, to dream, and to learn at will. I even had my own closet where I would go to play or to daydream, but most often to read without disturbance. I loved the cocoon in which I lived and had no desire for any transitions except my promotions in school. Indeed, my scholarly pursuits became the security cloak to protect me from having to enter the real world where I felt I could not compete with my dark skin and my long, very thin body. Besides, black was not beautiful in a predominantly white world.

I was colored, and there was no defined place for a colored woman in Boston except day work or day labor. Secondly, I was unattractive—or so I thought—because everyone called me "bean pole." Although I could do logarithms and figure out complex mathematical problems, I did not know how to "fix" being colored and unattractive. Of course, my family and friends did not view me that way, but I was observant enough to know that outside the safety of family and friends, that was the way I was seen.

I was proud to be colored, and I wanted to be a pioneer and help people. By five I knew that I wanted to be a doctor and by high school I knew that I wanted to be a psychiatrist, but the major intent was "to pursue the social good, to help others," particularly the poor colored people who went without education and health services. These ideas were generated from the Sunday school lessons and the lessons learned from my mother. Yet, she had had a difficult life, and I doubted that I could overcome the adversities and hardships she had. Although she did very well in con-cealing the vicissitudes of being a single parent raising five children, I knew I could never be as courageous as she.

Although outwardly, I was a quiet, shy, well-behaved, good student, inside I struggled with many philosophical, social, and religious beliefs far beyond my years. The contradiction of slavery and discrimination in a democratic society, the silent massacre of six million Jews, the hypocrisy of Christianity, and cruelty to the poor were just a few of the subjects I read about and pondered in the privacy of my closet. Adults only smiled when I posed such questions and said, "'Lizabeth's child is always thinking. Children shouldn't be thinking about such things!" It was never said harshly, more often with great admiration and a worried look, but I never received any answers.

Looking back now I can only feel very thankful for the protection and love that I received in spite of my differentness. However, my differentness was not as acceptable in the white world. In all of the literature on rites of passage, transformations, and adolescent development, few scholars have noted the effects or the distortions of discrimination or racism on that process, except, of course, the African Americans of the 1940s and then those African American scholars who began to uncover the issue again in the late 60s and 70s.[7]

What is now astounding to me is that my sisters and I, especially Alice, who was closest to me, never talked about the influence of race on our lives. My mother talked about her life in Virginia and the pain of segregation and discrimination she and her family experienced. But she did not talk too frequently about it, partly, I think, because she did not want to frighten or discourage us, but partly because Boston's colored people rarely talked about race relations. Boston was the promised land and most colored people were glad to be there. However, the very contradictions of living in the cradle of liberty were glaringly obvious to me, even though the subject was rarely discussed in my presence. I remember that my mother's friends chided her about encouraging me to be a doc-tor. She ignored their negative comments and responded, "Gloria can be whatever she wants to be if she works hard enough and is willing to work harder than her white classmates to get there."

Defining the Person within the Dark Skin

By fourteen I had no breasts, no menses, and I was still as thin as a rail—not intentionally or deliberately, but just naturally. Finally, one of the many doctors to whom my mother took me reassured her that I was not undernourished and had inherited my father's genes. Since I had a hammer toe like his, she finally began to accept the fact that tall and skinny was just part of me. However, she continued to buy my clothes a size larger, just in case I put on weight. It mattered little to me, because I had no interest in clothes and wore baggy rolled-up jeans and big men's shirts. It was the beatnik era; my mother always said I ushered it into vogue.

To my camp friends and school friends I was Glo-Jo, but to my older sisters' friends I was Alice's little sister, a nice way of calling me a pest. By sixteen, my mother began to worry a bit about my bookish ways and persuaded (more likely ordered) my sisters to include me in the dances and parties they attended. Of course, it was a total disaster. I didn't like to "slow dance" and no one liked to folk dance or square dance. Most of the time I sat in a corner and read a book until someone would turn down the lights. I would turn up the lights and then someone would take the bulb. Then, of course, I'd want to go home, which meant Barbara and Alice had to leave. The Johnson rule was you all go together and you all come home together. The difficulty was that ten to twelve girls at the party would have to leave as well because they had come with the Johnson girls. Consequently, when I decided to leave, it had a devastating effect on the party. I think the reader can well understand why none of my sisters' friends cared to know my name. I was just Alice's little sister—the bookworm and pest.

A great deal of my confusion about the social life of an adolescent had to do with school. Most of my best friends were school friends, but they were white. I was rarely ever invited to their homes, and when I invited them to my home, they never came. It was very painful to be so rejected and set apart. We were friends, but not really friends. They liked me, but they did not like my race, the color of my skin, or my slave heritage. I lived in two worlds and was not a major part of either one. I helped my white classmates with their homework (I was very good in mathematics) either after school in a classroom, or in a drugstore between my house and theirs, and on occasion at their house when their parents weren't there.

On the other hand, there was an anti-intellectual attitude among many of the colored youngsters in the neighborhood. Poetry, philosophy, and politics were subjects for white people not for colored people. There were African American youngsters who had the same aspirations for an education that I had, but the difference between me and them was the intensity of my interest and my complete involvement in my schoolwork. The duality of my existence—one black and one white—was confusing and painful. I never wanted to be white. I just wanted to be who I was—Gloria or Glo-Jo, the dark-skinned girl who loved to read and exchange political and philosophical ideas, who loved nature and being out-of-doors, who loved classical and folk music, who wanted to be a doctor and help the mentally ill, who wanted to find a place in the world where she could be who she was and what she wanted to become in spite of her skin color and her plainness. What was wrong with trying to live in both worlds or wanting to belong to both?

By the time I was in tenth grade, I was certain I was not a Christian with a capital "C," but more of an agnostic. By eleventh grade I decided I was a pacifist and owed my allegiance only to "God" or human love and I stopped saluting the flag. When the teachers at Girls' Latin School realized I did not salute the flag, they tried to coerce me by saying that they would write to all the colleges and tell them I was a nonconformist. Then I was suspended for the day with the request that I return with my mother. My mother asked me some very penetrating questions like: "Are you prepared to postpone going to college and work for a while because of your belief?" It was a very difficult question. I had been working hard since kindergarten because I wanted to be a physician. I knew I needed to get a scholarship to go to a good college or work and try to save enough money. It was my senior year and I was in the top ten percent of my class. However, after I had read a great deal about the concentration camps during World War II, I believed that

Nazism had arisen out of a distortion of nationalism. An individual's allegiance belonged to a higher order of moral–ethical commitment than one's country. One had to consider one's loyalty to humanity and humanism above and beyond one's loyalty to one's country, race, or place of origin. I believed fervently in one world and one people. I was ready to postpone college if the scholarship was denied me. My mother then went to school with me.

Mrs. Johnson was tiny but mighty and very articulate. I was, of course, readmitted without any obligation to salute the flag or sing the song designated by the school board to be sung in lieu of a prayer. However, there was a price I had to pay for defining myself differently. I was meant to be one of ten students selected to the National Honor Society. The principal refused to nominate me. As I cried on my mother's shoulder that evening she said, "Gloria, remember no matter what you do, do not for the glory of men who are very fickle, but for the glory of God—however you are defining God to be these days." I remember the twinkle in her eyes as she referred to my ever-changing definition of God. What I will always remember about Mrs. Johnson was her kindness, her sense of humor, and her complete trust and belief in me. She even enjoyed it when I stopped calling her Mama and began to call her Mrs. Johnson, the way the people in our neighborhood called her. She was "the wind beneath my sails" and I literally adored her.

That day I left childhood behind and took a giant step into adulthood. Having defined myself spiritually, in an existentialist sense, I had been able to find the real self within the dark skin surrounded by a white world, a world I then knew I would never be a part of completely.

Defining Myself for Myself: The Authentic Self

Kierkegaard in his book, *The Sickness Unto Death* describes several aspects of despair: the despair of not wanting to be a self, the despair of wanting to be a self, and the despair at defining the self. The despair, as he defines it, is the ultimate "sickness unto death" and the core of the existentialist dilemma. Put more simply by one of my favorite poets, Emily Dickinson, "Ourself behind ourself concealed, should startle most." And so, off I went to Mount Holyoke College determined to define myself by my own definition. It was a lovely setting—a small town surrounded by farmlands and rolling hills. There were very few minority students, certainly less than eight the first year, and the numbers declined each subsequent year. Yet for me it was the reflective environment that I needed, and I settled in and made friends. There was still the pretense that race did not matter, although the outside world that intruded upon us told us differently.

It was 1954, the year of the Supreme Court decision on school segregation. The topic was never discussed in my sociology class and never mentioned in the college newspaper or in any lectures on campus. It was as though there were two worlds: one at Mount Holyoke College and then the wider world. Rosa Parks began the Montgomery bus boycott—still, no discussions in college lectures about one of the most socially significant events of the century.

During my senior year, Gwendoloyn Carter, then a professor at Smith College, organized a four-college seminar on African Studies, and I was the only non-white student in the course. As we talked about the emergence of independence in Ghana and Nigeria and apartheid in South Africa, there was no discussion of the Civil Rights Movement in the South. Indeed, if I had not attended the NAACP Youth Program on Saturdays during high school, I would not have known anything about African American history or the major African American scholars, poets, or writers. These scholars were ignored in the history, sociology and English courses I took and no mention was made of them in the African Studies Seminar. It was strange and eery to me that the entire subject of African American history and writers was so completely ignored.

The invisibility of the issue of race conveyed a message to me about how I should define myself if I wanted to be acceptable in a world dominated by whites. Was I to pretend that I was not colored, that my skin was not dark? Was I to forget that my ancestors came to this country as slaves? Was I to ignore that there were places I could not go because I was colored? I had no desire to do so, but I wondered about some of the professors who clearly conveyed to me their discomfort with the issue of race, which meant if I was to be accepted by them, I needed to submerge that issue and thus conceal myself behind myself. I did not know how to do that. My mother, family, and friends had made me feel so proud to be me with my heritage of slavery and courage. Thus, to conceal myself and ignore myself was devastatingly egodystonic. Instead, I persisted in being Gloria—asking the unanswerable, raising discussions about the uncomfortable issues—politely, reflectively, but persistently.

And then, several serendipitous events changed the course of my life and set me on a path that I would pursue relentlessly both personally and professionally. First, I met a young colored man from Princeton, a Woodrow Wilson scholar, who had done his undergraduate work at Morehouse. It was with him that I could openly discuss all the issues of the Civil Rights Movement in the South, the atrocities of the Ku Klux Klan, and the course of school desegregation. These were the kind of discussions that I had longed for but never had at college, which was too white and too well-mannered to discuss such issues, nor in Boston, with colored people who felt they had no reason to be concerned because they lived in the cradle of liberty and had no such struggles to resolve.

Secondly, the summer between my junior and senior year, I applied for several positions as a campcraft counselor. I had spent eight years at a Girl Scout Camp in New Hampshire, two of which I was in training as a campcraft counselor. I had done as Mrs. Johnson had admonished, "Get your training and qualifications and then you can compete." I knew I was competitive.

The first call came from a camp in Maine. They were very eager to have me: my records from Girls Scout Camp were superb, so were my references. They told me that they wanted me to come immediately. I made arrangements to take the train to Portland, Maine and called to tell the director the day and time of my arrival. He assured me someone would be there to meet me and asked how they could identify me. I said, "I'm a tall colored girl and I'll be wearing a sailor blouse and a blue plaid skirt." There was a long silence and then he said, "A plaid skirt." I told my mother about it, and we both agreed that he had not expected a colored girl.

I arrived at the Portland station after a five-hour train ride, hungry and tired, and two young women identified themselves as the counselors who had come to drive me to camp. We drove another two hours to the camp and parked outside the director's office. He came out to greet me, but told the counselors to leave my bags in the car. I went inside his office to talk, expecting to fill out papers and hear about my tasks. The conversation that ensued left me in a state of shock. The essence of the conversation was that he had never expected a colored person to apply. The camp was a Christian camp and they had just started to accept Jews, but he did not think they were ready to accept colored people yet.

I cried the entire eight hours on the bus back to Boston. My experience, my training, my skills, my references—all my qualifications meant nothing. All he could perceive was the dark skin and that made me unacceptable. I thought of my resolve not to salute the flag and why I had made that decision. I knew then that I would never, ever be able to do so because of the sheer hypocrisy of "liberty and justice for all." I felt a new resolve to preserve my allegiance to a higher order than a country and pledge myself again to the pursuit of social justice and humanistic values.

My mother had never seen me so despondent, and when I told her what had happened, she cradled me in her arms and sang "On the Old Rugged Cross." Whenever she sang it, I knew she was feeling deep sorrow—"On a hill faraway stood an old rugged cross the symbol of suffering and pain." After that, we dried our eyes and then sang that most comforting and empowering spiritual—"Oh freedom, Oh freedom, Oh freedom for me. Before I'll be a slave I'll be buried in my grave and go home to my Lord and be free."

The next call came two days later from a camp in upstate New York. The camp director was staying at a downtown hotel and wanted to interview me immediately. My record and achievements were outstanding, so he said, and he was sure it would be a good match. I told him who I was and asked if he had any objections to having a colored counselor. There was a long pause and then he said, "This is an Ethical Cultural camp, would that bother you?" I then inquired about the meaning of Ethical Cultural and he explained. We met; he was pleasant, but surprised that a colored girl had such academic achievement, had attended Girls' Latin School, and was now a senior at Mount Holyoke College. I tried not to feel like some freak. I knew that my achievements were not unusual at Mount Holyoke College. It was just that I had had a "very white education" by his standards, both inside and outside of school, and he found this astonishing. I knew then what he expected of colored girls.

The next day he called and said that after thinking about it, he decided that it was not the right time to have a colored counselor. It had only been two years since they had started to accept Christians to the camp and he did not feel it was time to integrate colored people. However, he had given my name to a Girl Scout camp director who would be calling me. I went to the Girl Scout Camp at Buzzard's Bay and had a delightful time, but the pain of the rejection took a long time to go away.

When I went back to Mount Holyoke College in the fall, I applied to Meharry Medical College, as my friend from Princeton had suggested. I had never been South; I had never been in an all-colored setting; I had never had a colored teacher or seen a colored doctor. I felt I needed to understand and see for myself the most major social revolution of this century—the end of racial segregation, the Civil Rights Movement, and the fight for social justice. As a young child I had promised myself that I would never remain silent like the Germans while six million Jews were killed. I felt I needed to actualize that commitment. I needed to define myself and my life for myself, and not let it occur by happenstance or for the convenience of being accepted as the exception in a white world.

My Journey Home

Alice did not come to the airport to meet me. Joyce, my younger sister, did. She said simply, "At last you've come home." I had been away for thirty-four years. I hoped that it would not be too late for us to share some time together. She had just been diagnosed as having metastatic thyroid cancer. She was like my twin in that we looked so much alike, but she was not as tall and had always been prettier. Throughout our childhood I had protected and teased her, and she had adored me and still did. Mrs. Johnson and Barbara were gone but I was hopeful that Alice, Joyce, and I could enjoy some time together. Alice came the next day and the reunion in Boston began, only this time I would not be visiting and then flying away. I had come back to live.

Over the next year, the three of us talked about many things and reminisced about our childhood. Although life for each of us had been different, we all agreed our childhood had been very special. Alice and Joyce related to me the many changes in our old neighborhood. I knew the professional task that I had come to tackle would be difficult and I was thankful for my sisters' support and encouragement. It had been a long journey both physically and spiritually from our childhood home on Elbert Street to my new position in Boston. However, there were many professional and personal lessons learned that I hoped would be useful in developing programs for poor inner-city youngsters.

My childhood experience had been extraordinary. I was eager to create such experiences for other inner-city youngsters. However, was I ready for New England and Boston and the Yankee Racism? I remembered my confrontations with the hypocritical liberalism of New England, the distortion of self so prevalent among many New England African Americans. It startled me to see so many selves concealed behind themselves in order to be accepted according to nebulous white standards.

Although I knew that living in Boston was going to present many challenges, the beauty of New England had always remained fixed in my mind throughout my travels and it would always be home. I remembered my days in Nashville as I was sitting in, standing in, and freedom riding, and the words of the poet John Masefield, who said that when one struggles to have meaning in one's life, there may be great confusion, but to live life without meaning is "like a ship longing for the sea, but yet afraid."

I felt certain that my journey home would be meaningful in spite of the adversities I knew would come. I was no longer concealed behind myself. I was Alice's little sister but I had many other parts of myself that I had discovered. I had defined myself, and with that definition I had defined my life and my path.

Notes

1   There is no evidence that the early process of self-concept development is different for boys or girls. However, the identity stages of self-concept development do have sex differences. In these paragraphs I use the feminine pronoun to enhance the feminist perspective of the self-concept process.

2   Gloria Johnson-Powell. 1973. *Black Monday's Children: The Study of School Desegregation in Southern School Children*. New York: Prentice Hall. The northern data was published in a chapter in *The Assessment and Evaluation Of The Afro-American Family* 1980, B. Bass, G. E. Wyatt, and G. J. Powell, eds.

3   A chapter about my childhood was published in *Growing Up Female*, 1978, Clare Kopp, ed., New York: Plenum.

4   V. Turner, 1987. "Betwixt and Between: The Liminal Period in Rites of Passage," in *Betwixt and Between: Patterns of Masculine and Feminine Initiation*. L.C. Mahdi, S. Foster, and M. Little (eds,) LaSalle, Illinois: Open Court.

5   The places described in this section were part of a Boston neighborhood called Upper Roxbury or Sugar Hill. It is the neighborhood where Malcolm X lived, as well as Louis Farrakhan. It was a working-class Jewish neighborhood and at the time of my childhood African Americans were beginning to move there from Lower Roxbury and the South End. At the time (1930-1948) the African American population of Boston was less than ten percent. Upper Roxbury or "the Hill" was known for being home to many educated African Americans at that time.

6   William Strickland went on to Boys' Latin School and Harvard University. He is Professor of Political Science at the University of Massachusetts.

7   In *Children Of Bondage* (1940) authors Allison Davis and John Dollard explore the personality development of black youth in an urban southern city. The book relies on the field studies of W. Lloyd Warner (Yankee City) as well as Allison Davis and Gardner Burleigh (Deep South). Other notable studies include *Negro Youth at the Cross-ways: Their Personality Development in the Middle States* by E. Franklin Frazier; *Growing Up in the Black Belt: Negro Youth in the Rural South* by Charles S. Johnson; as well as *Color and Human Nature: Negro Personality Development in a Northern City* by W. Lloyd Warner, Buford N. Junker, and Walter A. Adams. In *The Psychosocial Development Of Minority Group Children*, 1983 (G.J. Powell, J. Yamamoto, A. Romero, and A. Morales, eds.) the chapter "The Psychosocial Development of Afro-American Children" provides an extensive listing of those scholars who have pursued this topic in more recent times.

6

Place and Kinship
A Native American's Identity Before and After Words
DONALD ANDREW GRINDE, JR.

I cannot order my early memories in any particular sequence—rather they swirl around me in an experiential place where time and space, as well as collective and individual perceptions, blur into an impressionistic totality (perhaps I will return to such a state upon my death). I do know that my parents dreamed of me before I was conceived, before such dreams I lived in a place without names and words. It was their dream that eventually enabled me to come into the world of words and then learn to be a human being. And so it was that I was brought into the world, and subsequently, through a barrage of seemingly random sights, sounds, smells, tastes, and touches, that concrete reality after birth gradually took on the shape of names and words. It was my parents and the rest of my family that named me when I was a child—not the outside world. That kinship identity and meaning was informed by the human and natural environments that I encountered in my formative years. As Native and mixed-blood people from the coastal Southeastern United States (we had another name for it, "Tama," when we lived in that place in another world with only our native relatives), we understood that we did not own the earth—it owned us. We were simply "Tomathli," or the people who live on the high ground or bluffs. Thus, the place of our birth vested indelibly in us, an identity, since we have always been and will always be there with the spirits of relatives of past, present, and future.

Our relatives, elders, and friends helped us to name the world and thus enabled us to "see" it and to dream about it. Thus kinship tells us that our biological and mythological grandmothers and grandfathers, mothers and fathers, sisters and brothers are reflected in the environmental mothers and fathers (Moon, Sun, earth and sky), sisters and brothers (plants and animals) and forces of creation (earth, wind, fire and water). From the start, a sense of unity existed for me in the small federal housing project where my parents and I lived during the early years of my child-hood—since we still lived in the land of our ancestors.

Before I went to school, I had lived in a world where there were no words (in the spiritual world and the womb of my mother) and after I was born I had lived in a world where you heard words.

When I went outside that world into the dominant society's schools, I learned that you could also see words, and this was called reading. As long as I can remember, I was intrigued by the idea of "seeing" words.

As a young child, my world was very personalized. Hours were spent looking at the transit of ants and praying mantis, and listening to the birds and the wind in the trees. I was raised to know that experience came first and then ideas, because we were encouraged to figure the world out for ourselves. My identity, informed by place and kinship, partially preceded notions of nationalistic ideology that I would receive in the educational environments of the dominant society. Ideological identities can be changed and reformulated in the media and education to suit the time and historical needs of a population, while traditional Native American conceptions of identity are rooted in place and kinship in a magical way that insinuates itself into your life from birth. I suppose that is why colonial societies have attacked American Indian identity from the beginning of contact. People who ritualize place and link kinship to that reality cannot be easily "moved" or "reinvented" for the sake of conquest and the marketplace.

My mother taught me that the place I inhabited nurtured me in a maternal way. When I complained about the hot Georgia sun she would tell me that since they had paved so much of the ground in the city, the earth, our mother, could not "breathe." From her I learned that the earth was a living and breathing organism and that we were a product and function of its existence! Life, as we knew it, endured because our mother endured. I realized that our spirits were all around us—not on some cloud in the sky—we just needed to understand the spiritual world around us and learn how it operated. We were guided by our personal and spiritual experiences, not faith. My personal relationship with my natural surroundings formed at an early age, was not symbolic but deeply experiential for me, and has remained with me throughout my entire life.

At the same time, I began to notice that other people had ideas about this world as a "vale of tears" and that true happiness existed in a far-off place separate from this world, called "heaven." These ideological notions of existence appeared to concentrate on human codes of behavior with little attention to learning from the physical place and historical time within which people lived. In fact, space and time are often compressed or obliterated in such ideological conceptions, since the only place that mattered was some far off "holy land" and the only time that was significant was a magical one that existed about 2,000 years ago. Coming from a humid subtropical environment, it was impossible for me to imagine such an arid place as the "holy land" where people herded sheep for a living. Thus, the message was not "grounded" in my spatial and personal experience. Such a "holy" place seemed far less vivid than my own personal and familial experiences with my surroundings.

Growing up as an only child, with a heightened sense of relatedness, did not prepare me for the bureaucratic indifference of the public schools. Although I was shy, I made friends. It was during this time that I also experienced the terror of gangs. For the poor, random and senseless violence was a hallmark of our existence, and, even in the first grade, bands of violent boys, six to twelve years old, terrorized those of us who would not join. In the first grade during recess, a student in another class knifed me in the abdomen, sending me to the emergency room. I never knew that the attack was coming. After taking a drink from the water fountain, I turned and felt the knife plunge into my stomach. I can still remember the smile on my assailant's face, the pain in my abdomen and my parents' panic and concern at the hospital. I can still remember my mother and father protesting to the school about the violence and very little being done about curtailing weapons in our elementary school.

I also remember observing group violence during my youth. As the Civil Rights Movement heated up in the mid-1950s, I saw African-American people demonstrating peacefully after a St. Patrick's Day parade and mounted police charging into them with tear gas and clubs. My mother observed that the Black man and the White man were locked in a struggle for equality and that in such struggles Euroamericans sometimes go crazy with violence—lynching people and killing women and children. It was obvious to me even as a child that while the state had a monopoly on "legitimate" violence, police violence was often far from being legitimate in its application.

As a student who was "different" in the American South, I received a rather spotty education in grammar school. Since I read a lot at home and my parents and relatives talked to me a great deal, I learned about language, politics, literature, and culture through family experiences. When I received standardized testing in the upper grades, it was revealed to the school's surprise that I was "gifted" and I entered an "accelerated" academic program. My years in the "gifted" program were basically oriented towards Math and Science—disciplines that appeared to be addenda to the Cold War defense education efforts.

During my years in elementary school, I established a firm relationship with my Grandfather, who taught me hunting, trapping, native agricultural practices, and the spiritual dimension to place such things in an appropriate context. My Grandfather had seven daughters, and my mother was his oldest daughter. As my mother's first child, I was almost the same age as his two younger daughters. In retrospect, it appears to me that I was not only my Grandfather's first grandchild but also the son he never had. I think my mother sent me to visit my Grandfather during the summer so I could learn things and so my Grandfather could have a son. The result is that I really had two fathers when I was growing up. Although I did not grow up in affluence, my family life more than compensated for any monetary shortcomings.

Grandpa had herbal remedies for most ailments. He believed that Indians should eat no grains except corn and occasionally rice and that wheat bread, refined sugars, and virtually every processed food was bad for us, both for nutritional reasons and because these foods were not part of a traditional American Indian diet. He grew corn, beans, and squash in "hills," stating that they were supposed to be grown together symbiotically. In the late summer and early fall we would run the razorback pigs out of the swamp into his cornfields to fatten them up for market. He would always take the leanest and strongest and slaughter them for our consumption before he fattened the others for market. I learned about the behavior of pigs, snakes, rabbits, deer, and insects from him. Everything had a place in creation, according to Grandpa. I watched wild pigs forage for rattlesnakes in the swamp. I learned how to avoid poisonous snakes and not to kill them, since we believed that if you kill one snake many more will show up in that same place in the next day or two. My Grandfather also taught me about the weather; I still remember learning about the high wind in the pines and the sound it makes in anticipation of a storm.

When I entered high school, I took a heavy academic load, which sometimes had an adverse effect on my health. But I was determined to do my best to gain a good education in order to bring honor to my family and to become self-sufficient. At the age of twelve, I began to have epileptic seizures. Although the seizures ceased by the time I was fourteen, the experience taught me about the fragility of life and the human condition. I remember my first seizure as if it were yesterday. As I was fading into unconsciousness, I wondered if I was exiting from this world. Awakening a few minutes later, I was pleased to still be on this earth, and yet I had experienced a peacefulness that defied description. From a practical standpoint, the seizures heightened my awareness that the world of ideas was where I would work, since many jobs involving physical labor were not suitable for epileptics.

My mother and father had graduated from high school during the Great Depression and going to college was not a realistic option for them. However, they saw in the early 1960s that a state university education for their son was within their financial grasp so they encouraged me to aspire to it. For awhile I entertained the idea of going to an Ivy League school, but the tuition was more than my father made in a year. It was unrealistic for me to seek something that was so out of reach for the class that I was born into.

I wound up going to Georgia Southern College, a state university just a few miles from my Grandfather's house and far enough away from my parents to secure the experience of residential college life. I began as a business major, then switched quickly to pre-law, seriously contemplated becoming a biology major (I really enjoyed botany) but then decided to go into history since it sought to comprehend human existence in very broad terms. College life in the early sixties was still a lot of "panty raids" and beer parties, but I do recall some defining moments, even in that environment.

In the fall of 1963 I remember sitting in Freshman English Composition and hearing a student run down the hall shouting that the President had been shot! We were writing an in-class essay and the English Professor (a kindly gay man with one of the biggest hearts I have ever known in the academic community) told us to finish our assignment and then leave quietly. After class, I walked down to the student union and watched on TV the grim news of President John F. Kennedy's assassination in Dallas. When it became apparent that he was dead, I went with several Asian American students and some white students to lower the campus flag to half-mast. As we were doing this, a group of white students told us threateningly that we weren't to lower the flag since Kennedy was a "nigger lover" and deserved to be shot. The ensuing shoving match, with racial epithets hurled from both sides, ended when a larger group of white students arrived with the intent to also lower the flag to half-mast.

Once again, I had faced the darker and violent side of American society, even in a time of national mourning. The next year I would deliver a paper in my International Relations class on the futility of American involvement in Vietnam. Most students hissed at the end of my presentation, and the only other American Indian at the school, a Seminole from Florida, seemed to be the only one who considered my views seriously. Through these experiences, I learned that speaking out and taking "controversial" stands had a cost, but I generally believed that the benefits gained by being true to yourself outweighed the costs levied by the dominant society.

Completing my undergraduate degree in 1966 at the age of nineteen, I obtained a graduate fellowship in American history to attend the University of Delaware in the fall. Although I had wanted to do American Indian history, there was no such thing at the time and no graduate advisor to help me. American Indian history was not considered a "legitimate" field and my graduate advisor told me that I needed to focus on an area such as American Economic history to secure employment. When I told him that I was an American Indian and thus still wanted to do research in this area, he smiled and murmured, "I thought that we had killed all of them." Since my advisor's interests were in the development of the American West, I wrote a dissertation on the DuPont Company's price-fixing practices in its western markets. At the time, that was about as close as I could get to a study of American Indians. But I resolved that I would create my own American Indian history course when I began my teaching career.

Realizing that American Indian history was not an "approved" subject, I knew that I would have to seek internal rather than external validation for my work. I still strove to complete my classes and degrees, but I understood that my professional life would be essentially different from many "mainstream" students. My quest was to create a discourse on Native American history that reflected the Native American viewpoint on the process of conquest, domination, and the struggle for self-determination. I reasoned that this would not be an easy journey, and there would probably be little appreciation for my work except amongst American Indian people. I also understood, from the start, that by sticking to a realistic interpretation of American Indian history from the Native American viewpoint I would not gain friends and influence people in the upper echelons of the historical profession which was marked by ideology, control, and the sanitization of American history for popular consumption. For me, the conquest of America clearly had winners and losers, while the official line was that nation-state formation was a bothersome process that eventually created a society that was "fair" to all who assimilated into its ideological inventions.

From my own internal identity produced by place and kinship, such ideological rationalizations repudiated the intrinsic worth of American Indian people and the genocidal struggles that we had undergone. Often, friends and colleagues exhorted me to give up my dedication to my group identity and pursue my academic career as an "individual" (that is, to do work that benefited me and not necessarily my group). Also I noticed during the 1960s that people whose identities were not grounded in place and kinship tended to develop and change ideological identities quite readily. For example, once when sitting with a group of Indians and non-Indians in a social event at a park, a young non-Indian woman dressed in 1960s fringed garb confessed to the group that she was trying to "find" herself. Her search was for ideas that would define her, and in doing so she thought she would find a place and people that would be better. Since the United States is a collection of ideas and not a homogeneous people, I suppose that this process was important for many people. But I never went through a conversion process and thus I was never an ardent "Marxist" or "Capitalist" or "conservative" or "liberal." Instead, I understood that these were the thoughts of the Europeans that structured and restructured their worlds in the whirligig of "politics." My own political inclinations seemed to defy conventional classification until academic scholarship began to focus more directly on race, class, and gender.

Nevertheless, I was still perceived by many as being "political." I was once asked by a colleague, "Don, as a radical American Indian scholar, what do you think of the concept of American Indian sovereignty?" I replied to his query by asserting that "If I were a member of the dominant society then I would not be perceived as a radical but a conservative, since I stood steadfastly for the preservation of the language, culture, traditional government, and land base of Native American peoples." I am not so sure that the colleague ever fathomed the full meaning of my reply since it would have required him to look at me as something more than a "marginal" person in his society.

By the late 1960s, protests against the Vietnam War were in full swing. Feeling strongly about the futility of U.S. involvement, I became involved in student protests against the war. My advisor chided me for my views since he was a conservative, but he truly believed that you had the right to your views and your only obligation was to logically substantiate them. Throughout my graduate studies, I never felt penalized for my political views by him, although I did not feel that this was necessarily so with regards to other, more "liberal," professors who talked one way and behaved another. This professional experience demonstrated to me the moral contradictions in liberalism, as the war in Vietnam split our society asunder.

At about this time, it also became obvious to me that refocusing the status quo to arrive at a consensus for all meant severe sacrifices for those of us outside the mainstream. Worse yet, becoming a part of the mainstream seemed a form of psychological, cultural, and intellectual suicide. However, listening to the social, political, and economic critics of the time enabled me to formulate a personal course that seemed to avoid some of the ideological pitfalls of the times. Abbie Hoffman, Jerry Rubin, Tom Hayden, Jane Fonda, Herbert Aptheker, Stokely Carmichael, and many student leaders were among the people whom I gained wisdom from during this time.

A few American Indian students were in attendance at the University of Delaware and we "found" each other in the course of our stay there. I remember a Nanticoke Indian from Delaware who lived in the university apartment complex. He had been in the Navy in the early sixties and had gained a security clearance in Naval intelligence since he was assigned to guard an admiral's office door in the Pentagon. By the mid-sixties, he was using the GI Bill to attend college, but he was always complaining that if Naval intelligence wanted him they could yank him back into the service years after he was out.

One balmy autumn day in 1968, this American Indian student ran up to me and said that he wanted to go fishing that afternoon. His manner had a certain urgency to it and we drove twenty miles to a secluded lake and then rowed out into the middle of it. Before I could get my line into the water, my friend produced a letter from a governmental security organization stating that, since he had been in Naval intelligence, he could earn money by joining certain "radical" student organizations at the University of Delaware and reporting on their activities. They offered him $6,000 per year for his reports, which in those days paid for his tuition, room, and board as an in-state student. Although he did not want to do such a thing, the letter also contained a thinly disguised threat that if he did not agree to their offer they might pull him back into active military service, which would disrupt his college career.

My friend anguished over being placed in the position of "ratting" on his fellow students or being forced to interrupt his college career. We discussed his options, and I told him to ignore the letter and make no choice, at the time, since it appeared to be a form letter. Finally, he agreed that doing nothing was the best course and, as far as I know, he was never contacted again about the matter. With this experience, I understood that we were being "watched" and that it was important to convey our awareness of what the government was doing to monitor our activities.

In 1969, I was elected to a second term as President of the Graduate Student Association at the University of Delaware. As a student leader I supported antiwar protest marches, the Students for Democratic Society, the Weathermen, protests against ROTC and defense research on campus, Earth Day, as well as the beginning of women's rights and minority studies.

Essentially, I was either an undergraduate or a graduate student throughout the 1960s, and I am thankful for that experience since it was such an exciting time to be involved in politics and university life. However, I was always aware that a significant number of the people involved in the antiwar movement were not interested in the other issues that I considered related or pivotal to changing American society. My role as a student leader became more focused as I gained a fuller realization of such mainstream political realities.

My decision to become a university professor sprang from an awareness that the ferment of the 1960s was driven more by people's personal concerns about the effect of the military draft on themselves than by a larger critique of American politics and society (race, class, and gender issues). With the intellectual baptism of the 1960s fresh in my mind, I began my teaching career in 1971 at a small Catholic college (Mercyhurst) in Erie, Pennsylvania. I was twenty-five at the time. Paradoxically, the first course I taught was not American Economic history (which my advisor had thought marketable), but American Indian history—a task I had been training myself for throughout my graduate career. I regarded the training to get a Ph.D. as the "union card" that allowed me to legitimately function within the historical profession while pursuing my own goals to create a usable past for American Indian people, and maybe for the dominant society. Teaching the course was a scramble initially, since I had to invent the course and create the lectures from scratch. I knew that conquest history, wars, treaties, and government policies were important, but I also included discussions on Native languages, culture, philosophy, and spirituality. Fortunately, the students responded favorably to this approach. I was virtually the only professor who gave them insight into the world of "marginalized" people from a personal perspective. People at that small Catholic college understood white ethnic differences and extrapolated their reality to reason that understanding American Indians' experiences was a similar process. While they were not right in their assumptions, their intentions were good and they were open to discussing ethnicity in America in a variety of contexts.

I worked in Native American community organizations wherever my career moves took me. My community work provided a fuller understanding of the practical sides of American Indian education and policies as well as the problems of developing an American Indian history that we could call our own—not one that rationalized and justified the behavior of the conqueror. Whether it was working at SUNY in Buffalo, UCLA, UC Riverside, or Cal Poly, this networking with other American Indian and minority scholars helped me to lessen the social and intellectual isolation from the institution that was the norm. It is through this interaction that I have been able to refine and hone my ideas, since talking to mainstream scholars usually involved shrugs and discourses on "standards" and "real history," as opposed to any meaningful interaction about content and interpretation.

This isolation, however, made me a better family man because my life as a social human became centered more and more on kinship, childrearing, and marriage. As a result, I have happy, well adjusted children and grandchildren. Since both my wife's tribe as well as mine are matrilocal and matrifocal, we have built a house on her reservation (Navajo) for summer use and retirement purposes. Our children have become educated and returned to the reservation to raise their children. As a consequence, when my wife and I go back to the reservation, life is a swirl of kinship and place-oriented activities. This process has greater and greater value for me as I get older. My writing and rewriting of American Indian history are more important for my children and grandchildren than they are to me personally these days.

It was in this environment that I had a series of personal crises that profoundly affected my life. The first of these was the murder of my sixteen-year-old son by a drug dealer. One Sunday afternoon, my second-oldest son went to play a game of pick-up basketball at the local neighborhood playground in the small, rural California town where we were living. He was playing with a group of boys when a car drove up and motioned to two of the boys to come over to the car. With the game interrupted, my son stood by waiting as the two boys talked to the men some thirty feet away. After some shouting, the men pulled out a gun and motioned for the two boys to get into the car. Seeing what was happening, my son tried to ease away, but the men yelled for him to get into the car since he had seen what was happening. The two boys in the car said that he had nothing to do with them, but my son was forced into the car. Taken to a deserted road, the marijuana growers placed the three boys face down and began to intimidate them by cocking and uncocking a pistol to the back of their heads—accusing the boys of stealing their plants. The other two boys as well as my son said he had nothing to do with such activities. Finally, the men shot my son in the back of the head at point-blank range and then got into the car and sped off—leaving the other two boys there with my dying son.

The resulting entanglement with the legal system showed me that justice, up close, is neither pretty nor blind—it reflects instead the values of the community, racism and all. Upon being informed of the crime and the capture of the perpetrator that evening, we were told that the murderer was a local businessman and that he was trying to plead "diminished" capacity (he claimed the shooting was accidental since he was on drugs at the time), and plea-bargain to involuntary manslaughter (about three years hard time). Initially, the District Attorney seemed inclined to agree with his reasoning—thinking initially, as he stated to me later, that my son was just an illegal "Mexican." When he found out that my son was the son of a local American Indian college professor, he decided to change his mind on the plea bargain and prosecute for second-degree murder.

I pressured the DA's office to fully prosecute the murderer while arranging for my son's burial and grieving with my family. I do not now understand how I did all those things and still kept my sanity. I remember being angry and disappointed in the way the justice system worked. My wife told me that she felt violated—like someone had opened up her womb and had begun to kill her from the inside out. The other children were in shock.

The trial was even worse. The local business community that we traded with presented a signed petition to the judge that my son's murderer was a local businessman and thus deserved special consideration. The defense tried repeatedly to prove that my son was, indeed, involved in stealing the murderer's marijuana plants, in spite of the testimony to the contrary by the two other boys who survived the incident. Towards the end of the trial, victim's assistance services called us and asked why we were not in court to see justice served. When I replied that I was afraid I would kill the murderer if I saw him on a regular basis in court, the court counselor suggested that I visit the murderer in jail and "forgive" him. When I told the victim's assistance counselor that we did not do things that way, there was a long pause and then a "good bye." Eventually, the man was convicted and served eleven years and he is out on parole now.

A few years after my son's death, I was stricken suddenly with diabetes. I lost a pound a day for twenty-five days before I was able to diagnose my condition. The health maintenance organization that I was enrolled in kept insisting I had the flu and that they did not need to run a series of tests on me. I thought I had cancer and might die soon and finally persuaded the HMO to run tests on me and to specifically run the diabetes tests over the protests of my doctor. Within hours, the doctor called me up and sheepishly informed me that I had diagnosed myself and had additional health problems from going so long without treatment. The experience was another lesson in death and dying and what's important in life—and it was especially helpful a few years later as I talked to my father in his last days as he lay dying of cancer.

These personal crises had coincided with my getting tenure, so I decided that speaking my mind and working to change an awful system were more important than climbing the ladder of success. The experiences redoubled my resolve to write American Indian history from an American Indian perspective for the record, and less for personal advancement. As a newly-tenured faculty member, my personal identity as a Native American was increasingly in conflict with my professional identity. An affirmative action officer at a university where I worked once told me, "Don, you have to think of yourself and your personal advancement and think less of the needs of American Indian people." As a person with strong group orientations, such conflicts between doing what was advantageous for me and not right for American Indian people became untenable. I reasoned that having tenure and job security now compelled me to use my freedom to free others.

As a result, I continued my research on the Iroquois influences on American government. In the early 1970s, as a young American Indian professor at SUNY–Buffalo, I was visited by several Iroquois elders. They told me that their tribal and oral histories testified to the fact that their ideas of democracy had a profound influence on the founders of America. They then asked me as one of the first Native Americans to receive a Ph.D. in American history to research the white man's documents and write about this historical fact in a way that non-Indians could comprehend. I told them that I was surprised at this thesis and request, since I had always thought that the U.S. Constitution was one of the primary instruments of oppression used against American Indian people. In a deliberate manner, the Iroquois elders replied that they were aware of the way the Constitution had been used against them but they wanted me to pursue such a line of research, "Because it is the truth." I began a preliminary survey of the historical and documentary literature and found some interesting leads for further research. However, grant money for the project was not forthcoming. Non-Indian foundations and professors discounted the idea out of hand in spite of an intriguing scholarly evolution of the idea (a former President of the American Historical Association had hinted at the use of Iroquois ideas in the quest for American union as early as 1754).

In 1977, having no research funds and using only the evidence I could garner in the libraries in Buffalo, I published a book, *The Iroquois and the Founding of the American Nation* which advanced the notion that the Great Law of Peace of the Haudenosaunee (Iroquois) was an intellectual factor in the development of American governmental ideas of freedom and democracy. Initially, the book fell stillborn from the press. Only interested American Indians and a few others read it—scholars and "friends" of the American Indians scoffed at the thesis of the book. Five years later, interest in the idea resurfaced as the Bicentennial of the Constitution approached. I then gained some research money from private foundations to further my work on the subject and published *Exemplar of Liberty: Native America and the Evolution of American Democracy* in 1991 (coauthored with Bruce E. Johansen). This book is now acknowledged as the definitive work on the Iroquois influence on American government. Without my internal validation and the personal crises I experienced, I doubt that I would have had the persistence to publish my second book given the derision that I received from the anthropological establishment after my first publication.

Fortunately, this research enjoyed and still enjoys a wide readership for those who want to survey the evidence and decide for themselves. The argument that there is no scholarly and documentary evidence relating to the Iroquois influence on American government is no longer tenable. Critics and neoconservative pundits claimed that such assertions were a product of an "invented" tradition that served the needs of "multiculturalism." They reasoned that, of course,

American Indian people (appealing to latent racism and implying that we were savages) could not have had anything to do with the development of American government. I was impressed with the absolute avoidance of historical and documentary fact and the *ad hominem* and racially biased critiques about my scholarship. They said that it was better that a good non-Indian historian examine the evidence, rather than I.

In the process of my research, I discovered important and heretofore unpublished notes relating to the first draft of the Constitution. As a scholar of the American Constitution, I approached the Constitutional Bicentennial Commission (chaired by former Chief Justice Warren Burger) and asked that they publish what was essentially the first notations and draft of the Constitution. They flatly refused such a request without even examining the draft that exists in a historical society in Philadelphia. It became clear that they were not interested in furthering scholarship on the Constitution, but rather their role was to make sure that the right "spin" on the Constitution was achieved in the Bicentennial celebrations. It was clear that the federal government and the "court historians" were more interested in rationalizing American history to support the present dominant ideologies than in broadening our historical awareness.

By the early 1990s, my arguments and scholarship could no longer be ignored as they had been in the 1970s. The result was both a media and scholarly argument that fueled the wars over "political correctness." I have concluded that the making of American history like the making of sausage is a messy and untidy business and if you have an uncritical appetite for either of them then you had better not examine their production very closely. Historical facts, interpretations, as well as historical inventions that we choose to examine, are functions of our present existence. Objectivity is a myth: we are "participants" in the creation of American history, and to pretend that we are not active in the construction of our "realities" is to deny our humanity, our place, and our time. Throughout this whole process, it has been American Indian scholars, my family, as well as many non-Indians like my co-author, Professor Bruce E. Johansen, who have been supportive of my ideas.

In the late 1980s, I spent a year in Washington D.C. pursuing my research and testifying before the Senate Subcommittee on Indian Affairs. During that time, Russian–American relations were thawing and Russian scholars were coming to Washington D.C. I became a part of the program that brought American and Russian scholars together in various people's homes and hotels to discuss common issues to speed the ending of the Cold War. As we met the Russian scholars, we were aware of the beige government vans that were always outside the hotel with men in trench coats standing around, watching our activities. These surveillance tactics clearly indicated that the Cold War was not completely over. Our discussions with the scholars, on the other hand, were very positive, and we realized that we shared very similar experiences, even though we lived under different ideological configurations. This was a significant experience in my life, as it reinforced my feeling that governments often stand in the way of meaningful interactions, even at such critical times as the thawing of the Cold War.

No discussion of my life could be complete without some mention of my activities in the American Indian Movement (AIM). For over twenty years, I have been a member of AIM. From the time that it was declared one of the ten most dangerous organizations by the FBI in the 1970s until today, I have believed that American Indian liberation is basically a conservative process (preserving the culture, language, and spirituality of American Indian people), but I also believe that political action and human liberation movements are crucial if indigenous peoples are to regain their lands, sovereignty, and autonomy. In most other colonized areas of the world, native peoples (India, China, Africa) have regained their lands and their freedom, but this has not happened in the Americas. Instead, American Indian sovereignty is obfuscated by governmental discourses on "jurisdiction," resource management, and assimilation. American Indian people have largely remained colonized entities within the neocolonial governments that have been created after independence movements in the Americas. Until this is rectified, American Indians will remain imprisoned in an ideological rationalization that denies them basic human rights. For example, site-based Native American spiritualities are given short shrift by the U.S. judicial system. When an American Indian spiritual leader states that a certain mountain is sacred, a non-Indian must corroborate that assertion. We do not go to Muslim scholars who study Christianity for outside verification when the Pope asserts that abortion is immoral in his eyes—people accept the Pope's word, although they may disagree. Only American Indians need "outsiders" to validate their religious claims about sacred sites and their spirituality. As long as American Indian people remain unfree and imprisoned within alien ideologies, there will always be a need for Native American liberation movements like AIM in the Americas.

* * * * * *

At the beginning of the 1980s, when my wife and I decided to build a house on her reservation (Navajo) we reasoned that our children needed to understand the place of their birth even though we lived in the non-Indian world as professionals. We plan to retire to this house because it is our place with our kin. Having built the house with my own hands and the help of my family, there is no other place quite like it for us. When my wife and I die, we expect to return to the place (mother earth) that is important to us and our kin. Since I have not talked to anyone who has come back from the dead, I do not know much about that world after death. Perhaps it is a world without words where everything and everyone is related. I suspect it will be very different in every way from this world, including the spiritual environment. At any rate, I will have lived my life here, and I will be content to leave the world and my place to my kin to make of it what they will. I hope that my words will inform them of what I know so they can better understand what they know. In looking back, I have been blessed by the creator through my family and my work. My life has been interesting and full, and there is still much to do.

Part II

PIECING TOGETHER
History

7

Locating Biafra
The Words We Wouldn't Say

Faith Adiele

I grew up thinking that *Biafra* was a curse word. Late at night in the living room, my mother and other grown-ups whispered the term under their breath, and it had a nasty, frightening sound. What made it different from other things my mother didn't want me to know about was the anxiety I sensed whenever the topic arose. My mother was not a woman who scared easily. The daughter of Scandinavian immigrants who had stopped paying her college tuition and thrown her out of the family for having a black man's child, she seemed to be immutably fearless. Nevertheless, when I was between the ages of four and seven—the years of *Biafra*—there were times the word would appear, perhaps slipping out during a quiet moment with Joan Baez on the phonograph, singing about Bangladesh, and my mother's voice would get that low, hushed urgency. I had no idea what the whispered word meant, but it frightened me too. Occasionally I had nightmares and vague, unexplained feelings of shame.

In time I came to understand that *Biafra* was more than a dirty word and referred to something specific. Because we didn't have a television and my mother limited my access to news magazines, I had no visual image to accompany my unease. It was years before I realized that *Biafra* was a war, one of the bloodiest and most controversial wars of the twentieth century, before I learned that *Biafra*'s starving children could have been my cousins and playmates, and that while I tossed in bed at night, first in a California housing project and then in a trailer home in rural Washington, restless from scenes of hunger, my father was missing, presumed dead on the battlefields I dreamed about. *Biafra*.

When I was nineteen months old, my father, an African graduate student studying in the West, received an urgent summons to return home to Nigeria. He left forty-eight hours later, his belongings spilling out of half-empty boxes scattered across the floor of a rented room. His intention was to attend to family business, scout out job prospects, and then come back. Though my parents had split up before my birth, and my mother was raising me alone in Seattle, they maintained a friendship for my sake. "I want you to know that this is not a good-bye," he wrote to my mother and me from a ship in the middle of the Atlantic. "I shall look forward to our meeting so long as we are all alive."

The ship docked in the capital Lagos on November 19, 1964—four months before my second birthday—and he disembarked to find Nigeria on the eve of general elections, with ethnic, regional, and religious tensions high. Fifty years earlier the British had shackled together three different tribal groups occupying two distinct geographic regions to create the fragile political entity known as Nigeria. The Hausa and other feudal, nomadic tribes inhabited the poor region of the North. Widely Muslim, they dominated the military and tended to eschew formal education. The lush, urban area of the South was divided into the Yoruba homeland in the West and the Igbo homeland in the East. Both Western-educated, predominantly Christian tribes, they controlled the country's massive civil service between them. The Igbo, in particular—my father's tribe—were known for their strong drive to educate and provide for their families. In my mother's political science textbooks they were referred to as the "Jews of West Africa"—an ominous prediction of events to come.

In 1960, four years before my father's return, Nigeria regained its independence. Forced to withdraw from the country, the British left political power in the hands of the heavily populated North, and the uneasy balance of Nigerian nationhood was struck. Now, on the brink of elections, the country strained under the heavy legacy of colonialism and a new, indigenous layer of political corruption.

Into this volatile situation my father the Igbo staggered, giddy from the long sea voyage, the tropical heat, and a decade-long absence from home. He was thirty-two, and it was the first time he had stood on independent Nigerian soil. I can't imagine how it felt for him, committed Pan-Africanist and Nigerian nationalist that he was, to find himself in 1964 a black man in a black-owned country, whatever its problems, to have been born under colonial rule and then be coming into adulthood just as his homeland regained its freedom. His heart must have felt as if it would burst to find itself in so large a landscape. The United States, the country he had just left, was barely four months into the Civil Rights Act. Harlem and other Northern cities were in flames, and in the South, the bodies of civil rights workers Cheney, Schwerner, and Goodman had been found in their shallow graves. He must have followed the news of the country that had been providing his education with fascination. Originally my parents were drawn together through a shared passion for current events. I imagined them on opposite sides of the ocean, devouring the newspapers, each hungry for word of the other's country.

The transition from the United States to Africa was nonetheless difficult. Ill for the better part of a year, my father awoke from a series of fevers in 1965 to find anti-Igbo sentiment spreading and no work in Lagos. He traveled home to Igboland, where he spent six months convalescing. Finally, in the fall, he was given an appointment at the University of Nigeria, a new university and the first to be modeled on an American system. Thrilled to be earning a living at long last, he spent his first paycheck on Christmas gifts for my mother and me. He sent cheery letters to us back in Seattle, referring to my mother as *My Sweetest Jo*, as if they were still lovers, and sending special wishes to *Dearest Faye*, his pet name for me, as if I could read.

On January 15, 1966, a revolutionary faction of the Nigerian military seized control of the country in a bold bid to reduce political corruption and regionalism. My mother must have learned the news from the African students she knew at the University of Washington or from the radio. The international press characterized the revolution as an Igbo-led coup, though they praised the civic-mindedness of the Young Turks and acknowledged that support for the new regime was widespread across tribal lines. In the Eastern Region where my father lived, a charismatic Igbo Lieutenant Colonel named Ojukwu became the new military governor. With the rest of the world watching, no one more carefully than my mother back in Seattle, the revolutionary council instituted a six-year recovery plan.

Two weeks later my father wrote to us:

Well my sweetest and fondest loved ones, I have been thinking very much about you these days. With Jo perhaps still unemployed and Faye growing up and not seeing her dad, oh I feel so so so! Hope you are happy. You are much on my heart. And of course with our country Nigeria in trouble, one gets the impression of tragedies everywhere. What do you think about it? What kind of news do you have in the States about the revolution? I tell you this: everybody here likes it. The whole country is rejoicing and there is so much support for the military regime. Oh Jo, the amount of corruption, nepotism, graft, dishonesty, complacency, laziness, and pride in the former regime! It was a disgraceful state of affairs. So let not the world blame us too much for the change. It came at the right time. I am sure you would have welcomed it had you been here yourself. We hope this will teach other nations, particularly African nations, some good lesson. For a few to dominate, trample, cheat and maltreat the many, is dangerous. What has happened here is the revolt of the masses, the revolt of the common man against oppression.

My mother must have been relieved to learn of my father's safety and hear his characteristic optimism. I wonder, however, if she sensed an edge of desperation to his letter. He claimed to be happy, and yet it were as if, in the face of the entire country's rejoicing, he alone were predicting the serious troubles to follow. And follow they did.

A few weeks later I turned three and a few months after that, in May 1966, the Nigerian revolutionary council issued a decree that would unify administration of the nation. Four days later my father wrote to us, congratulating my mother on having graduated college, apologizing for being unable to send money out of the country, and describing life under military rule.

At seven o'clock the very next morning after my father wrote his letter, anti-Igbo violence—instigated by northern politicians opposed to the revolutionary council's decree—swept cities in northern Nigeria. It was a Sunday, and Northerners armed with knives, clubs, and stones invaded local churches and attacked worshippers. More than 3,000 Igbo were killed, and a mass exodus of refugees began to the southeast—a chilling reminder of their standing as "West Africa's Jews."

Once order had been restored, the revolutionary council set up a tribunal to investigate the cause of the riots and determine necessary compensation for the victims. The North threatened to secede from the Federation rather than face the tribunal, and four days before the tribunal was scheduled to commence, a coup led primarily by Northerners took place. Members of the revolutionary council were executed, and both western and northern Nigeria fell. In the Eastern Region, Ojukwu managed to contain the coup attempt, but the coup leaders in Lagos would agree to a cease-fire only on the condition that Nigeria be partitioned into North and South and that all civilians be repatriated according to region of origin.

Between caring for me, reading about events in Nigeria, and protesting the United States' involvement in Vietnam, my twenty-three-year-old mother managed to secure a job teaching junior high school. We moved to a small town in northern California named Ceres. There were fields—worn plots labored in by thin migrant workers—but there any resemblance to the goddess of fertility and agriculture ended. My mother remembers Ceres as hot, dusty, poor, and racist, especially towards the Chicano migrant population, but to a three-year-old, it was wonderful: I had my own bedroom; there was plenty of dirt in the vacant lot behind the housing project where we lived; and at the bakery across the street, they knew my name.

My mother read voraciously, scouring what newspapers and magazines she could find in that small California town for information on Nigeria. As an adult I realize how difficult it must have been for her to come up with good news to tell me about my father. Somehow she managed, tucking away my father's letters to us, keeping her worries and what she read to herself. I remained happily unaware of the crisis in Nigeria, as I was unaware of the fact that every day gangs of boys harassed my mother as she walked to and from work. Each morning and each night, day after day, they followed her, shouting: *Nigger lover! Nigger lover!*

In Nigeria a full-scale pogrom against Igbos began. Between May and December 1966, at least 30,000 people lost their lives, and more than 50,000 others were wounded or maimed. Radio stations in the North broadcast music and speeches celebrating the violence: *We are off to kill the infidel and destroy his child,* one song bragged. Igbos attempting to flee the North were rounded up at airports and bus and railway stations and attacked by soldiers and civilians. The bodies were then sent down to the southeast. According to Igbo accounts of the time, "By early October the sight of mutilated refugees, orphaned children, widowed mothers and decapitated corpses arriving at our airports and railways stations [was unbearable]." If my mother could find a rare London paper, she would have read reports that: "Men, women and children arrived with arms and legs broken, hands hacked off, mouths split open." "Some were burnt and some buried alive. Women and young girls were ravished with unprecedented bestiality; unborn children were torn out of the wombs of their mothers."

During the main phase of the killings, my father somehow managed to write to us:

> *Oh you wouldn't believe it that my senior sister is one of the people who were killed. She was visiting some relations in the North during the time. It is hard to believe but ours could be any day now unless of course they disarm the soldiers who are killing innocent citizens. The country I love so much is in flames but I still hope it will survive!*
>
> *I am pleased to hear about Faith's progress. You must be complimented very highly for being a good mother. She would not be such a wonderful girl had you not been such a wonderful, interesting, willing and devoted mother. Thanks a million.*

Years later I still question how my father managed to remain so calm, so hopeful. On the brink of disaster, he found time to praise my mother on her parenting skills, as if nothing else were happening. He spent more time detailing her attributes than he did the ongoing atrocities against the Igbo. Was this his way of protecting us, I always wondered. Perhaps my father, like my mother, had chosen silence as a strategy of love. He censored his communication with my mother, and she in turn censored hers with me. I grew up in a shadow of unspoken words, one parent trying to shield me from the shouts of *nigger lover,* the other from cries of *kill the Igbo infidel!*

In his last letter, written right before the Christmas of 1966, my father admitted his reluctance to talk about what was happening:

> *I find it extremely uncomfortable to narrate my story regarding the mass killing of Easterners in Northern Nigeria. The Northerners just liquidated all Easterners living in the North and of course I lost a score of relatives there. The unrest is still with us. Nigeria is facing the worst crisis in its history and if we escape a complete disintegration, we are lucky indeed. We live in fear every day on account of the threat to our lives by the Northern Army. However, one has not lost hope in the capacity of Nigerians to solve their own problems.*
>
> *You remember that I used to have eight sisters and one brother. Two of my sisters plus my mother plus my father are all dead.*

To escape the pogroms, the Eastern Region and parts of the central provinces seceded from the rest of Nigeria, forming an independent republic. Ojukwu, since elected Head of State and Commander-in-Chief of the People's Army, sent out a call for all Igbos and minority tribes still left in the West and North to return home, and they came, often walking for days with their possessions on their heads and their babies on their backs. Amidst great jubilation, residents named their homeland *Biafra,* after the Bight of Biafra, a wide bay off the coast of Cameroon, and took the rising sun as the symbol of their new nation. On May 30, 1967, nearly three months after my fourth birthday, my father ceased being Nigerian and became instead *Biafran*. Students at the University of Nigeria, where he was teaching, were said to have "jumped out of their halls in their pajamas and nightgowns for sheer joy."

Africans cheered, praising Biafra as the first African nation based on self-determination rather than a legacy of colonial boundaries, the first nation where Africans were completely independent, both politically and psychologically, the first truly black nation. Biafra saw itself as a radical experiment in self-determination, a black African endeavor with universal implications. Linking Biafra to the situations in South Sudan, Vietnam, and Ireland, Ojukwu stressed that "for black, for yellow, for white, the pattern is the same whenever man . . . sets out to assert his dignity and freedom." In *Their Bones Shall Rise*, a treatise on the cause, he reflected on what seven years of independence had taught Biafra and predicted the dangers to come:

> We learn that the enemy is not simply white, not simply the colonial or ex-colonial master, but that the enemy is neocolonialism; it is everything that threatens to destroy African dignity both within the African state and without. We can be, and frequently are, our own enemies.

A month after Biafra was established, the Federal Republic of Nigeria realized the economic disadvantages to a partition which retained Biafran oil fields for Biafra, and declared war. In July Federalist troops invaded Nsukka, where my father was living, and destroyed the university. As they had previously rejoiced at Biafra's formation, Africans across the continent now wept to witness Nigeria, the largest, richest, and most important nation in black Africa—as well as third largest democracy in the world—turn upon itself. It signaled post-independent Africa's first loss of innocence. Thousands of Nigerian and Biafran students were trapped overseas, cut off from their families, reduced to angry scuffles with their former compatriots in college corridors. The country plunged into savage civil war, and all communication with the outside world was suspended.

At the time my father vanished to war, I was four years old and able to read. Fortunately for my mother, I had never shown particular interest in my father's letters. What I yearned for were things like photographs and gifts that I could see. So long as she produced the occasional treat and said it was from him, I was satisfied. I imagine that after four years of buying me gifts with money he may or may not have sent, it was easy enough for her to maintain a similar fiction when Biafra swallowed him up.

Nigerian Federalist forces had expected to conquer the upstart nation in a matter of days or weeks. They and the rest of the world were stunned at the full-scale opposition Biafran soldiers mounted to protect their homeland. Like their contemporaries, the Viet Cong, Biafran fighters were known for their clever guerrilla tactics and resourceful use of materials. Towards the end of the war, when Biafra could no longer afford to purchase weapons, engineers built ingenious homemade anti-aircraft and artillery guns that kept the resistance going several more months.

During the two-and-a-half bloody years of the Biafran War, July 1967 to January 1970, the rest of the world was also in turmoil. The old systems of power were shifting dramatically. In the United States, the Civil Rights Movement and various cultural revolutions were heating up, and there was mounting opposition to the government's intensified involvement in Vietnam. China was undergoing the Cultural Revolution; the Green Revolution was sweeping various developing nations; and in the Middle East, Israel surprised everyone by defeating the Arab States in the Six Day's War. In April 1968, nine months into the war, Martin Luther King, Jr. was assassinated, and U.S. cities went up in flames. In Ceres, California I sustained an injury, falling atop a heavy wooden table and nearly breaking my nose. I suffered extensive internal bleeding and spent the rest of the year bruised and swollen, with a shadow of darkened skin beneath my eyes. In the Fall, just as I started kindergarten, the Soviets invaded Prague, the Têt Offensive embarrassed U.S. objectives in Vietnam, and my father's ancestral village fell to Nigerian Federalist forces.

Though human rights groups had long protested the treatment of Biafran civilians, it wasn't until the starving children of Biafra crowded close to the camera lens in the summer of 1968, staggering slowly through the landscape of my five-year-old's nightmares on spindly legs, that the international community took notice of the brutal war in Africa. My mother had forbidden me to look at magazines like *Life* and *Time*, whose covers screamed *Biafra* in capital letters and promised shocking, graphic photographs within, but eventually, somehow, I managed to see some news photos, possibly from scraps of *Ebony* magazine she cannibalized to illustrate the African storybooks she made me. The scenes of horribly emaciated black children and babies with protruding ribs and distended bellies, their huge watery eyes staring into the camera lens, became the physical manifestation of my nocturnal anxiety.

The longer the Biafrans held out, the more ruthless Nigeria became. By instituting the notorious blockade of all air, sea, and land routes into Biafra, the Federal Government effectively cut off all medical and food aid. When the Red Cross and others condemned this action, the Nigerian military replied that the starvation of civilians was a legitimate weapon of war. The plight of Biafra's children and civilians received widespread sympathy and generous offers of private aid, yet superpowers like Britain and the U.S. were unwilling to challenge Nigeria's federal government and its policy of Igbo genocide. Despite the support of Israel and numerous European nations, attempts to get Biafra's case heard in the World Court failed.

By the end of the war, Biafra was completely without food, weapons, and money. Half of the seven million people still alive were in danger of starvation. The leaders spent the waning months of the war outside the country, desperately trying to raise funds for the cause. International relief agencies ran high-risk missions through Cameroon in attempts to evacuate as many of the children out of Biafra as possible. Fifty percent of all children between the ages of two and five died of malnutrition anyway.

In 1969, the year American astronauts walked on the moon, my mother's teaching contract ended, releasing us from the dry fields of Ceres, California. She had since reconciled with her parents and decided that it would be good for me to be near them. We moved to my grandparents' farm in Washington state and bought a trailer home. On the faint hope that one letter might get through to my father, my mother wrote repeatedly, informing him of our new address. Some of her letters returned months later, marked *Undeliverable*; others did not return at all.

I was now six years old, which must have made it harder for my mother to shield me from the words whispered after dark in the living room and the haunting photographs of Biafra. She hovered nervously near my grandparents' television, and truly, there was much to fear: In America, fire hoses turned against peaceful black marchers, angry whites spitting at black schoolgirls. In Asia, Buddhist monks set themselves on fire, and a small girl ran wailing down a road as napalm burned the flesh off her body. In Africa, I could see black children who looked like me but for their ribs jutting through their skin. I absorbed each of these images into my bloodstream, and at night, any one of them could have flashed into my dreams and triggered the occasional nightmare, the strange feelings of shame. *We can be, and frequently are, our own enemies.*

In January of 1970, Biafra's ragtag troops surrendered to Nigeria. The sun, originally so bright, had set on Biafra, and the repatriation of conquered Biafrans into the Federation began. Once again, my father was Nigerian. Almost immediately the price of oil skyrocketed, transforming Nigeria virtually overnight into one of the top ten petroleum-exporting nations in the world. The country's unexpected wealth helped minimize the trauma of post-war reconstruction.

Still my mother and I heard nothing from my father. It had been more than three years since his last letter. Much later I learned that my mother had written to him several times since the end of the war. Hearing nothing, she feared the worst, though as usual she said nothing to me. Late one night she took out the family album and wrote in pencil under his name on the family tree: *Deceased, Biafran War, 1970?*

One day in the fall of 1970, nearly a year after the end of the war, a letter, torn and battered, limped in from Nigeria. It was addressed to my mother and me, then, simply: *Sunnyside, Washington, U.S.A.* Numerous stamped and scrawled messages bled into each other, charting the envelope's circuitous route around the globe. For nearly half a year, the letter had crept and crawled its way from Igboland in the east to the federal government in the west, through U.S. Customs, along the streets of Washington, D.C., to Washington state, and finally to my grandparents' farm. It was from my father.

"Look!" my mother said, clutching the letter, laughing hard. "There's no address! The postman just happened to know us. Your father couldn't even know we moved from California. Somehow he must have remembered that Grandma and Grandpa lived in Sunnyside," she marveled. "He couldn't even be sure that they were still alive."

I watched my mother curiously. At age seven, I was now old enough to share her excitement at receiving a letter from my father, and yet her giddiness made me a bit uneasy. I wondered at the intensity of her reaction. As I tore open the letter, she pointed to one of the scribbles crosshatching the envelope like the lines of a map. *"Look,"* she said. "It went all over Washington, D.C. *That's* why it took so long!" Together we read the final, official pronouncement from the Postmaster General of Washington, D.C.: *"No such street as Sunnyside."* My mother began to laugh hysterically. "They sent it to Washington, D.C.!" she repeated, and something in the way her voice thickened sounded a bit like relief. "They thought Sunnyside was a street!"

> *Warmest Greetings, the letter began.*
>
> *I have been wondering how I can reach you just to let you that I am still alive. I survived the Nigerian civil war although I lost everything including my diary which contained your address. Our home, assets, properties, my library and all my books, certificates and diplomas, thesis, my Ph.D. dissertation, my academic gown and hood and everything you can imagine were destroyed. All I now have is the outfit I was wearing on the day the war ended.*
>
> *My hunger to contact you (even though I don't know how) has been so acute that I am just taking a chance and sending this through the Postmaster. If you ever receive it, please write back immediately . . . I look forward to hearing from you having lost every hope of hearing from or seeing you again.*

The letter was dated March 29, 1970, six months earlier. It came from the wreckage of the University of Nigeria. There was no way of knowing what had happened since then. My mother chose to believe that my father was still alive, though she didn't erase her penciled question in the family album. In the end she was proved right, and not long after a second letter arrived. It was equally delayed, equally poignant.

> *Just yesterday, one of the construction workers picked up an old file jacket in what used to be my house and lo and behold your address was right at one corner of it half faded! Then I decided to use it in the hope it will reach you wherever you may be in Washington.*
>
> *Indeed I have been thinking of you and throughout the war I had been very anxious about you even though no means of communication was possible. Now that I can write, I am taking the opportunity to inform you that I am still alive. . . .*

Again my mother and I wrote back, and in the spring, having established contact with us, my father sent a longer letter describing his role in rebuilding post-war Nigeria. It became clear that he was not going to return anytime soon. The casualties of war had swept him into a cause whose need was much greater than ours.

> *March 26, 1971*
>
> *Hope you got my last letter of September last year informing you about my appointment as Commissioner for Education since June 1970. In that same lengthy letter (four pages of long sheets of paper—not air letter cards like this one) I described the horrible experience of the war—the burning of our village and the terrible destruction of life and property. We lost quite a few members of the family and practically everything including a pin! I gave a catalogue of the post-war problems facing us just for your own "education" and understanding. I also described my job as Commissioner and asked for your latest photos since I don't have anything in my possession to remind myself about you. I stated what was left of the family and asked about yours. Do please write, won't you?*

We never received the long letter he mentioned about the war. My parents assumed that the Nigerian government had confiscated it. My father seemed almost to take this as a sign, and in his next letter he made a choice for silence.

> *June 28, 1971*
>
> *Conditions are far from normal over here. I still lack more than ninety percent of the essentials for work and living. . . . Money is in extreme short supply and my monthly pay can hardly sustain the large dependents I have acquired as a result of the civil war (orphans, cripples and all sorts) all for a week! . . . The degree of damage and devastation is so great and so overwhelming that whatever is being done is only a drop in a limitless ocean! . . . We lost quite a number of dear ones to air-raids, bullets and shelling! Tunde died. Mercy died. . . . Quite a number of our "clan" passed away and it is quite a torture to remember them and I would rather let the sleeping dogs lie (if I can help it). I find it quite unbearable at times to have to recall the tragedies we had to pass through and I wouldn't be doing Faith any good sending a catalogue of dead relatives! When she is older it will become part of the history she will have to piece together, I suppose.*

Reading these letters as an adult, I was furious at my father's decision to leave me in ignorance. I understood his desire to forget the past and his reluctance to relive his pain, but it was my story as well. I was tired to death of being protected against death, tired at not having been prepared for the world. My father claimed that he wouldn't be doing me any good by sending a catalogue of dead relatives, but he was wrong. I had become a black woman in America. History was the greatest gift he could give me. How many blacks in the New World could compile a catalogue of lost descendants in Africa, could walk through the remains of what used to be our houses, could, when the time came, find our way home to our ancestral villages? Our history had always been painful; the important thing was to remember it. My father knew this. Biafra had been founded on this: that the true measure of humanity is our ability to meet the challenge of history, a history of oppression. He knew this. In the same breath he had begged for photographs to replace those lost in the fire, bemoaning the fact that he didn't have anything in his possession to remind him of us. *For a few to dominate, trample, and maltreat the many is dangerous.* Memory is everything.

Out of this hunger, I began a journey, asking questions despite my father, not realizing that I was in fact fulfilling his prediction, his challenge to me: *The history Faith will have to piece together.* I was a mass of contradictions and half-articulated desires. I missed Biafra, a country that did not exist, and Nigeria, a country I had never seen. I was obsessed with being African and not-African, with being American and not-American, with being half-white and looking all-black. I moved to Boston, where every time I saw Africans on the street, laughing together and speaking a language I could not understand, I yearned for Biafra. Every time packs of boys trailed me, shouting *nigger*, I yearned for Biafra.

I looked for her in history, in books, re-reading my heroes, the Nigerians who had kept me company all the years of my father's absence: Wole Soyinka, the Igbo poet Christopher Okigbo, the novelist Buchi Emecheta. Chinua Achebe, my father's classmate and Africa's most famous writer, who became an expatriate after Biafra's downfall, explained that, "I had stayed in Nigeria because I didn't want to run away. But in the end we were beaten, and everything we had hoped for our country was destroyed." My father's letters made me cry as if Biafra had just happened yesterday. These were all the authors of my expatriate identity, and I studied their words like a strategic map to lead me home.

The Christmas of 1989, nineteen years after the end of Biafra, puts me on a southern Nigerian highway, headed east. Yet another Northern military dictator is in charge, and the country strains under stringent economic reforms imposed by the IMF and World Bank. Caught up in a frenzy of spending in the eighties, Nigeria found itself overextended when world oil prices plummeted. The country is bankrupt, and tensions are high. At twenty-six, this is my first trip "home." As with my father some twenty-five years before, the transition from America to Africa is difficult. I stagger through with a similar combination of élan and despair.

Okpu Umuobu, our ancestral home, is a sleepy little village nestled in the shadow of the largest tree I have ever seen. Its huge, gnarled roots twist high above the earth, forming a series of natural seats that conform to the human body and stretch a quarter of a mile along the forest floor. Every evening the villagers gather at its feet and lay the day to rest. At some point in all the greetings and telling of stories, the sun falls into a cluster of branches and the moon disentangles itself to provide some light in all that shade.

According to local lore, the tree saved the village during the war. Towards the end of Biafra, Nigerian troops finally made it this far south. They marched straight into the village and started looting and setting fire to houses and farms. My family's house on the main road was one of the first to go. When they saw the prize tree, the soldiers rushed to chop it down. The villagers say that wherever the Federalists' axes struck the tree, blood ran like sap, and the soldiers fled the village in terror.

We stay at Samson House, a small pastel bungalow named for my grandfather that my father built to replace the house burned in the war. One day my father casually mentions that during the war he was responsible for all refugees in the region. It is the first time he has mentioned Biafra, and I hold my breath to prolong the moment. "Every day they poured in with nothing," he tells me. "I had to allocate whatever clothes and food I could find. I also had my own dependents—more than a dozen of them." He waves his hand, taking in the entire compound. "People were sleeping everywhere." When I ask which family members died in the war, he changes the subject.

I switch tactics, talking to people around him, collecting stories and the merest scraps of stories. When I ask about my father's favorite sister *Nneka*, the one after whom my mother had almost named me but instead named my first doll, no one seems to know who I mean. People are vague about relationships in general. Everyone seems to be a cousin.

Taking an evening stroll around a friend's compound, I pause to inspect a few stones scattered under a leafy banana tree. "The eldest son is buried here," my friend tells me. "He was doing well at the university but left so he could fight for Biafra." The tone of her voice suggests disappointment or even distaste, and I'm shocked. I hadn't expected to find loved ones buried in the garden, but I had expected pride. Whenever I push too hard, the refrain is always the same: "No one talks about him."

No one talks about Biafra the war, but everyone talks about Biafra the political concept. Everyone argues politics in general. "Your father was the one responsible for bringing us electricity when he was Commissioner," the villagers tell me as we recline in the deep recesses of the tree. They point to the poles along the side of the road and say bitterly, "If left to this *cata-cata* government, we would have nothing." I find myself growing angrier and angrier at a federal government which appears to be still blatantly penalizing the East. Before I can even understand what is happening, the yoke of tribal oppression settles around my neck, practically choking me. It is as if all my child-hood nightmares had been preparing me for this moment, to be America's black, Africa's Jew.

I am thrilled when a friend gives me a collector's item—a one pound sterling note printed by the Republic of Biafra. "I know you'll appreciate this," he says, and I wonder if he is referring to my passion for history or my obsession with things Biafran. As I inspect the intricate brown and green designs of the bill, he sighs. "There's no room for the Igbo in this country," he says. "We're all just waiting for Biafra to rise again."

His friend, who would have been at most a toddler during the war, agrees: "All the opportuni-ties go to uneducated Northerners who grow fat on Eastern oil. Without Biafra we are nothing."

When I suggest that all black people need Biafra, they are stunned. "What," they ask me repeat-edly, "things are still bad in America? We thought that black Americans only wanted to be crim-inals and basketball stars!"

On the twentieth anniversary of Biafra's conquest, Nigerian news magazines put out special issues celebrating the country's remarkable post-war recovery. The British publications are the worst. They praise the inter-ethnic tolerance in urban areas and the fact that former Biafran leader Ojukwu was recently allowed to return from exile. Something in the way Nigeria's former colonial masters marvel at the so-called ability of Nigerians to throw their arms around their compatriots who dared secede reminds me of the remark General Westmoreland made during the Vietnam War about the "Oriental" not having the same regard for human life as the Westerner. It is equally suggestive of portrayals of happy darkies in the American South.

It is clearly time to go home. Ojukwu's words show me how to be an American African. His challenge in 1969 speaks to me today: "The old African was considered something on par with the animal. The present African is considered somewhat sub-human. . . . To be truly African in the present-day context is, at all times, to be proving to the world that you are a human being, no more, no less." The work of constructing home, of proving to the world that we are human, can be done anywhere. The questions are always around us, like history; the answers come at the oddest times.

In October of 1993, my father comes to the U.S. for medical treatment. It is three months after one military dictator was scheduled to return Nigeria to civilian rule, and a month before a sec-ond seizes power. I fly out to Chicago to be with him during his convalescence, and my moth-er phones regularly from Washington. The day before his flight home to Nigeria, he turns to me as we're packing. "You know I had a sister," he says. "Nneka. Your mother asked about her last night." He shakes his head, smiling. "She remembered Nneka was my favorite." His eyes veer away. "She died long ago. We don't talk about her."

I lean forward. I had begun to wonder if my mother had been mistaken about the existence of this supposed favorite sister. My father begins to rummage through one of his suitcases. "I told your mother we don't use her name because we've long forgotten her," he says. "She died in the war." My heart stops, as it still does—and always has—every time someone mentions *Biafra*. I marvel at the lie he tells himself, that we don't use her name because we've long forgotten her. My father pauses, looking sad, and I wonder, was she the aunt mentioned in his letters, the senior sister killed in the July 29 pogrom? I nod, trying to convey my sympathy, trying not to break the spell of hearing my aunt's name spoken.

He continues the story: "She insisted on staying in Nigeria. She went out with a boy, a Biafran soldier. He wanted to marry her. 'We'll be fine,' she said. She was staying with me at Nsukka," he explains, and I begin to understand his agitation. She must have been his junior sister. She was staying with him. He was responsible for her. My father shakes his head and rummages harder in the suitcase. "They went out, had plenty of food to eat, enjoyed themselves, but then the inva-sion came." He bends over the sea of sweaters and trousers, speaking slowly into the suitcase. "Someone saw them on their last day. They were running toward the river. The person said it would have been better that they just run into the river and die *there*—" He gives his head a sudden jerk and gestures with an upturned palm, as if trying to fix the scene exactly in his own mind. "Then to be carried off and—"

Bang! The suitcase slams shut with a loud finality that forces my heart into my mouth. "Queen!" he calls me by his latest nickname, his face pinched. "Come and deal with this bag!"

It takes me several full minutes to hear what he is saying, to will my body to move, to shift out of my reverie of dread and realize that once again, over two decades later, he has shut more than just the suitcase lid.

For the rest of the day I scheme. I plan different strategies for how to return to my aunt's story, how to double back and sneak up on my father, how to ask just the right questions that will jog his memory and override his objections at the torture of remembrance. Later, when walking to the drugstore to stock up on his prescriptions, I realize that I will not demand my catalogue of dead relatives. I have read and studied and discussed and dreamed about Biafran atrocities for years. They are so well imbedded in my psyche that I do not need to ask what happened to Auntie Nneka. I never needed to ask. I stopped breathing the minute my father said her name because I already knew the end. I have known since I was four years old, tossing hungrily in bed at night. I do not need to hear that my aunt too was raped, hacked to pieces, set on fire, disemboweled by the countrymen she would not fear. It is enough to know why I never heard her name—this aunt for whom I was to have been named. The one my father can never forget. The one who should have run into the river.

Still later I compile my own family catalogue: the words, the names, the things my parents wouldn't say out of love. Their strategy of silence spans three decades and two continents: the word *Biafra*, unutterable for years, and with it, my father's disappearance. My mother's fear that he had died. The names of those who did die—my hungry cousins and unknown aunts. Those whose names we knew but never spoke again—*Mercy, Tunde, Nneka.* Those whose names we never knew. The appropriate war cry to make us happily destroy each other—*oriental! infidel! nigger lover!*

Sometimes it is impossible to forget what we have not been allowed to remember, and so I carry with me the part of childhood that starved, the part still buried under a banana tree in the back-yard. Memory is everything. The question is how to be Biafran without being perpetually in exile, how to be African, something truly human. How to accept the silent way my parents chose to love, and then adopt a strategy that is the exact opposite and speak the things we claim to have forgotten. Above all, how not to be our own enemies.

When I now imagine *Biafra*, I see both sides. There will always be the nightmare of children who could have been me, who, despite my parents' great efforts, inhabited my dreams and left their bruises, whose hunger pains I still feel as strongly as my own. At night they still sleep with me, in rivers, in the shade of trees. *Their bones shall rise.* But there is also the dream: in it my mother and father stand separated by a river now, not an ocean, each of them looming taller than any tree I have ever seen. Barefoot, I climb high in my mother's branches and inhale the perfume of her whitest bark. As evening approaches, I stop at my father's blackest roots and lay the day to rest. My parents' broad arms stretch out to shade me, not quite touching, daring the world to attack. If ever someone tries, their branches take the blow for me, and the amount of blood they are prepared to lose would frighten anyone.

8

Afro Images
Politics, Fashion, and Nostalgia

Angela Y. Davis

Not long ago, I attended a collaborative performance in San Francisco by women presently or formerly incarcerated in the County Jail, and Bay Area women performance artists. After the show, I went backstage to the "green room," where the women inmates, guarded by deputy sheriffs stationed outside the door were celebrating with their families and friends. Having worked with some of the women at the jail, I wanted to congratulate them on the show. One woman introduced me to her brother, who at first responded to my name with a blank stare. The woman admonished him: "You don't know who Angela Davis is?! You should be ashamed." Suddenly a flicker of recognition flashed across his face: "Oh," he said, "Angela Davis—the Afro."

Such responses are commonplace rather than exceptional, and it is both humiliating and humbling to discover that a generation following the events which constructed me as a public personality, I am remembered as a hairdo. It is humiliating because it reduces a politics of liberation to a politics of fashion; it is humbling because such encounters with the younger generation demonstrate the fragility and mutability of historical images, particularly those associated with African American history. This encounter with the young man who identified me as "the Afro" reminded me of a recent article in the *New York Times Magazine* which listed me as one of the 50 most influential fashion (read hairstyle) trendsetters over the last century.[1] I continue to find it ironic that the popularity of the "Afro" is attributed to me, when, in actuality, I was emulating a whole host of women—both public figures and women I encountered in my daily life—when I began to wear my hair natural in the late sixties.

But it is not merely the reduction of historical politics to contemporary fashion that infuriates me. Especially disconcerting is the fact that the distinction of being known as "the Afro" is largely a result of a particular economy of journalistic images in which mine is one of the relatively few that has survived the last two decades. Or perhaps the very segregation of those photographic images caused mine to enter into the then-dominant journalistic culture precisely by virtue of my presumed "criminality." In any case, it has survived, disconnected from the historical context in which it arose, as fashion. Most young African Americans who are familiar with my name and twenty-five-year-old image have encountered photographs and film/video clips largely in music videos, and in Black history montages in popular books and magazines. Within the interpretive context within which they learn to situate these photographs, the most salient element of the image is the hairstyle, understood less as a political statement than as fashion.

The unprecedented contemporary circulation of photographic and filmic images of African Americans has multiple and contradictory implications. On the one hand, it holds the promise of visual memory of older and departed generations—both well-known figures and people who may not have achieved public prominence. However, there is also the danger that this historical memory becomes ahistorical and apolitical. "Photographs are relics of the past," John Berger has written. They are

> . . . traces of what has happened. If the living take that past upon themselves, if the past becomes an integral part of the process of people making their own history, then all photographs would acquire a living context, they would continue to exist in time, instead of being arrested moments. [2]

In the past, I have been rather reluctant to reflect in more than a casual way about the power of the visual images by which I was represented during the period of my trial. Perhaps this is due to my unwillingness to confront those images as having to some extent structured my experiences during that era. The recent recycling of some of these images in contexts that privilege the "Afro" as fashion—revolutionary glamour—has led me to reconsider them both in the historical context in which they were first produced (and in which I first experienced them) and within the "historical" context in which they often are presented today as "arrested moments."

In September, 1969, the University of California Regents fired me from my post in the Philosophy Department at UCLA because of my membership in the Communist Party. The following summer, charges of murder, kidnapping, and conspiracy were brought against me in connection with my activities on behalf of George Jackson and the Soledad Brothers. The circulation of various photographic images of me—taken by journalists, undercover policemen and movement activists—played a major role in both the mobilization of public opinion against me *and* the development of the campaign that was ultimately responsible for my acquittal.

Twenty-five years later, many of these photographs are being recycled and recontextualized in ways that are at once exciting and disturbing. With the first public circulation of my photographs, I was intensely aware of the invasive and transformative power of the camera and of the ideological contextualization of my images that left me with little or no agency. On the one hand I was portrayed as a conspiratorial and monstrous communist, i.e. anti-American, whose unruly natural hairdo symbolized Black militancy, i.e. antiwhiteness. Some of the first hate mail I received tended to collapse "Russia" and "Africa." I was told to "go back to Russia" and often in the same sentence (in connection with a reference to my hair) to "go back to Africa." On the other hand, sympathetic portrayals tended to interpret the image—almost inevitably one with my mouth wide open—as that of a charismatic and raucous revolutionary ready to lead the masses into battle. Since I considered myself neither monstrous nor charismatic, I felt fundamentally betrayed on both accounts: violated on the first account, and deficient on the second.

When I was fired by the UC Regents in 1969, an assortment of photographs appeared in various newspapers, magazines and on television throughout that year. However, it was not until felony charges were brought against me in connection with the Marin County shootout that the photographs became what Susan Sontag has called a part of "the general furniture of the environment."[3] As such, they truly began to frighten me. A cycle of terror was initiated by the decision of the F.B.I. to declare me one of the country's ten most wanted criminals. Although I had been underground for over a month before I actually saw the photographs the F.B.I. had decided to use on the poster, I had to picture how they might portray me as I attempted to create for myself an appearance that would be markedly different from the one defined as armed and dangerous. The props I used consisted of a wig with straight black hair, long false lashes, and more eyeshadow, liner and blush than I had ever before imagined wearing in public. Never having seriously attempted to present myself as glamorous, it seemed to me that glamour was the only look that might annul the likelihood of being perceived as a revolutionary. It never could have occurred to me that the same "revolutionary" image I then sought to camouflage with glamour would be turned, a generation later, into glamour and nostalgia.

After the F.B.I. poster was put on display in post offices, other government buildings, and on the television program, "The F.B.I.," *Life* Magazine came out with a provocative issue featuring a cover story on me. Illustrated by photographs from my childhood years through the UCLA firing, the article probed the reasons for my supposedly abandoning a sure trajectory toward fulfillment of the middle-class American dream in order to lead the unpredictable life of a "Black revolutionary." Considering the vast circulation of this pictorial magazine,[4] I experienced something akin to what Barthes was referring to when he wrote,

> I feel that the Photograph creates my body or mortifies it, according to its caprice (apology of this mortiferous power: certain Communards paid with their lives for their willingness or even their eagerness to pose on the barricades: defeated, they were recognized by Thiers's police and shot, almost every one).[5]

The life-sized headshot on the cover of the magazine would be seen by as many people, if not more, than the much smaller portraits on the F.B.I. poster. Having confronted my own image in the news store where I purchased the magazine, I was convinced that F.B.I. Chief J. Edgar Hoover had conspired in the appearance of that cover story. More than anything else, it seemed to me to be a magnification and elaboration of the wanted poster. Moreover, the text of the story gave a rather convincing explanation as to why the pictures should be associated with arms and danger.

The photograph on the cover of my autobiography,[6] published in 1974, was taken by the renowned photographer Phillipe Halsman. When Toni Morrison—who was my editor—and I entered his studio, the first question he asked us was whether we had brought the black leather jacket. He assumed, it turned out, that he was to recreate with his camera a symbolic visual representation of Black militancy: leather jacket (uniform of the Black Panther Party), "Afro" hairdo and raised fist. We had to persuade him to photograph me in a less predictable posture. As recently as 1993, the persisting persuasiveness of these visual stereotypes was made clear to me when I had to insist that Anna Deavere Smith rethink her representation of me in "Fires in the Mirror," which initially relied upon a black leather jacket as her main prop.

So far, I have concentrated primarily on my own responses to those photographic images, which may not be the most interesting or productive way to approach them. While the most obvious evidence of their power was the part they played in structuring people's opinions about me as a "fugitive" and a political prisoner, their more subtle and wide-ranging effect was the way they served as generic images of Black women who wore their hair "natural." From the constant stream of stories I have heard over the last twenty-four years (and continue to hear), I infer that definitely hundreds—perhaps even thousands—of "Afro"-wearing Black women were accosted, harassed, and arrested by police, F.B.I., and immigration agents during the two months I spent underground. One woman who told me that she hoped she could serve as a "decoy" because of her light skin and big natural, was obviously conscious of the way the photographs—circulating within a highly charged racialized context—constructed generic representations of young Black women. Consequently, the photographs identified vast numbers of my Black female contemporaries who wore naturals (whether light- or dark-skinned) as targets of repression. This is the hidden historical content which lurks behind the continued association of my name with the "Afro."

A young woman who is a former student of mine has been wearing an "Afro" during the last few months. Rarely a day passes, she has told me, when she is not greeted with cries of "Angela Davis" from total strangers. Moreover, during the months preceding the writing of this article, I have received an astounding number of requests for interviews from journalists doing stories on "the resurgence of the Afro." A number of the most recent requests were occasioned by a layout in the fashion section of the March, 1994 issue of *Vibe* Magazine entitled "Free Angela: Actress Cynda Williams as Angela Davis, a fashion revolutionary." The spread consists of eight full-page photos of Cynda Williams (known for her role as the singer in Spike Lee's "Mo Better Blues") in poses that parody photographs taken of me during the early 1970s. The work of stylist Patty Wilson, the layout is described as "'docufashion' because it uses modern clothing to mimic Angela Davis's look from the '70s."[7]

Some of the pictures are rather straightforward attempts to recreate press photos taken at my arrest, during the trial and after my release. Others can be characterized as pastiche,[8] drawing elements, like leather-jacketed Black men, from contemporary stereotypes of the sixties to seventies era of Black militancy. They include an arrest scene, with the model situated between two uniformed policemen and wearing an advertised black satin blouse (reminiscent of the top I was wearing on the date of my arrest). Like her hair, the advertised glasses are amazingly similar to the ones I wore. There are two courtroom scenes in which Williams wears an enormous Afro wig and advertised see-through minidresses and, in one of them, handcuffs. Yet another revolves around a cigar-smoking, bearded man dressed in fatigues with a gun holster around his waist, obviously meant to evoke Che Guevara. (Even the fatigues can be purchased—from Cheap Jack's!) There is no such thing as subtlety in these photos. Because the point of this fashion spread is to represent the clothing associated with revolutionary movements of the early seventies as revolutionary fashion in the nineties, the sixtieth anniversary logo of the Communist Party has been altered in one of the photos to read 1919–1971 (instead of 1979). And the advertised dress in the photo for which this logo is a backdrop is adorned with pin-on buttons reading Free All Political Prisoners.

The photographs I find most unsettling, however, are the two small headshots of Williams wearing a huge Afro wig on a reproduction of the F.B.I. wanted poster that is otherwise unaltered except for the words "FREE ANGELA" in bold red print across the bottom of the document. Despite the fact that the inordinately small photos do not really permit much of a view of the clothing Williams wears, the tops and glasses (again quite similar to the ones I wore in the two imitated photographs) are listed as purchasable items. This is the most blatant example of the way the particular history of my legal case is emptied of all content so that it can serve as a commodified backdrop for advertising. The way in which this document provided a historical pretext for something akin to a reign of terror for countless young Black women is effectively erased by its use as a prop for selling clothes and promoting a seventies fashion nostalgia. What is also lost in this nostalgic surrogate for historical memory—in these "arrested moments," to use John Berger's words—is the activist involvement of vast numbers of Black women in movements that are now represented with even greater masculinist contours than they actually exhibited at the time.

Without engaging the numerous debates occasioned by Frederic Jameson's paper, "Postmodernism and Consumer Society,"[9] I would like to suggest that his analysis of "nostalgia films" and their literary counterparts which are "historical novels in appearance only," might provide a useful point of departure for an interpretation of this advertising genre called "docufashion," as yet a further site for the proliferation of nostalgic images. "[W]e seem condemned to seek the historical past," Jameson writes, "through our own pop images and stereotypes about that past, which itself remains forever out of reach."[10] Perhaps by also taking up John Berger's call for an "alternative photography" we might develop strategies for engaging with photographic images like the ones I have evoked, by actively seeking to transform their interpretive contexts in education, popular culture, the media, community organizing, and so on. Particularly in relation to African American historical images, we need to find ways of incorporating them into "social and political memory, instead of using [them] as a substitute which encourages the atrophy of such memory."[11]

Notes

1   "50 Who Mattered Most," *New York Times Magazine*, Oct. 24, 1993, pp. 122–25.

2   John Berger, *About Looking*. New York: Pantheon Books, 1980, p. 57.

3   Susan Sontag, *On Photography*. New York: Farrar, Straus and Giroux, 1978, p. 27.

4   During the 1960s *Life* Magazine had a circulation of approximately 40 million people. (Gisele Freund, *Photography and Society*. Boston: David R. Goddine, 1980, p. 143.)

5   Roland Barthes, *Camera Lucida*. New York: Hill and Lang, 1981, p. 11.

6   *Angela Y. Davis: An Autobiography*. New York: Random House, 1974.

7   *Vibe*, Volume 2, No. 2, March, 1994, p. 16.

8   I use the term "pastiche" both in the usual sense of a potpourri of disparate ingredients and in the sense in which Frederic Jameson uses it. "Pastiche is, like parody, the imitation of a peculiar or unique style, the wearing of a stylistic mask, speech in a dead language: but it is a neutral practice of such mimicry, without parody's ulterior motive, without the satirical impulse, without laughter . . . . Pastiche is black parody, parody that has lost its sense of humor . . . . " Frederic Jameson, "Postmodernism and Consumer Society" in Hal Foster, ed. *The Anti-Aesthetic: Essays on Postmodern Culture*. Port Townsend, Washington: Bay Press, 1983, p. 114.

9   Jameson's essay has appeared in several versions. The one I have consulted is referenced in note 8. I thank Victoria Smith for suggesting that I reread this essay in connection with the *Vibe* story.

10   Jameson, p. 118.

11   Berger, p. 58.

9

Time Traveling and Border Crossing
Reflections on White Identity

Becky Thompson

In the documentary film "The Life and Times of Harvey Milk"—the story of the late, gay rights and coalition leader—one of the people who knew him tells of how he learned that Harvey died. When he heard the news that Mayor Moscone and Milk had been shot he immediately drove to downtown San Francisco, thinking as did thousands of others, that there was no where else in the world he could be at that moment in history. He ended up parking far away from city hall and took a back alley hurrying to get to the front of the building only to see police rolling Milk out on a gurney, his whole body covered with a black tarp except for his feet. In his craziness this man remembers that all he could think about was "I had no idea that Harvey's feet were so big." Having shown this film in my sociology classes many times, I have often wondered why the producers left that scene in, why the line about Harvey's big feet?

It has recently occurred to me that whether the producers intended it or not, that little detail has metaphorical significance. Harvey Milk needed big feet to carry his big vision and his courageous body through the streets of San Francisco, to work in his busy camera store, to traverse the state with Sally Gearheart debating conservatives about the Briggs initiative,[1] and to stand with open arms to greet Dan White before White shot him. Thinking about his big feet reminds me that the details of life often reveal much about time, place, politics, and change, details that often take years to comprehend. The vignette from "The Life and Times of Harvey Milk" also conjures up much about the specificity of border crossing—for Milk, the costs and consequences of his decision to cross district, regional, racial, sexual, and gender lines in his years of political activism.

I too am concerned about the details, the specific contexts and the exact scenes that reveal the pain, the pleasure, and the reasons for border crossing. I am concerned with why people cross borders, what bolsters our traverses and what we lose and gain in doing so. I began writing this essay in 1992 having just finished unpacking seemingly countless boxes in my new apartment in New Jersey—stacking up the empty ones, thinking that I may need them again, and glad there was enough room in the apartment for me to store them without having to break them down first. With this job done, I was left craving the means, the time, the insight and the courage to understand the border crossings in my life, and I was struck by how humor insinuates itself into life when least expected and most needed.

In the trip from Maine to New Jersey (from a one-year teaching position to a one-year post doctorate appointment), I drove a twenty-four-foot U-Haul, a beast of a truck that seemed just inches short of being a semi. I drove while negotiating lane changes according to whether or not anyone honked at me since I couldn't see cars on my right because the mirror didn't work— a symbol of a life in which I have often made changes without being able to see clearly whether the move would be safe or not. As I willed this truck down the Maine Turnpike, the Massachusetts Turnpike, and then the New Jersey Turnpike, I kept looking over at my two big dogs perched together on one small seat, avoiding the floor of the cab which was entirely too hot for them. When I had planned this drive with the dogs, I was sure that the truck would have one long front seat, thinking that bucket seats were reserved for souped-up Cameros, Alfa Romeos and other "boy" cars. Who would have guessed there would be bucket seats in a moving truck? I alternated between smiling at the dogs' ability to adapt and feeling sad that spreading out in space and time has been impossible for them and me. And as I moved forward, I began counting, and then repeated almost like a mantra, the houses and states where I have lived in my life. I realized that this was my fifteenth move as an adult, following eight moves as a child: twenty-three houses in my thirty-three years. When I was a child these moves had been punctuated by divorces, remarriages, promotions, demotions, battery, upward and downward mobility. As an adult, the moves have been instigated by love found and lost, jobs begun and finished, college and graduate school started and finally completed.

During this latest interstate border crossing I realized that all my life I have actually been crossing borders—state, religious, educational, sexual, body, racial and cultural. One of the most difficult and life-affirming has been crossing racial borders. But I have been unable to understand the complexities of this crossing, the intricacies of what María Lugones calls "world traveling," without scrutinizing other traverses as well.[2] So my telling of this racial narrative and my linking it to something larger than myself are wrought with circuitous routes, convoluted signposts, and tricky maneuvering over what have felt like both paved and unpaved roads.

In the last twenty five years, women of color have pioneered scholarship that chronicles the complex nuances and historical underpinnings of racial identity development. Scholarship by white people who have "interrogated whiteness" has established this scrutiny as a key component in antiracist activism. At the same time, this writing has underscored the need to tease out how whiteness is taught and institutionalized.[3] In the words of bell hooks:

> only a persistent, rigorous, and informed critique of whiteness could really determine what forces of denial, fear, and competition are responsible for creating fundamental gaps between professed political commitments to eradicating racism and the participation in the construction of a discourse on race that perpetuates racial domination."[4]

Such an interrogation counters discourse in which "race" becomes a code for people of color, as if white people were not "raced" as well.

White women who have examined their own racial identities have highlighted how whiteness is shaped by history, culture, region, sexuality, family, and class.[5] These writers/activists offer daring, new explorations of the reasons for and consequences of confronting racism. In My Mama's Dead Squirrel, Mab Segrest, a Southern, white, Christian-raised woman and granddaughter of a Klansman describes the experiences that most changed her own race consciousness and sparked her antiracist activism. Segrest also writes about how, in the process of becoming an antiracist activist, her lesbian identity became only one of a constellation of identities.[6] The collection of essays, *Yours in Struggle: Three Feminist Perspectives on Anti-Semitism and Racism* also offers courageous revelations about how Jewish identity and/or lesbian identity can be turning points in racial consciousness.[7]

When I first read these and other accounts, I remember scribbling copious notes in the margins of the books, realizing that I had been starving for roadmaps on how to re-orient myself racially and yearning for stories by antiracist activists. Scholarship that teases out intracultural relations among women of color encouraged me to interpret the ways in which differences in social location and family dynamics may affect white identity. I wondered how the formation of white consciousness within middle- or upper-class nuclear families (such as those described by Mab Segrest, Elly Bulkin and Lillian Smith) might differ from how whiteness is taught in working, mixed-class, or single parent families. How does childhood sexual or physical trauma shape racial identity? Why is the bulk of the autobiographical work on racial identity by Southern white women and Jewish women, and what does that suggest about race theory formation? How does being raised in the West or North, for example, shape racial identity? And, how might generational differences change the historical events that most profoundly shape white identity?

Seeking answers to these questions feels like wandering around in the wilderness, finding few familiar markers along the way. As I have written this essay, I have fought the voices that insist my autobiographical approach is egotistical, that my words just add up to a "white girl's" apology, and that my attempt to hinge analysis on specific experiences will have little or no use for people of different backgrounds from my own. My efforts to write in the first person have been halting and tentative as I struggled against the stifling socialization of academic training. In the moments when I have quieted these voices of doubt and fear I have reminded myself that this is hard partly because I am unearthing exactly what I have been taught to forget. From early infancy, white people are taught to deny the centrality of race. This makes only more difficult the possibility of a just society. Through socialization children are taught to deny their perceptive abilities to know when harm is done to themselves or others.[8] Intuitively, I know that what people learn as children about race often is repeated over and over again in slightly different versions unless these experiences and the emotions underlying them are scrutinized, put in a historical context, and challenged by both private and public critique. This work does not by itself undo racism, but it is a step.

As Thunderstorms Shook the Phoenix Sky

I was born in 1959 in a Mormon hospital in Logan, Utah to two teenage parents who were wildly in love but hardly equipped to parent or to see themselves through to a healthy marriage. A brilliant, spontaneous, and complicated woman, my mother began rebelling against Mormon expectations about women and sexuality early in life. According to her version of the story, by the time she was an adolescent she had been baptized one hundred and sixty-five times "to save the souls of the unsaved." At some point she refused any more dunkings. She named me Becky after Becky Sharp, an independent, tough-minded character in William Thackery's *Vanity Fair*; she was quick to reprimand the Mormon nurses when they suggested that my real name be Rebecca, from the Bible, since no child of hers would be required to carry that religious legacy with her.

As a teenager, my mother slept with the Mormon bishop's son, smoked cigarettes, drank vodka, and was sent to reform school. At sixteen she tried to kill herself. The church and psychiatric authorities reacted harshly, angered by her rejection of the strong Mormon tradition built on women martyring their way through life. While quick medical intervention saved her in the moment, she says having me and my younger sister, Ginny, soon after may have saved her for the long term. But then she was faced with the enormous task of raising two sometimes crying, needy children when she was still growing up herself. When I was a toddler, my mother would rock me in a big old rocking chair as thunderstorms shook the Phoenix sky, as she wished for a time when she would have money for a baby-sitter. As I grew up, she shared with me her love for poetry and literature, reading me Langston Hughes ("life for me ain't been no crystal stair") and Nikki Giovanni, teaching me that soulful literature can be a lifeline in hard times. She also let my sister and me know in myriad ways that we irreparably tied her down. Overwhelmed and saddled with too many responsibilities, she did not always know when others were injuring us, nor were there other adults who intervened. I was exposed as a child to relatives' alcoholism, physical and emotional violence, and incest, and I had neither the language nor the context needed to name this abuse.

My first father is an alcoholic who spent his life between jail, halfway houses, studio apartments, and the street. He rarely held down a steady job and never had any money. He had a wry sense of humor and the heart of a poet. He, like my mother, was raised a Mormon and saw marriage as a way to escape restrictive religious influences. He lived with my mother, my younger sister and me until I was three, when my mother packed us up in the back of her powder blue Falcon in the middle of the night and, without telling anyone, drove from Logan, Utah to Phoenix, Arizona, leaving behind my father, whose drinking problem had escalated. In Phoenix, she waitressed to pay the bills and put herself through college.

When I was five my mother married a man from an upper-class, Ivy League, Episcopalian family who offered her welcome financial stability but was unable to match her intellectually or emotionally. They soon had a son, my brother, Stuart Little, affectionately named after the rat in E.B. White's book by the same title. As my second father began to climb the corporate ladder, we moved to a bigger house in Phoenix, made a cross-country move to Boston when I was nine, and then, as is common for young professional families, moved back across country to Los Angeles three years later. When I was twelve, he and my mother divorced and we resumed living on her teacher's salary. With each marriage, geographical move, and divorce our social class status shifted, as income, values, and the priorities attached to class changed.

Crossing regional borders were mostly positive experiences for me. I proudly considered myself "worldly" and, although I had to constantly make new friends, being labeled smart in school helped inhibit the other students from picking on me.[9] Crossing class borders, on the other hand, was wrought with shame and confusion. As a young child I didn't know that life for others was different from my own. I didn't realize how profoundly the divorces limited how much money we had, in which area of town we lived, and which schools I attended. As a latch key kid, I lived in rented houses and got toted around in a beat-up old car—that my sister, mother, and I watched with awe as it caught fire in a mall parking lot. While this was just part of life from my perspective, my mother worried late into the night about how to pay all her bills and schedule her college classes around waitressing shifts.

I didn't start to feel hurt and excluded because of class divisions until I was an adolescent, when I became exposed to people from upper-class backgrounds. When we moved to California, my mother and second father bought a home in a wealthy, exclusively white suburb of Los Angeles. After her divorce, my mother struggled financially to stay in that town so that her children could continue to be in "good schools." (By that point I had attended six schools and lived in eight houses.) Attending the high school in this town gave me access to many resources—a good library, singing classes, sports, safe neighborhoods, and the name of a highly-regarded high school to cite on my college applications—which mattered increasingly as I started to understand how much I wanted to go to college. At the same time, staying in that school also meant I was surrounded by wealthy children who had their own cars and charge cards and, in the summers, headed for vacation homes and camps.

I made my way through high school waitressing at various twenty-four-hour restaurants, making french fries at McDonalds, cleaning people's houses, and babysitting for neighborhood children. On school mornings my sister and I routinely went through the ordeal of frantically searching for clean matching socks that didn't have holes in them. And I remember shame burning inside me when a woman whose house I cleaned stood over me whining about her life as she instructed me about how I should scrub her toilet. As most of my classmates automatically assumed they would go to college, I wondered how I was going to pay for it, not knowing how to ask for help to fill out college applications or financial aid forms. It wasn't until college that I learned that financial aid and scholarships even existed. The guidance counselors at my high school didn't think students needed that information.

My mother considered going to college full-time a luxury, doubtless because she had completed her B.A. as a single mother in bits and pieces. When my step-grandparents died they left college money for my brother, but nothing for me or my sister. Having everything to do with male birthright, this decision as well as my family's silence about it revealed one of the many ways class is gendered. When I was in college, I started to seek out other students who were putting themselves through, but in high school I had neither the language nor the confidence to find camaraderie from other students who had also ridden financial roller coasters. While outwardly I professed a disdain for what I called frivolous things, like cheerleading and prom queen contests, inside I yearned to be thought of as pretty and as one of the group. Secretly, I felt like the odd one out with my hand-sewn dresses and my developing (but unnamed) dyke walk.

Memory Dwells in Forgotten Language

The racial narrative in my life weaves in and out of the details about class and region, beginning in a small stucco house by the railroad tracks in a poor neighborhood on the outskirts of Phoenix where my mother, my sister, and I lived when I was very young. Gloria Anzaldúa writes, "Admit that Mexico is your double, that she exists in the shadow of this country, that we are irrevocably tied to her. Gringo, accept this doppelganger in your psyche. By taking back our collective shadow the intercultural split will heal."[10] Although I have only recently been able to understand why, this shadow is part of my history. For years I have repeatedly dreamed I am in danger of losing something vital to my life having to do with Mexico. I have also had a recurring dream in which I don't go to my Spanish class on time, show up late or not at all, or go to a test only to realize I know none of the answers. In each version of this dream I am exposed as a fraud.

I started piecing together the meaning of these dreams and Anzaldúa's idea of the double when I was twenty-five and had moved to Hyde Square—a Puerto Rican, Haitian, and Cuban neighborhood in Boston. Although it felt inexplicably very familiar, as if I were coming home, I had no idea why, until I eventually learned from my mother that I had spent the first few years of my life in a Chicano neighborhood (which, until she told me I had "forgotten completely"). We had been the only white people she remembered living in that neighborhood. I must have grown up hearing Spanish spoken, which explains why it has always felt familiar and I have been determined to become bilingual as an adult. In this instance, my mother's silence was fueled by a complicated combination of gender and class oppression. When I asked her why she never talked about the Chicano neighborhood of my early years, I quickly understood that, for her, thinking about that time meant remembering that the bathroom had no floor (it was dirt). In that house, she had to deal with my father's drunkenness and the violence that ensued when he came to visit. For my mother, "forgetting" the Chicano influence was part of trying to forget the poverty and the helplessness she felt as a single mother of two children.

Kachina Dolls and Historical Amnesia

With my recognition of the early influence of Chicanos/as on my sense of home and community, I also began to sift through what it has meant for me as a white child to grow up in Arizona, in Indian country. Partly because the separation between Hopi, Navajo, Zuni and white people is even more severe than between whites and Chicanos/as, the messages I received about Native people were both painful and confusing. I remember being taken to a children's art class at the Heard Museum in Phoenix, where a white teacher asked me to draw a Kachina doll, which is a Hopi figure that is considered an intermediary between the creator and human life. Kachinas are spirit essences of all things in the natural world, including plants, animals, cosmic forces, and ancestors. I started to draw a tiny stick figure when the teacher came over and drew a Kachina doll as big as the entire page. I was amazed by her ability to draw a figure that took up the whole paper. I painted the figure with bright colors—orange, green, brown and yellow. When my mother came to pick me up, she was so proud of the painting that I just let her believe I did it, even though I knew it wasn't really my drawing and that I could never do something that right or that big.

Although Hopi, Navajo, Zuni, and Apache influences are pervasive in Arizona, this experience was the closest I ever came to learning about Native American cultures. Yet, indirectly I learned about absence and appropriation. I learned that Hopi traditions and culture came from a museum and an Anglo art teacher. And, now, as a teacher and writer, I am searching to understand how these and other exclusions are institutionalized so that the attendant ethical issues may not even occur to the museum staff, patrons, and subscribers. What does it mean to exhibit Indian art in white-controlled museums while white people act as "experts" on Indian art? In this process of appropriation, Native art is typically segregated to "ancient art" sections of museums, reinforcing the lie that Native Americans are "vanished" people who are no longer producing art and hence, "culture."[11] However, cultural vitality is a matter of perspective. As the Navajo artist Joe Ben explains, "if there are any people who are vanishing it is white people, driving themselves out of existence with their destruction of the planet, irreverence for ritual, and unwillingness to see the interconnections between the land, culture and survival."[12] In fact, much contemporary Native American art addresses current political, social, ecological, and cultural issues in compelling ways and belongs in modern museums, alongside works by Georgia O'Keeffe, Sylvia Edwards, and other contemporary artists.

It wasn't until I was in graduate school and had begun to learn about Native American land rights that I understood the costs of my ignorance toward Native American cultures. I was watching the film *Broken Rainbow*, about the current U.S. government's forced "relocation" of 10,000 Navajo from the Big Mountain region in Arizona (a policy which renders them refugees).[13] For the first time, I saw what has been and continues to be done "in my name." On a personal level, this historical amnesia has profound public and political roots. The Mormons have a long history of stealing and swindling land from Native people, from the early founders of Mormonism in Utah to recently, when John Boyden, a Mormon lawyer, duplicitously represented both the Navajo people and Peabody Coal Company in a court case in which the Navajo lost almost all their mineral rights. In the 1800s, Mormon men acquired huge tracts of land that they divided up among their multiple wives who were then expected to bear many children to farm the land, support the Temples, and prosper financially. For example, my great-great-grandfather had eight wives in Utah. His wealth and power were built on immoral land acquisition and polygamy.[14] As a child, I was never taught a word about how the Mormons prospered at the expense of Native Americans.

Just as Mexican–Anglo connections are often rendered invisible in the construction of white identity, so are connections between Native Americans and white people. I sit here with the cheekbones of my sister, father, and grandmother, which are strikingly similar to the facial bone structure of many Southwestern Native people. To deny that miscegenation or rape of Native American women by Mormon men occurred is a lie and a symptom of historical amnesia. This amnesia also makes validating those ties nearly impossible. Although Mormons are well known for keeping extensive genealogical records, they have completely hidden information about interracial marriage or interracial sexual relations.[15] I can only imagine how different genealogical charts would be if they not only included marriages but also documented extra-marital sexual ties and abuse as well.[16]

On the Margins of a Movement

With the distorted messages I received as a child about Chicanos/as and Native Americans, I was also exposed to complicated messages about Black/white relations. During the years we lived in Phoenix, my mother taught English literature at a predominantly Black urban high school. Like many young people in the 1960s, she had rebelled against her parents and religious traditions and supported the Civil Rights Movement wholeheartedly. Since she was living in Arizona in the 1960s, she did not feel directly a part of the Civil Rights Movement whose center was in the South.[17] However, from as far back as I can remember, my mother's teaching, political affiliations, and intellectual interests reflected her opposition to racism and her commitment to integrated education. She often sparred with other teachers and administrators who used traditional text books rather than primary sources (based on the notion that the African American students were not bright enough to read and interpret literature on their own). She opposed the educational tracking system with its racist underpinnings, and raised her children to know African American poetry, literature, and history. She grieved about the murder of Martin Luther King Jr. and voted for Shirley Chisholm for Vice President.

I also remember a huge verbal battle between my mother and her father after she learned that he was going to vote for George Wallace for president. She stormed out of my grandparents' house, with me running to catch up, as she screamed that she didn't want to have anything to do with that "racist man." This was not unusual behavior. My mother would "go off" in private *and* public when offended by people's political positions. The genteel manners and the habitual politeness that many Southern women link to the maintenance of racism were social amenities my mother never taught me. It was not uncommon for her to kick her dinner guests out of the house before the meal was even over, furious with their conservative political stances on current or historical events.

During her second marriage, however, my mother's opposition to racism was clouded by a complicity that left me feeling ashamed and confused. When my mother remarried, she adopted the middle-class life of her second husband, which included hiring an African American woman to come in to clean the house. I can't even remember her name, which also indicates a form of historical amnesia. Although the "nameless" woman lived at least an hour's bus ride from our house, it was a relatively short drive and my step-father would drive her home when he felt like it. I remember wishing that he would be in a good mood when he came home from work so that he would drive her. I felt ashamed when she had to take the bus, although I don't remember ever having said anything.

I also remember a time when my mother realized that this woman had cleaned the oven with some household product that wasn't for ovens. My mother's tone of voice was both pitying and condescending as she explained that this had happened because the woman could not read. I remember thinking, "Well, why didn't you explain it with words?" I was six or seven at the time and young enough to know the frustration of not being able to figure out meaning from print. But most of all I remember feeling shame: shame for being there; shame about my mother's attitude; and shame that this woman had to clean our house. Later, I came to understand what was modeled for me in this instance: white people may be opposed to racism on a structural level, while simultaneously upholding it in private contexts. This contradiction was certainly not open for discussion.

My mother held two key convictions about race: white people had treated African American people so violently that there was no reason for an African American person ever to trust a white person; and because of the abuse Black people had survived historically, they were morally superior to white people. To her credit, my mother did not deny that racism existed, nor did she think that African American people were somehow responsible for racism. Even so, in the final analysis, her romanticizing of African American people was still problematic.

I extrapolated from her message that African American people will never trust white people, that I could never be worthy enough to have friendships across race, and that I was inevitably doomed to being a racist. As a white person, guilt was the unavoidable result of injuries white people inflict. I also believed that experiencing racism inexorably led African American people to moral superiority—that some kind of intrinsic virtue and moral agency results from facing discrimination. Within this framework, white people could never become moral agents because we had not been oppressed by racism. I grew up believing that I should grant authority to *whatever* people of color said. The logic I learned was, "It was the least you could do, after all that white people had already put them through." Within this construct, white people were inherently bad and African American people were inherently good: white people responded to inequality with guilt rather than by dismantling racism. In addition, partly because I had little first-hand exposure to the Civil Rights Movement specifically or grassroots activism in general. I believed that the responsibility for racism was to be individually shouldered rather than collectively burdened.

Body Crossing and Stolen Stories

Being a survivor of childhood trauma—and the body border-crossing that resulted—has also profoundly shaped my outlook on everything, including what I learned as a child about power and race. Recently, I came across a report I wrote in the second grade about slavery in the United States in which I included a picture of one level of a slave ship in which hundreds and hundreds of black people were strapped down in long lines, in rows that were so tight it seemed impossible for them to breathe. From the moment I found that picture as a child, it was imprinted on my mind. Mab Segrest, a white antiracist activist, tells of a similar experience when she was thirteen years old. She remembers hiding under bushes across from her high school to watch 200 Alabama Highway Patrol troopers surround twelve Black children who were the first to "integrate" the school. She recalls, "I have a tremendous flash of empathy, of identification, with their vulnerability and their aloneness inside that circle of force. Their separation is mine. And I know from now on that everything people have told me is 'right' has to be reexamined. I am on my own."[18]

I now know that the picture of the slave ship had such a powerful impact on my life partly because of the intense identification I felt with those chained people. When I was being abused when very young, I felt as if I was pinned down for what seemed like interminable periods of time. During this abuse, my limbs would turn to styrofoam. Starting with my toes and extending upward, the pores of the styrofoam would fill up with concrete until my arms and legs were completely immobilized. In that experience, my body was thoroughly "colonized," engulfed so completely that the only way I could cope was to leave my body, leaving the territory that had become unsafe for human life.[19]

By the time I was four years old I had also watched my father screaming that he wanted to die after he had become violently sick from getting drunk after having consumed Antabuse.[20] As the paramedics tried to save his life, he screamed incessantly that he just wanted to die, as he pulled I.V.'s out of his arms again and again. I watched with big, horrified eyes as paramedics tried to push me aside, trying to spare me from seeing what was already indelibly carved on my consciousness. At that moment, I remember slipping out of my body, having taken flight from the intense pain that filled the space. Like Pecola in Toni Morrison's *The Bluest Eye*, I left my body but my eyes were tragically left behind, a witness to the brutal scene I was a part of.[21]

Photographs taken of me from age four and older show a child with eyes off center, cast off, looking up and away, still seeing everything, but from a perspective not wholly of this world any more. By three years old I had also witnessed violence between my parents, followed by police coming to drag my father away. This is when I first learned that police presence often heightens rather than quells violence. If the police arrived after the fighting between my father and mother had calmed down, the struggle between the police and my father as they arrested him meant yet another round of physical violence.

The violence I witnessed and experienced left me feeling like an outsider at home, with other people, and even in my own body. By the time I turned five, I had already begun spending what felt like huge chunks of time alone. At noon each day I would walk home from kindergarten, let myself in, and stay in the house until 3:00 or 4:00, when my mother would come home with my little sister. At that point, my mother only had enough money for child care for one child. I was enormously proud that I could unlock the door and take care of myself until they came home. The responsibility I carried so young has given me a sense of independence that I carry with me constantly. But, looking back I know I was entirely too young to be alone for those long hours. By the time I came across that picture of Black people in chains, I saw my isolation as inevitable, and, as I imagined about the slaves on the ship, I knew that the "authorities" offered no protection.

What does it mean, however, for a white child to identify so completely with a Black slave? As a child I didn't know that seeing myself as a chained slave was a form of appropriation, that in my identification I did not recognize that white people, people of my own race, were the ones who put them in chains. I knew that white people were the ones who enslaved Black people, but no part of me saw myself as part of that white power. It makes sense that I didn't, at age four or five, have the language or skills to know the possible deleterious consequences of conflating stories. But, the fact that my memories of abuse and my identification with the black slaves were so tightly fused was a barrier to understanding my role in racism as I grew older.

It took me a long time to understand that my appropriation was part of a long history of white women's inability to understand our own complicity in the history of slavery and domination of Black people in this country. In the 19th century, white women used images of slavery and bondage to highlight the damages caused by patriarchy, while simultaneously creating a politics that avoided reckoning with their own complicity in slavery and lynching. In the current wave of the Women's Movement, white feminists have benefited from policies and scholarship about the family, wage labor, violence, reproduction, and religion (to name a few topics) that appear to speak to the needs of all women but which, actually, have been white-centered and have relegated women of color to the margins. I held onto the image of the slave ship for many years until I began to see the contradictions and complicity that desperately needed to be untangled.

The lessons I learned while growing up about race reveal many troubling and contradictory characteristics of white identity. The overarching message I learned was that white people are in charge and have been consistently abusive. The specific dynamics associated with this domination were multiple: white people deny or ignore people of color; appropriate their language, culture and work; act in contradictory ways and are not held accountable; do not deserve to be trusted; are not worthy of interracial friendships; are condescending and pitying toward people of different races; are morally inferior to Black people; and are vulnerable and lonely if they rebel against racism. I also learned that whiteness is not itself a positive assertion of race. Rather, whiteness exists only to the extent that it is not Black, Chicano or Native American.

This particular constellation of messages I learned may be more reflective of liberal than conservative ideology about race. For example, I was not raised to believe the conservative racial ideology which supports biological determinism, justifies continued violence against people of color, or espouses the "blame the victim" ideology.[22] In addition, although there are some major differences between conservative and liberal ideology about race (and I would argue that conservative ideology is, in the end, more damaging) below the surface of the liberal racial socialization I was raised with was unacknowledged doubt about my own self-worth. When my identity was predicated upon another's supposed inferiority, my sense of self depended upon constant justification and proof. My fear of admitting to the reality of white skin privilege turned out to be a mask which hid how access to unearned privileges and self loathing can co-exist. It is this self-doubt that fueled the projection and anger which I then used to deny my own racism.

Redrawing Racial Maps

As an adult, I have sought to examine the truth in these descriptions of white identity, seeking community, scholarship, and activism which scrutinizes and undermines whiteness as it is constructed. This has been both a profoundly personal and public process: personal because understanding racism requires me to look at the specifics of my own background and attitudes, and public in that during the fifteen years since I was first introduced to feminism, race has shaped almost every conflict, conference, and activist event I can think of.

My initial way of proceeding might have been described as two-headed and stubborn. During my first years in college, I would characterize myself as "kicking and screaming" my way through learning about race while I exhibited various intensities of denial, guilt, shame, and defensiveness. For instance, in a 1977 college course titled, "The Black Experience," I routinely chirped in with naive abandon that, "I am not racist because my mother taught in integrated schools," and "I don't understand why we can't all get along. Slavery is in the past." While outwardly resisting an examinination of my own racism, internally I felt that, as a white person, I didn't deserve to be in that class and that I was morally inferior to the Black students. Looking back on my behavior, chances are several students—as well as the teacher—might have liked to show me the door during the first week of class.

I stormed out of the first antiracism workshop I attended in 1979 at the University of California at Santa Cruz, furious that white women had the audacity to state that white people are racist. Had that indictment come from the Black women leaders of the workshop I might have stayed, thinking that *they* would know. In my head, no white woman had the right to claim authority about racism, as I lumped people of color and racism into one category and left white people out of the equation entirely. I attended a meeting in 1980 in which students from the University's Third World activist organization voiced their anger at white feminists who had organized a public confrontation with a Black man (whom a white woman had accused of rape) without first consulting with the Third World organizations. By the time this happened I knew enough to not protest their anger although I did not yet have the historical background I needed to know why that confrontation was so problematic.[23] While embarrassed by my methods of resistance and apologetic to those who had to witness them, the passion of my responses also signalled my investment in changing.[24]

Through my continued exposure to community activism and scholarship with people of color in the early 1980s, I eventually made a transition from what I am labeling my "kicking and screaming, 'I am not a racist' stage" to a period when I felt I needed to do everything I could to overcome racism—mine and everyone else's. During this period—my "'I don't want to be white' stage"—I had great difficulty accepting myself as a white woman as I shifted from denying the realities of racism to wanting to dissociate from white people entirely. At this point, close connections with other white people felt threatening. I felt as if I'd had more than enough of white culture and that I needed to spend all my energy catching up—learning from and being with people of color.

During this period, I recall feeling extremely self-conscious about showing my childhood photograph album to an African American friend because she would see that almost all of the people included in it were white. I felt unworthy of being friends with people of color, afraid that at any moment I would reveal my racist self and alienate them forever. Yet I thought that if I could not break through this fear, my intentions to stand up against racism would be fraudulent. I felt extremely self-conscious about being in all-white crowds and proud if I was one of the only white people at an event primarily attended by people of color. I believed I needed to take my direction from them and distrust most everything white people said. I felt jealous of African American women whom I thought could search for "their mothers' gardens" as Alice Walker has described it, without having to face the possibility of finding slave holders in their genealogies.[25] I remember riding on a bus in Boston when I was re-reading Barbara Smith's *Home Girls: A Black Feminist*

Anthology for a course and holding the book conspicuously on my lap in hopes that the Black woman sitting next to me would see it. I wanted her to know that I knew of the book—so I could be counted as a "cool white woman."

Looking back on these scenes, I see the distortions in my thinking glaring back at me and it still feels risky to admit them. At the time, I shared none of these feelings with anyone. On some level I knew I was in process and I feared embarrassing myself. By this point, I had had enough exposure to multiracial feminist politics, antiracism trainings, and scholarship by women of color to know that much of what I was thinking was racist. Yet, I didn't see a way out of my ambivalence about being white. When I tried to showcase *Home Girls* on the bus ride I did not yet understand that the particular Black woman sitting next to me might have felt absolutely no kinship with Black feminists, and might have been homophobic as well. Believing that Black women could search for their "mothers' gardens" without uncovering "oppressors," I was not yet accounting for how internalized oppression, colorism and classism—not to mention sexism and homophobia—have played themselves out historically in African American families and communities. These realities, in and of themselves, complicate notions of African Americans as "innocent victims." When I congratulated myself as one of the only white people in a social or political context, I was still seeing antiracism as some sort of competition—with only a few spaces at the table for antiracist white people. In my attempts to break away from living a segregated life, I was still measuring my credentials as an antiracist white woman through my association with people of color.

In the mid-1980s, I continued to participate in protests and civil disobedience against apartheid and U.S. militarism, and organize against racism on college campuses, and my writing and teaching became more centered in African American, Ethnic, and Women's Studies. During this period, what I found most challenging was understanding how to proceed as a white woman given the complexities of identity politics. I might now characterize this stage as "grappling for a steady position" intellectually and politically at a time when I—and I think many other white feminists—were fumbling to find ways to proceed.

By the late 1970s and early 1980s, identity politics emerged to shape feminist political organizing in significant ways. In 1979 the now-classic position paper written by the Boston-based feminist group, the Combahee River Collective was first published. The Collective concluded that "the most profound and potentially most radical politics come directly out of our own identity, as opposed to working to end somebody else's oppression."[26] Their stance came from understanding that no previous political movement had ever placed the liberation of Black women at the center of focus. They resolved that Black women must organize by and for themselves.

Many Latinas, Asian Americans, lesbians, working-class women, Jewish women, people with disabilities, and older women also considered identity politics central to their political agendas in the 1980s. The promise of this politics was the assertion that those who had been held down historically needed to be in charge of creating strategies for change. This position stood against the history of white people or Black men who have spoken for Black women or ignored them altogether. It countered the history of confining race in the United States to a "black–white" thing that rendered Latinas/os, Native Americans and Asian Americans invisible. This stance also made clear why establishing organizations by and for women of color (such as Casa Myrna Vasquez, a battered women's shelter in Boston, The National Black Women's Health Project in Atlanta, and Kitchen Table Women of Color Press) became a high priority for feminists of color nationally. Accordingly, race, class, and heterosexual bias in feminist demonstrations and conferences could be avoided if the perspectives of women of color, lesbians, and working-class women of all races were integral to the planning.

One consequence of this foundational politics—and perhaps an inevitable one—was an increased jockeying for authority, based on one's belonging to a subordinated group. In this distorted arithmetic, a white straight woman was "outflanked" by a woman of color, or a white lesbian had more "credentials" than a white straight woman. With this scenario, identity politics had been twisted into an essentialism which assumed that those from subordinated communities had "biological" or "natural" access to knowledge or ideas that people from dominant groups could never have. This essentialism fed what Elly Bulkin calls "oppression privilege," which assumes that certain criticisms can only be made by those who share a given identity. Within this construct, it is unacceptable, for instance, for a non-Jewish woman to criticize a Jewish woman or for a white woman to take issue with a woman of color.[27]

For some white women, an important step away from the traps of ranking oppressions occurred when we found ways to understand our own racial identities and unearned privileges.[28] Anti-racism groups for white women became one such step as they helped women wrestle with the shame and guilt we felt as white people—feelings that I think fed white women's silence and distorted interactions with women of color. In the antiracism group I was part of, I began to see how constantly beating ourselves up for racism was based on the notion that one person's actions are sufficient to change social relations. As the small group of us met together we also started to realize that it was no coincidence that most of us came from alcoholic homes and/or were survivors of sexual abuse. Both identities had fed our willingness to castigate ourselves about "our racism." Childhood experiences had taught us early in life what it felt like to be an outsider. Our task, then, was to learn how to use that knowledge without trying to appropriate the outsider status that women of color experience to explain our own. This group helped me take a more measured step in working on racism, teaching me that social change is much larger than singular efforts. It was during this two-year period in the late 1980s that I stopped feeling bad or wrong because I am white and I started seeing ways to channel my energies without trying to leave a piece of my identity behind.

A subsequent stage in my racial identity evolved as I began to understand the distinctions between identity politics and an informed consciousness—a stance based on one's political affiliations and relation to subordinated communities regardless of biology.[29] Some of this came about as I became more comfortable confronting racism, regardless of whether or not it was confirmed by a person of color. Leading antiracist trainings in biracial or multiracial teams gave me hands-on experience in seeing how each of us could use our own racial positions and experience in complementary ways. During these trainings we attempted to uncover daily forms of racism—both individual and institutional. This challenge catalyzed discussion about racism and internalized oppression as well as African American, White, Latino, and Asian American identity development. Often it was most effective to break up into separate racial groups. Typically, the people of color and white people were in entirely different places in terms of recognizing the centrality of racism in American culture. The separate groups saved people of color from having to listen to white people's rationalizations and denials, while giving white people space to speak with an honesty and candor rarely possible in racially-mixed groups. These separate groups also made it possible for a Black leader, for example, to discuss internalized racism among the Black people, a discussion that could not have taken place in racially mixed groups.

During the late 1980s, I also became more confident about my abilities to teach multiracial scholarship, largely because of the intellectual and emotional support I received from people of color—friends, lovers, and scholars. In this stage, those whom I could consider authorities and role models for understanding race and racism also broadened to include white people. My earlier competitive approach had been replaced by understanding that I didn't have to recreate the wheel in my own life. I began to actively seek writing by white women who have historically stood up against racism—Elly Bulkin, Lillian Smith, Sara Evans, Angelina Grimke, Ruth Frankenberg, Helen Joseph, Melanie Kaye/Kantrowitz, Tillie Olsen, Minnie Bruce Pratt, Ruth Seid, Mab Segrest, and others. I also realized I needed antiracist white people in my daily life with whom I could share stories, talk about complex "racialized" interactions (in the classroom, for example), and brainstorm about strategies. Most importantly, I needed white friends whom I could trust to give me honest feedback. In this, what might be called the "conscience doesn't have a color" stage of my racial identity, I no longer saw "whiteness" as inherently bad or good, any more than "blackness" is inherently so.

Over time, I began to realize that while the unearned white privileges afforded to me remain, my political and familial connections were changing. The process of becoming antiracist had coincided with creating a life that had become multiracial and multicultural. The neighborhoods I lived in, people I considered friends and trusted allies at work, my research interests, and, those whom I considered "family," were becoming increasingly multiracial. I had gone beyond "crossing the color line" politically, emotionally, and sexually to trying to create a livable space in the border between two worlds. This borderland had become much more than a political location, since whom I called family and what my culture looked and felt like was changing as well. My loyalties, my emotional, political, and intellectual sustenance, and my daily life had come to center around people of color and other white people who, probably not coincidentally, were also living in various racial borderlands.

"Structures that Can Support Us / Without Fear / of Trembling"[30]

There is much to be gained when white women whose racial identities have undergone major change find ways to recognize and support each other. In part, this will require us to name ourselves in positive terms. The demeaning terms imposed upon us—"wanna-be's" or "whiggers" (white niggers), and accusations that we are "slumming" or "committing racial suicide"—are obviously inappropriate descriptions. And yet, the term "antiracist" doesn't fully capture this identity or location either. Like the term "race-traitor," the term "antiracist" says who we are only by what we are against. In addition, many of us have come to our racial politics through an antioppression stance which assumes that racial justice must occur alongside dismantling sexism, poverty, anti-Semitism, homophobia, and other oppressions.

We also need positive terms for white people who see multiple points of view and whose community ties are multiracial and multicultural. We need to talk about what living in this borderland feels like, how we get there, what sustains us, and how we benefit from it. For me, this place of existence is tremendously exciting, invigorating, and life-affirming. It can also be complicated and lonely. It is certainly a place that nurtures my creativity and imagination, since there are few rules and a lot of room for improvisation. It is a place of "psychic restlessness," in the words of Gloria Anzaldúa, although for white people, this restlessness is largely voluntary and "chosen," which is quite different from the "restlessness" of border living for women of color.[31]

One benefit of the process of collective naming is its potential for supporting effective political organizing. Perhaps the most dramatic recent example of the possibilities of such organizing was apparent during the Anita Hill/Clarence Thomas hearings. Within days of that hearing 1603 Black women had signed a statement that ran in *The New York Times*. Collectively named "African American Women in Defense of Ourselves," these women protested the treatment of Anita Hill and the pervasive disregard for Black women's lives in the United States. There was no coherent nationally organized antiracist statement by white men or women, although there were regional responses. I cringed as prominent white women who supported Anita Hill emphasized the commonality of sexual harassment among women without simultaneously identifying and challenging the racism in this context. This was a haunting and painful indicator of my own and other white women's failure to create political consciousness and a national movement of white feminists who are confronting racial domination.

An increased visibility of antiracist white people could also reduce racial conflicts within multiracial alliances by providing contexts where white people could walk each other toward positive racial identities. This visibility could also counter the loneliness and confusion that some white people experience as they take steps to confront white domination. The displacement that white people may experience in the process (from their families and friends) is not the same as losing white privilege, just as the loneliness and confusion resulting from a chosen existence in a borderland should not be confused with the loneliness of forced exile. White people are trained not to see power inequities, while still benefitting from them. It is sometimes easier for white women to read ourselves into the victim/innocent scenario than the oppressor/guilty one even though white women occupy both simultaneously. In this instance, guilt becomes a safer response than taking responsibility for racial inequality. White women may be uniquely positioned to help each other see this and move beyond it.

For white people, making positive changes in racial identity often hinges upon identifying how being an "outsider" in life—a woman, a Jew, a lesbian, disabled—and an "insider"—a white person, a man, a Christian—both shape people's lives. Jewish-feminists have often led the way in describing this dual vision and how the "outsider's eye" can be a motivation for confronting racism.[32] Other experiences of being an "outsider" may also encourage people to question racial domination. There is much about white lesbian culture that is used to solidify whiteness.[33] However, one of the many strengths of certain lesbian communities is the room that has been made for interracial political alliances, friendships, and long-term lover partnerships. Multiracial alliances in some lesbian communities may have enabled more acceptance for lesbians who cross color lines and are antiracist activists than exists among heterosexuals. The power and comfort of this identification and the outsider vision it affords may be one reason why so many antiracist white feminists are also lesbians.

My own experience suggests that dealing with childhood trauma may be a necessary part of racial re-orientation for many white women. Surviving abuse is no guarentee of political consciousness. All that abuse promises is scars. The rest is left up to fate, resources, and the healing that may come from collectively naming and organizing to stop abuse. However, a radicalizing force in my life did come from understanding the origins of my own "outsider's lens" and beginning to see how that lens enabled me to question other injustices.[34] Because sexual abuse is so common—one third of girls across race and class are sexually abused, often very early in life—it may be the first experience of being an "outsider" that many white women face.

Understanding how early trauma can inform one's vision can also help white women avoid the "liberation by analogy" approach to fighting oppression (fighting someone else's fight because you can't acknowledge and fight your own). This feeds a "saving them" approach to organizing rather than a "saving all of us" perspective. Early traumas also often lead people to question what home means and provides. Questioning the notion of "home" as a unitary, safe haven is often at the root of subsequent scrutiny about power and inequality.[35] It is this questioning that may also fuel a desire to live at the borders and the willingness to live with the "psychic restlessness" this engenders.

Finally, I would hope that collective identification among antiracist white people might facilitate more multicultural living. My hunch is that the lack of collective identification and positive naming is a key barrier for many white people who, with support and models, might oppose racism and cross color lines. As white people carve out positive racial identities we need to grapple with the organizing strategies, codes of conduct, and political priorities required to live in borderlands. Several years ago someone who was both older and wiser than I told me that coming out as a lesbian does not involve a singular door but rather a multilevel maze. The steps required to negotiate through this maze fluctuate with political, economic, and geographic changes. These changes govern what seems possible, probable, and simply out of the question. To me, crossing racial borders demands a similar negotiation.

At the end of this century, I am left wondering what traverses it will take to stop us from backtracking. What structures do we need to build to make border crossing possible, even probable, and certainly not out of the question? Cherríe Moraga explains, "I am not talking about sky scrapers, merely structures that can support us without fear of trembling."[36]

Notes

The title of this essay is adapted from María Lugones. 1991. "Playfulness, 'World'-Travelling, and Loving Perception," in *Making Face, Making Soul: Haciendo Caras*, ed. Gloria Anzaldúa (San Francisco: Aunt Lute, 1990) pp. 390-402. I want to thank Sally Abood, Gloria Anzaldúa, Esther Brock, Elly Bulkin, Lynn Davidman, Patti DeRosa, Estelle Disch, Peter Erickson, Beth Fillmore, Ruth Frankenberg, Sheila Adams Hart, Mary Gilfus, Angela Giudice, Ginny Onysko, Gayle Pemberton, Betty Thompson, Sangeeta Tyagi, David Wellman, and the members of the Boston area women's antiracism group (1987–1988) for the many ways they helped me with this essay.

1   This 1978 California initiative sought to remove supporters of lesbian and gay rights from the educational system.

2   María Lugones. 1991. "Playfulness, 'World'-Travelling, and Loving Perception," in *Making Face, Making Soul*.

3   Elly Bulkin. 1980. "Racism and Writing: Some Implications for White Lesbian Critics." *Sinister Wisdom*. 13 Spring; Ruth Frankenberg, *White Women, Race Matters* (Minneapolis: University of Minnesota Press, 1993); Elly Bulkin, "Hard Ground: Jewish Identity, Racism and Anti-Semitism," in *Yours in Struggle*, Elly Bulkin, Minnie Bruce Pratt and Barbara Smith (Brooklyn, NY: Long Haul Press, 1984); Sara Evans, *Personal Politics: The Roots of Women's Liberation in the Civil Rights Movement and the New Left* (New York: Random House, 1979); Joan Nestle, *A Restricted Country* (Ithaca, NY: Firebrand, 1987); Marilyn Frye, "On Being White: Toward a Feminist Understanding of Race and Race Supremacy," in *The Politics of Reality: Essays on Feminist Theory* (Trumansburg, New York: Crossing Press, 1983); Minnie Bruce Pratt, "Identity: Skin Blood Heart" in *Yours in Struggle*; Adrienne Rich, "Disloyal to Civilization: Feminism, Racism, Gynephobia" in *On Lies, Secrets and Silences* (New York: Norton, 1979); Adrienne Rich, "Resisting Amnesia: History and Personal Life," in *Blood, Bread, and Poetry* (New York: Norton, 1986); Mab Segrest, *My Mama's Dead Squirrel: Lesbian Essays on Southern Culture* (Ithaca, New York: Firebrand, 1985); Lillian Smith, *Killers of the Dream* (New York: W.W. Norton, 1978).

4   bell hooks, *Yearning* (Boston: South End Press, 1990), p. 54. This passage was quoted in Kathryn B. Ward, "'Lifting as We Climb': How Scholarship By and About Women of Color Has Shaped My Life as a White Feminist," Working Paper 13, Memphis State University: Center for Research on Women, 1992.

5   See footnote 3.

6   Mab Segrest, *My Mama's Dead Squirrel*.

7   Elly Bulkin, Minnie Bruce Pratt and Barbara Smith, *Yours in Struggle*.

8   For a legal analysis of how children's understanding of inequality is muted see Patricia Williams, *The Alchemy of Race and Rights: Diary of a Law Professor* (Cambridge: Harvard University Press, 1991). Williams tells of a young boy who sees a big dog and is afraid only to be told by his parents that he need not worry since "there is really no difference between big and little dogs."(p. 13). Williams uses this scene to explain how the subject positions of children (and other subordinated groups) are denied. Until "educated" to the contrary the child acknowledged and understood differences in size and possible consequences of this difference. Williams writes that this represents "a paradigm of thought by which children are taught not to see what they see; by which blacks are reassured that there is no real inequality in the world, just their own bad dreams; and by which women are taught not to experience what they experience, in deference to men's ways of knowing."(p. 13).

9   My notion that living in several states in the United States was a sign of being "worldly" is a telling indication of how early ethnocentrism is internalized.

10   Gloria Anzaldúa, "La Consciencia De La Mestiza: Toward a New Consciousness," in *Making Face, Making Soul*, p. 394.

ОНreducers

11 See the poetry by Chrystos in *Not Vanishing* (Vancouver, B.C. Canada: Press Gang Publishers, 1988) especially, "I Have Not Signed a Treaty With the U.S. Government" (p. 71) and "Savage Eloquence" (p. 41).

12 Personal conversation with Joe Ben, Phoenix, Arizona, Summer, 1992.

13 *Broken Rainbow*, which is directed and produced by Maria Florio and Victoria Mudd, won the 1985 Academy Award for best documentary feature and is distributed by Direct Cinema Limited, 445 West Main Street, Wycoff, N.J. 07481. For information on the campaign to repeal the 1974 Public Law 93-531 which sanctions forced relocation write BMLO, P.O. Box 1509, Flagstaff, AZ 86002. See also, Wendell Waters, "Big Mountain: Facing Cultural Genocide," *Sojourner: The Women's Forum* (January, 1989) pp. 22-23; and Jerry Kammer. *The Second Long Walk: The Navajo-Hopi Land Dispute* (Albuquerque, New Mexico, University of New Mexico Press, 1980).

14 Mormon missionaries played a key role in dislocating Hopi youth from their families and forcing them to attend boarding schools. After Hopi parents protested, U.S. federal troops forced the children from their homes.

15 By raising the possibility of interracial blood in my family, I am certainly not professing any claim to a Native American identity. This clarification is important to counter the imperialist appropriation of Native American practices by white people who claim relations with Native Americans based on "past lives," "prophetic dreams," possible blood ties, or professed spiritual affinities. For an important analysis of these actions among some white gay men and lesbians see, Earl Jackson, "The Responsibility of/to Differences and Theorizing Race and Ethnicity in Lesbian and Gay Studies," in *Beyond a Dream Deferred: Multicultural Education and the Politics of Excellence*, eds. Sangeeta Tyagi and Becky Thompson (Minneapolis: University of Minnesota Press, 1993).

16 This genealogical documentation could expose the silence and erasure of homosexuality historically along with the idea of a "pure" white race.

17 Had she not been a single mother who was raising two children, she might well have traveled to the South with other students and activists at the time. Certainly, the dominant imagery of those who did become involved in voter registration drives and civil disobedience did not include single and/or pregnant divorced mothers.

18 Mab Segrest, *My Mama's Dead Squirrel*, p. 20.

19 The conceptualization of sexual abuse as a form of colonization is developed by Mary Gilfus, Assistant Professor of Social Work at Simmons College, Boston, Massachusetts.

20 Antabuse is a drug that is intended to deter drinking since it causes a potentially deadly reaction if it is combined with alcohol.

21 Toni Morrison, *The Bluest Eye* (New York: Simon and Schuster, 1970).

22 William Ryan, *Blaming The Victim* (New York: Vintage, 1972).

23 For historical analysis see Angela Davis. "Race, Racism and the Myth of the Black Rapist," in *Women, Race and Class* (New York: Random, 1981); Manning Marable, *How Capitalism Underdeveloped Black America* (Boston: South End Press, 1983).

24 My own resistance has been a helpful reminder for me as a teacher. Some of the white students who have been most feisty and resistant to learning about racism have also been the ones who, in the final analysis, have really changed themselves in some significant ways. I have also noticed that heterosexual students who are most resistant to learning about heterosexism and lesbian/gay identity are often gay or lesbian themselves (but have not come out) and/or are those who, in time, will take the issues most seriously.

25 Alice Walker, *In Search of Our Mothers' Gardens* (New York: Harcourt Brace Jovanovich, 1983).

26 The Combahee River Collective, "The Combahee River Collective Statement," *Home Girls: A Black Feminist Anthology* Barbara Smith, ed. (New York: Kitchen Table: Women of Color Press, 1983).

27 Elly Bulkin, "Hard Ground: Jewish Identity, Racism and Anti-Semitism," in *Yours in Struggle*, p. 99.

28 Peggy McIntosh. 1992. "White Privilege and Male Privilege: A Personal Account of Coming to See Correspondences Through Work in Women's Studies," in *Race, Class and Gender: An Anthology*, eds. Patricia Hill Collins and Margaret Andersen (Belmont, CA: Wadsworth Publishing) pp. 70-81.

29 Becky Thompson and Sangeeta Tyagi, "The Politics of Inclusion: Reskilling the Academy," in *Beyond a Dream Deferred: Multicultural Education and the Politics of Excellence*, eds. Sangeeta Tyagi and Becky Thompson (Minneapolis: University of Minnesota Press, 1993).

30 Cherríe Moraga, "The Welder," *This Bridge Called My Back: Writing By Radical Women of Color*, eds. Cherríe Moraga and Gloria Anzaldúa (NY: Kitchen Table Women of Color Press, 1983) p. 219.

31 Gloria Anzaldúa, "La Consciencia De La Mestiza," in *Making Face, Making Soul: Haciendo Caras*, p. 377. Anzaldúa refers to this psychic restlessness among women of color who occupy at least two worlds simultaneously (are bi- or tricultural, linguistically, ethnically, or racially).

32 Adrienne Rich, *Blood, Bread, and Poetry*; Elly Bulkin, "Hard Ground" in *Yours in Struggle*. Melanie Kaye/Kantrowitz, *The Issue is Power: Essays on Women, Jews, Violence and Resistance* (San Francisco: Aunt Lute, 1992).

33 While claiming an outsider status can be a step in the process of re-evaluating one's relationship to power racially, it can also do exactly the opposite. It is dangerous to romanticize outsider status as an inevitably radicalizing principle. A painful example of the "retro" use of lesbian identity is evident among white lesbians who use their position of marginalization as a means of defining their whiteness. In the early 1990s I saw a brochure for Olivia summer ship cruises that includes a picture of all the women who were on the previous year's adventure. In the sea of 200 or 300 lesbian faces, not one woman that I can remember was dark skinned. In this instance the power afforded through membership in an "outsider" community, as lesbians, galvanized and solidified white power. They could maintain segregation and yet deny the reality of it since they were marginal themselves.

34 There are many parallels (and piggy backing) between coming to consciousness about racial identity and understanding oneself as a survivor of childhood trauma. Both are fraught with denial. Both are discouraged by the dominant society. Both contain half-truths and half-memories. Unearthing details about surviving abuse and messages white women learn about race require deliberate digging. It takes conscious effort and patience and a willingness to forgive oneself for events that have been locked up in shame and denial. It is indeed scary to go back and conjure up the parts of that past that have been buried, and yet that work needs to be done.

35 For a profound examination of the meaning of home in relation to race consciousness see: Minnie Bruce Pratt, "Identity: Skin Blood Heart," in *Yours in Struggle*.

36 Cherríe Moraga, "The Welder," *This Bridge Called My Back*, p. 219.

10

A Hyphenated Identity

Harry Kitano

Growing up as a Japanese American means a constant search for an identity. Even if one is monolingual and can speak only English, and knows nothing about the Japanese language and culture, one quickly learns that there are questions concerning an American identity. Comments such as,"Where did you learn how to speak English so well?" or "Why did your people bomb Pearl Harbor?" are reminders that acculturation and identifying as an American are insufficient criteria for belonging to the host society.

The reality of being different came about very early in my life. My parents were from Japan and they opened a hotel in San Francisco's Chinatown, so that in the beginning, what mattered were not racial differences, but those of nationality. China and Japan were enemies, ergo, the Chinese and the Japanese in America were also hostile to each other. When I attended elementary school, there was this Chinese girl, Dorothy Lee, who would mutter "Jap," and try to pinch me. I learned to suffer these taunts in silence; I knew that my teachers would be of no help, and that my parents would only laugh and scoff at the idea that I was afraid of a Chinese girl. I was unaware of the word prejudice at that time, but whatever it was, it was uncomfortable. I tried to avoid any contact with Dorothy, and counted my days as successful if I could escape without being pinched.

There were only a few Japanese families living in or near Chinatown. They were concentrated in the small business sector; a dry cleaners, an art goods store, a pool hall, a restaurant, and small hotels and rooming houses. Most of their clientele were other minorities, especially Blacks, Filipinos, and other Asians. As far as I can remember, the racial tensions that are characteristic of present-day race relations among minority groups were not present then.

There was a closeness among the Japanese families, so that although we lived apart, we formed a community. One central gathering place was the Japanese school; most of the children attended this school after the regular school day. The Japanese classes met every day from 4 to 6, so for most of us, it was an extremely long school day. However, it was not all work and study; on the contrary, it was often disorganized chaos. One lone teacher had to deal with over 20 students, ranging from the very young to some who were in high school. Motivation to learn was not very high; I found it a chance to meet with my peers, to tease and nag the teacher, and to behave in a way that would not be tolerated in the regular school. I was quiet, obedient, conforming, studious, and turned in my homework in the regular school—I was the opposite in the Japanese school.

It was a situational orientation; I learned early in life that at least for me and my peers, the situation shaped behavior. We learned that we were to behave with much more reserve when dealing with the dominant group, and less so among fellow ethnics. However, I deeply regret that I did not take the opportunity to learn the Japanese language more thoroughly; my attendance for over ten years was not a total waste, but because I can speak only limited Japanese, it was obviously not a total success. The school involved the families, and ceremonies, dinners, meetings, and speeches fostered community cohesion. There were year-end pictures so that even today, looking back and wondering who went where remains a part of one's history. The school that I attended closed during World War II and never opened again.

The close network of the Japanese families constituted my first world. Parents would help each other; the reputations of all of the children were known, and the primary reference group was my family and the small Japanese American community in Chinatown. We shared experiences and were exposed to similar values, which were reinforced by the families and the ethnic community. Not all of us behaved according to the values, but we had a clear idea when norms were violated. I don't remember any dramatic clashes between the ethnic way and the American way, primarily because of the situational orientation. I did things the American way when dealing with the host society, and the ethnic way when dealing within the family and community. This was not too difficult since there was often a congruence between the two value systems. I had minimal voluntary contact with people who were not fellow ethnics. I went to school with children of Chinese, Italian and Mexican ancestry (it was the North Beach area of San Francisco), but never got to know them intimately. The public school was integrated, but my early life was within a structurally pluralistic ethnic group. For example, I was never invited to visit or play at any homes except by Japanese Americans, and never invited other than Japanese Americans to my home.

Growing Up in the 1930s and 40s

Life for a Japanese American growing up in the 1930s and 40s was, to use a current phrase, "not a piece of cake." I remember discrimination and domination quite well. We lived just below Nob Hill in San Francisco; there was a public playground next to the Mark Hopkins Hotel on the hill. I was told by my parents that I should not play there; no one would tell me why, so that when I was about 8 years old, I trudged up the hill with several of my ethnic companions. For a few times nothing happened, but one day, a stern, white lady came up and said we could not play there. Her presence was dominating—we never questioned her authority and we hurriedly left. We thought that she was right: that that playground was reserved exclusively for the whites who lived on Nob Hill. It strengthened the wisdom of my parents that certain places were off limits, and that I shouldn't raise questions, especially when there were no appropriate answers.

Another incident, at about the same time, remains strong in my memory. A close bachelor friend of the family used to take me and my brother fishing and to other activities. Once he took us to a swimming spa called Sutro Baths which was purported to have both hot and cold swimming pools. We were extremely excited—we endured a long streetcar ride across the city to the baths. However, when we got there, the cashier evidently told my friend that "Japs weren't allowed." My friend looked embarassed, never told us what was said, and muttered something about not wanting to go swimming anyway. I went along with his rationalization, even venturing that I didn't want to go swimming either, although I felt that the rejection had something to do with our ancestry.

Pearl Harbor and the Concentration Camps

If I had doubts that racism was a problem, they were quickly erased after the Japanese attack on Pearl Harbor in 1941. I had just entered Galileo High School; I remember attending the all school assembly where President Roosevelt gave his speech about the "day of infamy," and the declaration of war against Japan. There were just a few Japanese American students; we glanced at each other furtively, feeling that all eyes were upon us. It was a trying moment; I felt confused and even guilty that Japan had attacked the United States. But, nothing untoward happened; school continued and I thought that, aside from the war, I could live a relatively normal life.

However, soon afterwards, there appeared signs on the telephone poles addressed to persons of Japanese ancestry—that we were to register, assemble and be prepared for removal to "relocation centers." Newspapers, especially the Hearst Press, and politicians lead the charge—that all Japanese were traitors; they were dangerous to the war effort so they should be locked up and shipped to Japan. We were inundated by rumors, ranging from benign treatment by the authorities to permanent incarceration. It was an introduction to the next several years of my life, since rumors were an integral part of my wartime experience.

The FBI came and took my father away; it was a mixed blessing, since, while it gave him the status of being acknowledged as a community leader by the government, it meant he had to leave his family under crisis conditions. We were not to see him for several years; he never talked about his experiences in his camp, which I believe was in Bismarck, North Dakota. One irony was that since it was an "official" camp, under the Geneva Convention for prisoners of war, so that their food and treatment was better than what we were to experience.

Our worst fears were realized—that all of us, whether citizens or aliens were to be incarcerated. Disorganization was the order of the day. My mother, who had seldom been outside of the home, was left in charge and she panicked. She was sure that we were going to be taken out and shot, so she was prepared to die. (I should add that at the time of this writing she has reached her 102nd birthday.) We heard a variety of rumors. One was that that we were going to be shipped to Japan and traded for American prisoners of war; another more optimistic one was that once the United States realized that it had made a mistake, the evacuation orders would be rescinded. We lived by rumors, primarily because the government provided very little information. Perhaps they didn't know what to do with us, or, more likely, they kept secrets in the name of national security.

My family, and all others of Japanese ancestry, were ordered to close our homes, either sell or store our furniture and other valuables, pack what we could carry and assemble at designated sites. Although my past experiences had shaken my faith in my American identity, the forced evacuation lead to even more doubts about who I was. I still believed that I was an American; I belonged to the ROTC band at Galileo and played "The Stars and Stripes Forever," marched behind the flag, and had little identification with Japan. However, it was clear that my ancestry was viewed with suspicion, and that my government saw me, my family, and members of my community as enemies, or in simple terms, we were all "Japs."

To add to my discomfort, the initial assembly place was on Van Ness Avenue, just a few blocks from my high school. I tried to hide my face from the students who were walking by; several came to express their sympathy, but others came at us making airplane-like noises in order "to kill the Japs." An important-looking white man with a clip sheet began calling out family names to board the buses that were to take us to the train station. His pronunciation of Japanese surnames could be termed "state of the art," and perhaps would have come as a source of comic relief if the occasion were not so serious.

Life in a Concentration Camp

It is hard to recapture my feelings of being herded into railroad cars, drawing the shades, and seeing armed soldiers at every entrance, especially since over half of the "prisoners" were women and children. We didn't know where we were going, how long the ride would be, and what was at the end of the journey. The most vivid remembrance was that of crying children, confused parents, and the hot, stuffy car.

We quickly adapted to camp norms. We formed youth groups, a euphemism for gangs, and I belonged to the San Francisco gang. There were already established gangs from various parts of Los Angeles, so that the primary identification for adolescents was through groups from their former area of residence. The change for me was that instead of identification with the family, my primary identification was with my group. Food was one of the highest priorities; my gang quickly learned that if we gulped down our food, we could run to another mess hall and eat another meal. Not that the food was of gourmet quality; we quickly labelled it "slop suey," but for a growing teenager, a full stomach meant a degree of contentment. My adaptation was to "monku"; that is to develop griping to an art. There was plenty to gripe about—the food, the smelly horse stalls, the bedding, standing in line, and most important, the lack of freedom, and facing an uncertain future. My group argued constantly, even picking on whether jeans with a red tag (Levis) were superior to those without a tag.

Santa Anita represented a growing away from the family. Almost every waking moment was spent with my peers; we got up, washed, ate, went to the bathroom, played, and argued together. The small, crowded barracks were for sleeping only, so that the influence of the family became minimal. My primary identification was with the San Francisco group; we met other peers through their group identification such as those from San Diego, Hawthorne, San Pedro, San Jose, and the numerous gangs from Los Angeles. I heard of a few fights between gangs, but my San Francisco group was known to be relatively peaceful, so that we stayed out of any serious conflict.

Looking back, I marvel at the ability of the Japanese to organize a coherent community under concentration camp conditions. There were about 20,000 of us, hemmed in by barbed wire; Santa Anita was to be only temporary until more permanent inland camps were developed; we came from different parts of California and yet, the community was able to offer a semblance of coherent life. I don't know who provided the organizational impetus, but there were softball and basketball leagues, dances, talent shows, and other activities that kept our mind off living behind armed wire. There were some riots and some beatings, but Santa Anita was remarkably peaceful, given the unusual circumstances.

Camp life exposed me to a wide variety of identities. I met those with strong Japanese identities—so strong that they were convinced that Japan would win the war. They advised me to prepare myself for the future by learning the Japanese language, its values and its culture. One can't miss the irony of that advice—knowledge of Japan is extremely valuable today, but not because they were victorious in World War II. Then there were others who were 150 percent American, who said that it was our patriotic duty to cooperate with the United States Government in order to win the war over fascist Japan, Germany, and Italy.

I vacillated in my identity, most often leaning towards an American identity. But I found it hard to answer the question, "If you say that you're an American, why are you in the camp with the rest of us?" My only weak rejoinder was that there were imperfections in any system.

Although life in Santa Anita was short, from April to October, 1942, I had established some roots there. Even though it was temporary, there was an attempt to start a school, but since it was not mandatory and there was little organization, I did not attend school. Instead I roamed around and played most of the day, made friends from other parts of California, and began to have an interest in girls. The news that we were to be separated and sent to different permanent camps was met with tears and frustration. We were again to be pawns of governmental decisions; the feeling of being utterly powerless reinforced the cynicism that was a strong part of camp philosophy.

The move was to Topaz, a permanent camp set up in the middle of the desert in Utah. Here I got the feeling of being a real prisoner; at Santa Anita, one could see cars moving along the outside streets and some residents even had friends who would wave to them. But Topaz was in the middle of nothing, and the perimeters were sealed with barbed wire fences, guard towers, and armed soldiers. I lived in Topaz from 1942 to 1945 and graduated from high school there.

The relative shortness of the war meant that much of what I learned in camp was not internalized and permanently incorporated into my lifestyle. Nevertheless, many of the former residents still remember the feeling of being totally unwanted by the host society, and the hard struggle to re-establish themselves, once the camps were closed in 1946.

Release from Camp

There was a procedure that with governmental clearance we were free to relocate anywhere in the United States aside from the barred zones along the Pacific Coast. After graduating from high school in 1945, and talking over the decision with the remnants of my family (three of my sisters and my older brother had already left camp), I decided to apply for my leave. Armed with something like fifty dollars, a high school diploma, a one-way train ticket, and with fear and anxiety, I left my "home" with a vague idea that I would go to Milwaukee. There was no logical reason why I chose this city; I had no relatives, friends, or acquaintances there, although I could probably say the same of wherever I chose to go. I sometimes wonder if I would have the courage to make a similar move today, leaving a relatively safe "home" for an unknown, but probably very hostile society. But I was young, ignorant, and still believed in America.

I was extremely self-conscious when I boarded the train at Delta, Utah; I had not faced the outside world for over three years and the crowded train was filled with soldiers, sailors, and marines. I expected at any time to be spotted as a "Jap"; much to my surprise, I was totally ignored and even offered a seat. Everyone was more interested in their companions; some were even making love, which was a shock to one who had spent the last several years in a strict environment.

The War Relocation Authority (WRA) had set up an employment office in Milwaukee, and they referred me to a farmer whose specialty was erecting silos. Aside from disliking heights and hard physical labor, the job was mine for a short time. One of the things that I brought with me to camp was an old trombone, and I played in a number of dance bands that were organized in both Santa Anita and Topaz. I decided to try my hand at being a professional musician; I answered an ad in *Downbeat*, a magazine for musicians, and found myself traveling to Worthington, Minnesota to play in the Tiny Little orchestra. I was hired sight unseen, and given my two-weeks notice (fired), the minute I was seen. The manager was nice enough to refer me to a new band that was being formed in Austin, and so I began my career as one of the few musicians of "oriental" extraction playing in what is known as the Midwest territory. I had changed my name to Harry Lee and identified myself as of Chinese extraction, from San Francisco. Aside from some skeptics who could not understand why one would leave California to play through a Minnesota winter, no one raised any questions about my identity, although I always feared that I would be discovered. Occasionally some dancer would pull his eyes to achieve a slant, and mouth the word "Jap," but such displays were few and far between.

In one band, I was told that I was hired to replace a black musician; the musician was much more talented than what I could ever be (Oscar Pettiford, who later played for Duke Ellington and is one of the foremost jazz bassists), and I realized there was a pariah group even more the target of prejudice and discrimination than mine. There were also heated discussions about Jewish musicians; one trumpet player decided that Harry James was no longer his idol because he was Jewish. I suspect that if I had not been around, Asians would also have been the target of snide remarks. Nevertheless, I realized that there were also other groups that were not accepted. I strove very hard to belong, so that I dressed, talked, walked, acculturated, and identified as a jazz musician with a Chinese surname.

Berkeley

I returned to California to attend the University of California in 1946 and received my B.A., M.S.W., and my Ph.D. in 1958. Meanwhile, I continued as a part-time musician. On applying for membership in the San Francisco Musician's Union, I was faced with a dilemma. There was a white union, I believe it was Local 6, and a Black union, Local 669. I had a choice; I joined Local 6 but played primarily in black bands.

One incident stands out in my mind. I played for an all black band that had a "gig" in Redding, in Central California. On the way, we stopped for something to eat. Imagine my surprise when they turned to me and said, "Lee, could you find out if they'll serve us?" Here I was with a group of talented musicians acting as their spokesperson, even though I had been recently released from a concentration camp. I think that the restaurant sold us sandwiches "to go."

Academic Experiences

I regret being a quiet, nonaggressive student during my years at the University of California at Berkeley. I stuck around mostly with fellow ethnics and did not participate in campus life. It was the post World War II era where all-white fraternities and sororities ruled campus social life, and Asian Americans were viewed as outsiders. As a consequence, I felt that my role was to remain in the background and to be anonymous, even to professors. I was satisfied to sit and listen, and to not raise any questions. It was only after I graduated with my Ph.D. that I felt that I had not taken full advantage of the opportunities that were available on the campus at Berkeley.

I was trained primarily as a psychologist, with a major interest in Social Psychology. In a course in Clinical Psychology, we were to write our own psychological histories; I don't remember the details, but I know that I wrote about myself without once mentioning my years in a concentration camp. I thought that it would not be of interest to the professor, although by that time I was also acquainted with such terms as repression and shame.

Employment

There were two jobs, prior to my appointment to the University of California, Los Angeles in 1958, that were important influences on my way of thinking. One was as a caseworker at the International Institute in San Francisco where the emphasis was on working with immigrant groups and helping them adapt to the American society. My major task was to work with a variety of Asian immigrants, wherein I developed a detailed knowledge of the kinds of problems that were associated with moving, with old country values and experiences, to a new country. The problems of the immigrants' children, the second generation, were especially interesting, since I had also gone through these conflicts in my own upbringing.

I also worked as a therapist in the Child Guidance Clinic of the San Francisco Schools. Here I was exposed to psychoanalytic thinking; we were supervised by consulting psychiatrists with a heavy psychoanalytic orientation. My clientele was minority children who were acting out. Although I would have preferred to work with Asian American children, almost none were referred to the Clinic. While it was exciting to deal with some of the intricacies of psychoanalytic thinking, concepts such as discrimination and racism were seldom given high priority in our psychiatric conferences. It was difficult for me to believe that insight gained through verbal interaction would lead to a significant change in the behavior of my child clients.

Sociological input and sociological thinking came primarily after my employment at UCLA. While conducting research on Japanese American Crime and Deliquency, I worked closely with sociologists and their perspectives opened up newer ways of thinking for me. I received a joint appointment in sociology and taught courses on ethnic groups and race relations. The most influential sociologist for me was Milton Gordon. His view of acculturation in his book, *Assimilation in American Life* was extremely helpful in providing an organizational framework to my knowledge of my ethnic group. The idea of hyphenated Americans, the different stages in acculturation, the effects of discrimination and prejudice, and the role of structural variables went far beyond the social psychological and psychoanalytic models that were a part of my early training.

In 1969 I published *Japanese Americans*—a difficult book to write since it was the first book about my ethnic group after World War II and I had to cover material from many disciplines, history, economics, psychology, anthropology, sociology, psychiatry to name a few, and yet provide a coherent account of the experiences of an ethnic group. I used a sociological perspective to provide the basic framework, while my own life experiences were used to illustrate and add flesh to the frame.

The reaction to the book was very positive. I was especially pleased that members of my ethnic group reacted so well. Many called or wrote, with comments such as for the first time they began to understand something about their parents, themselves, and the Japanese American culture. It provided the impetus for lectures throughout the United States. The book was also translated into Japanese, so that on visits to Japan, I enjoyed a degree of celebrity status.

Experiences Abroad

There were a number of teaching and research experiences abroad which were helpful in clarifying my ethnic identity. While serving as the Director of the University of California Tokyo Study Center at the International Christian University in the early 1970s, I quickly discovered that I was more American than Japanese. I was different from my Japanese colleagues, and walked, talked, dressed, and behaved more as an American than a Japanese. Conversely, while spending a summer at the University of Bristol in 1979 it was difficult to escape from my ancestral heritage. Questions about Japan were more common than questions regarding Los Angeles. The category of Japanese Americans was not readily understood and as a consequence, my identity as a Japanese, rather than as an American, was reinforced.

Domination

My past experiences have lead me to develop my Domination Model in order to explain race relations. I tried to make sense of what had happened to the Japanese Americans, and whether such an incident could happen again in a democratic society.[1] The dominant group (D) has the power to erect barriers which limits the ability of the dominated group (d) to participate equally in the host society. The primary actions are prejudice, discrimination, and segregation, through such mechanisms as stereotypes, laws, and norms which result in the dominated group being avoided, placed at a competitive disadvantage, and isolated. These are the shaping factors, and the more severe actions, such as concentration camps, expulsion, and extermination can best be explained when these prior actions have been in place. The more severe acts can occur when the host society perceives a crisis—that its very existence will be in danger unless more drastic steps are instituted. The Japanese attack on Pearl Harbor and World War II were seen as such "triggers" on those of Japanese ancestry residing in America.

Once a group is incarcerated, there is always the danger of expulsion, exile, and extermination. Some Japanese Americans were deported to Japan; there was talk of using the internees as guinea pigs for "experiments," such as lowering caloric requirements and separating the sexes so that there would be no more "Jap bastards." Fortunately, more sane and humane forces prevailed.

There is also stratification in the lower part of the system (small d). I experienced these differences—that specific dominated groups are less acceptable than others. These are the conditions that lead to "middleman minorities,"[2] and model minorities.[3]

I suspect that if I were to write on my gravestone today, my epitaph would simply say, "a Japanese American who served as a Professor of Social Welfare and Sociology at UCLA." While changes in the dominant society have allowed a shift in what Ogawa (1971) calls From "Japs" to Japanese,[4] I also realize that it is my education that has enabled me to be comfortable with all of my identities—as a Japanese American, a college professor, a member of UCLA, a Los Angeleno, and a Californian. I have lived in Japan, Great Britain, and Hawaii and have retained all of my above identities.

Notes

1   Harry H.L. Kitano. 1991. *Race Relations*. Engelwood Cliffs, New Jersey: Prentice Hall.

2   Harry H.L. Kitano. 1974. "Japanese Americans: The Development of a Middleman Minority," *Pacific Historical Review*, November, XLIII, 4, 500–519.

3   Stanley Sue and Harry H.L. Kitano. 1973. "The Model Minorities." *Journal of Social Issues*, 29, 2, 1–10.

4   Dennis Ogawa. 1971. *From Japs to Japanese*. Berkeley: McCutchan Publishing.

11

Jews in the U.S.
The Rising Costs of Whiteness
Melanie Kaye/Kantrowitz

Before America No One Was White

In 1990 I had returned to New York City to do antiracist work with other Jews, when a friend sent me an essay by James Baldwin. "No one was white before he/she came to America," Baldwin had written:

> It took generations, and a vast amount of coercion, before this became a white country. . . . It is probable that it is the Jewish community—or more accurately, perhaps, its remnants—that in America has paid the highest and most extraordinary price for becoming white. For the Jews came here from countries where they were not white, and they came here in part because they were not white; and incontestably—in the eyes of the Black American (and not only in those eyes) American Jews have opted to become white. . . . [1]

Everything I think about Jews, whiteness, racism, and contemporary U.S. society begins with this passage. What does it mean: *Jews opted to become white.* Did we opt? Did it work? Was it an illusion? Could we have opted otherwise? Can we still?

Rachel Rubin, a college student who's been interning at Jews for Racial and Economic Justice, where I'm the director, casually mentions: when she was eight, a cross was burned on her lawn in Athens, Georgia. I remember the house I moved into Down East Maine in 1979. On the bedroom door someone had painted a swastika in what looked like blood. I think about any cross-country drive I've ever taken, radio droning hymn after Christian hymn, 2000 miles of heartland.

On the other hand, I remember the last time I was stopped by cops. It was in San Francisco. I was getting a ride home after a conference on Jews and multiculturalism. In the car with me were two other white Jews. My heart flew into my throat, as always, but they took a quick look at the three of us and waved us on—*We're looking for a car like this, sorry.* I remember all the stories I've heard from friends, people of color, in which a quick look is not followed by a friendly wave and an apology. Some of these stories are about life and death.

Liberals and even progressives kneejerk to simplistic racial—black/white—terms, evade the continuing significance of race, and confound it with class.[2] Race becomes an increasingly complex muddle.[3] Growing numbers of bi- and multiracial children. *Hispanic*—not a racial identity, but a cultural/linguistic category, conflating Spain with its former colonies. No one was *Asian* before they came to America either; the term masks cultures diverse and polychromatic as anything Europe has to offer; yet *Asian American* has emerged as a critical and powerful identity. In the academy, obligatory nods to issues of race/class/gender result in language so specialized it's incomprehensible to most people, including those most pressured by these biases, and students tell me "when Jews are mentioned in class, there's an awkward silence."[4]

Where is *Jewish* in the race/class/gender grid? Does it belong? Is it irrelevant? Where do those crosses and swastikas fit in?

Race or Religion?

"Race or religion?" is how the question is usually posed, as though this doublet exhausts the possibilities. Christians—religiously observant or not—usually operate from the common self-definition of Christianity, a religion any individual can embrace through belief, detached from race, peoplehood, and culture.[5]

But I have come to understand this detachment as false. Do white Christians feel kinship with African American Christians? White slaveowners, for example, with their slaves? White Klansmen with their black neighbors? Do white Christians feel akin to Christians converted by colonialists all over the globe? Doesn't Christianity really, for most white Christians, imply *white*? And for those white Christians, does *white* really include *Jewish*? Think of the massive Christian evasion of a simple fact: Jesus Christ was not, was never, a Christian. He was a Jew. What did he look like, Jesus of Nazareth, 2000 years ago? Blond, blue-eyed?

Of course Jewish is not a race,[6] for Jews come in all races. Though white-identified Jews may skirt the issue, Jews are a multiracial people. There are Ethiopian, Indian, Chinese Jews. And there are people of every race who choose Judaism, were adopted, or born into it from mixed parents. The dominant conception of "Jewish"—European, Yiddish-speaking—is in fact a subset, Ashkenazi. Estimated at 85-97% of Jews in the U.S. today, Ashkenazi Jews are those whose religious practice and diaspora path can be traced through Germany.[7] The huge wave of Jewish immigration from Eastern Europe was Ashkenazi (as was the earlier, much smaller, highly assimilated community of German Jews, who looked with dread upon the arrival of—from their perspective—an impoverished, Yiddish-babbling, superstitious horde). Ashkenazi Jews also migrated to the far points of the globe—to South America, Australia, Africa, Asia. They may be very fair or very dark.

Sephardic Jews are those whose mother tongue is/was Ladino (Judeo-Español) and whose religious practice and diaspora path can be traced at some point through the Iberian Peninsula (Spain and Portugal), where they flourished, unghettoized, contributing along with Muslims to Spanish culture, until the Inquisition (read, *torture*) forced conversion or expulsion from Spain of all non-Christians. Sephardim migrated to, and lived for generations and even centuries, in Holland, Germany, Italy, France, Greece, the Middle East, and the Americas. The first Jews in the New World were Sephardim: 1492 marks not only Columbus's voyage but also the expulsion of the Jews from Spain. Some Sephardi consider themselves the aristocrats of the Jews, and look with contempt upon the Ashkenazi history of ghettoization and persecution. They may also be quite fair or quite dark.

Mizrachi Jews are those who lived in the Arab world and Turkey (basically, what was once the Ottoman Empire), as minorities in Muslim rather than Christian culture. Their mother tongue often is/was Judeo-Arabic. *Mizrachi* means "Eastern," commonly translated as "Oriental," and is used by and about Israelis, often interchangeably with *Sephardi.* Spanish Sephardim sometimes resent the blurring of distinctions between themselves and Mizrachim, reacting with pride in their history and with Eurocentric bias against non-Europeans, referring to themselves as "true" or "pure" Sephardim.[8] The confusion between the categories is only partly due to Ashkenazi ignorance/arrogance, lumping all non-Ashkenazi together. Partly it's the result of Jewish history: some Jews never left the Middle East, and some returned after the expulsion from Spain, including to Palestine. Some kept Ladino, some did not. I imagine there was intermarriage. Mizrachim, though they may also range from fair to dark, are usually defined as people of color.

The point is, categories of white and color don't correspond neatly to Jewish reality. (What does correspond is Ashkenazi cultural hegemony: in the U.S., where they are dominant by numbers, and in Israel, where Sephardi/Mizrachi Jews make up about two-thirds of the Jewish population and strongly contest this hegemony.) Jewish wanderings have created a people whose experience eludes conventional categories of race, nationality, ethnicity, geography, language— even religion. Cataclysm and assimilation have depleted our store of common knowledge.

No, Jews are not a single race. Yet there is confusion here, and subtext. Confusion because we have so often been racialized, hated *as if* we were a race. Ethnic studies scholars have labored to document the process of racialization, the fact that race is not biological, but a socio-historically specific phenomenon. Observing Jewish history, Nancy Ordover has noted, offers an opportunity to break down this process of racialization, because by leaving Europe, Jews "changed" our "race," even as our skin pigment remained the same.[9]

> For the Jews came here from countries where they were not white, and they came here in part because they were not white. . . .

Confusion, too, because to say someone *looks Jewish* is to say something both absurd (Jews look a million different ways) and commonsense communicative.

When I was growing up in Flatbush (in Brooklyn, NY), every girl with a certain kind of nose— sometimes named explicitly as a Jewish nose, sometimes only as "too big"—wanted a nose job, and if her parents could pay for it, often she got one. I want to be graphic about the euphemism "nose job." A nose job breaks the nose, bruises the face and eye area like a grotesque beating. It hurts. It takes weeks to heal.

What was wrong with the original nose, the Jewish one? Noses were discussed ardently in Flatbush, this or that friend looking forward to her day of transformation.[10] My aunts lavished on me the following exquisite praise: *look at her, a nose like a shiksa* (gentile woman). This hurt my feelings. Before I knew what a *shiksa* was, I knew I wasn't it, and, with that fabulous integrity of children, I wanted to look like who I was. But later I learned my nose's value, and would tell gentiles this story so they'd notice my nose.

A Jewish nose, I conclude, identifies its owner as a Jew. Nose jobs are performed so that a Jewish woman does not look like a Jew.

Tell me again Jewish is just a religion.

Yet Nazi racial definitions have an "only a religion" response. Even earlier, the lure of emancipation (in Europe) and assimilation (in the U.S.) led Jews to define Judaism as narrowly as possible, as religion only: "a Jew at home, a man in the streets,"[11] a private matter, taken care of behind closed doors, like bathing.

Judaism, the religion, does provide continuity and connection to Jews around the globe. There is something powerful even for atheists about entering a synagogue across the continent or the ocean, and hearing the familiar service.[12]

But to be a Jew, one need not follow religious practice; one need not believe in god—not even to become a rabbi, an element of Judaism of which I am especially fond.[13] Religion is only one strand of being Jewish. It is ironic that it is precisely this century's depletion of Jews and of Jewish identity, with profound linguistic and cultural losses—continuing as Yiddish[14] and Ladino speakers age and die—that makes imaginable a Jewishness that is *only a religion*—only now, when so much else has been lost. But to reduce *Jewishness* to *Judaism* is to forget the complex indivisible swirl of religion/culture/language/history that *was* Jewishness until, in the 18th century, Emancipation began to offer some Jews the possibility of escaping from a linguistically/culturally/economically isolated ghetto into the European "Enlightenment." To equate Jewishness with religion is to forget how even the contemporary, often attenuated version of this Jewish cultural swirl is passed down *in the family*, almost like genetic code.

Confusion and subtext. *Jewish* is often trivialized as something you choose, a preference, like tea over coffee. In contrast with visible racial identity, presumptions of choice—as with gayness—are seen as minimizing one's claim to attention, sympathy, and remedy. As a counter to bigotry, *I was born like this* strategically asserts a kind of victim-status, modeled on race, gender, and disability: if you can't help yourself, maybe you're entitled to some help from others. . . .

What happens if, instead, I assert my right to choose and not suffer for it. To say, *I choose:* my lesbianism and my Jewishness.[15] Choose to come out, be visible, embrace both. I could live loveless or sexless or in the closet. I could have kept the name *Kaye,* and never once at Christmas—in response to the interminable "what are you doing for . . . ? have you finished your shopping?"—never once answer, "I don't celebrate Christmas. I'm a Jew." I could lie about my lover's gender. I could wear skirts uncomfortably. I could bleach my hair again, as I did when I was fifteen. I could monitor my speech, weeding out the offensive accent, as I was taught at City College, along with all the other first and second generation immigrants' children in the four speech classes required for graduation, to teach us not to sound like ourselves. I could remain silent when queer or anti-Semitic jokes are told, when someone says "you know how *they* are." I could endure the pain in the gut, the hot shame. I could scrunch up much, much smaller.

In the U.S., *Christian,* like *white,* is an unmarked category in need of marking.[16] Christianness, a majority, dominant culture, is not only about religious practice and belief, any more than Jewishness is. As *racism* names the system that normalizes, honors and rewards whiteness, we need a word for what normalizes, honors and rewards Christianity. Jews designate the assumption of Christianity-as-norm, the erasure of Jews, as "anti-Semitic." In fact, the erasure and marginalization of non-Christians is not just denigrating to Jews. We need a catchier term than *Christian hegemony,* to help make visible the cultural war against all non-Christians.

Christianism? Awkward, stark, and kind of crude—maybe a sign that something's being pushed. *Sexism* once sounded stark and kind of crude. Such a term would help contextualize Jewish experience as an experience of marginality shared with other non-Christians. Especially in this time of rising Christian fundamentalism, as school prayer attracts support from "moderates," this contextualization is critical for progressive Jews, compelling us to seek allies among Muslims and other religious minorities.

I also want to contextualize Jews in a theoretical framework outside the usual bipolar frame of black/white—to go beyond dualism; to distinguish race from class, and both from culture; to understand "whiteness" as the gleaming conferral of normality, success, even survival; to acknowledge who owns what in whose neighborhood; to witness how money does and does not "whiten."

> For in the eyes of the Black American (and not only in those eyes) American Jews have opted to become white. . . .

To begin to break out of a polarity that has no place for Jews, I survey the range of color in the U.S. People of color, a unity sought and sometimes forged, include a vast diversity of culture and history, forms of oppression and persecution. Contemporary white supremacists hate them all, but define some as shrewd,[17] evil, inscrutable, sexually exotic, and perverse, and others as intellectually inferior, immoral, bestial, violent, and sexually rapacious. If it is possible to generalize, we can say that the peoples defined as shrewd and evil tend to be better off economically—or at least perceived as better off economically—than those defined as inferior and violent, who tend to remain in large numbers stuck at the bottom of the economic ladder (and are assumed by the dominant culture, to be stuck there), denied access to decent jobs and opportunities, systematically disadvantaged and excluded by the educational system.

In other words, among the creeping fearsome dark ones are, on one hand, those who exploit, cheat, and hoard money they don't deserve, and, on the other, those (usually darker) who, not having money, threaten to rob and pillage hard-working tax-paying white Christians. In this construct, welfare fits as a form of robbery, the women's form; the men are busy mugging. Immigrant-bashing—whether street violence or political movements like "English-only" and California's overwhelming passage of Proposition 187—becomes a "natural" response to "robbery."

It is easier now to see where Jews fit: we are so good with money. Our "darkness" may not show, and this ability to pass confers protection and a host of privileges. But we are the model money-grubbing money-hoarding scapegoats for an increasingly punitive economic system. Jews, Japanese, Koreans, Arabs, Indians, and Pakistanis—let's face it: *interlopers* are blamed for economic disaster; for controlling the economy or making money on the backs of the poor; for raising the price of oil; for stealing or eliminating jobs by importing goods or exporting production.

At the same time, those defined as inferior and violent are blamed for urban crime and chaos, for drugs, for the skyrocketing costs and failures of social programs. This blame then justifies the oppression and impoverishment of those brought here in chains and the peoples indigenous to this continent. Add in the darker, poorer immigrants from Latin America and the Caribbean, and recent immigrants from China and Southeast Asia. Media codes like "inner-city crime" and "teen gangs" distort and condense a vast canvas of poverty, vulnerability, and exploitation into an echoing story of some young men's violent response to these conditions. Thus those who are significantly endangered come to be defined as inherently dangerous.

That is, one group is blamed for capitalism's crimes; the other for capitalism's fallout. Do I need to point out who escapes all blame?

When a community is scapegoated, members of that community are most conscious of how they feel humiliated, alienated, and endangered. But the other function of scapegoating is at least as pernicious. It is to protect the problem which scapegoats are drafted to conceal: the vicious system of profit and exploitation, of plenty and scarcity existing side by side.

The Cost of Whiteness

Aryan ideology aside, Jews are often defined as white, though this wipes out the many Jews who are by anyone's definition people of color, and neglects the role of context: many Jews who look white in New York City look quite the opposite in the South and Midwest. Radicals often exclude the category *Jewish* from discussion, or subsume us into *white*, unless we are by *their* definition also people of color, in which case they subsume us as *people of color.*

The truth is, Jews complicate things. *Jewish* is both a distinct category and an overlapping one. Just as homophobia is distinct from sexism yet has everything to do with sexism, anti-Semitism in this country is distinct from racism yet has everything to do with racism. It's not that a Jew like myself should "count" as a person of color, though I think sometimes Jews do argue this because the alternative seems to be erasure. But that means we need another alternative. The problem is a polarization of white and color that excludes us. We need a more complex vision of the structure of racism, one that attends to the sick logic of white supremacists. We need a more complex understanding of the process of "whitening."

It is probable that it is the Jewish community—or more accurately, perhaps, its remnants—that in America has paid the highest and more extraordinary price for becoming white.

Every time I read this passage, at the word "remnants," my hand moves to the hollow at the base of my throat, to help me breathe. *Remnants.*

What have we paid?

How many of us speak or read Yiddish or Ladino or Hebrew? How many of us have studied Jewish history or literature, recognize the terms that describe Jewish experience, are familiar with the Jewish calendar, can sing more than three or four Jewish songs, know *something* beyond matzoh balls or stuffed grape leaves? Many of us—especially secular Jews, but also those raised in some suburban synagogues where spirituality took a back seat to capital construction, where Jewish pride seemed like another name for elitism—many of us have lost our culture, our sense of community. Only anti-Semitism reminds us who we are, and we have nothing to fight back with—no pride and no knowledge—only a feeble, embarrassed sense that hatred and bigotry are wrong. I have even heard Jews, especially, "progressives," justify anti-Semitism: maybe we really are "like that," rich and greedy, taking over, too loud, too pushy, snatching up more than our share, ugly and parasitical, Jewish American Princesses, Jewish landlords, Jewish bosses, emphasis on *Jewish.* Maybe we really deserve to be hated. Thus Auguste Bebel, perspicacious, prophetic nineteenth century socialist named anti-Semitism *the socialism of fools.*

Do we even know the history of which we, Jewish radicals, are a part? As Trotsky's master biographer Isaac Deutscher explained "the non-Jewish Jew" to the World Jewish Congress in 1958:

> *The Jewish heretic who transcends Jewry belongs to a Jewish tradition. . . . Spinoza, Heine, Marx, Rosa Luxemburg, Trotsky, and Freud. . . all went beyond the boundaries of Jewry. They all found Jewry too narrow, too archaic, and too constricting. . . . Yet I think that in some ways they were very Jewish indeed. . . . as Jews they dwelt on the borderlines of various civilizations, religions, and national cultures.*[18]

Raised Orthodox, steeped in the tradition he rebelled against, Deutscher could grasp the "Jewishness" of his rebellion.[19] But typical "non-Jewish Jews" today, lacking Deutscher's knowledge of Jewish tradition, fail to see ourselves as acting within this tradition. We have even permitted the Jewish right to claim the term *Jewish radical.*

It is frustrating that those Jews best equipped to grasp what it means to choose *not to be white*—not to blend, pass, or mute one's differences—are the Hasidim (ultra-orthodox).[20] But because they are also separatist, and by ideology and theology do not value encounters with diversity, the Hasidim have rarely forged alliances around diversity and against bigotry. Instead, they tend to protect their individual communities and to blame urban chaos on their neighbors, often people of color, with law-and-order rhetoric and actions both racist and quintessentially American.[21]

The response of other Jews toward the Hasidim is instructive. Embarrassment, exposure, shame, rage; *why do they have to be so blatant?*—including *so blatantly Jewish* and *so blatantly racist*—as opposed to the discreet liberal norm of moving out of the neighborhood or sending the kids to private schools faintly integrated by race but starkly segregated by class. And somewhere, for Jews who care about Jewish identity, the Hasidim also represent a kind of courage: they dare to walk around looking Jewish.

Progressive Jews need to reconstruct an authentically American progressive Jewish identity, choosing from the vast storehouse of history/culture/religion which pieces we want to reclaim, which will enable us to be out as Jews with our own brand of Jewish courage. It's not that most Jews in the U.S. will endure the same unsheddable visual vulnerability as most people of color, though buttons and t-shirts, the *kipah* (skullcap worn by observant men)) and the *magen david* (Star of David—"Jewish star") may draw us into street visibility. But Jews, like all other people, make political choices. With whose interests will we identify and stake our future? With the dominant and privileged few—white, Christian, and rich, ensuring that poverty remains part of the American landscape, leaving bigotry unchallenged, to feed on the local minority of choice?

In 1993 a fabulous mix of some fifteen hundred people—all ages, all colors—attended a New York City conference on fighting racism. I had been invited to speak as a lesbian and a Jew on a panel about the relationship of identity to politics. To illustrate how identity can be used to divide or unite us, I focused first on my lesbian "side." I explained briefly why some queers might be reluctant to identify themselves publicly, due to fear of homophobia. And then I asked all those who self-defined as lesbian, gay, or bisexual, and were willing to identify themselves, to stand. A lot of people stood, and they looked around proudly, surveying the numbers of queers committed to fight racism. And then everyone, standing and seated, applauded.

Then I repeated the process with my Jewish "side." I explained briefly why some Jews might be reluctant to identify themselves publicly—whether because they feared anti-Semitism, or didn't feel connected to Jews (as in, *my parents are Jewish but I'm not*). Then I asked all those who self-defined as Jews, and were willing to identify themselves, to stand.

The rhythm was quite different. A few people popped right up, and then I could feel the tension, could see people looking around, and a few more stood. And more. And more. By the time the Jews finished standing up, practically every white person in the room was on her or his feet. Then came applause, scattered and nervous.

Instead of taking pride in the number of Jews committed to fight racism; instead of absorbing the plain fact that with a few exceptions Jews *were* the antiracist whites in New York City (New York has a huge Jewish community, but Jews are still a minority of New York's whites); instead of asking *why* so many Jews see the fight against racism as essential—there was fear. Classic Jewish fear of visibility. Fear we'd be seen by our antiracist comrades as too many, too powerful. Indeed, I did not hear our comrades in the audience celebrate our strength.

And how, one might ask, are we to fight as hard as we can if we fear our strength? Many Jews who work against racism and on various progressive issues do this work as progressives, as women, as workers, as queers, as whites, as people of color. We are invisible *as Jews*, while Jewish political conservatives are highly visible. We relinquish to the Jewish right wing the claim to represent the Jewish community, though the sheer number of Jews involved with progressive politics is stunning. We abandon Jewish culture to the religious orthodox: we think they are the "real Jews" and we are not. We neglect the powerful tradition of Jewish radicalism, a potential source of instruction, inspiration, and courage. Committed as progressives to the survival of people's culture, we stand, unseeing and uncaring, at the edge of a chasm opened by assimilation and infinitely deepened by the Holocaust. We facilitate the dwindling of the Jewish community—*to remnants.*

Is It Coming Again?

How can I concern myself with progressive coalitions and alliances when everyone—including progressives—hates Jews? When I speak in the Jewish community, people say this to me all the time. And they have a point. Look at the July 1994 bombing of the Jewish Community Center in Buenos Aires. The center had housed libraries, cemetery records, archives of 100 years of Yiddish theater, Yiddish newspapers, services of all kinds. Among the 95 killed, the hundreds wounded, were workers at the Center, students doing research in the library, and poor people in need of the services dispensed on Mondays, when the bombing took place. One of the oldest Jewish communities in South America was devastated.

I show up for a memorial service at a large synagogue on New York City's East Side, where I learn most of what I've just recounted (mainstream media do not report the destruction of archives, or Yiddish culture, or note the range of services provided by a Jewish community center). The crowd is older, well-dressed, many whose accents, language, or conversation mark them as refugees from Nazi Europe, or Argentineans with family in Buenos Aires. Rudy Giuliani, New Yor City's rightist neo-fascist mayor, stands at the *bima*. He says "we"—meaning him and the Jews. A chain of male *makhers* (big shots) link the bombing repeatedly to Iran, and claim the peace process as theirs—outrageously, since only a couple of years ago most of them were calling us *traitors* for working to end the occupation and protect Palestinian rights. Representatives from European governments rise to speak, including Germany, France, Austria, hardly historic friends to the Jews. Everyone repeats, like a litany, *Muslim fundamentalism, Arab terrorism, Iranian terrorism*. The World Trade Center bombing is invoked, as if that too were an attack on Jews. That anti-Semitic terror, whatever its source, is protected by Nazi and neo-Nazi strength in the Argentinean army, police, and government—this well-known fact goes unmentioned. All I can think as I leave the synagogue is the title of a poem I want to write: *If I Get Killed in an Anti-Jewish Terrorist Attack Here's What I Don't Want at My Memorial Service.*

At a recent Jews for Racial and Economic Justice meeting,[22] in a discussion which begins with the Buenos Aires bombing, we talk about how anti-Semitism is often used as a counterweight to progressive values, and how this use makes it hard to establish or sometimes even to feel solidarity with other Jews. We are often so busy reminding the mainstream Jewish community that Palestinians are killed all the time, that Gavin Cato's death was *also* a tragedy, we leave Yankel Rosenbaum and the Jews of Buenos Aires to the right wing.[23] It's as if anti-Semitism has been transformed into a right wing issue—paradoxically, since right-wing anti-Semitism is on the rise nationally and internationally; since right wing Jews periodically attack, sometimes with violence, progressive Jews.

Several people note the difference between New York City and the rest of the country; here Jews are hardly a minority, and most benefit from the privileges of white skin, while "in the Diaspora" at least one person present has been confronted with the question, *where are your horns?* Another says, "People are always asking me, *what are you?* They don't know I'm Jewish, but they know I'm *something*." Someone notes the casual New York City assumption that the main site of anti-Semitism is the African American community. We trade examples of how media bolster this assumption, headline the haters and separatists, erase the diversity of both communities, fail to report the many instances of cooperation and rapprochement.[24] Someone remarks that in the South and Northwest, Jews and people of color join to fight white supremacist groups as a matter of course. We agree that focusing on the seriousness and connectedness of right wing activity—racist, anti-Semitic, homophobic, and anti-abortion—helps us reach out to other Jews.

I am writing this at Rosh Hashonah, the Jewish New Year opening year 5755 of the Jewish calendar. We call the ten days following Rosh Hashonah *Yamim Noraim*, the Days of Awe, the most solemn time of our year, culminating in Yom Kippur, the Day of Atonement. If a Jew steps foot inside a synagogue once a year, Yom Kippur is the day. I am thinking about the danger, in this time of increased attacks on Jews, of stepping inside visibly Jewish spaces packed with Jews. At this time of heightened danger I feel intensely, paradoxically, the need to be among Jews in a Jewish space.

Elsewhere I have written, "to be a Jew is to tangle with history."[25] In the U.S. people tend to be both ahistorical and insulated from the impact of international events. From this tunnel perspective, Jews have it good. What are we worried about? And we *do* have it good. And we do worry. Jews have a history of nearly 6000 recorded years of repeated cycles of calm, then chaos: periods of relative safety and prosperity disrupted by persecution, brutal oppression, murder, and expulsion or exile for the surviving remnant to a strange land where the cycle begins again. Grace Paley reports her immigrant mother's succinct comment on Hitler's rise to power: "It's coming again."[26]

In the U.S. much of the bias against Jews has been mitigated by the development of some institutionalized Jewish power. This should be a cause for celebration. Instead it makes us nervous.

Jewish success is often used against us, as evidence of our excessive control, power, and greed, evidence which could at any moment topple us from the calm and, for many Jews, prosperous phase of the cycle into danger and chaos.[27]

Besides, Jewish success—like any other U.S. success—has been achieved inside a severe class structure, and Jews, like many other ethnic and racial minorities, have benefitted in concrete ways from racism against African Americans. Karen Sacks' brilliant investigation, "How Did Jews Become White Folks?" describes how "federal programs which were themselves designed to assist demobilized GIs and young families systematically discriminated against African Americans," and functioned as "affirmative action . . . [which] aimed at and disproportionately helped male, Euro-origin GIs."[28] Thus she convincingly explains post-World War II Jewish upward mobility.

History. In 1492 the Inquisition forced thousands of us to convert to Christianity or flee Spain and Portugal. Some of us ended up in the Americas and were forced to convert anyway. But many of us maintained our Jewishness secretly. We are called, neutrally, *conversos*, or, offensively, *marranos*—meaning, *pigs* (maybe related to taboos against eating pork).

In Northern New Mexico there are people who light candles on Friday night, they don't always know why. They don't eat pork and they don't always know why. They have names like *Rael*, which some say comes from Israel. Physically they are indistinguishable from their neighbors. But some of them know why they do certain things and they know it is dangerous to tell.

When I lived in Northern New Mexico in the early eighties I didn't know any of this, I was just hungry for Jews. My first Hanukkah in Santa Fe I made a menorah and lit the candles and said the blessing, alone but picturing Jews all over the world also lighting and blessing candles. Years later, I return to Taos for a visit. At a brunch, I meet a woman named Diana who grew up in Questa, twenty-five miles north. She tells me about the large number of Jews, more and less hidden, who live—and die—here. She indicates our host: "His mother lights candles on Fridays," she says, "he doesn't like to talk about it."

In 1993 I bring my new love to New Mexico. She is also a Jew. We drive to Questa to find the cemetery Diana told me about. We walk through the graveyard. There, among the crosses, every so often, a headstone with no cross. Many Raels. Names like Isaac, David, Sarah, Rachel, Moises, Aaron, Eli. On a few headstones we see the small stones which signify a Jew has visited a Jewish grave.

Passing. I get to choose when to disclose I'm a Jew. It doesn't show, at least not blatantly or automatically. If I need to, I can hide. Clearly, this applies to some Jews and not others, a benefit something like that "enjoyed" by the conventionally feminine-looking lesbian vis-à-vis the stone butch; or by the lighter skin, English-speaking Chicana. In other words, Jews benefit from not looking Jewish.[29] That many Jews walk safely down the streets of North America because our Jewishness is not visible is a fact, but not necessarily a comforting one. Many of us would prefer to be both visible and safe. Sometimes it's hard to find each other (why confirmed atheists like me, when we live rurally or outside large Jewish communities—join synagogues; how else would we find the Jews?). Passing/invisibility has a double edge.

Yet any time I feel whiny about passing's double edge, I picture myself in a car, any car, with a cop pulling up alongside. I think of all the times I didn't get followed around stores with someone assuming I was about to rip them off, even when I *was* about to rip them off.

I also think of my father changing his name from Kantrowitz to Kaye before I was born, pressured by the exigencies of being a Jew in the forties, even in New York. "It was easier," he'd explain, "people always called me Mr. K. anyway, they couldn't pronounce or remember it." (But when have you heard of a Gloucester, a Leicester, a McLoughlin changing his name?) When he died, in 1982, I took back Kantrowitz. I just didn't like the name going out of the world, and a certain incident weighed on me: a white gentile lesbian who knew my writing exclaimed upon meeting me, "Oh! I expected you to be tall and blond." I knew if my name were Melanie Kantrowitz, no one would ever expect me to be tall and blond.

But I have recognized in some situations exactly how I need to stiffen my spine to say (and then spell, though it is perfectly phonetic) *Kantrowitz. Kantrowitz. Kantrowitz.* And sometimes when I just don't have the *koyekh* (strength), I say *Kaye*, and feel grimly close to my dead ghetto-raised father.

To Discover Water

My father. *My father loved all things Jewish,* I wrote after he died in a poem I called *Kaddish,* which is the Jewish prayer for the dead.[30] My father who changed his name. My father *who loved the sound of Yiddish but would not speak it.* And my mother: hates bagels, hates matzoh balls, never went to *shul,* is careful to distinguish herself from *those others,* has spent her lifetime hating her nose, her Jewish nose. Yet says, repeatedly, *scratch a goy* (non-Jew) *you'll find an anti-Semite.*

My grandparents immigrated from Russia and Poland early in this century. My father, a teen-ager in Brownsville (a poor Jewish ghetto in Brooklyn) during the Depression, joined the Young Communist League; as an adult his major hero remained his friend Aaron, a communist who had spoken on street corners and died fighting in the second World War. My mother had circulated petitions against the Korean War, walking up to people on the streets of Flatbush during peak McCarthy period, and she had been spat on.

My mother often says, "When Melanie was three years old, I knew it was Melanie against the world, and I was betting on Melanie." One of her favorite stories about me dates from 1950, when my class and my older sister's had been given dog tags—issued in a Cold War frenzy to New York City schoolchildren as to soldiers—so that in the event of a bomb, our bodies could be identified. My sister, seven years old, asked what the dog tag was for, and my mother told her. I listened. And had bombs ever been dropped?, Roni asked. Imagine the discussion, my mother explaining to a seven-year-old about war, about Hiroshima and Nagasaki. The next time the 5-bell signal rang for a shelter drill and my kindergarten teacher said, "Now, children, it's only a game, remember, under your desk, head down," I, five years old, stood up and said it was not a game, it was about dropping bombs on children and our own government had dropped bombs on children and their eyes had melted and people were burned and killed. The other five-year-olds began crying and screaming, and the principal summoned my mother to school. "What are you, crazy, telling a kid things like that?" the principal is reported to have said, and my mother to have answered, "I will not lie to my children."

My mother's version of this story emphasizes my role: as class conscience and as rebel. But what delights me in the story is *her* courage: though a good student, she had dropped out of high school at fifteen and was always convinced that educated people were smarter. Yet she had the political and intellectual backbone to defend me and defy authority.

This was my Jewish upbringing, as much as the candles we lit for Hanukkah, or the seders where bread and matzoh shared the table. My father had been raised observant, my mother, not. But to us breaking religious observance was progressive, the opposite of superstitious. When we ate on Yom Kippur, it never occurred to me that this was un-Jewish. I knew I was a Jew. I knew Hitler had been evil. I knew Negroes—we said then—had been slaves and that was evil too. I knew prejudice was wrong, stupid. I knew Jews believed in freedom and justice (the screaming arguments at extended family gatherings never challenged my belief that we, the un-prejudiced, were the "real" Jews). My parents' attachment to Adlai Stevenson was such that I grew up sort of assuming he was Jewish, while a photograph of FDR hung on our living room wall, surrounded by reverence, god in modern drag. When Eisenhower-Nixon ran against Stevenson in 1952, I noticed Nixon's dark, wavy hair, like my father's, and said, "He looks like Daddy." "Nothing like him, *nothing,* how could you think such a thing," my mother snapped. She then explained in detail how Nixon got elected to congress only by redbaiting Helen Gahagan Douglas (the liberal Congresswoman). I was seven years old.

I remember my mother crying when the Rosenbergs were executed, and I was terrified, because I knew they were good people, like my parents, with children the same age as my sister and me. *Who would take care of their children?* Soon we would get our first TV, so my mother (and I) could watch the McCarthy hearings. I knew the whole fate of humanity hinged on these hearings, as surely as I knew McCarthy and his people had killed the Rosenbergs. It literally did not occur to me that real people, people I might meet, people who had children and went to work, hated the Rosenbergs or liked McCarthy. Nor did it occur to me that there were people who thought unions were bad, people who did not know you never cross a picket line, did not know prejudice was wrong and stupid. I could not even conceive of someone voting for Eisenhower: *how had he won?*

That this set of principles was Jewish never occurred to me. Around me was Flatbush, a swirling Jewish ghetto/community of first and second generation immigrants, including Holocaust survivors (though they were noted in my mind simply as the parents who brought umbrellas to school when it rained, spoke with my grandparents' accents); there were clerks, trade unionists, salespeople, plumbers, small business people, radio and TV repairmen, people like my parents (small shopkeepers) "in the middle," apartment dwellers where the kids shared a room, and fathers worked 60–70 hours a week; and people poorer than us, who lived in apartments where kitchen smells lingered on the stairs, someone slept in the living room, and summers the kids swam in underwear instead of bathing suits. There were teachers and even doctors who were rich and lived in what we called "private houses" in the outreaches of the neighborhood at the point where not everyone was Jewish.

But where I lived, everyone was, or almost. Jewish was the air I breathed, nothing I articulated, everything I took for granted.

Not-Jewish meant, for the most part, Catholic. Catholics were plentiful and scary: if you married them they would demand your children, and the pope could tell you what not to read. My high school, Erasmus Hall, the oldest and largest in the country, in theory integrated, was so severely tracked that the mostly Jews, Italians, and African Americans who attended rarely had classes together. As for WASPs, I knew they were the majority somewhere, but where? I knew *Jones* and *Smith* were someone's idea of an ordinary dime-a-dozen name, but I never met one: my idea of the commonest name on earth was *Susan Goldberg.*

I was 17 and a high school graduate before I met privileged WASPs, and that was in the Civil Rights Movement in Harlem. Before Harlem, I barely thought consciously about either whiteness or Jewishness (though I straightened my hair and performed unspeakable obscenities on my eyebrows). In Harlem the world divided up into white and black and there was no question what I was. I barely registered the large proportion of Jews among white people working in the Civil Rights Movement.[31] Nor in years of activism on the left did I note the extent of Jewish participation as something to take pride in, or understand that my rebellion against traditionalism had been enacted simultaneously by thousands of young Jews. Not until the early seventies when I moved to Oregon and encountered white Christian anti-Semites, did I even understand that to them I was not white: I was a Jew.

In 1972, I had just moved to Portland, Oregon, and was attending a feminist conference, talking with a woman while we waited for the elevator. I have forgotten the context for what she said: that she did not like Jews. Jews were loud and pushy and aggressive. This was the first time I had heard someone say this outright. I was stunned, didn't know what to say—"no, they're not?"—and I couldn't believe she didn't know that I was Jewish. My voice came out loud and flat: "I'm Jewish." To this day I can't remember how she responded or what I did next.

In Portland, I heard for the first time the habitual use of *Christian* interchangeably with *virtuous: Act like a Christian.* Even among leftists, it was tricky: liberation theology was sometimes a contemporary version of *Christian* equals *good.* As for feminists, the one thing they knew about Jews was that Jewish men thank god every morning for not making them a woman (this prayer exists, but is hardly a core ritual). Actually, feminists knew something else about Jews: that we had killed the goddess, a bizarre tableau in which Christianity emerges as the meek and innocent younger daughter. Crusades, witchburnings, inquisitions? That wasn't *their* Christianity. Their Christianity was a sweet white church and Grandma Jones's special Christmas cookies.

And *my* Jewishness? I had never articulated it. I began to think about it.

That first year in Portland, I read Hannah Arendt's *Eichmann in Jerusalem*, and realized something I had somehow up to this point managed not to notice: I would have been killed. My family, everyone I grew up around, practically, would have been killed. Random family tidbits clicked into place: my grandparents' families *had* been killed. I assigned the book to my freshman honors colloquium, and asked the class—as an exercise in ethics and in resistance strategies— whether, given the opportunity, they would have killed Eichmann. I can still see one of my students, Kathy, a nice woman, her large eyes framed in deep blue shadow, her pixie haircut giving her head a slightly bowling-ball shape. I can hear her answer quickly, without thinking, *why would I? I'm not Jewish.*

Only I and a couple of others gasped.

What is clear is this: the more outside of a Jewish ambience I was, the more conscious I became of Jewishness. Like Marshall McLuhan's perhaps apocryphal remark: *I don't know who discovered water, but I'm sure it wasn't a fish.* Inside a Jewish environment, where I could take for granted a somewhat shared culture, an expectation about Jewish survival, where my body type and appearance were familiar, my voice ordinary, my laughter not too loud but hearty and normal, above all, normal . . . in this environment, I did not know what it meant to be a Jew, only what it meant to be a *mentsh*. I did not know that *mentsh* was a Jewish word in a Jewish language.

To Create Solidarity

The more conscious I became, the more I thought and talked and came to write about it and act visibly and politically as a Jew, the more I encountered both blankness and kinship, anti-Semitism and solidarity—the more I came to locate myself in a tradition of Jewish women.[32]

Initially I felt most connected to women like myself, with thick dark eyebrows, sturdy legs, full mouths, big teeth, wild hair, skin full of oil glands for the desert. Secular, Ashkenazi, from Eastern Europe. English modelled on Yiddish inflection. Laughter explosive and frequent. We interrupt. We argue. We take for granted that the work of this lifetime is to seek justice; that if you're not a *mentsh*, you're a *shanda* (shame).

Emma Goldman lectured frequently in Yiddish. Clara Lemlich, at sixteen, cut short the speechifying at the famous Cooper Union garment workers meeting by calling for a strike vote (it passed). Rose Schneiderman first spoke the demand for bread *and* roses adopted by second wave feminism (could feminists have noticed *this* as Jewish, along with that obscure prayer?). Pauline Newman, Mary Dreier, Lillian Wald were open lesbians and important labor activists and social reform advocates.[33] Anzia Yezierska wrote in Yiddish-inflected English about the struggles of immigrant women for education, independence and love. Lil Moed and Naomi Kies devoted their lives to the struggle for Palestinian rights and peace between Israel and Palestine. Grace Paley and Vera Williams create wildly original stories and continue to slog along in the trenches of social justice.[34]

But the list goes on, to encompass the women *not* "like me"—rabbis and theologians whose critiques of traditional Judaism, or fights to include women in a transformed Judaism, have made it possible for a secularist like myself to go to *shul*. Scholars Judith Plaskow and Susannah Heschel demand the presence of women in the Jewish religion. Rabbi Julie Greenberg reinterprets Jewish practice and, as a single mother and a lesbian, raises her three joyfully-chosen children. Rabbi Susan Talve leads her St. Louis congregation into justice-seeking partnership with an African American church. Poet/translator Marcia Falk creates highly evolved feminist blessings and prayers, using traditional imagery but taking back the source of divinity, the power to bless.[35]

Sephardi women. Susan Talve and her grandmother Sarika, from near Salonika. The amazing sixteenth century figure Doña Gracia Nasi created an "underground railroad" to help Jews flee the Inquisition, and supported the translation of the Hebrew bible into Spanish, for those who lacked the opportunity to learn Hebrew.[36] Feminist scientist Rita Arditti's research into her own heritage brought Doña Gracia to me and many others. Poet Emma Lazarus is best known for her Statue of Liberty inscription, "Give me your hungry, your tired, your poor, your huddled masses yearning to be free." Therapist Shoshana Simons, of mixed Sephardic/Ashkenazi heritage, whose workshops and words suggest an enlargement of Jewish possibility.

Mizrachi women. Israeli film critic Ella Shohat argues eloquently and provocatively for the relocation of Sephardi/Mizrachi experience from the margins to the center of Israeli experience. Iraqi-American feminist activist Loolwa Khazzoom, founder of the Student Organization for Jews from Iran and Arab Countries, insists passionately on preserving the culture of Middle Eastern Jews, and on claiming all her identities. Poet and peace activist, Yemenite-Israeli Bracha Serri, exposes the damage done to women by men's violence. Therapist Rachel Wahba and poet Nava Mizrahhi each explores the complexities of being both Arab and Jewish.[37]

Mixed-race women who bring to the Jewish community lessons, language, culture of other peoples, if we are not too closed to welcome these. Puerto Rican/Jew Aurora Levins Morales, fifth-generation red-diaper baby, writes fierce, lyrical stories of working women's struggles. African American/Jew Josylyn Segal skillfully articulates her "unique and invaluable perspective on Jewish racism and Black anti-Semitism,"[38] asserting her right to be fully Jewish and fully Black.

This list is only a beginning.

And what is this new Jewish tradition we are creating and which, in turn, creates us? I once heard Judith Plaskow respond to someone's discomfort with new prayers reformed to eliminate male god language—"Those aren't the prayers I grew up with," the woman said, "I don't feel comfortable with them." And Plaskow responded, "We're not the generation that gets to feel comfortable. We're the generation that gets to create a tradition so the next generation grows up in it, and for them it will be the authentic tradition, and they will feel comfortable." No, we are not the generation that gets to feel comfortable. But we are the generation that sometimes gets to feel whole.

On the evening of Election Day, 1992, I was driving down from Seattle to Portland, Oregon, where Measure 9, the most vitriolic of the homophobic hate measures, was on the ballot. Measure 9 would have sanctioned discrimination explicitly and violence implicitly; would have banned from public libraries and schools books that deal positively with gay and lesbian experience; would have blocked funding of any public institutions that aided gays and lesbians—for example, AIDS counselling.

In the early seventies I came out as a lesbian in Portland, and lived there for seven years. I still feel deeply connected to the Portland lesbian community, and as I drove from Seattle to Portland, I felt like I was returning to Berlin, to the Weimar Republic in 1933 on the eve of the election; I was coming back to be with my people in their time of trouble.

As I pulled into my friend's neighborhood, Northeast Portland, a neighborhood mixed by income and by race—not especially gay—I saw signs on every lawn—NO ON 9. I started to cry, and I realized I had no concept of allies. Even though the friend I was going to stay with was heterosexual, and I knew she'd been working very hard on this issue, I had still somewhere assumed that no one would stand with us—that we would be fighting alone. And I knew this came from my history as a Jew.

I had heard about the escalation of violence against Oregon lesbians and gays. But I still was not prepared for what I found. I saw antigay propaganda that copied actual Nazi cartoons which showed Jews controlling the economy, substituting gays instead. Powell's Bookstore, which had been featuring displays of books endangered by 9, had received bomb threats, as had individuals working against 9. House and car windows had been smashed, cars tampered with. Physical attacks on lesbians and gays had skyrocketed, and in Salem a black lesbian and a white gay man had been murdered. It was like walking into a war zone.

I heard bits and pieces of this struggle: how some people in Portland or Salem didn't want to bother organizing rurally, how some white people did not understand the need to build coalitions with communities of color. Yet despite some reluctance and ignorance, a vast broad coalition was created. People told me not about the ease of creating this coalition but about the clarity and desperation and drive. Suzanne Pharr, a gentile lesbian from Arkansas who came to Oregon to organize against Measure 9, told me: "the radical right is a gift." And I knew what she meant exactly. Out of something ugly and outrageous has come something astonishing and inspiring, a model for the rest of the country, for the continued struggle against hatred—for survival.

A model for Jews as well. Oregon's Jews stood unanimously against Measure 9: every synagogue, every community organization and institution, every rabbi—the story goes that one rabbi didn't want to take a position, and that all the representatives went into a room and six hours later they came out unanimous.[39] Here is an excerpt from the Oregon Jews' statement, deeply informed by Jewish history, and by Jewish recognition of the intolerably high cost and inevitable slippage of any safety based on "whiteness":

> [The Holocaust] began with laws exactly like Ballot Measure 9. Those laws first declared groups of people to be sub-human, then legalized and finally mandated discrimination against them. Comparisons to the Holocaust must be limited. But clearly, this is the start of hatred and persecution that must stop now.

At the victory rally the night after the election, all the coalition partners spoke to celebrate, warn, rage, and comfort. There were representatives from the Jewish community, African American community, Native American community, labor. . . . Two voices especially stand out in my memory. One was a Chicano organizer from the Farmworkers Union, who said, "In this, we were there for you. Now we're organizing our strike, and I need to ask you to be there for us." The other voice was a white lesbian activist, who answered the farmworker: "Su lucha es mi lucha." Your struggle is my struggle.

I may be secular, but I know holiness when I hear it. One of its names is solidarity, the opposite of "whiteness." The more you claim it, honor it, and fight for it, the less it costs.

Melanie Kaye/Kantrowitz
New York City, 1994/5755

Notes

I thank Esther Kaplan, Roni Natov, and Nancy Ordover for substantial critical feedback. Sections of this essay are drawn from earlier writings: "To Be a Radical Jew in the Late 20th Century," "Class, Feminism, and the Black-Jewish Question" and "Jews, Class, Color and the Cost of Whiteness," all published in *The Issue Is Power: Essays on Women, Jews, Violence and Resistance* (San Francisco: Aunt Lute, 1992).

1   "On Being 'White' . . . and Other Lies," *Essence* (April, 1984). Sharon Jaffe, activist extraordinaire, is the friend who sent me Baldwin's essay.
2   "Closing Pandora's Box—Race and the 'New Democrats'", in Michael Omi and Howard Winant, *Racial Formation in the United States,* 2nd ed. (New York: Routledge, 1994), pp.145ff. Omi and Winant point out Lani Guinier's fatal flaw, from the Clinton neoliberal downplay-race perspective: "her willingness, indeed her eagerness, to discuss the changing dimensions of race in contemporary U.S. politics," p. 156.

3   Steven Holmes, "Federal Government Is Rethinking Its System of Racial Classification," in *New York Times* (7/8/94), explores the confusion from a bureaucratic perspective.

4   Students tell me, on one hand, that they learn in their women's studies classes not to make a hierarchy of oppression, but, on the other hand, that these classes rarely contain anything Jewish.

5   Christians usually see this as a generous feature of their religion—after all, anyone can become one, forgetting that not all of us wish to.

6   On the other hand, Karen Sacks, "How Did Jews Become White Folks?" in *Race*, eds., Steven Gregory and Roger Sanjek (New Brunswick: Rutgers University Press, 1994), points to "a 1987 Supreme Court ruling that Jews and Arabs could use civil rights laws to gain redress for discrimination against them . . . on the grounds that they are not racial whites."

7   *Ashkenazi* comes from the word for Germany; *Sephardi*, from Spain.

8   For Sephardi in the former Ottoman Empire, see Interview with Chaya Shalom in *The Tribe of Dina: A Jewish Women's Anthology*, eds., Melanie Kaye/Kantrowitz and Irena Klepfisz (Boston: Beacon Press, 1989: 1st pub., *Sinister Wisdom*, 1986), pp.214–226. Shalom, a fourth or fifth-generation Jerusalemite and a political radical, was raised in a traditional Ladino-speaking family to identify as *samakhet*—pure Sephardim. She describes Ashkenazi racism against Sephardi, *samakhet* racism against Arab Jews, and the complexities of passing and assimilation in Israel. See, also, Ella Shohat's analysis of Israeli Eurocentrism, *Israeli Cinema: East/West and the Politics of Representation* (Austin: University of Texas, 1989).

9   Nancy Ordover, oral critique, December, 1994. For an excellent discussion, see Omi and Winant, *Racial Formation in the United States*.

10   See Aisha Berger's poem, "Nose is a country . . . I am the second generation," in *The Tribe of Dina* (note 8). pp.134–138. One of Berger's many illuminating images: "this unruly semitic landmass on my face." The era of Jewish nose jobs is not over, though Barbra Streisand broke the spell that mirrored Jewish noses as inherently ugly.

11   First expressed by Moses Mendelssohn (1729–86), the central figure in the German Jewish *Haskalah* (Enlightenment), as the ideal of Jewish assimilation.

12   At least partly familiar; Sephardic and Ashkenazi practices often use different cantillation (chanting the prayers), and there are also variations between Reform, Conservative, Orthodox, and Reconstructionist.

13   One is, however, hard put to be a Jew without Jewish community. Even in religious practice, the unit of prayer is not the individual but the *minyan*, at least ten adult Jews, the Jewish quorum—in Orthodox Judaism, ten men.

14   There is painful irony in the fact that Yiddish, the beloved *mame-loshn* of Jewish socialists, is dwindling to a living language only for the ultra-orthodox Hasidim. For information about the Bund (Jewish socialists, for whom Yiddish culture was an important aspect of political life), see Irena Klepfisz, "Secular Jewish Identity: Yidishkayt in America," in *The Tribe of Dina*, and in *Dreams of an Insomniac* (Portland: Eighth Mountain Press, 1990); Klepfisz, "*Di mames, dos loshn*/The mothers, the language: Feminism, *Yidishkayt*, and the Politics of Memory," *Bridges* IV.1 (Winter/Spring 1994/5754); and Jack Jacobs, *On Socialists and "the Jewish Question" after Marx* (New York: New York University: 1992).

15   In this discussion I am indebted to Nancy Ordover, "Visibility, Alliance, and the Practice of Memory." unpublished paper (Berkeley: University of California, 1993).

16   Ruth Frankenberg's *White Women/Race Matters* (Minneapolis: University of Minnesota, 1993) offers useful insight on whiteness as an unmarked racial category. But Frankenberg misses opportunities to note the significance of *Jewish* as a category, although she and a disproportionate number of the white anti-racist activists she interviewed are Jews.

17   This group is often defined as especially smart—witness *The Bell Curve* singling out Ashkenazi Jews and Asians.

18 Isaac Deutscher, "The Non-Jewish Jew," in *The Non-Jewish Jew and Other Essays* (London: Oxford University Press, 1968). pp. 26–27. Deutscher's essay is fascinating, though distressingly blithe in its analysis of anti-Semitism.

19 Deutscher was unable to see the ethical dimensions of Judaism—a Jewish liberation theology that might support progressive politics.

20 In appearance, immediately identifiable as Jews because of distinct dress (black hats and coats for the men, arms and legs fully covered for the women) and hair (*peyes*—unshorn sideburns—for the men; hair cropped and covered by a *sheytl*—wig—or headscarf for the women), the Hasidim are magnets for anti-Semitism. Similarly, anti-Semitic graffiti, vandalism, and bombing of synagogues demonstrate that identifiable Jewish places are also vulnerable.

21 Though the Hasidim are vulnerable as individuals to acts of bigotry and violence, in New York City the Hasidic communities (Lubovitcher, in Crown Heights, and Satmar, in Williamsburg) wield influence. This is not a function of numbers; the Hasidim comprise a tiny percent of the world's Jews. Nor is it a function of wealth; indeed, a great many families in the Hasidic communities are poor, partly due to family size (as in all fundamentalist religions, the use of birth control is prohibited). Hasidic influence is a function of social organization: Hasidic leaders can deliver votes in an election and bodies in a demonstration (all they have to do is bus their students from their yeshivas in their buses). Here is a lesson for progressive Jews about the need for *progressive* Jewish visibility and organization.

22 Jews for Racial and Economic Justice monthly Coffee House, August 21, 1994.

23 I'm referring to the incident that triggered the Crown Heights riot of summer, 1991. Gavin Cato is the Caribbean American child killed by a car driven by a man in the Lubovitcher rebbe's entourage; Yankel Rosenbaum is the Australian rabbinical student killed by a mob shouting "Kill the Jew."

24 For example, when Lemrick Nelson was acquitted in the Yankel Rosenbaum murder trial, the press quoted Lubovitchers and city council members using the most inflammatory language, claiming that justice in the city was simply slanted in favor of blacks (whatever your opinion of the trial verdict, this claim is ridiculous beyond belief). Other Jewish voices were not reported. The New York Board of Rabbis and African American Clergy issued a joint statement calling for justice, healing, and reconciliation; the American Jewish Congress, American Jewish Committee, and Jesse Jackson did likewise—none of this was widely reported. So you would never know that there was a diversity of opinion. You'd never know that there are Caribbean and Lubovitcher teenage boys playing basketball together in Crown Heights; that there are programs of cultural sharing taking place. You'd never know for that matter that any women live in Crown Heights—you certainly never hear what they think about any of this.

Compare what happens when the extraordinarily gifted Anna Deaveare Smith gathers the diversity and complexity of Jewish and African American voices to explore the Crown Heights explosion. See her performance piece *Fire In the Mirror* (available on video and in book form)—an African American woman, she speaks in the voice of each character.

25 In "The Issue Is Power: Some Notes on Jewish Women and Therapy," *The Issue Is Power: Essays on Women, Jews, Violence and Resistance* (San Francisco: Aunt Lute, 1992).

26 Grace Paley, "Now and Then." *Tikkun* (May/June 1989), p. 76. In particular, European medieval and Renaissance history from a Jewish perspective reads like a disaster chronicle: expelled from here, massacred there, forced conversions someplace else. Occasionally there is a bright spot: "Jews return to Worms" (from which they had been expelled the year before); "Jews allowed to settle in England" (from which they had been expelled some centuries earlier). The late nineteenth and early twentieth century, especially in Eastern Europe, presents a similar wave of persecution, dwarfed only by the magnitude of what followed. Grievous official and unofficial oppression of Jews was a common feature of modern pre-Holocaust Europe.

27 I do not mean to claim a new and special status of victimization by uncertainty, which may even look appealing to those who face the relative certainty of extreme poverty, high infant mortality, etc.

28 Karen Sacks, note 6.

29 Jews who could pass as gentile, because they looked less Jewish and could speak the dominant language fluently, were more likely to survive the various swings of anti-Semitism. Thus to tell a survivor of the European Holocaust "you don't look Jewish" is to probe a painful truth—had the person looked more Jewish, s/he would probably be dead.

30 "Kaddish," in *Nice Jewish Girls: A Lesbian Anthology,* ed., Evelyn Torton Beck (Boston: Beacon Press, 1989), pp.107–11; first published in *Sinister Wisdom* 25 (1984).

31 See Melanie Kaye/Kantrowitz, "Stayed on Freedom: Memories of a Jew in the Civil Rights Movement." in *Narrow Bridge: Jews and Multiculturalism,* ed. Maria Brettschneider (New Brunswick: Rutgers, University Press, 1996). forthcoming.

32 When Irena Klepfisz and I edited *The Tribe of Dina* (note 8) in the mid-eighties, we chose to include photographs of the authors. We felt Jewish women literally needed to see what we looked like: the range as well as the commonality.

33 "It has taken over 65 years for historians to reacknowledge what the community knew all along, that lesbians were at the center of organizing on the East Side, and that their relationships influenced radical politics and strategy." Sarah Schulman, "When We Were Very Young: A Walking Tour Through Radical Jewish Women's History on the Lower East Side 1879—1919," in *The Tribe of Dina* (note 8). p. 271.

34 See *The Tribe of Dina* (note 8), tribute to Naomi Kies: interviews with Lil Moed and Grace Paley, Sarah Schulman (note 38); and Irena Klepfisz, note 14.

35 Judith Plaskow, *Standing Again At Sinai* (San Francisco: HarperSanFrancisco, 1990); Susannah Heschel, *On Being a Jewish Feminist* (New York: Schocken, 1983); Marcia Falk, *The Book of Blessings: Re-Creation of Jewish Prayer* (San Francisco: HarperSanFrancisco, 1994); for Julie Greenberg, "Seeking a Feminist Judaism," and Susan Talve, "Sarika." see *The Tribe of Dina* (note 8).

36 Rita Arditti, "To Be a Hanu." in *The Tribe of Dina* (note 8) p.23.

37 Ella Shohat (note 8); Loolwa Khazzoom, "A Bridge Between Different Worlds," *Bridges* 4.2 (Winter 1994–95). 49–56; Bracha Serri and Nava Mizrahhi, poems in *The Tribe of Dina* (note 8); Rachel Wahba. "Some of Us Are Arabic," *Nice Jewish Girls: A Lesbian Anthology* (note 33).

38 Aurora Levins Morales and Rosario Morales, *Getting Home Alive* (Ithaca: Firebrand, 1986); Josylyn Segal, "Interracial Plus." in *Nice Jewish Girls: A Lesbian Anthology* (note 33).

39 Portland New Jewish Agenda organized the meeting. This speedy mobilization is evidence also of magnificent anti-homophobia and coming out work done for years in the Jewish community by Jewish lesbians and gay men and our allies.

12

Chattanooga Black Boy

Identity and Racism

Calvin Hernton

I

My grandmother and I are hovering around a crib, a baby is in the crib. My grandmother is feeding the baby with a spoon. From time to time she lets me feed the baby too. I am aware that the baby is a boy. He has been crying furiously. But now the house is quiet. There is only the gulping sounds of the baby eating spoon after spoon of my grandmother's pumpkin pie. My grandmother and I marvel at how hungry the baby is. We enjoy his enjoyment of eating the bright yellow, mushy pumpkin pie. In addition to its being a boy, I am aware of the blackness of this hungry baby. Then, for the first time, I become aware of my grandmother's complexion, and that I am not black like her or this baby. I am more brown than black. We marvel at the blackness of the baby, who my grandmother says is my brother.

Although I did not know it then, I later realized that when this incident happened I was two years old, because I am two years older than my brother. For the first time it occurred to me, then too, that my mother and I were lighter complexioned than my grandmother and brother. But I do not remember having any negative or positive feelings about our different colors. Nor did my grandmother's behavior and comments communicate to me any such feelings. What I remember experiencing was that we had different complexions and features. But, at first, there was no significance attached to these alone.

I recall another incident that happened one or two years later. It is a vague but lingering memory of playing with a little boy about my age, three or four years old. He had a new red and yellow wagon. We enjoyed the wagon immensely. Taking turns, I would sit in it and he would pull, then he would get in and I would pull him. The wagon was easy to pull. Often we would get up great speed, one running with the other in the wagon—Wheeeee!— running along the sidewalk back and forth in front of my grandmother's house and the grocery store just across the street that the boy's parents owned. Sometimes we tumbled over and got scratches. We did this a lot, falling out of the wagon, and generally having a good time. This particular time we were in front of the store and the boy's mother suddenly appeared. I have a stark memory of this incident and particularly that the boy and his mother were *white*.

Of course, I already knew that both the mother and her son were white. My grandmother bought groceries in their store, and I bought candy and pop. They were always very nice to us and we to them. This time, however, it must have been the particularly harsh expression on the mother's face that fixed her and her son in my memory as being white. She made him come inside. Then, pointing at our house, she told me to "go home."

Later that evening my grandmother told me I had to stop playing with the boy. I remember knowing that he and I would never play together again. He stopped playing altogether on the sidewalk in front of the store. I have no clear memory of my grandmother or the boy's mother giving any reason for what happened at the time. I have a vague "sense" in me, however, that later my grandmother explained that the Ku Klux Klan had issued a warning to the boy's parents. What I did know was that the prohibition against our playing together had something to do with our being colored and the boy's family being white. I had no understanding as to why. It was just another unexplained event. Yet it caused a certain void to occur in me.

Little did I know then that I would experience it from time to time throughout my life. I felt a void open up inside whenever I felt rejected, scorned, or ridiculed. I would experience it, for example, every time a white person looked at me with what we called the "hate stare." I know now that feeling of emptiness—of denial and pain—is part of the individual and collective emotional experience of all black people in America. In order to escape the damaging effect of racial hatred, one has to develop a strong, viable sense of identity. I think I had this strong sense of self instilled in me by virtue of the love and kindness I received from many of the people with whom I had contact during my formative years, especially my grandmother.

My grandmother was and is my first and deepest influence, mentor, and teacher. I lived with her the first sixteen years of my life. When I was four or five years old, we moved from Chattanooga to a much smaller town called Tallahoma. The town and the people were quite "countrified," as we used to say. There was a vacant lot full of weeds down the road from our house. I remember that I was aware of white people living in the first house beyond the lot. Many children were there. One day while my grandmother was at work, some of the boys came to our house. I do not recall how or why they came, or whether I had made their acquaintance before. Soon we were romping out back among my grandmother's grapevines. My grandmother was proud of her grapes. There were lots of them and she tended them lovingly. They were a large, luscious green. We romped in the vines for hours, grapes were all over the yard and on the back porch, and many were squashed on the floor in the kitchen. The floors and the yard were soaked with sticky juice. I got so caught up in the fun that I completely lost track of what was happening—until it was too late.

My grandmother came home from work, but not before the boys had suddenly vanished. They were not there, and my grandmother was. I do not recall if she put her strap to my backside or not. I do know she gave me a tongue-lashing about "good-for-nothing peckawoods." Then she marched down to the white people's house and gave them a strong piece of her mind. From that day onward the white people gave us the utmost respect, and the boys kept their distance.

While my grandmother was chastising me, she told me that our neighbors were "po white trash" who were envious of her grapes, that the boys had deliberately destroyed the vines and they had done it because we were colored. "Peckawoods don't want to see colored folks have anything for ourselves," she had said.

A flash of recognition shot through my consciousness. Toward the end of our destructive foray, I had suddenly seen the damage and was visited by the horror of what we had done.

Then the feeling swept through me that the boys had come there intentionally to do mischief. Prior to the incident, I passed their house daily going to and returning from school. In passing, we might have spoken, as is the custom in the South, even between white and black people. But the boys had never offered to play with me before. Now, uninvited, they had come to our house.

During this time, I vaguely remember being about five or six years old and somehow knowing that black people and white people did not associate. No white people were in the school I attended. White people were in the world, I saw them, I moved among them along the streets and in the stores. I was aware that even though colored people and white people might be in the same spaces or places together, they were nevertheless somehow apart from each another. The white people who came to our house came only to collect money, such as rent, insurance payments, and to sell us things.

I saw white men and black men working on the same jobs. Garbage collectors, for instance, were both white and black. But the bosses were always white men and they drove the trucks, while the blacks ran alongside picking up the garbage containers and heaving them upon the trucks to other black men who emptied the containers onto the pile of garbage in which they stood knee-deep.

It was like this in every type of occupation. Whites were the bosses. The best and highest paying, most prestigious jobs belonged to them. And the blacks, both men and women, were relegated to menial occupations, such as janitors, laborers, domestics, ditch diggers, shoe-shine boys, and waiters. Within the segregated world, there were black professionals, mainly teachers, doctors, and preachers. Other professionals I knew of were insurance men, a truant officer, a lawyer, and numbers runners, all serving a segregated black clientele. I saw these things and observed them, but I was without comprehension and had no insight into them at the time.

East and West Ninth Street was the "black strip" in downtown Chattanooga. There were segregated businesses, taverns, hotels, theaters, restaurants, lodges and the colored branch of the YMCA. A lot of the colored businesses were owned by white people. Here and there, however, some black-owned enterprises would thrive in black neighborhoods, or the odd black-owned business would exist on the border-line separating whites from blacks. I remember feelings of pride and puzzlement regarding a black-owned grocery store over which we lived for a while on the Westside, across the street from which was the familiar white grocery store. The black store had once thrived, I gathered, but by the time we lived there, the store was a dingy, dark cave harboring its aging proprietor.

Every system of subjugation and discrimination has its "quirks." In the Jim Crow system of the South, one or two Negroes might have enjoyed a "white man's job," such as, for example, a crane driver in a factory, or a salesman in an otherwise all-white store. Such positions were privileged and at the same time they were hazardous. Racist whites begrudged these jobs because they felt all good jobs belonged to them; they were anxious to remove such a black holder of a "white man's job" any way they could, including by the use of physical harm.

In the middle of the intersection of Central Avenue and East Main Street, a black man was the owner of a "foot-long" hot dog shop which was famous and did a lively business. The shop served a drive-by black and white clientele. Customers entered through the same door. Outside and inside, everybody was served on a first-come basis regardless of their color. But the black proprietor had to "keep his nose clean," or his license might be revoked. Just one step over the line and his business would surely have been burned to the ground.

I remember the buzz of comments and raised eyebrows when the first black policeman was hired in Chattanooga. He was given no gun and he could arrest black people only. His "beat" was confined to East Ninth Street. If a white man committed a crime, the Negro policeman could not arrest the white criminal, he had to phone for a white policeman. On the other hand, any white man could and frequently did behave toward blacks like the "po-lice."

Generally, principals of black schools were Negro. But the superintendent was always a white man.

I do not remember the precise moment that I became *race conscious* of myself and others. But by the time I was a teenager in the eighth grade, I began to *hurt* inside and feel a bitter resentment toward the white superintendent who strolled into our classroom and sat in judgment over us and the teacher. The void would open up in me. It was about this time that I remember experiencing feelings towards white and colored people in general that were racial. A sense of being colored, or of being a Negro, had become a persistent aspect of my self-consciousness as a person. I became aware of identifying with people of color, while I tended to fear, feel mystified by, and resentful toward, the whites. I was a witness to white people regarding black people as being inferior. I was aware now that this did not make me feel good. It made me feel bad inside toward myself and all the rest like me. Yet I never really believed that black people were inferior. I knew we received degrading treatment on account of our color and features, but I did not believe that we deserved the treatment. On the other hand, although I was aware of whites who despised me and called me a "nigger," I did not have a comprehensive understanding of and insight into white racism and how it worked in the development of my identity.

From early childhood, I lived in a small world of my family (my grandmother and I), which was situated in a larger world of a town (Chattanooga) within the still larger world of the "Deep South," which, in turn, existed in the bigger world of the United States. At first, without my knowledge or consent, this world imposed on me the conditions and consciousness that would make me a member of something called a "race." The psychological product of the imposition of these conditions on me would be an image and concept of my self consistent with those of white racism. This "raced-identity," and the process by which it was to be realized in me, involved a social and cultural process that made me unconscious of myself as a product of and response to a thoroughgoing system of racism. I cannot recall, for example, when and how I became acquainted with such epithets as "nigger," "coon," "darkie," "peckawood," "cracker," and similar terms. Suddenly they were familiar to me, as though they had always been there, and their origin constituted an unexplained part of my life. It is like trying to remember when you first learned your name.

II

In writing this piece, I am relying a great deal on memory, on recall, the hazards of which are ever present. Memory consists of recollections, in between which are blanks. This is especially true of early childhood memory. But blanks occur throughout one's entire lifespan; and there is the mystery of why certain incidents, scenes, and episodes are remembered and others are not. We have memories that are hidden, they lie sleeping for many years, to be awakened by some triggering mechanism. There are blanks throughout my childhood years where I have no memory of myself whatsoever.

For example, between the incident of my brother eating the pumpkin pie and the time the white boy and I were made to stop playing together, there is a blank, I have no memory of anything. I vividly remember, however, that three major events colored the times of my youth. They include the Great Depression (1930s–1942), the case of the Scottsboro Boys (which began in 1931 and lasted throughout the decade), and the Second World War (1942–1945). The "Scottsboro Boys" were a group of black youths sentenced to death on the charge of raping two white women in Scottsboro, Alabama. Years later, the charge of "rape" was proven false. In recent times, one of the women came forward on television and told the world that they (the white women) had falsified "rape" because the white men (including the police) had pressured them into making the charge.

During my early youth, from the 1930s into the 1940s, I learned—and I do not know exactly when—that the terms I mentioned above ("nigger," "cracker," and so forth) were racist epithets. In ways of which we are at first unaware, we internalize elements that shape our identities. The epithets of racism issue from and signify an entire system that fosters hatred and alienation between whites and blacks.

> *My grandmother and I moved from Tallahoma back to Chattanooga. I was about seven years old. I walked several miles to school. I began to meet up with another school child, a girl, carrying books, on her way home like myself. At first we did not speak, but we saw each other, we knew the others were there on the street alongside. Eventually we started talking. We were curious about one another. Where did the other go to school? Why were there no children like the other in our respective schools? One afternoon we got stopped by the police. I do not recall what happened to the girl. I was taken home to my grandmother where the police warned us about the "crime" of a "Nigraboy" playing with a "Whyetgurl." After the policeman left, my grandmother cried, and warned me of the danger of getting lynched or sentenced to life imprisonment for rape, "like what happened to the Scottsboro boys," she said.*

During the latter part of the 1930s, throughout the 1940s, and into the 1950s, I grew from a child into my teens. In Chattanooga, as well as throughout the South and in most of the North, Jim Crow was the order of the day, and there was no escape—schools, stores, restaurants, eating places, businesses, churches, streets and neighborhoods were segregated. On washroom doors and on water fountains, and in all buildings there were "White" and "Colored" signs designating which entrances, which fountains, and which seats were for whites and blacks. We existed in the wretchedness of circumscribed spaces made that way by the whites, and the "colored" spaces were completely surrounded and dominated by the "white" spaces. There was also the Ku Klux Klan which stood for terror and violence against any one of us who committed the slightest infraction against the system.

We read the colored newspapers—*Chicago Defender, Pittsburgh Courier, Baltimore Afro-American*. Not only in Chattanooga but throughout the United States, we bore witness to the fact that we were a people against whom acts of violence were committed with impunity. Daily, we existed under the ominous threat of harm. But we struggled and survived.

Another blank in my memory is that I do not recall exactly when and how my grandmother and I left Tallahoma and returned to Chattanooga. Did we travel by train, bus, truck, or car? What happened to our furniture? All I recall is that suddenly we were back in Chattanooga, living with my grandmother's three sisters—Aunt Frances, Aunt Sis, and Aunt Delonie—in the upstairs apartment over the colored-owned grocery store on West Main Street. I have often wondered if the incident involving the schoolgirl is part of her memory as it is of mine? What did she feel? What happened to her?

During the Depression and war years, the Franklin D. Roosevelt administration instituted many welfare programs, along with rationing of goods, to assist the masses of poor and hungry people. On a certain day my grandmother and I went to the station where food was being distributed. We joined the long line of colored folks. The whites were standing in their line, which extended down the street in the opposite direction from the "colored" line. We had to wait until every white person who arrived had gone into the building before a single one of us was permitted to enter.

Hours passed. My grandmother hummed spirituals. Finally, about sunset, she and I were in front of the counter where potatoes and other provisions were being distributed. The woman behind the counter, really a teenage girl, informed my grandmother and the other black folks that we were too late, all the rations had been given out and nothing was left. My grandmother just stood there and stared at the young woman. Some of the others grumbled and made burdensome sighs. I could see sacks of potatoes only partially hidden beneath the counter. My grandmother saw them too, so did the others. Leaning over the counter and pointing, I yelled out that there were potatoes. The girl held her ground. She insisted that they were closing, and she ordered us, along with the others, out of the building.

My grandmother occupied a larger-than-life place in my world. She was truly a Christian woman; she respected people and demanded they respect her, whites as well as blacks. She didn't take no stuff from nobody. I had known her to accomplish all sorts of feats. I will never forget the time that:

> I went with my grandmother to make the last payment on the piano she had purchased for me several years before on the installment plan. When she gave the woman the final payment of seventy-five cents, the woman said that my grandmother owed three more payments. Tensely I watched as my grandmother dug in her bag and counted out every single receipt over a three year period—she had paid weekly. I recall the image of the woman as a mean-looking, bulky, white women with a chalk-white face. When my grandmother finished counting out the receipts, the woman's face had turned blood-red with consternation and defeat. Walking back home, waist-high beside my grandmother, I identified so intimately with her that I think I became her, and I floated upon a cloud of sheer racial pride.

Now, at the ration station, I was expecting my invincible grandmother to challenge this lying girl. Instead, she left the building without a word, which was totally uncharacteristic of my grandmother. At least she was supposed to give the girl a good piece of her mind. On the street I heard her singing an old spiritual. "Sometimes I feel like a motherless child, a long ways from home."

The spiritual seemed to comfort my grandmother. But it did not comfort me. I was livid with anger and feelings of being wronged. I felt resentment and hatred toward the girl. I remember distinctly that her whiteness was important to my rage, and I became mad at all white women. I became mad at my grandmother, too, and indeed, I was mad at all black women and all black people for accepting such treatment from a mere teenage girl. I do not remember the rage continuing much beyond the actual incident. It had subsided perhaps by the time we reached home. But the *raceness*—the whiteness and the blackness—of the incident was indelibly lodged in my consciousness. Without knowing it, a sense of *race inspired by racism* was becoming an integral factor in the way I identified myself.

III

Who and what one becomes is a significant part of how one is perceived by the eyes of the world in which one is born and lives. We were made absolutely visible in and by the Jim Crow signs of "colored" and "white" that were everywhere. We were forever under the white gaze from which there was no escape. Our ways and modes of living and expressing ourselves, which reflected our culture of origin in Africa, were degraded and denied. A black gospel quartet could perform in a white church, but no black people were permitted to enter. We stood outside on the Sunday afternoon sidewalk, degraded, yet proud because the singers were superb.

On the other hand, we were completely invisible, denied all but the most menial qualities in our own right. I do not remember that it ever occurred to me in a conscious manner that my childhood heroes in the comics were white—Superman, Dick Tracy, Captain Marvel, and the "classic comics"—*Jane Eyre, Oliver Twist, The House of Seven Gables*. Straight through to the eighth grade, elementary, and high school, I do not recall any teaching about the history of Negro people. The important people in history were white men, George Washington, Abraham Lincoln, Benjamin Franklin, and even John Brown. The only black men we learned about were George Washington Carver, the scientist, who invented various products from peanuts and gave his formulas to white men for nothing. The other black man was Booker T. Washington, whom white people liked very much, because Washington believed that Negroes should stay in their place. Only one woman was mentioned in history, a white women, Betsy Ross, who sewed the first American flag. I graduated from high school in the top of my class. I knew nothing about Frederick Douglass, Nat Turner, Sojourner Truth, Harriet Tubman, W.E.B. Du Bois, or the NAACP.

I heard about slavery from my grandmother, and perhaps she mentioned that we had all been brought originally from some faraway land called "Africa," where we were a proud people. But the black men and women I saw in the movies consisted of maids, mammies, servants, clowns, and buffoons who said "yessum" and "nawsum" to white folks and who rolled their eyes and ran from ghosts—Butterfly McQueen, Hattie McDaniel, Mantan Moreland, Rochester, Stepin Fetchit.

My first image of Africa came from the Tarzan movies, in which the virile, macho white man, white boy, and white woman, lived in and ruled over the jungle, its animals and the "savage natives." The American Saga portrayed invincible white men called "Cowboys." There were super heroic role models like Randolph Scott and John Wayne—the latter slaughtered thousands of "injungs" without reloading his rifle. There, in the atmosphere of the picture show, Chattanooga black boys and girls vicariously experienced what white men really thought of black men and women. We also watched and laughed at the manner in which white men portrayed white women. In the film series, "The Perils of Pauline," a fleshly, blond white woman was bound and tied to the railroad tracks over which a smoking train, huffing and puffing, sped toward her.

On East Ninth Street, the Negro Street, I sat in segregated theaters owned by white men and watched Negro gangster films in which light-skinned Ralph Cooper stopped "acting" and stared in the direction of the off-camera director every time the director gave him a cue. I listened to the light-skinned Negro Cowboy, Herb Jeffreys, sing "home on the range." Then there were the entertainers, who entertained us (me) the most—Bojangles, Cab Calloway, the tap-dancing Nicholas Brothers, Billy Eckstine, the absolutely white-looking Lena Horne and the sensuous, seductive, "naughty" performer, Eartha Kitt, whose voice was like sandpaper marinated in maple syrup. When Sidney Poitier came along, I was awed by his handsome blackness and thrilled by his naturalistic ("method") acting.

IV

Eventually the formation of a self-conscious Negro identity came to include feelings of both shame and pride connected with being a member of a race that white people themselves despised and which black people despised and loved simultaneously. The color hierarchy ("pigmentocracy") that whites established between whites and blacks gave rise to a secondary hierarchy among black people themselves. I learned at some point during my youth that if you were white you were alright, if you were yellow you were mellow, if brown you could stick around, but if you were black you had to get back. I learned that Caucasian features were valued over Negroid features. The noses, lips, and body types of white people were held to be ideal and therefore better than those of black people. I learned that white people had "good hair" and black people had "bad hair." I learned that the first black woman millionaire made her fortune from selling a product that straightened black folk's "nappy hair." In short, I witnessed that white skin and white features were considered beautiful, while the very idea of black beauty was believed to be a contradiction in terms.

The colorism syndrome within Negro society and culture gave rise to resentments by darker Negroes towards the lighter ones. That is what we, especially middle-class Americans of African descent, called ourselves then with racial pride—"Negroes." Light-skinned Negroes were given more access to the American Dream than dark-skinned Negroes. Sometime during my high school years I became aware of the number of light-skinned Negroes in high positions, with better jobs than black-skinned Negroes. My high school principal was indistinguishable from a white man. It seemed that many professional men and women, preachers, doctors, business people, politicians, and leaders of the race were light complexioned. I remember the shock I experienced when the president of the NAACP, the foremost race organization in America, was a "white Negro." His name was Walter White. There seemed to be a connection between color and the opportunity to climb up the socio-economic ladder. Fairer skinned members of the middle class, and those aspiring to it, viewed themselves as the "better class" of blacks, and tended to look down on and separate themselves from the masses of darker Negroes. Many of these Negroes boasted of their white ancestry and formed so-called "blue-vein" societies which excluded dark complexioned members of their race. These Negroes were the object of much criticism from their darker brothers and sisters, as well as from certain disaffected members of their own group. The light-skinned and middle-class blacks persisted in being ashamed of black folk culture and modes of entertainment, along with everything remotely connected with having been slaves. The spirituals and blues, for example, were not valued by middle-class Negroes. A black complexion itself was viewed as a drawback to racial representation and progress. I believe this was why attitudes of both pride and shame were expressed by a lot of Negroes in regard to Dr. Mary McLeod Bethune. Although she was a proud leader of the race and the only black woman in the Roosevelt adminstration, many Negroes felt she was too "black and ugly" (she had "nappy hair" and thick Negroid features) to be representing the race nationally and internationally.

In school, too, light complexioned female and male students were accorded higher status and displayed greater self-esteem than darker complexioned students. This was also evident among the teachers in a subtle but recognizable way. As a result, lighter complexioned Negroes were at once envied and resented. In addition, intra-racial color prejudice tended to be rampant in the world of teenage dating. Light complexioned boyfriends and girlfriends were envied and resented, but nevertheless carried a higher premium than dark complexioned ones. I know this went on because I distinctly remember that I resented the deference people showed to me in reference to my brother and myself. He was put on the spot for being blacker than I. But I was also on the spot for having fairer skin than he. Years later, one of his wives, upon first meeting me, looked back to my dark complexioned brother and quipped, "What happened to you?"

I observed this *pigmentocracy* operating within black families as well as in black society at large. "Marrying up" in Negro society consisted of getting married to someone lighter than oneself. At the other end of this polarity of light complexion versus dark, there were those who took pride in their color. Dark skin and Negroid features were viewed with esteem and African culture and the culture and ethos of the black masses were cherished. Resistance and defiance against the system of racism was lauded. High achievements were occasions for racial praise and the people who accomplished them were symbols of pride.

In college, and after I graduated, the development of my identity would be affected by the racial struggles going on about me, such as *Brown v the Board of Education*, the desegregation decision of 1954; the Civil Rights Movement of the 1960s; and the Black Power Movement. But while growing up in Chattanooga, my sense of racial pride and awareness of Negro achievements was formed and informed by the struggles and achievements of contemporary black individuals, like Jesse Owens (winner of four Olympic gold medals), Joe Louis (heavyweight boxing champion), Marian Anderson, (renowned concert singer), and Jackie Robinson (first major-league baseball player), to mention a few.

Because he knocked out so many "great white hopes" in the boxing ring, during three decades—1930s, 1940s and 1950s—Joe Louis was the foremost symbol of Negro pride. Like all Negroes, I became extremely proud of him. White people liked Joe Louis, too, because for them he was symbolic of American power in the war against Germany. This was particularly so in the match between Louis and the German heavyweight boxer Max Schmeling in 1938. The night of the fight, June 22, every radio in America was tuned in. I was a mere child at the time. But in my mind, and in reality, Joe Louis loomed extraordinarily large as a Negro hero, so much so that many years later I celebrated him in a poem, entitled, "A Ballad Of The Life And Times Of Joe Louis, The Great Brown Bomber."[1]

I portrayed how the white people felt:

> *Beat That German, Brown Bomber,*
> *Beat The Nazi, Beat Him For The Morale Of*
> *The American Democracy!*

In contrast to the whites, I portrayed how the black folks felt:

> *Whoop Him, Joe, Baby, Whoop*
> *Him For The Sake Of Colored Folks*
> *All Over Dhis Forsaken Land!*

Pride of race was rife in Negro folklore. Themes of defiance against white people and their racist system were a mainstay. When I was growing up the saga of "Shine" was best known among Negro males and was most often recited by them. According to the saga, "Shine" was the only Negro admitted aboard the greatest luxury ship ever built by white people, the *Titanic*. Shine was the janitor and when an iceberg sank the unsinkable vessel, he swam the entire ocean to safety. Before the news of the disaster reached shore, Shine was back home in his neighborhood tavern long enough to have drunk many bottles of beer and to have caroused with ninety-nine women.

The lore of Negro defiance and rebellion against the apartheid-like system of southern Jim Crow was inspired by both creative wishful thinking and actual occurrences. Chattanooga black girls and boys lived in the celluloid houses of make-believe, the "movies," especially on weekends. While Hollywood films that included black characters patently reflected the stereotypes and fantasies of white racism, there were the occasional films based on the aspirations and fantasies of black folk. I recall a certain cartoon about the adventures of, I think, "Jasper," featuring a little black boy and a scarecrow. The scarecrow advised and guided Jasper, the hero, on various adventures. Not only were the features of these characters Negroid, but their voices were distinctly of the Negro folk type.

I was amazed that these characters were recognizably black. I sat riveted in my seat, as the voices of my parents and neighbors spoke proudly from the mouths of the characters. Then, one day, a "short features" was shown between the main features. The short feature was called "Heritage." Beautiful jungle scenes appeared and torrential rains poured down, and a lion roamed among the trees and foliage and along the river bank, as if in search of some irresistible prize. As the scenes flashed on the screen the voice asked the question of what Africa means to him, or to us? Was it copper sun or scarlet sea? Was Africa a star in the jungle or just a jungle track? Was Africa some kind of garden in Eden where the men were bronzed and strong and the women were Black and regal? The man behind the voice did not know, for it all had happened too long ago to remember, 300 centuries ago, in fact. We had been removed from the African culture that our forefathers and mothers loved. In America, slavery and racism prevented us from inheriting the African past. So the question remained, what did Africa mean to us?

The voice was that of the Negro actor, Rex Ingram, and the scenes upon the screen illustrated Countee Cullen's famous poem about the mystery of the African past. I was so affected by this experience that years later when I came across the poem in a book in the library, I began reading the poem out loud, imitating the manner I had heard years ago in the movies.

I remember the jubilation of black girls and boys during a certain scene in a movie starring Paul Robeson, "Sanders of the River." The colonial white man and Paul were in a confrontation scene, when Paul ("Sanders") faced the white man squarely and declared, "WHITE MAN, I'M BOSS HERE!" Then he dove into the river and swam away, not unlike I imagined "Shine" of the *Titanic* had swum the ocean. It took the ushers nearly an hour to quiet our spontaneous, prolonged outbursts of racial pride. A big black man had cursed out a white man and told him that the black man was the boss.

In the real world of Chattanooga, a group of black high school teenagers boarded the city bus that took us from downtown far out to East Third Street. Upon boarding the bus, there were no seats for us because Negroes could sit only behind the whites, and the whites were seated everywhere, from the front to the back of the bus. But a single seat was vacant, it was beside a white girl. For about a half-mile several dozen black teenagers stood in the crowded aisle of the bus and stared at the vacant seat beside the white girl, who had begun to show nervousness. Suddenly, without any sign or word to any one, a black boy sat down in the seat beside the girl. The bus got so quiet we could have heard a pin drop on a carpet in Russia. Bubbles of sweat popped upon the boy's face and upon the girl's as well. But neither of them moved or glanced at the other. They held their heads and eyes straight ahead. Everybody, including the bus driver, pretended it was not happening. Yet all of us were intensely aware of the situation. Eventually enough people got off the bus along its route, leaving vacant seats in the rear, and the driver stopped and told the boy there was room in back now. The boy complied. But the point had been made. No one said anything. We felt the energy of racial pride radiating among us.

V

The hatred that black people experience from white people has tended to breed a counter-hatred on the part of many blacks. But racial hatred never developed in me, and thus it never became a part of my identity. I attribute this to the Christian teachings that were imparted to me by my grandmother. She was a religious humanist and in many ways the philosophy of Martin Luther King, Jr. reminds me of my grandmother's teachings and the way she lived. I knew and still know that racist white people carry out the enmities of racism against blacks. But I did not hate them back, because I learned from my grandmother that hatred was a sinful, self-destructive emotion for a person to carry in his heart. She always said, "Love, not hate, is the better medicine." So I only feared white folks and tried to keep out of their way; at least, I feared most of them, for Negroes in the South are very sensitive to which whites are more dangerous than others.

One of my first jobs was as a delivery boy for a neighborhood store. Delivering groceries to white homes, I entered their neighborhood and their houses, and sometimes I had to enter by their front doors and carry the groceries through the rooms to the kitchens. I saw the way middle-class as well as poor white people lived. I saw their living rooms and bedrooms, their toilets, and their kitchens.

Other jobs I held also put me in close contact with whites. I worked at various intervals as a shoe-shine boy at a major shoe-shine parlor in downtown Chattanooga, and as a pin-setter in the largest bowling alley, and in a steel erection and plumbing supply plant which employed about a hundred white and black men. I learned that there were different types of whites with different personalities, which altered, however slightly, the way white people behaved toward me and other blacks within the Jim Crow structure and its racist etiquette. In other words, there were "mean" white people and "good" white people.

Part of my job at the steel erection and plumbing supply plant was as a helper to the drivers of the two delivery trucks. Doug was an older white man of the stereotypical "white trash" vintage.

I had to address him as "mister," while he called me "boy," which meant "nigger," because frequently to my face he would actually refer to me and other Negroes as "nigger." Riding along he would often make obscene comments about black women on the streets, I was supposed to sanction his comments. But when his comments were about white women, I knew I was supposed to behave according to what Richard Wright termed "the ethics of living Jim Crow." I would say nothing, I would bow my head and not even glance at the white women. I viewed Doug as revolting, and I definitely did not want to become like him. But I did not hate him because I remembered what my grandmother taught me—that if I returned this man's hatred with my own hatred, I would become just like him.

The driver of the other truck, John, was a younger man of about twenty. He was quite lazy and he operated according to a scheme in which we "rested" a great deal in-between making deliveries. No matter where our delivery took us, John always ended up stopping at his house. Leaving me in the truck for at least an hour and sometimes longer, he would visit his wife and small children, including several babies. He introduced me to his wife, who was friendly. Frequently he would eat and bring me a portion out to the truck. I had to remain in the truck, he said apologetically, because the neighbors would cause trouble if a colored was seen socializing in a white home. We would discuss how someday this would not be the case. By way of reciprocating, we would always stop by my house on the way back to the plant and I would have a sandwich and a little nap, after which I would bring a sandwich out for John. Unlike with Doug, I could speak, act and behave relatively freely in John's presence.

Ordinary human interaction with whites happened even more freely with the owners of the grocery store where I worked. Mr. and Mrs. Shuman behaved as though they were not white, nor I a Negro.[2] Their nonracist disposition took me completely aback. The demeanor and behavior of Mrs. Shuman caused me considerable anxiety until I grew used to it. In the small, crowded aisles of the store, as we unpacked cartons and filled the shelves, she often brushed against me as if I were just another person. This was against the most explosive taboo of the South, physical contact between a black male and a white female.

VI

Toward the end of my senior year in high school, I took a test and was awarded an academic scholarship to attend Talladega College. I brought with me to Talladega College the raw material of an identity that was already in process. The college had been founded largely by members of the New England American Missionary Association in the 1880s, during the post–Reconstruction period. Situated in a small, isolated Alabama town, Talladega College had been designed to be a sanctuary where black men and women would be prepared to overcome the odds in a world set against them. Over the years, the institution maintained its original charge and character.

When I arrived during the 1950s, Talladega College employed an interracial faculty of dedicated women and men, nearly all of whom were considered radical. Many of the professors were white. My first two years there the president was white and his son was a student. Several other whites were students, and they frequently received threatening messages from racist whites in the town, to vacate "that nigra college."

During the heyday of the House UnAmerican Activities Committee—the mid-1950s—the college came under scrutiny and several of its professors received summons to appear before the committee. Not unflatteringly, in those days Talladega College was often referred to as the "back door to the Kremlin." The students came from all over the country, with different backgrounds and personalities. Studying and socializing with them vitalized my development, especially in regard to those with whom I formed intimate friendships.

VII

It is inescapable that my Talladega experiences informed the racial factor in my identity and contributed to the kind of human being I have become. My race informs my identity, but my race-conscious identity is first informed by the quality of my humanity.

It was at Talladega that I first realized who Jews were. Many Jews lived in Chattanooga including Mr. and Mrs. Shuman, the grocery storeowners for whom I worked as a delivery boy. Before Talladega, however, I did not know Jews were Jews—I mean, I did not know what it *meant* to be a Jew. This was despite the fact that I grew up hearing black folks talk about, make references to and compare themselves with "Jews." Jews were in the Bible, they suffered oppression and persecution. Feelings of affinity and identification with Biblical Jews on the part of the blacks were dramatically expressed in the Negro Spiritual: "Go down Moses, tell ol Pharaoh to let my people go." This song was familiar to every black person in Chattanooga. Yet, before I left Chattanooga for college, I have no memory of making a connection between Jews in the Bible and Jews in Chattanooga and had learned nothing about Jews as a people, their history and culture, or the *final solution*, Hitler's barbaric scheme to exterminate them.

As far as I remember, Chattanooga Jews were merely a "different" kind of white people, they were "good" white people. Most of the stores in Chattanooga black neighborhoods were "Jew stores." Jews provided credit for poor black people when no one else would, and they gave credit to poor whites as well. I heard talk about Jews having money and being hated by the regular whites because Jews were smarter than them.

It was at Talladega that I gained insight into things which I had experienced, but only partly understood, including racism and anti-Semitism in America. The summer following my first year, I returned to Chattanooga and went to see Mr. and Mrs. Shuman. When I entered their store, the Shumans greeted and embraced me. Despite the ethics of living Jim Crow, I no longer experienced anxiety because they had white skin and related to me as a human being. They inquired about my education, my ambitions in life. They hired me that summer as a clerk, even though there were obvious signs that the store was failing because of competition with the "supermarkets" that were coming into style. When it was time to return to Talladega, they gave me presents, and counseled me to leave the South and go North, where racism was not as bad and opportunities were greater.

It was during these years that I came to realize that the boy with the wagon and his parents were Jews. My grandmother had explained that the Ku Klux Klan had sent my playmate's parents a warning that in the South whites did not play with niggers, "Jew or no Jew." The experience and my grandmother's explanation of it had more meaning for me after my freshman year at Talladega College.

In addition to residential property rented to blacks, Jews owned bars, nightclubs, and theaters along West and East Ninth Street, and on West Main Street as well. They were also in the "rackets," including the numbers racket, whose clientele was almost one hundred percent Negroes. Big Bill Grooseman was famous as the leading racketeer in Chattanooga. He operated from a combined bar-pool-hall-gambling joint on West Ninth Street. It was a "funky joint," exuding an unctuous downhome atmosphere. I visited Big Bill's place that first summer from college, and several other similar places on East Ninth Street. The "clandestine" interracial socializing in these joints, and the expensive decor of, for example, the Brown Derby on East Ninth Street, were right out of New York's Harlem. That first summer back from college, I also stood in front of the synagogue and understood the full import of it having been defaced by a Nazi symbol when I was a boy.

What I am getting at is that on both the individual and group levels, Jews were among the whites who had a positive influence on the way I came to feel about myself as a black person and conceived of my identity in a world of racism. The relations Jews had with Negroes were client-like and helpful to Negroes. Many Chattanooga Jews stood between the whites and the blacks, and frequently defended them. Jews also served as inspiration to blacks in their struggle for equality and justice. For example, the only plant in Chattanooga where a black man had the most coveted job—Master Crane Operator—was owned by a Jew. The only downtown Chattanooga store that employed a black man as a clothing salesman was the Jewish haberdashery. If I am not mistaken, it was Miller Brothers, the largest most prestigious department store in Chattanooga at the time, that first hired a black saleswoman.

VIII

The hostile, degrading gaze of racism is a gaze that does not see the black person as a person; it is a dreadful gaze. The white "hate stare" can damage the self-esteem of an individual as well as an entire group of people. Growing up in Chattanooga, and later in college, I came in contact with non-Jewish white individuals who behaved like human beings in their relations with black people. But relations between Jews and Negroes let me see how a whole group of white people did not hate black people, and that they could be victimized by other white people because of their race and religion. Whether we like it or not, in the Jim Crow South, the friendly attitude of some white people toward a Chattanooga black boy was meaningful to the integrity of that boy's identity, an identity not merely as a raced self, but as a human being, regardless of race and racism.

I do not mean to downplay the role of racism in the making of my sense of who I am. But consciousness of myself as an African American is not all that constitutes my identity. Rather, humanity is the essential nature in which race, or having an African American identity, occurs or happens. And my identity is an ever-expanding process of discovering and becoming.

First and foremost I am a poet and writer. My identity as an African American does not determine what and how I write, unless I choose to make it so. Frequently I have chosen to write directly as an African American. Much of the rage I have felt for myself and for black people as victims of racism has been expressed in my writings. But neither my identity nor my writings are informed by racial experiences and feelings alone. I believe that identities founded on or rooted in exclusive notions of race are fallacious. Such identities diminish ourselves as well as the racial others who are excluded.

I recognize that people feel the necessity to embrace identities, and that identities are right and proper. Presently, identities based exclusively on race are a powerful urge in the world. But these identities are things that people invent, they are like garments people make, clothes they dress themselves in. But what is invented can be un-invented. That which is imposed can be resisted, subverted, uprooted, changed. To forge an identity and a consciousness that includes all other human beings, rather than excludes them, is an everlasting struggle in this world. But it can be done. Forty years ago the passion of this idea made me write "The Distant Drum":

I am not a metaphor or symbol.
This you hear is not the wind in the trees.
Nor a cat being maimed in the streets.
I am being maimed in the streets.
It is I who weep, laugh, feel pain or joy.
Speak this because I exist.
This is my voice
These words are my words, my mouth
Speaks them, my hand writes.
I am a poet.
It is my fist your hear beating
Against your ear.

Notes

1   See Calvin Hernton. 1976. *Medicine Man*. Berkeley, California: Reed, Cannon & Johnson, p. 21. All subsequent references to and quotations from this poem are from the same source.

2   Names throughout this section may be misspelled, as I am spelling them based on how I remember hearing them pronounced at the time.

Part III

LOVE LETTERS
and Conversations

13

My Dear Niece

Pam Mitchell

I picture you as you were during our last visit, almost a year ago, shortly after your twenty-fifth birthday and before my forty-second. I see you with your best friend negotiating the streets of Hermosa Beach. You're in little pressed white shorts and a sleeveless white blouse, your golden brown toes with nails painted red sticking out of leather sandals. Behind big sunglasses, your glowing face is perfect except for those charmingly crooked front teeth of yours you're so self-conscious about—a reminder that there was no one to put thousands of dollars into orthodontia so you could have a Regulation California Smile. We talked a little over lunch that afternoon. You wanted to know why your mom turned out as she did, and why I'm so different from her. I'm not, Betsy. The next day, you drove me south to meet up with a friend of mine—brash East Coast, Jewish, "dykey," loud, fat and dark. As I introduced you, I watched two worlds collide and held my breath, feeling at that moment that she'd become the stand-in for the me you'd rather not see. And you didn't: you waved at me, flashed a toothy smile in the general direction of my friend, and had your car back onto the Pacific Coast Highway in record time.

This is so hard, Betsy. You are a believing Christian (a Lutheran, right? Forgive my ignorance about the distinctions among Protestant sects), a petite southern California blond who lives a block from the beach in an affluent neighborhood. From outer appearances, you seem to belong there. You've told me the image you project is a facade, a face you put on because you're not sure who you are. You're a survivor; you know how to find a bargain rental in a community of property owners, how to carry your head high and buy clothes that won't immediately identify you to your upscale neighbors as a clerical worker who takes orders all day from people like them. Yet you live with inner turmoil, a legacy of our fragmented family that had no place for you and no money to make up for absence of place, and with the imprint of all those foster homes. I know you feel like a poseur, a fraud, like you belong nowhere.

It's a family disease. I visit you and feel like I belong nowhere also, like there is something very, very wrong with me. Ours is a family of misfits, of secrets, of questions left unanswered because there are no reliable witnesses and very few external artifacts. My adult life has been an archeological expedition through memory and psyche, in therapy and also through a more political process of putting my childhood experiences into a larger context. I've been aided in finding this context by the many writers and activists who have been mining their own histories and cultural identities for information about how to make themselves whole and the world a better place. Because our family is such a painfully fractured one, this process of discovery has often felt to me like I'm removing layers of skin. I offer you the information I've excavated as a gift. Although I know it won't spare you all of the pain, maybe it will make your own efforts at understanding yourself and your place in the world a little easier.

Because you're the only offspring of my only sibling, you and yours will be the only travellers remaining on this road. (I've never had or wanted to have children. Much that I'll tell you about our family might help explain why.) You should know what there is to know about the nexus of individuals that put you on this earth and played such a significant role in getting you where you are now. It's stretching it to say you have a family—there are individuals you're related to by blood, but they've rarely functioned as a unit or provided what families are supposed to provide. There have been too many betrayals, too many ties severed by distances, poverty, unbridgeable cultural differences, deaths at early ages.

You and I share genes and the social meanings others attach to them. We are white, we are Californians, a quarter of your tradition and half of mine is immigrant Jews from Eastern Europe, a quarter of yours and the other half of mine is West Virginia, white, Christian people—self-described "Mayflower stock gone to seed." We come from struggling people, working people, people not given the opportunity to work, and people too physically or emotionally disabled by the circumstances of their lives to be able to work.

Our people come from two communities that place a high value on family. Yet our own recent past, the story of your grandparents and their parents, is the flipside of this, the story of what happens when those all-important families cease to function, because of conflict or abuse or disability or untimely death. People flee across oceans or to the other end of continents. Or they run for other reasons—economic, political—and it's that which causes the family to break. Because these breakdowns run counter to cultural ideals about what family "should" be, they aren't talked about or even acknowledged, though certainly they're as much a part of the history of our people as are the stories of the families that "work." Rootlessness, displacement are, ironically, a part of your heritage even while they conspire to hide it from you.

Some of the stories I tell you might already know. Our relatives in my parents' and grandparents' generations scattered throughout not only the West but New York City, West Virginia, or wherever else they may have wandered in search of work or escape. People didn't fly much back then, especially poor and working people like us. People took trains or they hitchhiked. Your grandparents—my parents—each migrated during the Depression to Washington, D.C. to do clerical work with the U.S. government. That's where they met. Your grandpa was already involved in labor activism; your grandmother recruited him into the Communist Party. Travelling cross-country was still a major undertaking when they packed up and drove to L.A. shortly after World War II ended. It wouldn't be until after you were born that your grandma would get together the cash and the gumption to return to New York City for a visit. As far as I know, your grandpa never did see West Virginia again.

Had there been more contact among members of each of these families in my childhood—had I spent time on the farm in West Virginia or on the streets of the Lower East Side—I might have had a sense of familiarity and connectedness. This might have been enough to offset the fact that

I'm the hyphenation between two mutually exclusive, antipathic cultures, each of which has been ridiculed and despised by mainstream U.S. culture.

I don't want you to be ashamed of either of them, or of me, or of yourself. I say to you—and remind myself—that there is a lot to be proud of in each tradition, even though sometimes it feels to me that the common denominator is the displacement and the poverty and the alienation: an absence. In the tradition of too much of white America, this void is "supposed to" be filled by hating African Americans and by worshipping the almighty dollar. To their credit, my parents weren't willing to go along with the program. They became a part of an alternate vision, a movement that tried to create a place where working people from disparate cultural, ethnic, and racial backgrounds could join together instead of hating and competing with one another. That vision and that movement were destroyed in the '50s; that story is an important part of your heritage.

"Californification"

Yours is a family that's not so unusual, although it's not reflected in the public lore. The specifics are unique. But the effects of poverty and need and violence, the culture clash between two disparate backgrounds, each wracked by its own oppression—that's not such an atypical Southern California, story if you get below the surface. Of course, L.A. tries to be about the surfaces, because underneath it's so much about severed roots, about people who moved westward until there was no place further to go, people running from or running out.

Trying to find something to assimilate *into* is always a struggle in a place like California—or like Long Island, or like some other places that sprouted up out of deserts or potato fields after World War II. But California was further away geographically, the continent stretching out almost like an ocean. If one was poor or working-class, one might never see the family again. Which sometimes was the point.

I can't write about us without writing about region. This is story that belongs to Southern California, with its shifting sands and silly giraffe palms and tinderbox eucalyptus and grasses that came from elsewhere, replacing lifeforms that could handle the climate better and wouldn't self-destruct or conflagrate from the sun. There were cultures here before, of Gabrielinos and other indigenous peoples, but you and I aren't related to those. Our stock was moved in on top of theirs, without regard for the local eco-system. We *do* have roots, however splintered, hidden, and tangled and mangled and stretched beyond capacity they may be. Two wildly different species cross-pollinated. Do you relate at all to the hills of Appalachia or the shtetls of Eastern Europe? I look at you, golden blond and crisp and tan, like they dipped you in batter and threw you on the griddle (do you even know what a potato latke is?)—the picture of health, of Southern California success. I wonder what you know about Braxton County, West Virginia or Galicia, Poland/Russia. I assume you know even less than *I* knew about these at your age—who was there to tell you? By the time you were old enough to start asking questions you were being shunted from one foster home to another—Christian homes, Republican homes. Child Protective Services makes an effort—albeit an inadequate and problematic one—to place children in homes consistent with their "race" or "religion." But the categories that would have meant something to us—Communist, atheist—mean less than nothing to them.

"Red Diaper Grandbaby"

I'm sure you don't remember, but when you were barely talking I was helping you form those tiny fingers of yours into a fist and you were repeating after me: powa peepo, powa peepo! All power to the people. I wanted to make a miniature warrior out of you because I knew what we were up against, which side I hoped you'd recognize as your own. I got that from my parents, your grandparents.

Down through both lines of your heritage, your forebears were surrounded by people like themselves who had a rough row to hoe. Too often people in this predicament allow themselves to be bribed and manipulated into accepting the petty benefits racism confers on them without seeing the invisible tradeoffs: the violence that becomes a part of our lives, the toll it takes on our individual humanity when we look the other way in the face of obvious cruelty and injustice. But in both the cultures you and I share, alongside these ignoble traditions of racism are legacies of rabble-rousing for social justice. Finding alternatives to the vicious, self-defeating pecking order was the guiding principle of your grandparents' politics; in a very real sense, their politics was their religion.

I hope at least a touch of your grandparents' religion rubbed off on you. For all I know, you grew into a registered Republican. We've never talked politics. Despite all the brainwashing I'm sure you've been subjected to about the "evils" of communism, I hope you can take some pride in the fact that your grandma and grandpa were a part of that tradition. You've paid a price for it indirectly. When I was tiny, the FBI came snooping around the neighborhood poisoning the neighbors' minds against our family; and before I was born—when your mother was an infant—your grandfather lost a job he sorely needed in a purge against communists. These were events that had a major impact on you although you probably know nothing about them: that your mother's earliest years were spent breathing in her parents' terror, economic insecurity, hopelessness, and being shunned by many neighbor kids for her parents' politics has a lot to do with why she was ill-equipped to provide you with the kind of mothering you richly deserved.

It could have been different. A whole community, a whole culture of summer camps, folk music, friendship networks grew up around the people who shared left-wing politics. Your grandparents had been a part of that world, but as your mom and I were coming up, they were cut off from it by their own disillusionment and by the smashing of the communists by our goverment, by all the congressional hearings and the trials and imprisonments, the lost jobs and suicides, betrayals and bitter aftertastes. Your mom and I knew nothing about that whole community built on hope and vision. We fought our little battles in the schoolyard and classroom: war was wrong, the Russians were people just like all of us, you could be a good person and not believe in god, people should join unions, Black people were as good as anybody else. We always believed we were right, but thought we must be the only kids in the world who knew these things. We were unbelievably isolated in Pasadena in the '50s; it wasn't until the '80s, at conferences and gatherings for "red diaper babies" (children of communists) that I found out that thousands of other kids were having those same arguments in their own schoolyards, and fighting back as stubbornly as we did.

One red-diaper gathering in particular comes to mind as I describe our family to you: a meeting in an apartment in Cambridge where someone mentioned having one Jewish and one gentile parent. I said "me, too"—and so did each of the other seven people in the room. The communist movement was its own kind of melting pot, then: a culture that could have been a link between unlinkables. I have since read about the Communist Party USA's conscious efforts to cross ethnic and racial boundaries and incorporate disenfranchised peoples—including Yiddish-speaking Jews, as well as African Americans and other peoples. In practice inclusion in this new left culture was both positive and negative: it meant recognition, but it could also mean pressure to assimilate, to abandon communities and traditions. Some of our story got lost that way.

Violence, the Eraser

Your grandparents passed along to your mother and me certain ideals about justice and peace and people taking care of one another, principles that they and we have lived up to sometimes in the way we've conducted our own lives and sometimes have failed to—sometimes failed miserably. I can understand your anger at your mother. I still feel rage at my parents for all that they spent and spilt on me, their violence and abuse, even while I can also understand the pressures they were under. You are no stranger to such brutalities yourself, so I don't suppose I have to tell you how trauma can act as an eraser. When we numb out and forget details about our lives which have been unbearable, some of the other details fade with them. In the process, context and ethnic heritage can lose their shape, grow fuzzy and indistinct. I can say what I'm saying in this letter only because I have had counselors and friends to believe me and support me through a process of reliving and surmounting the ugliest moments of a nightmarish childhood.

I won't go into graphic detail, but we were targets, the family was, as Jews, as communists and as atheists. And, because our family was ostracized and too weak and disorganized to back us up, your mom and I were also targets of sexual and physical abuse in the neighborhood. Occasionally violence was perpetrated against us by people of color because we were white people, we were the white people living up close to them, there to receive their rage against racism. We were also forced to witness racially motivated crimes by whites against Black people and Mexican Americans. And members of our family acted out their self-hate and desperation on each other and on others; we were, some of us—your grandmother, your grandfather, your grandmother's father, and others—child-rapists and worse. I wish it weren't true. But if that abuse, the incest and the torture were nails in the coffin of our "family" as family, the cause of death was social forces that were beyond any individual's control and started long before any of us was born. I doubt you learned a whole lot in your high school history classes about the pogroms and persecution of Jews that brought your great-grandparents to New York, or about the poverty and expropriation and exploitation, the black-lung disease and company towns and murderous Pinkerton goon squads that forced your grandfather's people off their land to scatter from the West Virginian hills, moving to industrial areas to find work.

What's Class Got to Do with It?

You hadn't yet been removed to foster care when your grandfather died, but you were still a toddler, too young to attend his memorial service. He had called himself agnostic. His funeral was one of the very few times I ever saw him in a church. His eulogy, delivered by a Unitarian Universalist minister in love-beads who barely knew him, began with an injunction that was vintage 1970: "Let us not be uptight."

Nothing against love-beads or Unitarians, but your grandmother and I were, indeed, "uptight." And with good reason. Dad had dropped dead suddenly at 53 of a heart attack, leaving us to scramble around looking into welfare and government surplus food. He was bankrupt when he died; I inherited only his penny jar and his debilitated car that I never could get to run again. He left a small insurance policy, which my mother and his second wife haggled over for years and which ended up splintering into pennies to be divided amongst them and all the lawyers. I watched in disgust at the spectacle of my mother and another middle-aged woman fighting like vultures over the carrion that had been my daddy. I despised my mother for it. Now I can understand the panic she must have felt, losing alimony and child support so unexpectedly and suddenly; she, a "housewife" on the margins of the paid workforce for so many years, an anxious, phobic woman who never had a chance to heal from her own traumatic childhood. I "understand," but to this day I don't feel compassion. To this day I believe that every penny of that damned insurance policy should have ended up invested in your future. If there had been enough money to go around, your story and your relationship with the family would have been a very different one.

My own grandmother, your great-grandmother—you told me you don't remember her, but she watched you often and loved you a lot until her death—died a year or so after her younger son, your grandfather, did, when you were about four. Following your grandfather's death, I had gotten a phone call from a cousin of his named Bonnie (his mother's niece) of Ida May, West Virginia. Ida May was the kind of place I'd never been to and could hardly imagine, the kind of place where they still needed operator assistance to place a call to Pasadena in the early '70s. I promised to keep her posted on your great-grandmother's health, willing myself to be capable of being the link between unlinkables. But when my grandma got mugged on the street the following year and wound up in a convalescent hospital, I wasn't around. I didn't attend her funeral shortly thereafter. I don't even know if anyone in Ida May was ever notified. I had gotten the hell out of my hometown and my childhood on a scholarship within a matter of months after Dad died. It had been all I could do to throw a laundry basket full of clothes, a canvas backpack and garbage bags stuffed with belongings into the back of a friend's old station wagon. It would be decades before I could look back. Unfortunately, that meant leaving you behind along with my grandma. I'm sorry I had to do that.

Your mom almost got away, too. Did she tell you about that? When you were still an infant, she got offered a scholarship at UC Berkeley, but opted instead for the immediate security of a job as an eligibility worker for the state welfare department. But she just couldn't make the social leap to acting and dressing the part of social worker, and couldn't quite get the knack of refusing people refrigerators and emergency shelter just because they didn't get the paperwork right. She lost that job, and was back to asking eligibility workers for refrigerators herself. So much for upward mobility. . . .

So you and your mom stayed behind in a small rented house a few blocks away from the "home" I left behind—the tiny two-bedroom apartment I had lived in with your grandmother. That proximity to a family home base might have provided you with a bit of continuity had it remained in place. But your grandmother had other needs. Too anxious a person ever to learn to drive in a region where "no car" can mean "no paycheck," she didn't see much of a future for herself in Los Angeles, a place the New Yorker in her could never call a city. She moved to San Francisco just weeks after I left for college in Santa Cruz. To thwart the bill collectors, she left no forwarding address. Taking along only what she could carry, she sold or junked the other physical manifestations of your mom's and my childhoods: furniture, clothing, bedding. One of the suitcases she took north with her was full of family snapshots, report cards, school pictures, birth certificates, immunization records, and other papers and portable memorabilia. Less than a year later, bedridden by anxiety and on disability from the shock of one too many major upheavals, she called me from college to her bedside in a residence hotel amongst the porn shops and tobacco stores of San Francisco's Tenderloin. She told me then that this suitcase full of my childhood had mysteriously disappeared. Eventually your grandmother recovered enough to return to work, but that lost baggage never *did* come back.

Hence, we have few artifacts. You can hear stories from your mother and me about what growing up was like, but you have scarce opportunity to see or scratch or smell or touch any reminders of it.

Where Class Meets Race, and Where It Doesn't

I was never one for material possessions anyhow. Throughout my childhood we kept moving every couple of years, from one rented house to another, whenever a house got sold or one of us got into a fight with the landlord. With every move we lost some of our belongings, so I learned not to become too attached to things.

We always seemed to remain within the same square mile or so, though, in a working-class corridor through the center of the city. We would see faces of many colors there, at the matinees at the neighborhood theater, on the merry-go-round at the park, in the checkout line at the grocery store. But at school most of the faces were white. To our bewilderment, we headed to school in the morning in the opposite direction from many of our after-school playmates; gerrymandering of school districts "protected" us from some of our own neighbors. I was heartened when a federal judge finally ordered desegregation of the city's schools around the time I entered high school.

You shared that neighborhood for the first few years of your life. Then, when you were a few years old, your mom moved with you to a "safer" neighborhood in a more affluent neighboring town; given the realities of racism and economic inequality, that meant you spent those years almost exclusively among white people. In the end, her decision is part of why you were taken from her: she and you—the "family unit" the two of you made up together—didn't fit in with that orderly neighborhood full of financially stable people in nuclear families. I can't say whether you should have been taken away or not: was it the "right" decision? Would you have been even worse off if you hadn't been? It *is* clear that your mother would have needed help if she were going to continue to be your caregiver/caretaker. She should have had child care. She should have been allowed to finish college. I bet you remember all the times she tried, signed up for classes and then something would happen: her old shitbox of a car would break down, or there'd be a health crisis or an unwanted pregnancy, then something else and something else again. (You know the story; you've had to drop out of college more than once yourself.) She'd pick up low-paying, insecure jobs whenever or wherever she could, without a career or defined skills (as she's still forced to do).

When she couldn't find work, she tried to support you and keep herself afloat on those welfare checks, where they figure out a person's most basic need level and then give them a percentage of it, telling them it's against the law to earn any "extra." They have a complicated formula; your mom knew all about it because she'd been on the other side of the window, back when she was a probationary eligibility worker, but knowing didn't help much. Being white didn't help much, either, but it helped a little. I've come to realize that it almost always does.

I want to say to you, Betsy—yes, we're white, and that *does* mean something. It means you can blend in, it means you can stand on the shoulders of other white people to help yourself out, at the expense of others if you choose to (and sometimes when you don't). The way I see it, to press our race advantage not only is unfair, unjust, cruel, but also ultimately exploiting other dispossessed peoples is to the detriment of those from whom we really come, and—unless you're one of the lucky few who leap into a different economic stratum—to the detriment of those who'll follow you.

It's not a bad thing, being "white." I mean, you're not a bad person for being it. But it *is* fiction, a covenant to camouflage the differences amongst those of us who share by accident of birth in one or more of many European cultural heritages and share light-skinned genes, to ensure that we can count on one another. We belong to "the white race," the world's biggest street gang. But your family is at the periphery, vulnerable to doublecross not only because of economic disadvantage but because on your maternal grandmother's side you're a Jew. You are a Jew in a lifetime and a country in which European Jews are regarded as white people, at least for the time being. The rules can change abruptly, though. As a people, we've learned over the centuries to keep our bags packed.

"We were slaves in Egypt." Jews repeat this every year at Passover, and that historical fact, along with my parents' involvement in a movement committed to Civil Rights, meant I was taught to identify with African Americans—sometimes to over-identify. I was the smart but brainless child who didn't have the good sense to make sure my own ass was covered and got it kicked; got punched and called "fatso kike" and "nigger-lover" when I spoke up for the two African American girls in my class in grade school. I was trying to "rescue" Clemmie and Wilhelmina in part because I needed rescuing so badly myself. The truth was, neither of them liked me much or showed signs of needing my "help" in dealing with the brat-boys who shouted racist shit at them. Clemmie was as tough and strong as a third-grader could be, and Willie could run like the wind.

Years after Clemmie and Wilhelmina, I remember my teenaged raped and beaten and battleweary self lying in bed with my little transistor right up in my ear. I listened to the Watts riots leap from one block to the next across L.A. from me, thinking: go, team, go! Yes, act out my rage for me, feel my pain for me. When it was over, of course, the "team's" neighborhood was in ashes while mine was still standing. Now I know enough to ask myself, "what kind of 'team-work' is this?" and to admit that it's the righteous, well-intentioned, but nonetheless racist kind too often practiced by liberal white people.

Given your upbringing, I doubt you have this tendency to over-identify. I only hope you weren't trained to do the opposite: to distance yourself from people of different races. I worry you might buy into the anti-immigrant lunacy that has a chokehold on our state, that you might not be able to see in your Asian and Latino neighbors a part of your own story reflected back. Although you and I have both had our share of struggles, we've also shared in the California good life, a lifestyle built in large part on the labor of those so-called "illegals." I doubt you know this. Who would have told you?

When I was a pupil in the California public schools, I was misinformed about our state's Latino roots. In class I heard nothing about the "Bracero" program, about the Mexican people then being brought across the border at the whim of farmowners to work for poor wages under horrible working conditions. I was fortunate to have your grandfather to tell me all about it, to explain to me how it was designed to keep wages down for U.S. workers while exploiting Mexicans. Meanwhile, we went on school fieldtrips to some of Father Junipero Serra's thirteen original California Missions. I'll bet you were taken to the same missions to hear the same lies about the Spaniards and Indians when you were in school. The "padres" were presented as the ones we should identify with, as though they weren't slavemasters, rapists, and thieves. And as though they were our ancestors. Do you know that the same year that Columbus sailed the ocean blue, our Jewish ancestors were forced either to turn their backs on their people's way of life or to leave Spain under penalty of death?

I'm a Jew, You're a Jew

I'm a Jew. Well, my mother is, so I am. (Your mother is, so you are, too.) It took a long time for me to understand and accept that, partly because I didn't want to—because I had learned to be anti-Semitic myself, because I hated my mother, because I was afraid, but also because it didn't seem to "fit" somehow. What makes a Jew a Jew? Religion? But I was an atheist raised by an atheist. A relationship with Israel? I was a non-Zionist internationalist raised by a non-Zionist internationalist. A feeling of community? I had known so few Jews growing up. A race? To Hitler and much of Europe, yes, but here, mostly not, although a few white supremacist groups in the U.S. do include Jews among those they would destroy in order to protect the so-called "racial purity" of Euro-Americans. Jews came originally not from Europe but from the

Middle East. Whatever else I am, I'm *not* "Eastern European." Your mom's blue eyes and my own, passed down to us from our Jewish mother, bear silent witness to mass rapes by Cossacks, by other Europeans down through the generations. Our people pass the torch of Jewishness down through the female line because rape has been too much a part of Jewish life for anyone to rely on Jewish paternity. Still, because of genetic intrusions, some of them by force, and because our forebears' cultural experience was, for a number of generations, a European one, and because the boats they came in arrived here from Europe, Jewish members of our family and other Jewish immigrants in the U.S. in this century were received as a type of white people.

Your grandmother and her sister were raised as observant Orthodox Jews. Your grandma turned against her parents' religion when she joined the communist youth movement at sixteen. The way my mother recounted the story, when her mother saw that the world didn't tumble from not observing the Sabbath (Saturday, when Orthodox Jews don't do any work), her mother stopped observing, too, and started working from sunup to sundown that day, too. My mother's mother never forgave my mother for taking away her day of rest—or so my mother told me.

Most of what I know about the traditions of Judaism I've learned from friends as a grown-up. I knew nothing about the High Holy Days, the Jewish New Year celebrated in autumn. A couple of winters your grandmother tried to light the Channukah candles, but the eight-day ritual required more sustained concentration than she could muster. I knew about Passover only because I heard about your mother's humiliation when a teacher put her on the spot asking her to explain the holiday to her whole class. I believe she was in fourth grade at the time. Thankfully, your mom wasn't quite as lost as I would have been; she at least had gone to a Jewish pre-school and could remember some of what she'd heard about the Exodus of Jews from Egypt.

I didn't go to that pre-school, I think because we had moved too far from it for your grandmother to get me there on the bus. What little I learned about Judaism when I was a small child I associated with your great-grandfather on my mother's side—I don't know his first name, it might have been Saul but I'd be guessing. I have an image of myself as a very young girl sitting in his lap and touching his face, feeling the tie I had to him like no other, sensing the control he had over my mother who was otherwise a person completely out of control. From what I can gather he did horrible things to your grandmother when she was little. I recall him being present when horrible, unspeakable things were done to me. These atrocities were connected with Jewish ritual, grotesque distortions of Judaism carried out in its name. I remember this now in flashbacks that I can only bear to look at with the support of others who have survived similar ritualized torture carried out in the name of religious or political ideologies. For over thirty years I'd forgotten about those rituals and, in the process, forgot a lot about being Jewish. I forgot about my grandfather, too. To this day, I don't know what he was doing out in California, when he returned to New York, or when or how he died.

As a child, if I was asked whether I was Jewish, I wouldn't deny it. "My mother is," would be my answer. I thought that meant I wasn't. I didn't say "my mother used to be," although I knew she'd rejected her parents' religion. Yiddish was her first language, the one she spoke until she started first grade. I guess I knew somehow that you could reject a religion but not your mother tongue and all that it implies about your culture and identity, about meanings and humor and worldview. Somehow I knew that there could be no such thing as an ex-Jew.

Echoes of Yiddish, a language virtually annihilated by Hitler, live on in my own vocal inflections, my convoluted sentence structures. That and my dark, frizzy hair and "zaftig" (full-bodied) shape have given rise to that frequently asked "are you Jewish?" question. Another version of that query, shaped by West Coast ignorance and stereotypes, were "Do you come from New York?" I was asked this often enough as a teenager that it became my dream to visit the Big Apple, which I assumed must be full of millions of people just like my misfit self.

I spent my first financial aid check from college on an airline ticket to New York City to see this place that might be home. Still breathless from my first plane ride (and from getting my purse stolen before I even arrived from the airport!) I walked into a roomful of our cousins in Queens. The first words I heard as I was pinched on my gentile-looking cheek was "Such a shiksa! She looks just like her father." I'm not even sure I knew myself at the time that "shiksa" is a not-very-nice but mildly affectionate word for a gentile woman.

Some People Call Them "Hillbillies"

Ida May, West Virginia—as far from me as the moon. What cord ties me to these people? One random item I still have from childhood (I have no idea how I came to own it): a driver's licence, issued in the thirties in Parkersburg, West Virginia to one Miner Mitchell. Although I'm not certain and there's no one I can ask, I presume this "Miner" fellow was my paternal grandfather whom I never met; the date and place of birth fit (1898, in Braxton County). I also presume that his name came from the kind of labor he had to do for part of the year because working the land couldn't support his family, the kind of work that killed one of his brothers. I never knew the name of that great uncle, but I learned the names of those who killed him: black-lung disease and the coal company. I don't know what your great-grandfather died of, or when.

My grandmother, your great-grandmother Lettie: when I was six or so she left the farm and came to California to be near your grandfather. During those early years, I remember she'd get a small check every month from people who were searching for oil and coal and god knows what-all on that land. I don't know when she sold it, only vaguely remember her talking with my father about trying to hold on to it. I wish you or I had it now.

Grandma Lettie had one son besides my father, my Uncle Bruce whom I never met. He died a few years before my dad did (neither one of them reaching his mid-50s), not too long after my father visited him in Montana where he'd moved for work. It was a big deal, my father taking a vacation; I'd so rarely seen him when he wasn't at work, either in his little cubby in a brick building downtown, doing clerical work for the carpenters' union, or in his office in our house, moonlighting with his own small bookkeeping business. He couldn't afford to take me or your mom along, but he brought me back one of those glass globes with the snowflakes in them. I remember how impressed I was that I had relatives living out there in the world where it snowed.

I don't have any pictures of your great grandmother, but I'll describe her to you. She was a handsome, long-limbed woman with fair skin like your mother's and yours and impressive bunions from a lifetime on her feet in shoes that didn't fit. I spent a lot of time with her when she was in town. She'd be around for a year or two, then she'd leave on a Greyhound to visit relatives in other states, then come back again and move back into a room in Mrs. Rose's boarding-house.

She'd make me popcorn and buy me my favorite cookies and we'd watch TV together. "The Beverly Hillbillies" was one of our favorite programs. There I sat, twenty miles outside "them thar Hills of Beverly," watching this farce with my grandma, a "real live" refugee from the Appalachian hills. Never did I call her Granny. And she never acted like a fool.

Although we were her only relatives within a thousand miles or more, she never set foot in our house. My mother wouldn't let her enter. No reason was ever given to me, although I'm sure I asked. I remember at some point I heard a whisper of a rumor that anti-Semitism was somehow the cause of this exclusion, but I don't know what form this might have taken; nor do I know whether it was actually your great-grandmother who was the guilty party, or someone connected to her. I personally never heard any ethnic or racial slurs come from her lips. I *do* remember her telling me once that she wouldn't consider living near her brother in Baltimore or the wife of my dead uncle in Mississippi because she could never live in a place where Black people had to use the back door.

My grandma would show me photographs of these places named Baltimore and Enterprise, Mississippi, of southern Ohio and Billings, Montana, and of the people who belonged in those places. I remember the locations, but I never could quite get the names of all those strangers down, or comprehend their relationship to me.

My grandma was a practicing Protestant Christian, like you. I recall how she put on a hat and cheap white gloves every Sunday and went off to church, although I couldn't tell you whether it was a Baptist Church or a Methodist one. She belonged to one of those two churches, her husband had belonged to the other, and they baptised their sons as one of each; I never knew which of the churches could claim my father.

. . . And Some Would Call Me Christian

I suppose that technically this side of our family is "WASP," White Anglo-Saxon Protestant. That would make you and me WASPs, as well. Funny, I think of WASPs as the people who own things like banks and run the country and go to church on Sunday to provide their white-bearded, white-skinned Father with the opportunity to thank them for these contributions. Certainly they aren't God-fearing, impoverished, West Virginian dirt farmers like my dad's people or god-rejecting communists like my dad. Certainly they are not like me. To acknowledge the privilege that comes with being a WASP means grappling with the undercurrent of shame at being the wrong *kind* of WASP—the "failed" kind, the "white trash" kind.

As a child, more often than not I could and did "pass" as Christian; that is, I was most often presumed to be Christian, in the absence of evidence to the contrary, even though *I* knew I didn't belong. The community—meaning nearly everyone but us—had their Christian thing. To me it seemed like *one* Christian thing, although in fact the kids I knew were Roman Catholic and Eastern Orthodox and every variety of Protestant. On Friday afternoons the public school cleared out, all my classmates trudging off to their respective "religious education" classes, which were conducted discreetly a block or two from the school in order to maintain the fiction that our public school was not supporting organized religion. I was one of the few kids left behind, godless and at loose ends. Our teachers made no secret of the fact that they resented having to babysit us until the other kids returned. At those moments I suppose I was the hyphen between church and state.

For a brief time I had "converted." When I was four or so, I insisted on attending Sunday School at the Protestant church our landlords' children attended, so taken was I with the cut-out pictures they brought home of a blond stained-glass Jesus with an exceptionally cute little lamb. A look of amusement passed between my parents who figured—rightly—that if they indulged me I'd get bored and quickly stray from my path of Christian righteousness. If I remember correctly, I lasted less than a month. Still, it was the only formal religious instruction I've ever received, and it served to bolster my tenuous ties with the Christian world around me even as it distanced me from the Jewish world of my mother and her people.

Aware that your mom and I felt left out of that Christian world, our parents chose to observe the Christian-based holidays celebrated by virtually all of our neighbors. We grew up coloring Easter eggs and wearing Easter outfits and putting Christmas gifts under Christmas trees. Christmas was my least favorite day of the year. I felt like a fraud. I kept forgetting what it was that we were supposed to be pretending: that this really wasn't some little guy named Jesus' birthday we were celebrating, or that it was? That we were just like all the other families, except that they went to church and said grace and believed in the president and the pledge of allegiance and the arms race and we didn't? That if we could just keep playing out this same drama every year, the family would finally be a family and this holiday of theirs would finally be ours?

What "Tore It" for You and Me

I hadn't seen you for nearly a decade when you and I both showed up in San Francisco three years ago to acknowledge the death of my mother, your grandmother. We had met only once after you were taken from your mother: that day when you were sixteen. I was passing through Southern California and your foster parents let me take you to Disneyland. Searching awkwardly for words that neither of us had, we were both delighted to stumble upon a rock band in Fantasyland. We played together on the dance-floor, just as we'd played together when you were a youngster. Alas, a Disney employee soon approached me (because I was the grown-up?) and tapped me on the shoulder, admonishing me, "No same-sex dancing." You were incredulous, Betsy. You didn't have much experience with homophobia. You couldn't have known about the role it had already played in keeping us apart.

Eight years earlier, in Cambridge, I'd received a notice from the state of California. You were in a temporary foster placement at the time. I was notified that a hearing would be held the following week to determine whether you should be permanently removed from your mother's care. I was just coming out then, at a time when lesbians were having their *own* children taken from them by the government. (They still do pretty often.) I couldn't even conceive of myself as an alternative to foster care. I couldn't yet see how "lesbian" and "family" could go together.

Perhaps if I'd been more financially stable, more respectable, I would have considered myself a potential guardian for you and could have impressed the government as a worthy exception, an "exemplary" lesbian. Middle-class, white, two-parent gay and lesbian households have been fighting for respectability in recent years, with some success. But my class situation was murky; I had just dropped out of graduate school and was scraping along on odd jobs and unemployment. My ability to support you financially or emotionally was tenuous at best, made even less tangible by my shame at what felt to me like a personal failure. I'd flunked upward mobility, even though I still found myself moving in an alienating middle-class universe.

I was not only three thousand miles away but moving in a class universe light-years away from where I came from. That financial aid that enabled me to leave separated me from the family and our history, not only geographically but culturally. This is ironic, considering that the money was made available by the government in response to "urban unrest"—to the militant demands of working-class and poor people of color wanting their share of '60s prosperity. Your grandparents lacked the wherewithal to put me through a four-year university; in a very real sense, it was the Black Power and La Raza and Native American movements that gave me my college degree.

So I had the privilege of going off to a well-respected university, which at the time was chock-full of rich white kids studying the Third World and supporting revolutions for the hell of it. I never told classmates anything about my family. They must have thought I dropped out of the sky, and I suppose I believed that myself. It wasn't until I went on to a Ph.D. program in Boston that I hit the class ceiling and realized how much I didn't belong in that world. The next step was a process of seeking that ill-defined world I *did* belong in, a world that includes you.

Finding the Names I Call Myself

I couldn't assimilate into the competitive middle-class world of academia, and left graduate school when my funding was pulled out from under me. I chose to remain in Boston with the droves of other students who come to that city every year from all parts of the U.S. and end up staying. These "colonizers" are primarily middle- and upper-class white people. They have minimal contact with the Irish-American, Italian-American, African American and Puerto Rican folks who live in working-class neighborhoods like Southie, Charlestown, Roxbury, and Dorchester, although they never tire of ridiculing their accents.

I suppose the locals must have perceived me—not entirely inaccurately—as belonging in the colonizers' camp. But although I was a long way from home and didn't really belong to Boston, much besides my precarious financial situation distinguished me from this affluent influx: my values, my beliefs, my insecurities. It took me a while to grasp where these differences came from, but by the '80s I had found some names to call myself: working-class, lesbian, Jewish.

I floundered around for a while (it being easier to float then, in the relative prosperity of the '70s), and started poking around into my childhood memories. I began to participate in a form of peer counseling that delved into early-life traumas as a means of understanding identity and oppression. Through this, as well as through more traditional therapy and through support groups and study groups, I started recognizing some of the ways in which I had been in hiding from myself, began to feel the shame and terror and unexpressable rage that had come along with the territory of being treated as "less-than" by reason of class, gender, ethnicity. I began building on the liberation struggles of the '60s, books and articles about reclaiming identity were being published, particularly by feminist presses. These were notably by women of color; members of other marginalized groups began to follow their lead, including Jewish women and working-class women. In this search for a place to call home, a place from which to take a stand, it became necessary to choose among the many threads of identity, to pick one as primary. Hyphenation was just too complicated.

By the late '70s and early '80s, Jewish feminists had begun to define themselves and bond together. I'd met my first serious lesbian love that summer after dropping out of grad school, and found myself a part of a burgeoning lesbian feminist movement, which gave me a sense of community and place. This lover was Jewish. Since then I've surrounded myself with Jewish women as lovers and friends; they've felt comfortable and familiar. From a string of Jewish lovers I learned the range of what being Jewish could mean. I learned that Jews of my generation tend to share my own concern that they're "not Jewish enough." I learned about the holidays, responding to the more festive and secular of them—Passover, Purim—but never developing a deep connection with Judaism as a religion. I learned that in this I was part of a long history of secular Jewishness, a Jewishness based not in religion but in culture. I took comfort from the identity itself and from my relief in getting past my fear of accepting it.

I marched and rallied under a "Nice Jewish Girls" banner, went to countless meetings and discussion groups, and read and wrote about what it meant to be a Jewish dyke. December 25 came to mean a Jewish women's potluck, followed by a movie and a rowdy late-night dinner at a Chinese restaurant.

Although there are, in fact, many working-class Jews (including a lot of our relations in New York whom you've never met), the women in the particular Boston subculture I joined tended to be a part of that city's middle/upper-class infusion from elsewhere. Furthermore, as tends to be true of any group, the most visible spokespeople were predominantly professionals and/or the children of professionals. Finding a way to be simultaneously a lesbian feminist in general, and a Jewish one in particular, while also claiming my working-class identity turned out to be quite a challenge.

At a conference on fighting racism, a group of white working-class women found each other and began comparing notes. We couldn't relate to the guilt of our more affluent white sisters, whose minimal contact across racial lines seemed so distinct from our own. We were more likely to have been in direct competition with people of color—for housing, for jobs, for schooling—although we recognized that the fight was rigged, that our white skin gave us an unfair advantage. The brand of racism we were out to eradicate from ourselves and our people was no less virulent than its white middle-class counterpart, but it was shaped differently.

Though I learned a lot from these women and some of them became my friends, the sense of commonality I experienced with them was a cognitive one, one of connections made more in my mind than in the heart. I had difficulty relating to their particular ethnicities, their regional identifications, their predominantly Christian upbringings. Despite the class divisions, Jewish women felt more like home to me.

A chapter closed when your grandmother died three years ago and I decided it was safe to return to California. My sojourn East—which in my childhood image of the world was where the Jews were—had ended. In this time of more dislocation, of recombinant hyphenation, I reclaimed that part of my identity that is about region, about place. I held on to my hard-won Jewish identification. My new friends here are, just like my old friends back East, mostly Jewish dykes. I joined a Jewish lesbian writing group. But I also came to realize the extent to which I had looked to Jewish identity and Jewish women in a quest for the mother I never had; I knew finally that I never would have her. She's ashes in a box now. Memories about my early experiences of Judaism that couldn't surface while she was alive stare me in the face now.

And that other "part" of me, the shiksa/goyishe/gentile part that was parked away in the drawer of a mausoleum when your grandfather died: what about that? If you work at it, you'll discover that the Appalachian region of your great-grandparents has an honorable and vital history of radicalism and unsurpassed folk art traditions—in music, in cooking, in fabric arts. But I've had to dig for this knowledge. You certainly wouldn't know about it from the media; and any sense of it I might have gotten as my own identity was forming was hidden from me by my father's shame. I heard nothing about his upbringing. His speech bore not a trace of West Virginia, although his mother's twang and "reckons" were quite pronounced.

Often now I take pen to paper and try to conjure up your great-grandmother Lettie again, to sit quietly with her and listen better this time and take notes. I work with early memories, remembering a calm, handsome woman who couldn't protect me from her violent son, but tried mightily. I can vaguely recall her prayers and her minister, although I never got to know her God personally.

Last winter I loitered around a Christmas tree lot near my apartment on two separate occasions debating whether I should buy myself a Christmas tree. Would my Jewish friends feel betrayed if they saw it in my home? Would the ghosts of Christmases past, of old family ties and family lies, return to wreak havoc on my hard-won emotional equilibrium? I decided not to risk it, but next year I just might. Maybe I'll invite you up to help me decorate it.

In the meantime, I've noticed that although I claim I don't observe the religious holidays of Judaism, *they* somehow seem to observe *me*. Although I didn't consciously plan it this way, I've written this letter to you during the Jewish Days of Awe, the ten days between the Jewish New Year and Yom Kippur (the Day of Atonement), days for reflecting back and for seeking forgiveness. So, my dear niece who has likely never set foot in a synagogue, I hope you will accept this gift along with my wishes for a prosperous New Year—the year 5755 on the Jewish calendar.

When I visited you last year, you told me your goal is to be a lawyer who helps foster kids. I wonder silently: can you get there from here? It's so much more difficult for a working-class kid to get through college these days, much less law school. I fight the urge to apologize, facing not only my personal failure to make a future for you, but the failure of my parents' movement and my own. We thought all our work would mean that the world would be a more just place by the time we approached the millenium. Instead it sometimes looks to me like we've been travelling backwards. Still, I keep on fighting, in part because of you. And I give you this: finding these words and these stories about families and peoples—not the Hallmark or sit-com versions but the raw truth—is an act of resistance, an affirmation of all that I was raised to believe and want for you to know.

Note

The author would like to thank Elly Bulkin for her invaluable assistance in the writing and re-writing of this piece.

14

Oxydol Poisoning

Earl Jackson, Jr.

When I moved from Santa Cruz to San Francisco in 1992, my boyfriend Gilberto and I agreed that he would follow as soon as a decent job presented itself. In December, 1993, Gilberto accepted an administrative position at a dance company in the city, and we began to make plans. When Gilberto drove up two weeks before Christmas, however, he arrived empty-handed. Instead of laying down the rugs and imagining furniture arrangements as we had discussed on the phone the night before, he came to tell me the relationship was over. He could no longer tolerate my emotional unavailability and the way my obsessive devotion to my work dominated all other aspects of our lives. Since that weekend, I have made it a priority to understand and overcome my workaholism. Ironically, writing the present essay occupies a middle ground—somewhere between part of the recovery process, and part of the resistance to that recovery, or at least part of the confusion I at times feel about where work stops and life begins.[1]

I pose the following stories as questions as much as I offer them as explanations; my narratives neither presume nor will they propose an essential nature for any of the social identities they adumbrate. The personal history I venture here is thus also an interrogation of its own key terms, including "identity," "race," "gender," and "class." Although I do not attribute to any of these concepts a substantial "truth," I insist upon the dynamic reality of their operations in all areas of personal and social life. I delineate this reality of effect most dramatically when I describe how Gilberto and I negotiated race, sexuality, class, and gender within our relationship, and how these terms conditioned that relationship and overdetermined its failure. Beyond the intellectual and political agendas that motivate and inform this experiment, I write this essay as a means of self-understanding, a reflective act within the very practice that occasioned my loss. I also believe both Gilberto and I deserve an analytical account of my emotional inertia that does not excuse it. This essay, then, is a critical inquiry traversed by a personal reassessment within the processes of mourning and healing; it is in places a recuperative commemoration of the joys and the victories within the relationship that its end should not efface; it is here and there an apology; perhaps a step toward self-forgiveness, and running throughout the text and sustaining its audacity, it is a love letter.

Oxydol Poisoning

I am a white, gay male academic from a lower working-class, blue-collar background. I was born and raised in inner city Buffalo, New York, the third of four children. Both parents were from deeply rural Pennsylvania. My mother was raised Seventh-Day Adventist; my father was the youngest of nine children of a Pentecostal minister. Neither parent finished high school. I am the only child to attend college; to the best of my knowledge, the only other member on either side of the family to hold an advanced degree is a much older cousin, a doctor in Florida who became wealthy in the 1960s prescribing diet pills.

Between the ages of three and five, I hovered close to my mother when she did the laundry, watching intently as she poured the Oxydol into the measuring cup. It twinkled with green, orange, and blue crystals. The powder reminded me of the parti-color cake mix that the neighbors used for their kids' birthday cakes. From the T.V. commercials I habitually memorized, I knew that Oxydol's "color bleach crystals" were especially formulated to give you the "whitest wash ever." This frustrated me, because I wanted my clothes to emerge from the washer spangled with Oxydol rainbows. It seemed wasteful to have those beautiful gem-like hues vanish without a trace, and unjust that the crystals not only added no color but actually took color away.

Borrowing this child's fascination and disappointment, I can refashion Oxydol into a double-duty critical metaphor—first as a metaphor for the contradictions at the heart of dominant conceptions of "whiteness," and secondly for the local politics of psychological structuring within my family of origin. To be "white" is generally conceived of as having no racial specificity; far from being considered a deficit, this absence of characteristics reflects the identification of whiteness with a transparency to a fundamental "human essence," just as western Euro-American culture is considered "civilization" itself, whose male agent is the embodiment of the "universal," as attested in the use of "man" and "he" to include everyone in a by-no-means disinterested abstraction. The privileged ineffability of "whiteness" is an effect of hierarchized binaries of "white" and "non-white" wherein the visible particularities of the latter mark that position as the "incidental," the "local," the "particular," the "inessential." "Whiteness" therefore is a metaphysical nothingness whose transcendent vacancy depends upon the peoples of color to secure at once the white race's discursive self-erasure and its cultural monopoly, just as Oxydol's *white powder* subsumes the color crystals that are the secret catalyst of the detergent's *"whitening power."*

In my personal history, the macropolitical construction of whiteness is intricately bound up with the micropolitical idiosyncracies of my family's particular forms of racism and sexism, as well as its psychopathologies and its whitening out of the internal violences. My religious upbringing was the first area in which I noticed the two functions of the Oxydol principle at work—the erasure of internal differences, and the universalizing of the dominant peculiarities (of our family). I was raised Seventh-Day Adventist, which meant I followed the dietary prohibitions against pork and shellfish, and kept the Jewish Sabbath. From sundown on Friday to sundown on Saturday we were forbidden to watch television, to exchange money, or to take public transportation for the purpose of "idle pleasures." The dietary laws and Sabbath were never explained or given any cultural context; they were merely presented as rules enforced with threats of certain damnation. The potentially interesting relation to Judaism was completely elided, and these elements of Jewish religious doctrine were reduced to the literalist dogma of fundamentalist Christianity. We were taught, in fact, that the Jews lost the right to be the chosen people because they danced, which was an act of carnality God could not tolerate.

My mother's family was ruled by the iron hand of my grandmother, a humorless and vehemently sexophobic woman, in all likelihood psychotic, whose random acts of cruelty were excused, or whitened out as "Godfearing" parental guidance. Similarly, my mother's actions, however bizarre, were "whitened out"—if not through appeals to her piety, then simply by silent consensus. This is most vividly illustrated in the reception and transmission of one of my mother's memories of my infancy, part of the folklore of me. When I was a baby, I would not go to sleep without something to hold. Because I constantly played with boxes of detergent, my mother put me to bed every night with a box of Oxydol. Since she was out of Oxydol one evening, my mother substituted a box of chocolate cake mix. The next morning I was covered head to toe in the mix, looking, in my mother's words, "just like a little colored baby." She realized then that I had opened the cake mix because it smelled good to me. She concluded that she should only give me harsh smelling boxes such as detergent to prevent similar mishaps. As I grew older, my amazement and horror grew with each retelling of this story. No one listening to the story (the immediate family or relatives) ever wondered why, if the baby "needed something" to hold, he was not given a teddy bear or stuffed animal, rather than a box of detergent; neither my mother at the time of the incident nor any of her listeners ever inferred that if I could open a box of cake mix, I could also have opened a box of Oxydol, which might have injured or killed me.

A memory of my own that indirectly supports my mother's Oxydol story also indicates my resistant adaptations of the images imposed on me. For several of the years I was in grammar school, every late January I bought a box of hard-powder candy Valentine Hearts, as multicolored as the Oxydol crystals, but emblazoned on each piece with a phrase such as "Be My Valentine," or "O You Kid." The box itself also pictured the hearts and their messages. After finishing or throwing out the candy, I kept the box in my pillow case, hiding it when my mother did the laundry, keeping it there several weeks until it finally fell apart. It helped me to sleep to know there was something against my ear that said "I love you."

My disappointment in the Oxydol color crystals was an early sign of a tendency that figured in the circumstances surrounding my parents' first discussion of race with me during a visit to my paternal grandparents in Pennsylvania, when I was about five years old. When we arrived in my father's hometown, everyone was talking excitedly about the upcoming visit of the "wonderful colored preacher" to my grandfather's church. I also became excited to see him, imagining someone entinselled and stippled like a rainbow trout.

On Sunday morning, I was marched up to the guest speaker to be introduced before the service. While shaking his hand, I turned to my parents and said in a perfectly loud, obviously disgruntled voice: "He's not colored—he's just brown!" I remember the minister's warm laugh and hug, and my parents' and grandfather's horrified frozen pallor before I was whisked away. That was the first time it was explained to me that some people are "colored" and that while some white people call them bad names, they are "as good as anyone else." The "anyone else" in my parents' lesson exposes the reinscription of white supremacy within liberal gestures toward racial justice. While ostensibly expressing a belief in "racial equality," the "anyone else" presumes that the white multitude is both the standard against which others are to be measured, and the final court from which (qualified) validation of these others is granted or withheld.

Other seemingly "liberal" anecdotes subliminally supported the dominant discourse on race while promoting the family's private pathologies. At least one of these stories was a particularly overdetermined complex of associations for me, because of the Seventh-Day Adventist indoctrination in which I was immersed from early childhood until age eighteen. Because I had been born with jaundice, I spent the first two months of my life in the hospital, under the care of a young black nurse. When my parents came to take me home after I had recovered, they had to pry me screaming from the nurse. In telling this story, my parents stressed how "yellow" I had been, how much I loved "that colored nurse," and how much she loved me. She made them promise that they would "take care of her little baby." Because this story was repeated so often in my upbringing, I internalized new meanings according to each stage of my childhood history when I heard it. The messages included: I was born "wrong"—a particularly glaring example of the "original sin" emphasized in Sabbath School; my illness prompted my parents not to take care of me, but to abandon me; the illness was considered an unacceptable difference from what I should have been, a difference marked by an inappropriate skin color; because of my difference, I was entrusted to someone else, also visibly marked as "different." When my parents finally claimed me (when I was "white"), they were people I did not know, taking me from someone who had cared for me. They not only did not love me, but they devalued the person in the story who had loved me (my first caretaker has no name in the story, she was simply "a colored nurse" who lost her rights over me once my skin no longer marked me as "different"). The Seventh-Day Adventist worldview through which my origin was narrated further burdened my jaundice with meaning. The Adventists believe that a "yellow race" will overrun the earth, bringing about Armageddon. This fantasy supported the general anti-Communist hysteria of the late 1950s and early 1960s, since at that time everyone assumed the "yellow race" in question was Chinese. Therefore, being born with jaundice marked my birth as a conspicuous symptom of original sin and a portent of the agents of the end of the world.

During the years I watched the Oxydol crystals by day, and slept hugging the box by night, my best friend was Angie, a woman who ran the dry cleaning shop several houses down from my parents' apartment. I spent afternoons listening to her stories as she pressed clothes with what looked like two hot ironing boards. I loved her laugh (she was a very large woman, and her laugh resonated through her body), but most of all I was fascinated with her ability to chew gum and smoke at the same time. My parents also turned this into an official memory. As they tell it, whenever they could not find me, they would look in the dry cleaners, where I'd be with my "big colored girlfriend." Apart from the racist trivialization of the woman and her kindness, this story also diverted attention from dangerous information about the family. We moved from the apartment near the dry cleaners in 1959. This means I was between the ages of four and five when I was regularly disappearing, from a third story apartment with steep, dark stairs, down a street with extremely heavy traffic. Their neglect was hidden by the "charming" story of the "nice colored lady." This story, like the previous one also expressed my parents' indifference to their own failure to care for me and their devaluation of the person who showed me love in their place.

The majority of my baby pictures (from several months to one to two years old) show a child in various crawling postures alone on a large metallic kitchen table. In most of these, the table is bare; in some there are stacked cans of evaporated milk. There are no other figures in any of the pictures. There are several pictures of a woman holding a baby as far away from her body as her arms could stretch. I only know this to be my mother from her statement to that effect. She hated the glasses she wore in those years so much that she cut her head out of every photograph before placing them in the album. Although I can picture the living room of the apartment in which we lived at the time, I cannot locate any member of my family there with me. I can see, however, Ann Southern emerging gracefully from the revolving doors of an office building, pausing to let the words "Private Secretary" lattice their way across her wicked, "I-know-more-than-I'm-telling" smile. And Gale Storm defiantly gripping the rails of a tugboat as it bleats out "Oh Susannah!" And Ann B. Davis, hands on her hips in a gesture of goodnatured exasperation, in her role as Schultzy, the neutered lesbian housekeeper for Bob Cummings on "Love that Bob!"[2] My sustained memories of either of my parents begin around 1963, at least five years after this period. At this time, my mother was the blur on the other side of the Oxydol; my father was a rumor connected with the black steel lunch pail and coffee thermos in the sink in the morning. They were the shadowy stagehands for the incandescent reality of Lucille Ball and Imogene Coca.

My imagination was populated by less savory characters as well, because of my mother's habit of taking me to horror films, beginning with *The Creature from the Black Lagoon*, when I was three. I experienced my first unwieldy erection in the Ellen Terry Theater one evening in 1959, during a screening of *The Brides of Dracula*. The other film that had a powerful influence on me that year was *Thirteen Ghosts*, in 3-D. *Famous Monsters of Filmland* did a cover story on *Thirteen Ghosts* the month of its release, and after I had seen the movie, my brother, with my mother's permission, cut out the cover photo and hung it over my bed. The image was a woman's living corpse, in such an advanced degree of dessication that the skin and the skull had fused into one gnarled texture the color of burnt toast—or cake mix. Her eyes were simply holes that gaped on tremulous pools of blackness, like the shadows that percolated from my closet when the door was left ajar.

The horror films fit into a larger construction of the world as inherently menacing, thus justifying the agoraphobic isolation in which my family encased itself. Although it was actually sterile and devoid of nurturance, my parents constantly portrayed our "home" as a unique oasis of safety and security in a perilous universe. Any need for real emotional support was deferred by and displaced onto an exaggerated survival instinct, conflating the absence of physical threat with the presence of love. The geography of terror was structured around the binaries of "Them/Us," "Outside/Inside" and "Danger/Safety." These spaces increased in relative safety levels as they decreased in size and moved closer to the constrictive circle of "home" itself. The largest division was between the East Side of Buffalo, which was the black ghetto, and the West Side of Buffalo, which waas where we lived. Here the family's pathology was perfectly congruent with the prevalent discourses of racism and fear-mongering that characterized city politics and white working-class attitudes of the time.

The public "East Side–West Side" macrocosm, however, broke down into "the Neighborhood–Our House," divergently paralleled by "the Relatives–Our Immediate Family." My cousin Marion and my aunt Bonnie had married physically abusive alcoholics, Murray and Paul, who beat both women and their children frequently, at times severely enough to require hospitalization. Neither of the women ever pressed charges. Bonnie's husband often kicked her out of the wheelchair to which polio had confined her, forcing her to crawl on her stomach to the phone for the ambulance, in front of the children. My parents would go to the hospital and commiserate, but they never did anything, since it wasn't "their business." They often would congratulate our "immediate family" by contrasting the placid calm of our house to Marion's and Bonnie's. We were often asked, "Aren't you glad you have Dad for a father and not Murray or Paul?" or, "Aren't you glad we don't get drunk and beat you up?" I wondered why there wasn't a third choice. At family gatherings, however, Paul and Murray were treated just as if they were any other family member. I interpreted this to mean that none of us children would be protected from violence or abuse if it were to occur. I was right.

The Tints of Gender Troubles

I often forgot my father was alive. I raised my hand when the class was asked who did not have a dad. I was always on the verge of asking my mother to sign me up for the Big Brother program. Even I considered my faulty memory peculiar, since my father came home from work around 4:30 every afternoon, ate supper with us, and spent the rest of the evening behind a newspaper. Although my father was traditionally masculine, he was very quiet and extremely withdrawn. He had no friends, preferring to spend his leisure time fishing by himself or rebuilding the house.[3] My father's non-presence did not provide an alternative model of "masculinity" to that which my psychotic uncles represented for me. I wanted no part of that, nor of the boys on the street who seemed well on their way toward that kind of manhood. Like their fathers, they seemed rough, dull, and needlessly aggressive and cruel. I hated sports and competition, and tended to stay by myself; I preferred reading comic books and making friends with the squirrels in the backyard and the neighborhood dogs. I even trained a crow to eat out of my hand and sit on my shoulder.

Evidence of the social changes of the 1960s trickled into Buffalo; which were sporadically noted with perfunctory bewilderment by my mother and other neighbors on their porches.

Whenever the subject of interracial couples came up, my mother, or another neighbor would say, "It's always a white woman with a colored guy. You never see the other way around. That's because men have more sense." This puzzled me, given my parents' earlier assertion that "colored people are just as good as white people." It also encouraged my already growing identification with "women," first of all, because the women in interracial relationships seemed to be operating on the nonracist belief that my parents espoused more than my parents were, and secondly, because I did not want any part of the "sense" I saw displayed by the men in my neighborhood or in my family.

Like other aspects of the family-society interface, this public declaration of allegiance to the norm was marred by occasional intimations of a private deviation. Whenever the peculiarly recurrent rumor arose that there was "Indian blood" in our family, it was usually dismissed with the joking refrain, "Of course, on your mother's side." I assume this qualification derived from and supported the idea that racial mixing occurred through women, since men "had more sense." Note, however, that this association itself does not make sense, because the assignation to the matrilineal family does not indicate the sex of the person or persons who had brought this blood into our stock. Furthermore, such fingerpointing neglected another unspoken aspect of family history: my paternal grandmother was from the Louisiana Bayou, and her first language was French Creole. Nevertheless, the idea appealed to me greatly because I wanted something that guaranteed an identifiable physical difference from my father and all other "men."

My initial fascination with my (matrilineal) cousin, Yvonne, lay in the way she embodied this promise of a difference within. Yvonne claimed she had been told at an early age she was part Ojibwe. Of Marion's five children, one was a pale brunette, three were blonds. And Yvonne was beautiful. Her skin was the color of café Mocha, and she had long, chestnut colored hair, and huge dark eyes that glistened in ways she could control. I loved playing with her because she was an incurable tomboy, which meant she had all the good qualities of "boys" without the brutish machismo. She was very handy with tools, strong, imaginative, and very brave. She had defended me from bullies more than once. I always felt protected in her presence—even the day I sat with her on the curb where she was vomiting her grape Nihi into the sewer grating because her father had just broken her ribs with a baseball bat for dressing like a boy. We were outside waiting for the ambulance, hoping he had passed out by then. I assume Yvonne got the majority of the beatings because of her color, her exposure of one of the secrets.

My father was color blind. Even as a small child, this was a source of smug satisfaction for me; I associated the sex-linked gene for color blindness with a congenital grimness that for some reason was celebrated as a masculine ideal on this planet. My nuanced color sense I considered a gift developed outside the grey regime of the men without color. My passion for colors and their spectacular display founded my long history of disappointing my father. When I was five I used to help my father tend his garden by sprinkling cinnamon on the ants attacking his peonies. The spice is instantly fatal to the insects. One week when we had run out of cinnamon, giving the ants time to bivouac and recoup, I promised my father that I would use my savings to restock our cinnamon supply that Friday at the grocery store.

But when I discovered a kaleidoscope in one of the aisles, I decided to let the peonies fend for themselves. My father allowed me to buy the toy, but sighed and sadly observed that without the cinnamon the flowers had no protection against the ants. Although he did not buy any cinnamon himself, his resignation clearly exonerated him from my act of criminal negligence. Guilt nagged at me as I peered down that long, magical tube. As my eye revelled in the prismatic effects of these florescent shape-shifters, their riotous splendor confirmed my vision as *other than and richer than my father's*, whose masculinity impoverished his spectrum, robbed him of rainbows. But the spectacular excess of the kaleidoscope also was the mark of shame for my complicity in the destruction of the more orderly beauty of my father's cultivated flowers. My indulgence at the lens tokened the weird appetites that would overflow and corrupt the abstemious peonies because of my betrayal.

As I grew older, this conflict between the extraordinary and the natural evolved into the more publically current metaphorical systems of normative sex and gender constructions. While my mother's sexist mode of condemning interracial relationships inadvertently encouraged my cross-gender identifications, my parents invoked racial stereotypes to discourage my infractions of gender norms when the child's hope for the Oxydol crystals evolved into a young teen's flamboyant fashion sense. On seeing the clothes I bought or admired, one of my parents would warn: "Do you want people to think you're colored? Only colored men wear clothes like that. And they can get away with it—they all carry knives." The message here was manifold: (1) certain colors broke gender codes; (2) these colors also suggested a cross-racial identification; (3) an identification with or (even unintentional) emulation of the cultural expressions of another race is self-evidently negative and to be avoided; (4) black men are armed and dangerous.

Conjoining two usually unrelated stereotypes of black men ("colorful dressers" and "knife carrying") places the burden of literal self-defense on a man who wears certain colors rather than questioning the right of the hypothetical assailant to attack someone because of his mode of dress. Here racist discourse functions to foreclose from interrogation a gender system that condones brutal enforcement of an arbitrary cultural code. Using these racial stereotypes also allowed my parents to regulate gender norms within the family without directly addressing issues of gender or acknowledging that I was transgressing rules I should have internalized and accepted as so natural that neither correction nor coercion should have been necessary.

My mother occasionally gave voice to the otherwise unarticulated familial concerns over my "gender trouble." Whenever my potential infractions were too obvious, my mother would say, in the presence of my father: "Your father is going to have to have a talk with you one of these days." Although the anger with which she said this made it sound like a threat, I always wondered what was taking him so long. He never responded to this statement, usually remaining behind his paper or staring out at the garden, wondering how the roses were doing. As time went by, she said this with more urgency and an exasperation I think partially directed at my father for his complete uninvolvement in these conflicts. He never ultimately found time to "have that talk." During my rather slow puberty, concern gave way to anxiety, flaring up more violently in my mother's responses. When I was between the ages of twelve to fourteen I was a rather effusive storyteller. At times, when I was in the middle of telling a story I was particularly enthusiastic about, my mother became enraged, slapping me as hard as she could and shouting, "Why hasn't your voice changed yet! You sound like a girl!" My father merely receded farther into the distance beyond his newspaper.

At about the same time, my cousin Yvonne was also the subject of familial "concern" over gender issues. Marion was "nice" and long-suffering and "really loved" her children, but didn't know what to do about her husband. She did, however, know what to do about her daughter. When Yvonne was twelve, Marion found a love letter Yvonne had written to another girl. Marion had her committed to the State Mental Hospital in Buffalo, a locked ward. She was there three months and Marion refused to visit her or allow her to come home. Eventually they transferred her to a juvenile facility on the Hudson River (where most of the other girls had either been heroin addicts or convicted of violent crimes). She spent three years incarcerated there, when her grandmother, Gretchen, signed release forms and had Yvonne transferred to her guardianship, saving Yvonne from at least two more years there and a possible prison term. I was elated. We started seeing each other again right away, and when I was sixteen, Yvonne began sneaking me into the lesbian bars downtown practically every weekend for almost two years. These bars provided a more supportive environment and a more complex sexual politics than gay male bars would have. For a variety of reasons, moreover, the lesbian bars were far more racially mixed and highlighted the daily realities of class dynamics more openly than gay male bars of the mid-1970s (or, in most cases, of the early 1990s).

Double Bind/Original Sin

By the time I entered school, I was a rather morbid child. In the images that composed me, I was stranded on a desert of stainless steel and formica, raised at arm's length by a headless woman who bundled me up with toxic substances and consigned me to the graces of a ghoul gibbering above my crib. In kindergarten, when the other kids wanted to play house, I wanted to be the maniac holding them hostage. Or, I told them to be bugs, and I was a can of Raid. When I pressed the top of my head and hissed they were to belly-up and die. My favorite game was "vampire"; my mother let me wear her black apron as a cape. None of the kids really liked these games, and I became a loner, a tendency reinforced by being the only Seventh-Day Adventist child in the class. In my solitude, the games took on variations. The cape occasionally came off my shoulders and became an apron again. Or a skirt.

I was also an unusually bright and intellectually curious child. I taught myself to read beginning when I was three years old, memorizing how words looked on the screen during commercials when the voice said them. Someone must have helped me after that, but no one can remember who. The first book I ever read from cover to cover was called *It's Johnny's Birthday!* which I carried around with me until I was in kindergarten. I treasured that book because it signified my achievement and because it was about a boy whose parents, friends, and family showed their love by celebrating his birthday—the fact of his existence. In the back of my mind I knew I had never had a birthday like the one Johnny had. While reading the book made me realize this (the association between the Oxydol powder and the parti-colored cakes of other people's children was not accidental), the act of reading was an accomplishment I hoped would gain me the love and attention I had not yet received. When this failed to win my parents over, it only made it more obvious there was something missing in the family itself. Actually there were two things missing: love, and the kind of recognition and encouragement in intellectual pursuits a child with my curiosity needed.

The only books my parents owned were the Bible, a child's illustrated version of the *Old Testament*, and a set of *Do-It-Yourself* manuals. My parents and many of my relatives freely admitted that they had never read a book in their adult lives, and could not see the interest in doing so. The only outlet for my hunt for knowledge was Sabbath school and the Seventh-Day Adventist self-study correspondence courses. My studiousness further enmeshed me in the Seventh-Day Adventist doctrines of self-loathing and fetishized misery. These lessons were followed by written examinations that I took and sent in. With the corrections came specific instructions to guide my moral development. One of the questions was: "If you really enjoy something, what should you do?" The correct answer was "Fear It." In my answer, I mentioned that I collected comic books and loved reading them. When the exam was returned to me, the accompanying evaluation read: "Any sense of personal pleasure should arouse suspicion and prayer. The devil enters our minds through our sense of enjoyment. Therefore, anything you enjoy is a likely potential for sin. It is better to give it up than risk losing the true rewards of New Jerusalem." They then instructed me to sell my comic book collection and give the proceeds to the Church, which I did. For several months I refrained from buying any more comic books, and when I finally did relent, I did so with a profound and nagging sense of guilt that stayed with me for years.

A similar guilt was given me about being "proud" of accomplishments or talents. I was told I should be ashamed of my pride in my ability to read, particularly because overwork in learning, like any self-interested focus upon the functionings of the mind (these included therapy and consulting *ouija* boards) was an invitation for demonic possession. My erudition tragically facilitated my internalization of these lunatic notions instead of their rejection. This paradox informed my ambivalence toward my own intellectual energies, even to the extent of focusing my "religious" humility on a point of my personal history—my birthday, for at least two reasons. First of all, the topic of the first book I had learned to read fixated my guilt over my intellectual pride on that image. Secondly, if I could be ashamed of my excess pride in my reading ability and in my desire for a birthday celebration, I could rationalize my parents' disinterest in me as religious right-eousness in action.

My birthdays became ritual dramas of my acceptance of the cruelest judgments placed upon me, as expiation of my dual sins of pride in my intelligence and my need for people to acknowl-edge me as special. My eighth birthday was "celebrated" in Shinglehouse, Pennsylvania at my cousins' house—Althea and Ken. It was Ken's birthday party too. In the middle of the party, the radio announced that Marilyn Monroe had been found dead of an overdose in her home. This was the end of the party for me, and somehow the end of all parties. A few months later, I began crying uncontrollably watching the duet between Marilyn and Jane Russell in *Gentleman Prefer Blondes*, broadcast for the first time on *NBC's Saturday Night at the Movies*.

My older sister Sandy had married when I was in kindergarten, but lived only a few houses down the street. She had never finished high school, and had very little sense of the world, but she was a formidable figure with an ineluctable will. For my ninth birthday, she decided to throw me a large party in my parents' backyard, in order to get me out of my shell. She invited thirty kids (with whom I never played and whom I generally either detested or feared and hid from). It was an excessively hot day. I was not participating in the games with the enthusiasm that Sandy expected. When I told her I wasn't feeling well, she picked me up by my neck and pulled me into my parents' family room where she shook me until I was dizzy (I was on the scrawny side; Sandy was tall and around two hundred pounds), telling me what an ungrateful child I was, how much she had done, etc. She worked herself up into such a righteous frenzy that she beat me up to calm herself down. She swore I would never have another birthday party again. Later that evening, when it occurred to someone to take my temperature, it turned out I was running a fever of 102°. I had chickenpox. Somehow, my sister's uninformed "curse" had already been internalized by my family and myself, and in spite of the subsequent discovery of the cause of my unappreciative demeanor, no one ever attempted to celebrate my birthday again. Even in my adult life, I have never allowed myself to celebrate it either.

An Unsentimental Education

By kindergarten I was reading at approximately a third-grade level, and the teacher used to bring in other teachers for demonstrations of my ability, something which made my parents very uncomfortable, and increased the other children's disinterest in playing with me. By third grade I was thoroughly bored with grammar school. I used to watch the fourth grade teacher, Mr. Williams, talk with the other teachers in the hall. I had heard him speak French once, which seemed to me like a magic act I dreamt of being able to manage myself one day. I prayed that I be assigned him for fourth grade. He had a reputation of being a "hard" teacher, which I assumed meant he would offer more and be more challenging. He was also somewhat scary, too. Beyond being the only male teacher in the school, he was famous for his corporal punishments: whacks across the palms with the top edge of a triangular ruler, and making the offender squat on his or her haunches with outstretched arms on which he then placed dictionaries.

The last day of the school year, along with the final report cards we received a note announc-ing the name of next year's teacher. I lucked out. I had been assigned Mr. Williams and so had my best friend Patty. I was elated, but still a little nervous. But Patty started crying. She said her father would have a fit when he found out she was going to be taught by a "nigger." (Her father did in fact have several fits in reaction to the news; the fit in the principal's office secured his daughter's transfer.)

Mr. Williams was wonderful. He had a florid style of speaking that was rich in vocabulary, and resplendent with detours and asides that were for the most part lost on me except for the proof they offered that the world was larger and more complex than the one I had seen so far. I was an extremely attentive student, and responded well to the challenges he offered the students, challenges it never seemed to occur to him would be met. He noticed me immediately and took an active interest in my education in his class and in getting me out of the public educational system, if possible, thereafter.

One lunch hour, Mr. Williams took me with him to Sears where he had several errands to run. I had never seen a teacher outside of school, and I never saw them do things like "drive" or "shop." I was thrilled. Through this glimpse of his "private life" I got the sense that his eloquence and multilayered wit had several purposes. In class they enhanced his storytelling, encouraged vocabulary building, and supplemented the blandness of the textbooks with a more three-dimensional skepticism. In his interactions with the smug and suspicious store clerks, Mr. Williams was neither patronizing nor apologetic, but his modes of speech expressed his recognition that his presence as the only black customer in an all-white world challenged their worldview in ways they could not articulate, and his intelligence and erudition was itself an act of creative and defiant survival. I loved being seen with him, and identified with him when their questioning looks drifted from him to the little white boy holding his hand.

Mr. Williams had several conferences with my parents, first to convince them that I was an "exceptional child," but that my potential needed to be developed in special schools. They listened politely, but it was evident nothing was sinking in. At home my parents discussed what Mr. Williams had said exclusively in terms of "those colored" who "know about their social programs." At the third meeting, Mr. Williams detailed the procedures of entrance exams to private schools where he had some influence and assured them I would merit a scholarship. They assured him that I only "seemed smart" in a "normal" environment and that a new school would probably be too scary for me, since one where everyone was really "smart" would make me seem "dumb." This was the only occasion I had ever seen Mr. Williams plead with someone. The repressed incredulity with which Mr. Williams listened to my parents was the first external corroboration of a suspicion I never wanted verified: there was something fundamentally wrong with the people who had absolute authority over me; they were not qualified to make decisions concerning me that no one else would have the power to correct. In saying goodbye to them, Mr. Williams glanced at me with a look of helpless compassion, hoping that someone would succeed in saving me from the fate to which my parents were so complacently consigning me.

Mr. Williams lived up to his reputation in dealing out corporal punishments to those who broke rules, but it was relatively easy to stay inside them. Toward the end of the year, however, most students who had never been hit with the ruler started to disobey on purpose, in a counterphobic parody of their earlier fears. Mr. Williams must have been aware of this too, but went along with it. Perhaps it happened every year. When I did it, as I stood in line waiting, I knew that my deliberate talking out of turn was an attempt to get Mr. Williams to punish me for what my parents had done to him, for their refusal to take him seriously, and for their refusal to take me seriously. I wanted to be punished for being a white lower-class statistic, for being unable to escape the injunction to become "anyone."

An eighth-grade social studies teacher also tried to persuade my parents to allow her to arrange for my admission into a private high school. She knew that Lafayette High School, the public high school in my district, was one of the worst in the city and would not provide the kind of educational challenges I needed. I feared going to Lafayette because of the reputation of Mr. Lefkowitz, a former Marine drill sergeant who was one of the gym teachers there. Again my parents refused to consider it. Throughout my childhood, my family's patterns of interaction tended to reinforce for me the social ideology and the religious dogma of my environment. Now that I was older, however, my parents' decisions about my schooling seemed to me a wanton assertion of authority that freed me from all personally felt obligation to such authority—both in terms of behavioral control and in terms of the "truths" asserted. The utter disregard for my education and my intellectual curiosity intensified my skepticism regarding the family's opinions on gender and race to a complete repudiation of them. These messages were enmeshed in the family fantasy geography of safety and danger, that had been now conclusively exposed as a hoax. All the violence I saw occured on the West Side, where my uncles lived. The only place I knew of where a child had been nearly poisoned was my own house. The only person who physically assaulted me was my mother.

My skepticism led me to investigate both the larger social systems in which I was growing up and the family's history that was whitened out in its official self-delusion. Quite unexpectedly, my mother herself volunteered important information about the family I had not previously suspected: my older brother and sister were not my father's children. My mother's first husband disappeared in 1943, leaving her with a two-year old boy (Gary) and an infant daughter (Sandy). She obtained a divorce decree in 1945. In the 1950s she received word that her ex-husband was serving time in a State Penitentiary for masterminding a car theft ring. During his disappearances during their marriage, he had been impersonating a minister in several outlying towns, performing bogus marriage ceremonies. This item was invaluable in my early demystification of both the family's "normality" and the morality of compulsory heterosexuality. My mother's ex-husband's charade meant that many couples married between 1941 and 1959 in the upstate New York–Erie, Pennsylvania region lived in "sin" their entire lives, spawning a generation of bastards. Even a marriage between two "godfearing" Christians could be the result of a criminal's sick sense of humor.

In the whitened out version of my mother's family history, she was one of six children: Keith, Genevieve, Gretchen, Marion, Lois (my mother), and Bonnie. Once when Marion was a senior in high school she had said that one of her teachers was "pregnant," which enraged my grandmother, who struck her violently and told her never to use that word in her presence again. The hypocrisy here is particularly invidious, because Marion, although raised as my grandmother's daughter, was actually her granddaughter. My mother's older sister, Gretchen, had conceived her illegitimately. Marion was simply raised as Gretchen's sister. (Even as a teenager and adult Marion was never allowed to call Gretchen "mother.") The same fate befell my mother, meeting a traveling salesman in 1934. Pregnant, she left high school. In 1935, Bonnie was born and raised as my mother's sister. Bonnie was born in 1935, and contracted polio only a few weeks after the vaccine had been approved and distributed nationwide. Given the polio epidemic at that time, was it simply the family's rural isolation that prevented Bonnie from receiving the vaccine in time? Or was it the family's shame that kept her out of public notice? And why, as a little girl of seven, was she sent to an institution over 100 miles away from her home for five or six years? More whitening out the family's history at the expense of its children? She spent several years in The Crippled Children's Guild and was confined to a wheelchair her whole life. I did not find out she was my half-sister (instead of my aunt) until 1977, when I was in graduate school. Therefore when my parents wrung their hands helplessly over the battered crippled woman in the hospital, and when they compared our family favorably to Bonnie's, they suppressed the fact that the woman abandoned to the maniac she married was my mother's daughter.

Hard Knocks

I made two friends my first semester at Lafayette High School who were as alienated from school life as I was. Hoak was a mildly retarded boy who commuted to school from the orphanage in which he had been raised since infancy. Manuela had recently moved to Buffalo from New York City, and was horrified to learn that less than five percent of the student body was "Hispanic." I liked going bowling with Manuela's family because their laughter at my game had none of the derision that I had come to expect. I also loved to hear the ease with which Manuela and her parents glided from English to Spanish, reminding me of Mr. Williams's magic act with French.

Lafayette was approximately thirty-five percent black and sixty percent white. Between 1967 and 1969 there had been significant unease and occasional violence between black and white students. My gym teacher, the dreaded Mr. Lefkowitz, began the year with a bizarre means of diffusing the racial tension. In one of his early "pep talks," he said something like this: "Some of you guys are white, and some are colored. But I don't want to hear anybody calling anybody 'nigger.' You all come from families and are just regular guys whatever color you are. The only guy who might be a 'nigger' is one that's so useless even his folks didn't want him. . . . Right, Hoak?" Hoak laughed nervously. This launched a weekly campaign of focused abuse, including a medicine dodge ball game whose only rule was to "hurt Hoak as much as you can." Hoak had tremendous stamina, but the strain showed increasingly as the semester wore on.

One day in the locker room we had another "pep talk." Lefkowitz took on a tone of good-natured "pal," that reeked of venom and usually forebode a cruel denouement. In this talk, Lefkowitz occasionally addressed Hoak as if he were his "buddy" and his cruel treatment had been a means of "toughening him up," turning Hoak into "a regular guy." As if this line of argument had convinced himself and Hoak, Lefkotwitz concluded, "See, I did all this for you. I did you a favor. You'll do me a favor now too, won't you? It's only fair. We're buddies now, right?" Hoak nodded eagerly, but the rictus of his smile and the overly bright glaze in his eyes betrayed his fear. He knew he had no choice but to go along with whatever was coming next, but he was hoping against all reason that it would not be more of the same. Lefkowitz continued, "This dodge ball is a little flat, and my air pump is broken. Can you finish blowing it up for me, for your old pal, Mr. Lefkowitz?" Hoak said, "Sure." Standing in front of Hoak who was seated on a bench, Lefkowitz secured the ball between his legs, and extended the tube to Hoak's mouth. While Hoak was thus engaged, Lefkowitz winked at the other boys and motioned with his one free hand toward the shadow on the wall. It looked as if Hoak was fellating Lefkowitz. Lefkowitz began encouraging and complimenting Hoak on his ability: "That's great Hoak. You got a great set of lips." The next week Hoak was not in school. During roll call in a gym class a week later, Lefkowitz announced that Hoak had suffered a nervous breakdown and would be transferred to a "special school" after he was released from the hospital. Lefkowitz added, with mock regret, "Once a reject, always a reject."

I made it through the first semester without serious incident. One afternoon shortly after Christmas break, however, Mr. Lefkowitz was waiting for us in the locker room. He told us not to change because we were going to the auditorium instead. Everyone was seated in the first rows of seats, and the place was semi-dark except for the stage. One of the seniors who assisted Lefkowitz "manned" the spotlights. Another put a chair on the side of the stage. Lefkowitz told me to sit with all my books on that chair. He announced to the class: "Today we're going to teach Jackson how to walk and act like a man." I was ordered to walk across the stage, carrying my books. Whenever he or one of the class decided my walk or way of holding the books was too effeminate (every time for about ten times) one of the senior assistants leapt to the stage and knocked all the books out of my hands. I had to scoop them up, and start all over again.

Finally Lefkowitz directed me to pull the chair to stage center and sit on it. The assistant turned a pin spot on me. There were whispered instructions to the oldest of the senior assistants, muffled laughter, and then a momentary silence. Then the assistant spoke from somewhere in the row of boys that was only sporadically and vaguely distinguishable as shapes in the blackness. The voice told me what masturbation was and how to "do it." Thanks to my sheltered Seventh-Day Adventist upbringing, I had never heard of this before. I concentrated on remaining expressionless. I would not acknowledge the voice with so much as a movement of a muscle in my face. My eyes focused on nothing. I stared blankly ahead, without the expectation or desire to see anything beyond the inane blur of the footlights and the inky emptiness of the auditorium. I was on a spaceship looking out the window, in a cheap, unconvincing sci-fi movie. All alone. Hearing nothing except static on the radio, an unintelligible message from an irrelevant ground control.

Whether or not Lefkowitz turned the class attention to me in order to maintain the racial truce he had established by scapegoating Hoak, my situation was fully implicated in the prevalent discourse on racial, sexual, and gender identities.[4] It was one of the "Oxydol" functions of whiteness that facilitated strategic value in the choice of victims. Both Hoak and I could be considered racially unmarked because we were white. Denouncing a black child as a "reject" or a potential "fag" would have still meant inciting white student hostility against a black student, something Lefkowitz knew would have been counterproductive. Because "whiteness" has no "characteristics" (in its privileged self-definition as universal) both Hoak's and my racial identity could be ignored in favor of the intolerable "difference" that eclipsed it. Therefore, even if black kids were bullying either one of us, the white kids would not perceive it as a race-related conflict. This strategy, however, was subtended by the tragic irony that the adult leading the gang of young men in his charge against an unarmed person whose only crime was the appearance of "difference" was a Jewish man who came of age during the Holocaust. This irony was particularly painful to me because I felt an affinity to Judaism as a religion that my mother's church had at once imposed on and withheld from me.

The forms my persecution took demonstrated the horrible adaptability of the logic of hatred. Hoak was hated because he was "stupid" and his "imbecility" was the grounds for the suspicions he was a "faggot" because he didn't know any better. I had just made the honor roll, and my "brains" and my bookish habits were now the symptoms of my "faggotry"—I could be despised for being bright with the same intensity as Hoak could be for being dumb. The white picket fence and meticulous garden surrounding my house, my abhorence of dirty jokes and the religious stringency of my upbringing were circumstantial evidence for doting and attentive parents. The students used this misconstrued "parental over-protectiveness" as a focus of their hectoring of me, just as his parents' neglect had been the cause and vindication of their aggressive contempt for Hoak. My relationship with Manuela became a mark of my sexual/gender confusion. Being seen with a girl was usually regarded as a sign of heterosexual conquest and butch assurance. My friendship with a girl betrayed an identification with women and unorthodox sympathies with them.

The absence of a "Hispanic" student presence allowed the white students to use racial slurs against Manuela in taunting me. They would not have done this had she been black, not only because there would have been swift retribution from the black students, but also because the victimization of me had as one of its purposes the maintenance of an equilibrium between black and white *male* students.[5] But I suspect that the use of Manuela's race also figured in the covert communication and the stabilizing functions of this form of terrorism. By attacking me for an interracial friendship as a symptom of my homosexuality, the white boys could join the black guys in a truce on the basis of a common enemy of masculinity, while obliquely setting the limits of that truce to a peaceful coexistence within the contexts of the school environment. My friendship with Manuela transgressed both gender and racial boundaries; by touting these transgressions as stigmata of my sexual perversion, those boundaries were resecured. Heterosexuality required dating women but not liking them. Similarly, the provisional racial harmony between blacks and whites precluded cross-racial understanding. The foreclosure of real interracial relations as a structural necessity for the school's black and white "unity" was expressed at the expense of a third race, so that the assertion could be made and denied at the same time.

Needless to say, the news of the incident in the auditorium spread throughout the school, and open season was declared on me. I had to have several alternate routes both to school and on the way home to avoid packs of boys who would jeer, jostle or beat me. In the cafeteria, chairs and occasionally tables were turned over on me, my tray was often kicked out of my hands, my bag lunch trampled. The student monitors were among my most violent attackers, and the teachers on duty were often "jock" types who pretended they thought this was innocent horseplay in which I was participating and finding as funny as everyone else.[6] Like my family, the school was an institution of arbitrary but rigidly enforced discipline that paradoxically offered no real protection or security. Hallways were monitored heavily, and movement was severely restricted. During the cafeteria hour, students were allowed only in the cafeteria or the basement in which the cafeteria was located. We were not permitted to go outside, to go to other floors, or to use empty classrooms. Whenever I eluded my attackers by going upstairs or using an emergency exit, I was subject to disciplinary write-ups and detention, if caught. I started skipping school frequently.

The first time I was suspended for skipping school I was amazed at the logic on which the officials operated: they punished me for not attending classes by denying me permission to attend classes. To me this just meant three days without the risk of getting beaten up at school and without having to hide in the streets all day, since I was ordered to stay home. After returning to school, I was required to take a day-long battery of tests, to discover if there were some particular reason for my truancy. Administered by the itinerant school psychologist who made the rounds of several inner-city schools, the tests included interviews, Rorschach, coordination, and so on. At the end of the morning, the psychologist determined that there was indeed "sufficient indication" that I was seriously emotionally disturbed. He assigned me to weekly appointments with a therapist at a nearby clinic. The therapist was a dashing young man, whom I immediately trusted and, of course, for whom I suffered a deep transference love. I admitted that I was gay. He insisted that homosexuality was a neurosis that could not support a healthy relationship or lifestyle and that it could be overcome with work. His central focus was to convince me that my conflicts were not with the school or my family, but arose from my laziness in not giving heterosexuality a chance.

In my sophomore and junior years my skipping increased in response to the increased violence against me and the utter boredom I experienced in most of the classes. Latin was the only class I attended regularly and in which I participated wholeheartedly. Although I was barely passing everything else, I maintained a 99-100 average in Latin for three years, and in my junior year, when I was at my most desperate, I won a New York State Classical Association commendation for excellence in Latin. Home life became more tumultuous as my disciplinary problems with school continued. When I was a junior, my sister entered Lafayette and also began skipping school. This was actually one of the first major signs of the severe agoraphobia that would soon render her totally housebound. My mother, however, believed Michelle was just copying her older brother's behavior. Therefore I was subject to my mother's rage whenever I skipped school, but also whenever Michelle did.

One afternoon shortly after the tensions began surrounding Michelle's school attendance, my father astonished me by taking me aside confidentially. He told me that we had to be very careful not to "worry" Mom, because she was going through "the change of life." He did not specify what this was, but his hushed tone meant that it was one of those things never mentioned. What at first seemed like my father's admission that something was "wrong" with my mother's way of dealing with situations, turned out to be the Oxydol defense yet again. Instead of drawing attention to my mother's lack of control, the once whispered innuendo of "the change" functioned to excuse any of her excesses and enjoin us to silence. It also placed the responsibility for my mother's behavior on the children who were the targets of her terrors. The real event of menopause cannot account for the frequency and intensity of the "attacks" nor the duration of the condition its invocation supposedly covered (approximately three years).

Weekday mornings became so fraught for my mother that the anxiety over whether or not Michelle and I would go to school that day triggered attacks before either of us had even awakened. School days often began by being jolted out of bed by my mother's screams. Running downstairs, I found my mother lying face up on the kitchen floor, eyes glassy, shrieking like a parrot. She quieted down as soon as I began rubbing one of her hands. I continued rubbing her hand until her eyes looked as if they were registering her surroundings. This ritual sharpened my

---

observational skills and developed my physical reflexes because my mother often swung at me once she was aware of my proximity.

On two occasions, after reviving my mother on the kitchen floor and dodging her punches, I ran down to my older sister Sandy's house, where Michelle was standing rigidly behind the swing set, staring into space, unspeaking, with her hands gripped tightly around the swing chain. I had to pry each finger from the chains one at a time. She remained unresponsive or partially incoherent for several minutes. Although I remained outwardly calm in order to revive her, I was terrified that Michelle's state would set my mother off again, who would take it out on me as the cause of Michelle's difficulties. These scenes did not leave me much fortitude to face my own traumas awaiting me at school, or for my duties as a stockboy in a drugstore after school. My sister stopped going to school at all before her freshman year was finished. That year and several years thereafter I tried to convince my parents to take her to therapy. They insisted there was nothing wrong with her except that her older brother taught her how to drop out. My father told me that I must have been "born mean." My sister stopped leaving the house when she was sixteen. At the time of this writing she is thirty-seven. She has still never left my parents' house, except for two annual visits to my older sister's house, five doors down the street. Even in the dead of summer, this journey requires slacks, a longsleeve shirt, a full-length coat, and a hood.

I spent most of my junior year in the park between the Albright Knox Art Gallery and the Historical Museum, reading for hours on end. I still get a chill picking up Proust, because I read all of *Rememberances of Things Past* in that park through a Buffalo winter. My progress was slowed by the gloves that made turning pages difficult. But the frostbite I got when I decided to take them off put the gloves back on for the rest of the season. At work in the drugstore, I scooped up any pills scattered on the floor and either stockpiled them in my jacket or swallowed them by the Coke machine in case the random combination might make me feel better. At the end of my shift, sitting on the basement steps of the pharmacy above the rat traps, I wondered if it were time to kill myself yet. But I could not give the kids and teachers at school the satisfaction of knowing they "had been right" about me "all along." My contempt for everyone I knew saved my life several times.

By the first month of my senior year the school had had enough. I was expelled. As part of their compilation portrait of me as an incorrigible offender the school officials disclosed the reason the psychologist had found me "seriously disturbed" two years previously. During the initial interview the psychologist had asked me what I wanted to do professionally. I told him I wanted to make films. I said that I was fascinated with the technical aspects of filmmaking and that when I went to the movies, more than the plot, I was interested in the editing techniques, the lighting, the relations between image and sound tracks, and so on. He wrote on the evaluation that this was the sign of a very troubled youngster. According to his expert testimony, "Normal people watch a movie for the story—they couldn't care less about how it was made." On the official record of my expulsion I was listed as a "detriment to the morale of the school." The head of the English department added her own assessment: "I feel sorry for any college stupid enough to accept this boy. He should get a job sweeping in a garage and try to stay out of jail." The truant officer and whoever else was in the room seemed surprised and disappointed that I was not crestfallen, or even particularly discouraged at this news. My initial response, in fact, sounded closer to elation than despair. "You mean I never have to come back here?" I cooed. "No, we mean you *cannot* come back here. Don't look so happy. We're ruining your life." "I don't think so," I replied, mustering my best Barbara Streisand bravado.

At least the mortification my parents suffered at my expulsion explained why my eighteenth birthday was not celebrated, if not the previous seventeen. I intended to celebrate this one myself, because I now had my draft card, which then was legal proof of age accepted at liquor stores and bars. The liquor stores had a special fluorescent lamp by the cash register that somehow verified the draft card's authenticity. With that card in my pocket (despite the dread of its other implications) I went off to the downtown library, where I spent a great deal of time. I met a black guy in his thirties there, very smooth talking and really nice. He reminded me of Mr.Williams. He asked me to come home with him, but I bowed out, uncertain of the nature of his interest and not really wanting to experiment sexually. I was also afraid of his neighborhood, the "East Side" of my parents' nightmare-ridden cosmology. I said I had things to do, but I would be back the next day around the same time.

The following day we talked in the library lounge for a while and then he offered me a ride home, saying his friend with a car was waiting for him at the back entrance (facing the east side of Buffalo—the main entrance being on Main Street). I accepted and got in the back. We were driving for quite a while when I mentioned that the direction was wrong. They informed me they had other plans and everything would be fine as long as I stayed cool. They took me to a basement apartment whose inside door was guarded by a German Shepherd on a chain. The shades were all drawn tight. We were so far in the East Side I wasn't sure if I was more afraid of remaining in the basement with them or risking the street by myself. They took turns raping me. I felt guilty about not resisting, but I didn't know how or what good it would do. I also became angry with them for interfering in my attempts to free myself from my parents' racialized horror stories. At one point I made a mental note to observe the exact address when I left (however that would come about) so that in a few weeks I could send them an anonymous chocolate cake that would have poison in it. I wondered what kind of poison couldn't be tasted through the mix. I thought better of it, realizing I couldn't kill anyone just for raping me and because it might be misconstrued as racist. And I was afraid they would give it to the dog.

Eventually I heard them tell me it was time to go. They drove me as far as the parking lot of Sears, which, like the Library, bordered the East and West sides. This was the same branch to which Mr. Williams had brought me nine years earlier. Once the pair drove off, I decided this was a good chance to get my draftcard plasticized. I always liked the popcorn at Sears, in the long bag imprinted with a man's head in the shape of a popcorn cylinder. The popcorn vender was directly next to the card plasticizer. It was my lucky day. Not typical for a birthday. I walked home, eating the popcorn, occasionally checking to see if the blood that was darkening the top of one of my socks had dried.

One year after I was expelled I snuck back into Lafayette High School, found a room where the proctor did not know me, and took the New York State Regents Scholarship exam. The school had done its job so miserably that of the over 400 students who had taken the examination that day, I was the only one to win a full Regents scholarship. The school officials were furious and tried to block the award, but they had no legal grounds to do so, since there had been no precedent to make a ruling against an "expellee." I enrolled in SUNY at Buffalo and was ecstatic about studying. I worked very hard, excelling at German and my English literature classes and earning a 4.0 average my first semester. My mother said, "That's nice, but you know you will fail. You know you'll start getting in trouble just like you did before. Why not save us the grief and embarassment—Dad can get you a janitor's job at Chevy." I continued to get 4.0s and each time it was met with similar dismissals. I decided to leave the country.

I went to school in Austria. I was enchanted with Europe. Growing up where I did, it had never occurred to me that one could live in a beautiful environment. I won a *Deutsche Akademische Auslandsdienst* (DAAD) scholarship to the University of Würzburg. Living in Germany, I wrote home telling of travelling to Egypt (sailing the Nile in the Sudan), touring the Soviet Union, and so on. My younger sister answered my letters with synopses of television shows she clipped from *TV Guide* and mounted on cardboard, to show me what I was missing. Hearing of my decision to study Japanese in graduate school, my aunt Genevieve (the sole remaining devout Seventh-Day Adventist) wrote me to tell me that I was wasting my time on frivolous things. If I came back to the Church and studied the teachings, when New Jerusalem was established I wouldn't have to settle for trips from country to country, I could fly on my own power from planet to planet. She also reminded me that it would be a yellow race that would overrun the world before the Second Coming. My aunt was prescient. This was 1976. It would be a few more years, when Japan emerged as an economic superpower while the U. S. steel and auto industries collapsed, before the title of apocalyptic monster would be transferred from the Chinese to the Japanese.

I escaped, but not entirely. Outside of my particular academic interests, I failed to compensate for, or even sufficiently monitor, the areas of knowledge and skills that had been excluded from my upbringing. In September, 1980, I entered a Ph.D. program at Harvard. I had lived in two European countries, travelled all over Western and Eastern Europe, Northern Africa, and Japan, and held a Master's Degree from Cornell University. Nevertheless, I decided to open a checking/savings account at the local bank that had an "IRA" sign in its window, marvelling at the daring of a financial institution that would so publically announce its support of the Irish Republican Army. I attributed the bank's politics to the large Irish community of Boston and the radicalizing influence of the two universities in this part of Cambridge.

Such lacunae in my education supported the class-based shame that I carried with me long after graduate school. In fact, my lower-class background has been a far more serious hindrance in my professional life than my homosexuality. I am not referring to an elitism I have perceived or any deliberate exclusions I have suffered. Often the "lower-class subject" has internalized her or his disqualification so thoroughly that direct oppression from "above" is rendered virtually redundant. In my case, I exacted oppression where there would have been none forthcoming. Like many working-class people who have become academics, I suffered from a feeling that I was a "fraud" for many of the first years of my teaching career. After overcoming this feeling, I still suffer from a reticence to initiate sustained social contact with colleagues and others in my field on a basis of assumed equality. It never occurs to me that I would be afforded the same respect or collegiality that most fellow (at least the white male) faculty members I know take for granted.

This pattern is reinforced by my internalization of the rhetorics of self-defacement in Japanese social interactions. While these strategies of behavior are not "neurotic" in their original contexts, the thoroughness with which I embraced them repeated the contradiction of my intellectual history in that my capacity for learning supported a tendency to internalize self-deprecating psychological templates (such as my Seventh-Day Adventist correspondence courses). My extension of these forms of social communication to non-Japanese contexts combined my familial psychopathologies with my class-based shame.

On the other hand, I am a very performative teacher and lecturer. This is primarily because I love teaching and have developed this teaching persona as an integral part of my pedagogical strategies, but it is also because I can be more comfortable in my position of "doing my job"— certainly a characteristic of a working-class psychology. The stark contrast between my colorful presence at the podium, and my shy, rather retiring tendencies "off stage," make me seem aloof or disinterested, a misperception that might encourage the very snubbing I mean to avoid. On top of this, my psychosocial conditioning can also lead me to misread acceptance as rejection. These contradictions also determined some of my difficulties with personal relationships, most clearly my relationship with Gilberto.

Gilberto

On the bus downtown I told myself that there was no sense in placing a "Personals Ad" if I resented the time required to meet the people who responded. This guy in particular sounded worth the gamble of a couple of hours on a Sunday afternoon. But Sunday was a premium work day. I was teaching two rather demanding classes, and my play, which was going up in three weeks, still needed script rewrites. I couldn't even think about the book. Arriving at the Java House early, I spread my books and papers out on a table facing the entrance.

Seeing him in the doorway, my first thought was, "I hate that shirt." It was an Hawaiian shirt of glossy silk that seemed to pick up the cacophony of the street glare framing him and twist it into floral truisms. But his smile belied that noise. Once Gilberto sat down, I realized the garishness of the shirt had been a trick of the light. If his shirt revealed an elegant simplicity, Gilberto's apparently easygoing, almost guileless demeanor invited the closer engagement necessary to appreciate the gradual efflorescence of a complex and often reticent personality. He was sizing me up, but I was not aware of this right away. I did notice that my enjoyment of his company increased as time went by. Two hours passed. I didn't look at a bus schedule. He suggested a walk. I thought I'd go as far as the bookstore, check in there, and head home. It was on the way to the bus station anyway. Gilberto loved book browsing as much as I did, and I found my usual pleasure in roaming among the shelves amplified and refracted through his. He suggested, very shyly, that we have dinner together, and I was surprised to hear myself agree so enthusiastically. He offered to cook, and I didn't even mind shopping with him, something I usually deplore. It was fun.

Dinner was wonderful. He drove me home, and I invited him in to meet my cat, Jane. He stayed quite a while. While we talked, he lay on his stomach on my futon couch. I sat on the floor across from him, by the TV. I thought there was something deliberately inviting in the way he was situated and the quality of his lingering, but it seemed too delicate, too special to acknowledge or even to attempt to verify at all. The next day, when I told my friend Benjamin I had spent so much time with a blind date on a Sunday and I didn't have a panic attack about not getting work done, Benjamin asked if the guy performed any other miracles, like rainmaking.

Gilberto's present and past impressed and moved me. He was born in Texas, the youngest of nine children. His mother grew up in a Texas border town and his father had immigrated from northwestern Mexico. While Gilberto was still a baby, the family moved to a small town outside Fresno, California. In his preschool years, Gilberto was his mother's constant, effervescent companion. He loved to dance to the radio while his mother ironed clothes. She tied the toddler to the bed-post with her apron strings so he could dance and jump on the bed without falling. Like me, Gilberto learned to fear and dislike traditional masculinity, identifying more frequently with the women in his family, who seemed more loving, reasonable, and imaginative than the men. Also like me, Gilberto was the only one of the children to leave "home" in order to create a kind of life impossible to imagine within the world of his upbringing. He studied Art History at the University of California, Santa Cruz, and then stayed on in Santa Cruz, beginning a successful career in arts administration.

My identifications with Gilberto in these aspects of his life were tempered by my awareness of the differences in our respective histories, an awareness that was the source of my admiration for him. The tendency of his family to stay together cannot be reduced to the same inertia and agoraphobia prevalent in mine. The relative stasis of Gilberto's family can also be attributed to the restricted opportunities for Mexican Americans, and to a need for economic and cultural solidarity.[7] Although Gilberto left home, he took with him a sense of the importance of preserving his heritage and culture against Anglo-dominant homogenization, a struggle he learned about in grammar school.

In second grade, the teacher gave the class a special assignment. Each child was to ask her or his parents from what country or countries the family had originally come to the U. S. The next day each child in turn was to go to the map in the front of the class, place the tiny flag provided in the country of origin, and tell the class a "fact" about that country. When Gilberto's turn came, he dutifully placed the flag in Mexico. Before he could begin his sentence, the teacher interrupted him, demanding to know why he had placed the flag where he had. Frightened and confused, he replied, "Because my family is from Mexico." The teacher made a sound of exasperation and waved him away, saying, "Sit Down! You didn't understand the assignment. No one is from Mexico. I meant you were to find out where *in Europe* your family was from. Next time get it right." He never mentioned Mexico or Mexican customs in school again, and he never spoke Spanish if any of the other students or the teachers might hear.

Unlike many children traumatized by such treatment, Gilberto persevered in speaking Spanish at home and retaining it in his adult and professional life, even after moving away from home and a Spanish-speaking community. He admitted that while he was proud to be Mexican American and to have retained his fluency in Spanish, he was shy and uncertain about using Spanish in front of "native speakers" of the language. I lent him a copy of Gloria Anzaldúa's *Borderlands*. His response touched me deeply. He was staggered by her discussion, description, and examples of the various kinds of "Spanish" she used in daily life, and her valorization of the hybridized Spanish typically spoken among Tejanas and Tejanos. He had never seen his form of Spanish in print before, and this was very important to him, particularly because much of it was the language of his mother.

On our second date, I invited Gilberto in for tea, even though I detested tea, and had no idea if I owned any. Remarkably, there were some tea bags in the cupboard. But I did not manage to do more than note their existence. Gilberto never got that cup of tea, although that faculty rental townhouse essentially became "our space" beginning that night. But there was little time for a "honeymoon." In the first months of our relationship, I was extraordinarily busy. The following year I was coming up for tenure review. It was imperative to have at least a book contract in hand by January. Since coming to UCSC, I had never been awarded either course relief or a sabbatical, so I needed that summer to write enough of the book to send it to the press for review by August, to allow time for readers' reports and a decision. I also loved my work and relished the total immersion the summer afforded. I worked from early in the morning until early evening, when Gilberto arrived. I was usually either exhausted or still preoccupied with the work I had been doing, but Gilberto was angelic in his understanding and support.

Gilberto considered a primary relationship the most important thing in his life, and he devoted himself to each relationship wholeheartedly. He was giving and understanding to the point of self-sacrifice, certainly characteristics he had seen in the women of his family. But he was not merely repeating a pattern unself-consciously. One of the reasons he worked so hard at a relationship was precisely because he had seen how unhappy these women were within the relationships to which they were resigned. He was determined to have a relationship that was completely fulfilling, a kind of relationship he had never seen growing up. Unfortunately, his earlier efforts met responses similar to those his mother and sisters experienced. His boyfriends treated him appallingly, essentially taking him for everything he had to give and abandoning him when they had used him up.

But now Gilberto was with me. I could not believe my luck. I mean this (and meant this) quite literally. I could not believe someone so wonderful would want to be with me as much as Gilberto did. I had not done anything to earn it. Therefore, in the back of my mind, I did not believe Gilberto's feelings for me. In fact, the very profusion and clarity of his demonstrations of those feelings I interpreted as evidence to the contrary. The horror stories about his exboyfriends also supported my skepticism of the devotion Gilberto showed me almost immediately. He wanted to do only what he assumed I wanted, and our schedule was structured according to my needs. He was happy, even gleeful in arranging things this way, and resistant to my attempts to make the decisions more mutual. My healthy misgivings about Gilberto's attentiveness to me, however, also disguised my unhealthy suspicion of anyone's attraction to or affection for me, stemming from my own insecurities. I could not see what Gilberto saw in me, and instead of trusting his perception, I diagnosed it as a symptom of his unresolved psychological conflicts. I told myself that what he seemed to think was love was an obsessive pattern that at the moment we both enjoyed, but was bound to burn itself out over the summer. If it did not, I would probably have to persuade him to see a therapist. In my defensive fear of love, I dismissed Gilberto's affection as a psychopathology. While I believed my affection for Gilberto to be genuine, I felt obligated to express it "unselfishly," by leading him to treatment for the illness of lov-ing me. I foresaw the sign of his recovery as his abandonment of me. I had already entrenched myself in defenses against this outcome, although it was these defenses that ensured it. Even his patience with my work schedule and my forms of withdrawal only made me doubt his feelings for me all the more.

Just as in my family's history, the psychopathological systems supported the oppressive politics of class–race hierarchies in Gilberto's and my relationship—liberal politics and "political cor-rectness" at first served personal neuroses. During the early stages of our courtship, when Gilberto's descriptions of my features he found appealing included the whiteness of my skin—a kneejerk silent speculation about possible "internalized racism" protected me from really hearing him. My qualms about sounding like a neocolonialist exoticising the "racial other" excused me from responding to him reciprocally. I did not hold on to these defenses very long, however.

The first week we met, Gilberto encapsulated his personal–political philosophy for me: he hated men, especially white men. In the context of his other statements and considering the objects of his affections, it is easy to unpack this declaration. By "men," he meant the kind of dominant heterosexual male who not only fit the standard definition, but who also found ulti-mate value and meaning in fulfilling that ideal. That "ideal" admitted cultural variants, ranging from the overly developed sense of entitlement of the white yuppie to the agonistic paranoid vigilance of the jock, to the *machismo* of his father and brothers. Gilberto's emotional and sexual bonds with certain men evince a distinction he made between biological sex and ideological gen-der identities.

An analogous distinction can be discerned in his "hatred" of white people and the erotic and aesthetic attraction he admitted his lovers' pallor held for him: for Gilberto, "white" was not so much a genotype as a belief in the naturalness of white dominance and white Euro-American cultural monopolies. In other words, if the skin color of his love object was one focus of Gilberto's erotic investment, it was not the determining feature of a uniformly politicized racial category. The critical difference between "white" as a racial characteristic and "white" as an ide-ology also structured a specific pattern of affection between us. He often told me he did not consider me "white," meaning he did not see me as a proponent of that ideology. I hasten to emphasize, however, that I locate the significance of Gilberto's statement solely within the idi-olect of our relationship; I do not extend this to any illusory extra-racial exoneration, nor do I imply that I refuse "to identify" as white. I introduce this merely as one of the ways in which we each negotiated our respective racial identities—as well as each other's—in the configurations of our intimacy. While Gilberto occasionally expressed his affection by disassociating me from the "white race," I expressed my affection for him by facilitating his reintegration with his Mexican-American "identity."

The first summer we were together, one evening we were out having a beer and the subject turned to birthdays. I winced, because I always avoid telling people when my birthday is. This time it was particularly uncomfortable for me, because that day happened to be my birthday. When he asked me when mine was, I named a date at random. "November 1," I lied. He jumped—"That's amazing—mine's October 31! We can celebrate ours together." I kicked myself under the table, but decided not to tell him the truth until it was too long after my actual birth-day to celebrate it. Instead of slipping into my habituated depression over my own birthday, I focused on Gilberto's. I promised him that on his birthday we would be in Mexico, the first time for both of us. I wanted to share his first experience of Mexico with him, and wanted it to be a birthday gift from me.

The trip proved a unique convergence of several miracles. I initially conceived of it as a cele-bration of Gilberto's birthday (his "identity"), as well as a celebration of his Mexican heritage and his mother's language. We undid the damage of his teacher's ignorant pronouncement, reminis-cent of my sister's reckless declaration of my unworthiness to have a birthday. Gilberto's initial amazement at how well he could function in Spanish there soon filled out into a new sense of confidence and a confirmation of all aspects of himself. I was so proud of him. I could no longer ignore the fact that I had fallen in love with him, too. In other words, I had to admit to myself he was in love with me, and it wasn't necessarily a mistake or a neurosis.

We rented a car and explored the Yucatan. I got very good at map reading and "investigating." Off the beaten track of a beautiful tiny beach town called Akumal, I discovered a tucked away grotto called Yalku, famous for its nesting parrot fish. We drove to Akumal, and followed my map into the bushes until we reached this beautiful secluded lagoon, technicolor with all sorts of marine life. We also were enchanted with Akumal. We promised each other to stay in Akumal for his birthday the following year, which we did. Once in Akumal, Gilberto took a snorkeling lesson and then taught me. We snorkeled all over our beach and then borrowed rickety two-speed bicycles from our hotel and rode eight miles through the jungle on horrendously rocky dirt paths to Yalku. Snorkeling there was like entering the kaleidoscope, but this time the world was both fantastic and real, in all the colors that my father would never see, including the color of the lover who had taught me how to breathe in this world. We saw barracudas basking underneath us, constellations of triggerfish, damsels, and blennies. I got nipped by a moray eel, in front of whose cave I had been dangling my leg. Mexico was a miracle.

Both trips to Mexico were rare breaks in my all-consuming fervor for work. Writing the book took twelve to sixteen hours a day. Once I had moved to San Francisco, it frequently happened that Gilberto drove up on Friday, only to spend the weekend on the living room couch reading, while I continued to type on the computer, occasionally pleading "just one more hour." The first deadline arrived and I sent the draft manuscript and outline to the press. Now all I had to do was wait, and while waiting, do the rewriting, the polishing, and draft the projected chapters. Therefore, I was just as busy and obsessed after the project's first goal had been met as before. Now the chapters took even longer, I frequently stayed up all night writing, or got up at three or four AM to begin, leaving Gilberto to sleep alone. In January I received the contract, which increased my intensity of work because this meant that the book would actually be published. This also meant I wrote during every waking moment and all weekend every weekend, because I was now back teaching. Gilberto was still understanding, and, although disappointed, he forebore.

Because I had realized early on that my parents had never loved me, I faced adult emotional life with a contradictory sense of despair and entitlement. Since the only people who could arguably be considered under obligation to love me had not, I had no basis for expecting anyone else to love me. On the other hand, *precisely because my parents had not loved me*, I was also susceptible to an unconscious belief in a sympathetic magic, thinking life owed me someone to love me, to restore the balance of justice my parents had thrown out of whack. My response to Gilberto was often structured around these two effects of my emotional deprivation. I at times simultaneously, at other times alternately, refused to accept his love, and yet took it for granted as my due. While the origins of these attitudes are understandable, neither of them contributed to responsive capacity conducive to a mutually fufilling relationship. Both left Gilberto out in the cold. The refusal to accept his love was far more common. My taking his love for granted, while initially the rarer of the two responses, however, was actually the one that Gilberto cultivated, eliciting it through both positive and negative reinforcement.

Gilberto loved acting as the caregiver, the one lavishing attention on the other, but hated it when the attention was returned, or if he were made the focus of special attention. One of the first times I tried this was a disaster. I took him out to a new, fancy restaurant that had just opened, and laid it on thick that I was doing this "for him." It was the first time he was aggressively unappreciative, petty, surly, and in general unkind and abusive. When I finally protested, "Gilberto, you have never treated me like this before," he seemed to realize what he was doing and snapped out of it. After apologizing he reminded me of the many times he had told me that he could not tolerate such attention.

If, coming home after a meeting or a late class, I became overly expressive about my happiness in finding him there, or told him how much his support and love meant to me, he pushed me away, dismissing what I said in a good-natured rebuff that also carried a peculiarly ominous tone of conviction in his voice, calling me drunk or saying that he wasn't going to listen to sweet-talk from a bottle. Although I had told him stories of my heavy drinking days in years past, he had never seen me in such a condition and in fact he knew that my obsession with the book made me abhor the idea of being mentally impaired, however pleasant, and that I limited myself to one or two beers a week, if that. Therefore I took this to be another message that such direct expressions were intolerable and would not be acknowledged as valid. This conscious interpretation was supported by my own aversion to being blamed for something I did not do. Now what I did not do is to tell him I loved him. I also hate rejection, especially rejection of a feeling I find difficult to offer in the first place.

I should have pushed him to examine the motivations behind his rigid altruism and to consider the effects on the relationship if such attentions were to be exclusively unidirectional. Instead I let the vehemence of his response reinforce my tendency to withdraw; I assumed my covert expressions of love and appreciation were understood and found satisfactory. I retreated into my work for several reasons now: as a defense against his love; as a protective response against the rejection I felt from his refusal to accept from me the attentions he gave me; and as a way to demonstrate the love he would not let me utter directly. This was going to be the greatest, most stunning book ever written in gay studies, so that it would honor the dedication to Gilberto that I kept rewriting on a secret file when he slept or when he was not home. I was like a ten-year-old riding my bike past my "sweetheart's" house, calling out "Look, no hands!"

Gilberto started complaining in our second year. He had decided to give up on the relationship while I was away for a week as a visiting scholar for the Center for Japan Studies at the University of Michigan, Ann Arbor. I could tell something was up when I called him. He was very cold and unresponsive. He was even worse when he picked me up at the airport. I talked him into trying again, and promised to try myself. I still wanted more than ever to take two weeks off for Mexico instead of one, even if I had to lend him most of his fare. I also promised to find a therapist for my workaholism beginning in January, when the insurance cycle would permit it. In the meantime, Gilberto decided to see a therapist in Santa Cruz shortly before we left for Mexico, to clarify some of his ambivalence toward his family and to come to terms with his childhood. This astonished me, because he had always said he did not believe in them. He had two sessions with the therapist before his work schedule, our vacation, and then preparations for his move to San Francisco in December made it impossible for him to continue with her.

When Gilberto confronted me on my return from Ann Arbor with his unhappiness great enough to make him willing to leave me, I was able to look more closely at a fear that was at the heart of my pain and confusion at the restaurant when Gilberto had responded so negatively to my expression of affection. At the point I knew I had to acquiesce to his refusal to accept such expressions, I began to worry about the relations between Gilberto's one-sided giving and the fate of his other relationships. I feared that some of the exploitation and neglect Gilberto suffered at the hands of his ex-boyfriends (which is what made them "white" in his narratives) was to some extent—if not elicited, certainly supported by his insistence on their participation in his altruism. Such unbridled giving eventually spoils the recipient; it may have even conditioned shifts in Gilberto's boyfriends' deportment to levels of selfishness that Gilberto deplored in his father's and brother's behavior. I wondered when my capitulation to this rule would exceed his level of tolerance, rendering me the kind of bastard my predecessors had eventually proven to be. At what point would my compliance guarantee Gilberto's dissatisfaction? And how could this relationship, however "individual" and idiosyncratic, remain isolated from the racial makeup of its agents, and how could Gilberto be expected not to feel his personal anger confluent with a social and cultural anger at the history of Anglo exploitation of Mexicans and Mexican Americans, even if the disequilibrium in our relationship was initially of Gilberto's express construction? We had reached that point. I am not suggesting that I had been trapped, nor do I attribute the cul-de-sac at which we arrived to a no-win situation of meeting a demand and accepting the anger that meeting such a demand incites. This is not a neurotic conundrum, but a sociopolitical contradiction, not merely a personal victimization from a repetition compulsion, but a particular, local instance of the incessant yet metamorphic tragedy of institutionalized racism as a fundamental cultural horizon. Retrospectively mapping the ways the "personal" and the "political" intermeshed in my years with Gilberto leads me to conclude that one of the reasons race is such a profound dynamic in interracial relationships is, paradoxically, because of a kind of default social epistemology that facilitates the reconstruction of any interpersonal situation in terms of racial politics, even if race was not a principle element in the minds, motivations, and actions of the parties involved.

Even when the intrapsychic and/or interpersonal dynamics have no discernible (or merely tangential) relation to issues of race, these moments, and the subjective and intersubjective complexes constituting them, can be retroactively resignified (or reinterpreted) in terms of racial politics. Neither our individual social histories regarding race nor the histories and contemporary situations of the larger social order (and of the embedded, subordinated, and contestatory subcultures therein) will allow any moment of our relationship to remain insulated from racial meaning. When people who knew Gilberto see me with one of the white men I have dated since our breakup, they often comment, "Oh, I thought you liked Latinos." But when people who had not known Gilberto see me, they do not say, "Oh, so you like white men." The discrepancy of inference is another example of the epistemology of white hegemony that renders "white" an essence without particulars, and white men beings without characteristics. (I assure you that the white men I date have plenty of characteristics far more compelling than the incapacity of their skin to retain pigment.) When I had first met Gilberto, he had only dated or had been in relationships with other white men. Mexican, Chicano, and Latino gay men in the area who had seen Gilberto with his partners at the gay bar in earlier years assumed that he was "white identified" and repressing his identification with his ethnic heritage. Given that Gilberto was only twenty-eight at the time I met him, and that he had been in a series of monogamous relationships lasting from several months to several years, and considering the paucity of eligible gay men in Santa Cruz—and the far smaller number of "out" gay men of color, the racial make-up of Gilberto's partners cannot be immediately ascribed to an exclusive preference for white men or an internalized racism. Furthermore, even if he had made a conscious decision not to date Chicano/Latino men, this choice may have been based not on racial identity but on gender politics, since Gilberto associated Chicano male styles of self-presentation with the oppressive and homophobic behavior of his father and brothers.

On the other hand, even if there is no discernible racial determination in Gilberto's object choices—even if we could prove their shared whiteness coincidental—it is impossible to foreclose racial politics from these relationships and Gilberto's erotic life. Why? Because the tension between the "fact" of his partners' race and the signifying excess of "race" that can never be reduced to a "fact," structures a contradictory and heterogeneous discursive field in and through which these relationships develop and articulate their multidimensional particularities.

I learned this lesson viscerally through the certain loss of Gilberto and from facing the enormity of his hurt and anger then and thereafter, beginning that Sunday in December, when it turned out that one of the other agendas in Gilberto's therapeutic sessions had been to clarify his resolve to leave me. He needed more out of life than our relationship promised and he could no longer wait for me to find time to live. In insufficiently exorcising the most abject self-identifications any dominant ideology would impose on its lower-class subjects, I acted in ways that made me a "white male" in Gilberto's lexicon. The long-term effects of my "Oxydol poisoning" obscured from my critical awareness the peculiarity of my obsessive ambition and its monstrous costs; the long-term exhaustion and rage from struggling against an Oxydol-whitened world left Gilberto little option but to leave. In a ghastly irony, my neurotic fear and shame-based behavior drove Gilberto to the very act my insecurities had coincidentally predicted at the beginning of the relationship: he found a therapist to cure him of me. Realizing now that his love was not a symptom, I know too late Gilberto's giving up on me is not a "recovery," but a loss for us both. It is not a loss that a critical insight can ameliorate, nor a political conviction vindicate. But it is nevertheless crucial to develop a new analytic understanding and articulate a politics through my reflections on this loss, if I am to resist this class subjectivization and disengage from this mode of my racial identity.

Dream Work

July 21, 1994. Yesterday morning the dentist told me I had to have an emergency root canal within the next two days. I crawled into bed as soon as I returned home. Despite my anxiety and the pain in my jaw, I fell asleep quickly and dreamt that I was back in Akumal. It was early morning and I had just started snorkeling. I pulled the banana I smuggled from breakfast out of my swimming trunks and was instantly swarmed by the yellow and black sergeant majors. A few yards beyond, they were joined by the more graceful and furtive jackknives, just as always. When it got a little deeper, individual fish cruised by: a jewel fish, a Spanish hog, a neon goby. Beneath me I saw some grouper and just ahead was that queen Angelfish nested in the anchor I told Gilberto about the day before. I hoped she would stay put until he came. Swimming a little to the side, I catch sight of the black and green triggerfish that Gilberto discovered the first day we tried snorkeling. One of them had just blown a sea urchin over, exposing its belly. The other trigger was poised, ready for the kill.

I suddenly realized I had not yet surfaced, and I was still breathing regularly through the tube. I finally got the hang of Gilberto's lessons. I felt safe and warm in the sea, but mostly because even though I could snorkle by myself, I knew Gilberto would be by any minute, tapping me on the shoulder and pointing at the surface. When I came up, he'd say, "Hey Doc! How's your mask? Does it need adjusting? Breathing ok? Guess what? Over toward the pier I saw three big yellow cow fish. Wanna see?" He was always spotting cow fish, but I could never find them. Soon we'd walk back to the shore for a piña colada in the sun. Later when we walked over the rocky areas, I'd see if I could still get him to squeal by petting the big iguanas. I doubt it—unless just to make me laugh.

Then I woke up, strangely refreshed and much calmer. I still felt the warmth of the sea in the dream. And the sense of safety, even though I woke up before Gilberto appeared. But then again, he taught me to snorkle. So I was already safe, and he was already there. With me. In the safety he taught me how to create for myself.

Most of these reminiscences are sad—some very sad—stories. But amid, before, and beyond all these sad stories, there are a few stories that are still true, stories whose miraculous "have happened" cannot be erased or undone. There was once a lonely boy in upstate New York who made friends with crows. Years later, in central California, a mother would secure her baby son near her in order to indulge yet protect him from his wild dancing joy. When her baby son grew older, he would take the crow's friend to bed and whisper "I love you" in his ear, so that the older boy would never need to resort to an empty Valentine again. And the older boy, in return, would take the dancing young man south for his birthday, to prove once and for all that you can most definitely be from Mexico. I address this belated love letter to these two little boys, and the young men, and older men they became; they remain for me the not altogether lost heroes of a romance whose possibility says more than I can write.[8]

Notes

1   When I first met Gilberto, I told him repeatedly that I wasn't always this preoccupied and unavailable - he just happened to meet me in the middle of finishing my book. I would be "better" once it was done. I left him sleeping alone night after night, getting out of bed to work on the book, keeping the cats quiet who insisted on getting up with me and sharing my chair. Now I tell Ken I'm not always this preoccupied, he just happened to meet me as I'm finishing this difficult autobiographical essay. I will be "better" once it's done. Tonight, like several other nights, I have gotten up, leaving him alone in the bed, to work on this essay, I sit poised on the edge of the seat, shushing the cats as they snuggle between my back and the back of the chair.

2   Davis would reprise the character in the 1970s for the Brady family, but tone down the butchiness.

3   My father was a genius with his hands and could build or fix anything, but never attempted to teach me even the most rudimentary of his skills. When my older sister's male children were growing up, however, my father taught them carpentry, let them help him with various projects, and took them fishing. My mother would often say (in front of me) that the grandkids were good for Dad—they were like the son he never had.

4   The racial truce Lefkowitz concocted presumed a sense of a shared, normative heterosexual masculinity underlying and thus subsuming racial differences, a gendered and sexual identity that was entirely fictive—a fantasy created by the enjoined animosity against that individual posited as this masculinity's antithesis, when in fact it was this oppositional or negative relation the "queer" represented that constituted that masculinity.   Dominant male heterosexuality is a deadly hoax—in that it requires violent acts of defense against non-belligerent, non-seductive others, suggesting that male heterosexual identity is so tenuous and its maintenance so costly, that the mere existence of alternatives must be viewed as a threat.

5   On the other hand, if Manuela had been black, I could have been the target of the heterosexual "territoriality" that it was rumored black male students acted on if they saw a white boy with a black girl. This is another element in the gender-specific construction of interracial relations that my mother and her neighbors observed from an entirely different perspective, albeit both factors militated against interracial relations for white heterosexual males.

6   In neither the bullying of Hoak nor myself, did any of the black students take an active or initiative role. It seemed to silence them.

7   Arturo Islas's novel *The Rain God* depicts this phenomenon beautifully. For a formal schematic of the differences between "identification" and "empathy" that constituted my positioning to Gilberto, see "Responsibility," pp. 150–52.

8   I would like to thank: Becky W. Thompson and Sangeeta Tyagi, who are the only two colleagues who could have persuaded me to attempt this experiment and the only two editors to whom I would entrust this text; Samuel R. Delany, whose inspiration is legible throughout my narrative; Steve Johnstone, who lovingly endured all the symptomatic behaviors the writing process caused, and still made my fortieth birthday a very happy one; Jérémie Elisha Curtis, who woke me one night because he was afraid, and one morning because I was; and Kenyon Brown, who, along with my cats Gus, Jane, and Ron, offers me the most effective antidote to Oxydol poisoning any boy could hope for.

15

Writing Life
Beth Brant

I'm wondering if it might be a good time to make bread. The writing is not going well. Truthfully, it's not going. Perhaps the soothing action of mixing and kneading would get me back to a good place. The writing. THE WRITING. It takes on large proportions in my mind. It is not easy to write. Nor is it fun, and pleasant is not a word I would use in conjunction with writing. Yet, it is hard to relax when I'm away from the computer and my desk. I keep thinking about the stories. I dream at night about the people in the stories. I see their faces in odd places—the grocery store, on the street, sitting on a subway, lurking behind a tree or bush. They are like ghosts. But ghosts have had a life. These people are looking to me to help give them life.

In the kitchen I assemble the yeast, the flour, sugar, oil and take down the large stainless steel bowl. Turning on the tap, I empty two packets of yeast into the bowl. Running my wrist under the water to test the temperature, I judge it to be right. I measure two cups of water into the bowl. The yeast bubbles up, then sinks to the bottom.

This is a metaphor.

I stir the yeast and water with a wooden spoon and think about my dad. Daddy. I think of him often, missing him, wondering what he is doing in the Spirit World.

I add sugar, dry milk, and a little oil to the yeast-water. I stir, adding flour by the handful until the dough is a good consistency. I dump the mixture onto the cutting board and add still more flour to the spongy mass. I begin to knead—pushing it away with the heels of my hands, pulling it towards me—I make a rhythm.

When my dad was young, he discovered music—a certain kind of music. He was walking in a neighborhood in Oshawa, Ontario, and heard music coming out of a window. He'd never heard music like that. He wanted to walk up to the house, ring the doorbell, and ask what that music was. But he was a little Native boy, and little Native boys didn't ring doorbells and ask questions on a street that was white. He never said what he was doing on that particular street and I never asked—the story was enough.

The story is always enough for me, but editors insist on explanations, details. Does it matter how he got from here to there? Does it matter? Isn't story why we are here, no matter the mode of transportation? Daddy said that when he grew up and was earning some money, he found out the name of the music he had heard on that Oshawa street—Beethoven's Ninth Symphony. He bought the recording, then a year later bought a record player, played it over and over, and sang "Ode to Joy" ever after. I like that story. It testifies to a number of things that Daddy taught me— beauty is possible, and beauty is found in unlikely places. All his stories were about that, all of my stories are about that.

I knead the dough and hum "Ode to Joy." I never planned on being a writer. It was not even a fantasy of mine. Born in an urban Mohawk family, story was a given, not something to search for or discover. But the gift of *writing* came a long time after my birth. Forty years after. That year I was on a search for the spirit of Molly Brant, Clan Mother, elder sister of Chief Joseph Brant and the architect of diplomatic relations between the Mohawk Nation and the British. My lover, Denise, and I were, at that time, caterers and bakers. We worked in our home (illegally) making desserts, quiche, breads, and various other items for small, local restaurants. We also were called upon to cater political events—conferences, seminars, benefits, readings, visual artists' openings. We did not make a lot of money, but enough to pay the bills and take care of our family, consisting of us and my three daughters. We had planned a camping trip in the East, stopping at Tyendinaga, my Reserve, then moving on to New York State. I wanted to visit all the homes in which Molly Brant had resided, just to see where she had walked, where she had slept, where she had dreamed. Her story has always been neglected in favour of her brother's, Joseph—just one more example of sexist racism at work. I didn't know what I was going to do with this knowledge or the feelings I would uncover, but I just wanted to *see* her with my own heart. Grandma Brant always told us that Molly was the true warrior and truth-carrier of the Brant history. We proceeded on our trip, stopping at Brantford, on to Six Nations, to Tyendinaga (where Molly Brant never lived, but where my family did and does), on to New York State and the towns where Sir William Johnson and his "country wife" had made homes.

I wash out the bowl, oil it, and place the mound of kneaded dough inside, covering everything with a tea towel. That trip changed my life, changed what image I had of myself, intensified my love of all things Native, all those things that make culture alive and real. It was while we were coming back to Michigan that we decided to take another road through what used to be Seneca land. The dirt road looped through stands of White Pine and deciduous growth. We were coming around a curve in the road, Denise driving, when a great shadow blocked out the sunlight and the tip of a wing touched the front windshield. A Bald Eagle made his presence known to us. Denise stopped the car, I opened the door and stood, transfixed, as Eagle made a circle around us then flew to a nearby White Pine and settled himself on a branch. The branch dipped low from his weight, his dark wings folded around him, his white head touched by a flash of sun-light through the needles of the tree. I remember how his great talons gripped the branch as I moved closer and stood in front of him, my heart drumming inside my human body. We were locked together in vision. I could feel his heart beat take over mine. I felt my hands curving and holding onto the branch. I felt the sunlight flashing on my head. I heard the thoughts; the deep, scratching thoughts of blood, bone and prey, the thoughts of wind carrying me along, the thoughts of heartbeat. He blinked his eyes, unfolded his wings, and flew away. I watched him as I slowly came back to myself, to the smell around me, the breeze picking up and scattering dust in my face, my legs growing so weak I could hardly walk back to the car. When I got home, I began to write.

I was born in 1941, in the house of my Grandma and Grandpa Brant—the house where my Aunt Colleen still lives. It was a hot May morning, when my Irish-Scots mother pushed and willed me out of her womb. The story goes that Daddy had bought an ice-cream-on-a-stick for my mom, but in the excitement, put it in his pocket. It wasn't until Grandma was doing the wash that she discovered the mess and made Daddy wash his own pants. I grew up in a family that had strong women and sweet men. Mama's family was not thrilled to have her marry an Indian, in fact her father refused to give her away at the wedding and railed and stormed about having a "nigger" for a son-in-law. In time he came around, but those kinds of wounds were not easy to close or heal.

I have a photograph of my mom and dad around the time they were newly married. They were ages eighteen and twenty. The old black and white photograph shows my mom wearing shorts and a halter top, daddy dressed in a short-sleeved shirt and pants. They are leaning against a honeysuckle vine, daddy's arms around mama's bare waist. She is leaning against his chest, head thrown back with laughter. She is holding his hands that encircle her waist. They look so young, so sensual, so in love, so happy to be touching and smelling the honeysuckle that twists around Daddy's dark hair and comes to rest on Mama's blonde head. I came from this—this union of white and Native.

Mama and Daddy came to live with the Brant family. In the old way, the traditional way, Daddy would have gone to live with the Smiths. But since Mama was a white woman and feelings were bad on their side, it was the natural course of things that the Brants would assimilate her and all offspring of the union. Thus, I was born in the Little Room of Grandma and Grandpa's house in Detroit, the room that was alternately used as a birthing room, a sick room, a room to put up various members of the family when they came to visit or to live.

Memories are stories—pictures of the mind, gathered up and words put to them, making them live and breathe. My memories are good ones. I was loved.

There were a lot of us, living in that small house. Grandma, Grandpa, Auntie, mom and dad, and their three children. At other times there were more—aunts, uncles and their children, relatives from Tyendinaga with their families. I wonder to this day how we all fit, how we managed to all sit around the kitchen table (The young kids usually ate in the Little Room off a card table. It was a rite of passage when we became old enough to sit with the grown-ups. Like most of what Grandma did, she had her own way of deciding who was old enough. I think I sat with the adults when I turned twelve, but others got there before their twelfth year, and some had to wait much longer.) When my cousins and I get together, we inevitably get around to talking about that card table and the question of space. How did we all fit? Was there some magic involved?

There were books. Both Grandma and Grandpa knew how to read and write. They considered it a blessing. They read a lot and always bought the newspaper. Grandma was a Methodist and read a verse from the Bible every night before she went to bed. And she insisted on saying grace before meals. "Our Heavenly Father, we ask you to bless this food for the use of our souls and bodies. In Jesus' name we ask it. Amen." Grandpa was not a christian, preferring the old way, the Mohawk way. Yet, for all of Grandma's high-mindedness about christianity, she believed most fervently in the power and beauty of Earth. Her garden was a testament to that belief.

The first inklings of connection and intimacy with Land came from watching and helping Grandma and Grandpa work the garden. Getting the soil ready, using the planting stick, seeds drifting from their hands, I felt the devotion and care they lavished on that small piece of land. When we would take trips to Tyendinaga (our Territory and the place they were born and raised) I felt that connection even more deeply. This is where they came from. This is where Daddy came from. This is where I came from. This is where our people's bones are buried and revered. This is *home*.

Grandpa taught me Mohawk and the idea of what men are supposed to be—loving, hard work-ers, giving, secure, respectful of women, playful with children. Grandma taught me manners, how to make corn soup and fry bread, and the idea of what women are supposed to be—strong, fierce protectors of family and land, independent of men while respecting them. (If they war-ranted respect. She held no affection for men who drank, neglected family, or hurt children and women.) Grandma never needed a man to tell her how to fix a toilet, clean a well, or butcher a deer. And her daughters, my aunts, followed her counsel. Even my mother became like that. She must have gathered the knowledge by osmosis. Those two grandparents formed many of my val-ues and the beliefs I hold to.

I get up to check the bread. It has a smooth, glossy look to it. I poke my finger in gently and the bread rises up to cover the hole. I punch it down, cut it in two pieces, make two loaves and place them in the bread pans.

When I began to write, I wrote about my family. At first there were funny stories about my grandparents' Indian ways. Nice stories, full of loving description of their ways with each other and with the world outside them. Then something happened. The writing got more serious—my family was not just fun, they were also survivors of colonial oppression. I began to figure out, through the writing, that what I remembered was not necessarily the complete truth. I was still viewing the family through the eyes of the child I had been.

What happens when I sit in front of the computer (or, in those days, the typewriter)? This desire to peel back the husk of memory, the hungry need to find the food that is waiting inside. There are times when I feel as if *I* am the seed, being watered and sunned by the keys I press to make words. The words are the shoot, wandering across the screen, stopping then starting, coming from my mouth, my fingers. I speak aloud as I write—the words being from mouth to hand. Somewhere in that activity is the nucleus of writing, of truth. I no longer feel that the words come directly from me. There are spirits at work who move my lips, my fingers. Who call me, who take over my clumsy attempts to put one word after the other to make some kind of sense. An automatic writing of sorts. I used to fight the spirits. Now I accept them.

I check the loaves. They have risen nicely. I place them in the oven at 375 degrees, close the door and think about the work that is piled on my desk. There are deadlines for articles, corre-spondence to write, a book to finish, another book making itself known at the edges of my mind. I procrastinate. I avoid the inevitable confrontation with the spirits of writing. I have been known to clean the whole house to the extent of cleaning cupboards, just to keep from doing what the screen asks me to reveal. Why? At this point in my life, I have written about most things that others might shy away from—my life with an abusive, alcoholic husband, my life with Denise, my lesbianism, sexual lovers—yet there is always the modesty, and the fear of being judged, and therefore, all Mohawks being judged. The writing spirit has no fear, has no human failings that waste time procrastinating. There are times when I think the spirit is the collected consciousness of those Native writers who have passed on—Pauline Johnson, D'Arcy McNickle—they can't stop writing, even in the Spirit World, and have to make visitations to those of us on Earth who call ourselves writers. And while I have accepted their presence in my life, I still want to ask—why me? They do not answer.

There was a time when I was ashamed to be Indian. This happened around the time I was in the fifth or sixth grade. I was a pale, blonde child, I wore glasses, and had lots of baby fat. Up until then, I was ashamed of my lightness, my paleness. The family was dark—dark skin, dark hair, dark eyes—and then there was me. I used to wonder if I was the right child, or if I was somehow switched at birth. Since I was born at home and there were no other babies around, this fantasy didn't last long. I was very jealous of my cousins who "looked" Mohawk. They had the dark hair I envied, the brown or dark grey eyes I wanted to peer out of my own face. I resented my mother—somehow this was her fault. But as I grew older and caught the drift of racism, I hid my Mohawk self from the schoolmates who might have become my tormentors had they known. It was enough that I was fat and wore glasses; taunting and teasing waited for me if I made myself noticed. At home, life went on pretty much as usual. The family was not aware of my " other life" as a white girl. My girlfriends in the neighborhood didn't give a whole lot of thought to the family. Anyway, they had grown up on the street that had the only Indian family. This was nothing new or different to them. But the other kids in school were to be feared, cajoled, envied.

My writing soon took an autobiographical bent. I got published fairly quickly, a fact that causes me amazement even today. My work in those days was raw, not as free from cliché or roughness, but editors saw something. There was a substantial network of feminist journals and magazines in the early `80s. They took chances on women like me—women who had no prior publishing experience, women who were not "educated," women of color. Taking chances was the hallmark of these publications, and I am very thankful for their existence.

It seemed that Eagle had many plans for me. In 1982, I was asked to edit a special issue of *Sinister Wisdom*, a feminist journal at that time published and edited by Adrienne Rich and Michelle Cliff. I took on the job, not because I knew anything about editing, but because the issue was to be about Native women. This caused me a lot of excitement *and* fear. In the first place, up until that time, there had not been an anthology of exclusively Native women's work. All other Native anthologies had been edited by whites. *A Gathering of Spirit* was a groundbreaker in those two areas, but also in another equally important area. Of the sixty women who had contributed to the book, ten of us declared our lesbianism. This was a new day in the history of Aboriginal writing. This time around, we were actively saying who we were—all parts of us—no coyness, or hiding, or pretending to be something we weren't. It was a great political and personally courageous act on the part of those nine women who stood with me. I will always be thankful to them and blessed in knowing them.

Another wonderful thing about *A Gathering of Spirit*, is the humanness of the book. This is not just another anthology of well-known and well-published authors. There are first-time writers, letters, voices from Native women in prison, oral histories, artwork. This was a special book in 1983. It continues to be a special book today. Native women write to tell me how the book changed their lives. Many of the women who were published for the first time now have their own books. And many Two-Spirits thank me for shaking the stereotype of what makes good writing, what makes good Native writing—it is not all male, or heterosexual, or necessarily from the pen of someone who had formal western education. I am very proud of that book. Not because I edited it, but because it changed the face of Native literature forever. It became its own entity. It became what it had to be—a brilliant and loving weapon of change.

I published my first book of poems and stories, *Mohawk Trail*, in 1985. Although I like this book and continue to read some of the work in public performance, I am always chagrined when people mention a piece from it. I want to say, "That old stuff," not because I don't like the work, but because each *new* work seems better to me, more full and mature. Perhaps this is the way with writers. My book of short stories, *Food & Spirits*, was published in 1991. There was a long gap between books because I am not a prolific writer—I don't write every day—yet I write in my head every day. I listen to people's conversations, not because I'm a voyeur, but because I am fascinated with people's voices—the rhythm, the phrases they use, the accents, the music. I keep these some place inside me; even in sleep, words from a conversation flash by; people's faces pop up, some I've never seen before. Linda Hogan once said that she used to think she was crazy, but then she realized that the craziness was due to being a half-breed in a white world. I believe that too. I also believe that being a Native writer induces its own madness. We are trying to make sense out of the senseless. We are trying to tell a truth in a culture that dishonors truth-tellers and the story behind the telling.

Grandpa died when I was quite young. I remember the wake, his body laid out in the wooden box, the family and strangers all over the place. I hated it. It scared me. I wasn't quite sure that he was really dead, or if he would rise up (like one of the stories in Grandma's bible). If Grandpa was really dead, who would talk with me in Mohawk? (By one of those generational twists, a result of colonialism, my father and his siblings didn't speak the language but understood it. I suspect that Grandma had a lot to do with this. Although she remained adamantly and vehemently Mohawk, she also felt that it was okay to assimilate "a little," for safety's sake.) If Grandpa was really dead, how would we all survive? We depended on him for so much, not just economically, but emotionally and spiritually. Who would counteract Grandma's forays into christian platitudes? Who would hug me tight and call me his "masterpiece"? Who would make the raspberry jam every year, the bright red jars decorating the fruit cellar?

Grandma died when I was eighteen, newly married, and a mother. My husband had been in the Navy and we were living in a forsaken town in Georgia. There was no money for me to come home, so the family decided they wouldn't tell me about the death until after the wake. I was furious. I felt that I was given no choice. It's true there was no money, but I would have liked to have said goodbye to Grandma at her moment of death, not after she was in the ground. It was years before I found myself at the cemetery where they both were buried. It had taken me that long to be able to see that place, that land of death. And many years after that, I took my two oldest grandsons, Nathanael and Benjamin, to visit. They rolled on the markers, picked up leaves and threw them at each other, shouted and laughed. I wondered how often a cemetary gets to hear the laughter of children. I tell my grandsons about their great-great-grandparents. My memory will shift to theirs, and they will keep the stories alive and moving.

My marriage was not a good one. I was seventeen and pregnant. My dad didn't want me to marry. My mom did. She often would have these attacks of caring what people thought of her. I suppose her great rebellion in marrying my dad took its toll on her in little ways. She would compensate by drilling us in proper behavior and morals. I don't know what I wanted. I guess I wanted to be grown-up and living a grown-up life. I thought that marriage guaranteed that. Also, my mom and dad genuinely loved and liked each other. I had no idea that my marriage wouldn't be the same. But, in the first place, my husband wasn't a sweet Mohawk man. We were to live out the fourteen years together in anger, violence, alcohol, hatred. But I had three daughters—Kimberly, Jennifer, Jill—and they were in turn the only sweetness and beauty that was visible to me during those fourteen years.

Leave him I did; or rather, told him to leave us. I went on welfare, looked for work, tried to hold it together. My parents were wonderful—buying food, buying the kid's clothes, taking care of things when I felt I couldn't. They had always been there during the course of my marriage, but I couldn't bring myself to tell them of just how many times he came home drunk—the marital rape, the screaming and shouting. I was ashamed to tell them, as if I had brought this into being. Daddy, slow to anger, would have erupted and probably done harm to my husband and brought harm to himself. My mother would have wanted to find a way to take care of it that would reduce me to a child again. I kept all of it secret, only daring, years later, to expose the secrets through writing.

I do not believe that all writing is autobiographical, or that a writer has to use words as a confessional. In fact, I think that type of writing is unique to white North America. I do know that as a Mohawk woman I was born to and grew up in a culture that persists and resists, but also carries its load of colonialist untruths. As an Aboriginal woman, I have internalized these untruths. Writing helps me to let go. The spirits of writing bring comfort, assurance, righteous anger, deliverance. I am alive, quivering, in front of the computer. I dredge but also bury. I face the monsters of racism, homophobia, and woman-hating with the spirits beside me. I am protected at the same time as I open myself to rage. I find salvation while uncovering horror. Writing is the place to feel all senses commingle and cohabit, bringing forth something new, giving birth to words, to beings that will inhabit story, that *are* story. This is what the spirits bring—verdant sensuality, lush panoply, a garden.

I check the bread. It is rising, developing a golden crust. It is almost done, almost there.

I met Denise Dorsz in 1976. I immediately loved her. For me, it was simple—I wanted to make a life with this woman. I wanted to share my life with her. Denise has brought many gifts to my life; we have also had to struggle and fight for the ability of each of us to be separate and unique while building a partnership of love and continuity. Denise is white—Polish-American—and is also twelve years younger than me. The romanticizing of the lesbian and gay community is hard to dispel. We often believe the myth that is not exclusive to hetero-sexuals—fall in love, live happily ever after. As of this writing, in 1994, we have been together for eighteen years. There was a period of time when we were separated, and I wrote exhaus-tively and excessively during that time about our relationship, about our separation. None of this was for publication, but then, none of what I write is consciously or unconsciously for anyone else but me and the spirits. My point is that I was able to use writing to heal a wound that was very deep and festering. I was angry—writing brought me calm. I was obsessing about the past—writing gave me insight into the future. I was in pain—writing cooled the pain, brought me out of that condition. Writing was/is Medicine. It is the only thing I know that brings complete wholeness while it is making a visitation. Making love comes close—orgasm, like writing, is a spiritual communication.

I never went to university. My circumstances were such that it was unthinkable to even imag-ine going. Yet my father had worked days in the auto factory and gone to college at night. Formal education was not unheard of or dismissed in the family. My grandparents thought high-ly of it, Daddy and Mama worked tirelessly to achieve it for my father. My siblings and I were encouraged, prodded, to achieve a degree of some kind and my sister and brother worked extremely hard to get those degrees. Instead, I married and gave up all desires for expansion of myself. It was 1959, this is what women did, especially self-hating ones like me. Why did I hate myself? There is no simple political polemic that can explain or describe my actions. I was loved by my family. I had solid and sturdy role models. I had culture. I had language. I had a spiritual base. Then again, I inherited secrets. They wore me down. I learned to be silent rather than reveal the family I wanted to idealize.

The secrets of Indigenous life are not secret. Alcoholism, family violence, the internalized vio-lence of self-doubt, self-loathing. My father, who was a brilliant man, used to say in serio-comic fashion, "What do I know, I'm just a dumb Indian." He knew he wasn't, yet *did not know* if he was just that. I have also made that statement, but more than that, I have thought it and felt it. Writing has changed my perception of myself. Eagle has changed my way of being in this life.

Writing. This mysterious and magical act that brings possibility of transformation. I do not believe that what I have to say is more important than others' words. At the same time, there is a reason why I am able to bead words together to make language. It makes me able to be of use—to my people, to the many families I am connected to—First Nations, feminist, gay and lesbian, working-class, human. I love words. When I was in the sixth grade, I won a spelling-bee and my prize was a dictionary. I loved that book—so many words to choose from, so many words to play with. To this day, I write with a dictionary beside me, sometimes forgetting what I'm writing as I turn the pages of that book, reading the meanings, the way words came into being. Yet, there are times when English words are not full enough or circular enough to encompass a thought or feeling I am trying to convey. It is then that I mourn for the loss of my Mohawk language. With no one to speak it with after Grandpa died, I have forgotten the words, but not the wholeness and richness of the meaning behind the words. I believe my language is hovering somewhere inside the place where the writing spirits dwell. They will bring it back to me. And there are times when Mohawk words jump into the computer, a surprise, a lovely gift when I least expected them to come.

I loved to read. I began reading at age four, taught by Grandpa and my dad. I remember the book, *Johnny Had a Nickel*, a book about a kid who had a nickel to spend and the long list of things he could buy with it (this was 1945, don't forget). Johnny ended up going for a ride on a carousel, but I ended up with an obsession for words, and a great respect for books. I had a library card when I was five. The library was fascinating to me—still is. I thought people who wrote books were creatures different from us. I didn't know until I was well into adulthood that Native people wrote books, and that Pauline Johnson, a Mohawk writer, had been published in the last century. My family didn't know either, or we would have had those books in our home. I read everything and anything I could get my hands on. It's cliché, but books were my friends. Along with movies, they shaped my view of the society I lived in. I always knew that my family was not a part of that society, didn't *want* to be a part of that society. Ah, but how *I* wanted to be (at least during my childhood and teenage years). I wanted to be an actress like Ava Gardner, Rita Hayworth; I wanted to dance like Marge Champion, sing like Ella Fitzgerald or June Christy (I seemed to have a lot of confusion about where my loyalties lay—with the white girls or the women of color! Maybe this is what being a half-breed means). I wanted to be acceptable. It wasn't until I was grown that I picked up a book by James Baldwin and found the kind of words and world that had meaning for me personally. Though he wrote from the culture of African Americans, he wrote about the effects of racism, the effects of colonialism, and I found the missing words that had left me bereft of meaning in my life. Later on, I was to "discover" Scott Momaday, James Welch, Simon Ortiz, Paula Gunn Allen—people of my own kind—people who wrote about *us*.

The timer is ringing. The bread smells are permeating the house. I open the oven, the heat fogging my glasses. For a moment, I can't see, caught in another way of being. I lift my head, hearing the faint whispers of spirits gathering together. My glasses clear, I remove the bread from the oven, tapping it, hearing that hollow sound that signifies a good loaf of bread. I turn the loaves onto the counter and return to the computer. I turn it on—a low hum emits as I tap in the code to lay the screen bare and accepting.

In most of my work, especially the short stories, I attempt to show breakthroughs in people's lives. Much of my own life has involved breaking through existing scenarios that have been programmed into my head. Despite the loving and culturally rich messages I received from the family, the cacophony of the dominant society made an even louder noise. Through writing, I "come back" to the family, come back to who I am, and *why* I am. The noise of dominance recedes and gives over to the music of my ancestors, my history. The people who inhabit my stories inhabit my life. They have made a home inside me, inside the computer, on the page. The people who live in story are, like Native people everywhere, struggling and dreaming, caught between the beauty of what we know, and the ugliness of what has been done to our people, our land. It seems as though I give these people choices—like the choice I make every day—to resist the ugly and go with beauty. I say, "it seems," because I never know what the people are going to do—they tell me. I feel as though they are speaking, "Write me, write me," and I have to struggle against what I have been told from white society, free myself, and give myself over to the singing and whispering that is my world, the world of Indigenous being.

When I was finishing up a book of essays, my father, whose physical body died in 1991, came to sit with me. My father, who never wrote a book, but wanted to, oh how he wanted to, was with me, chastising me over sentences that wouldn't live, "Now, Bella, you know that doesn't sound right," praising me when I got it right, "That's good, Daughter, that's good." His life, which was often so circumscribed, was one of hope and faith. He believed in the continuation of the

People. He believed in the old way, the *Onkwehonwe* way. He believed that the best was always to come. He left Earth with that faith gleaming in his eyes, transported to the Spirit World where he probably sings "Ode to Joy" to his relatives. It is my turn, my inheritance to sing an ode to the continuity of Mohawk ethos.

The bread is made. Later on tonight, Denise and I will cut it, slather on the butter, the same butter I am told is bad for my arteries. I'll save some for my grandsons, four examples of how story continues in the blood.

The computer is humming. The cursor blinks and talks, calling me into the sacred territory of story and meaning. They are gathering more forcefully now, the alchemy about to begin. Alchemy—from the Greek word Khemia, meaning Black Land—the Black Land of these words appearing on an electronic machine, soon to be transmuted into words on paper, the flesh of trees. What happens after no longer has to do with me. I've done my job.

16

Birth of a Negation
A Love Letter

Andrew Spieldenner

Visits to Vietnam

My lover and I are in a prison camp together.
We are in love in wartime.

A young soldier working as a guard has befriended us.
We ask him honestly—the truth—are we going to die?

He answers, yes, it's almost certain. I contemplate escaping. Ask him to help us. He blanches. That is impossible, he says. I regret asking him, fearing recriminations.

I see the forest through the fence on my right. I think, the place between the trees—I could burrow through there—toward freedom? Two of us would surely be spotted. One of us has a slim chance. I think of leaving my lover, imprisoned. But immediately I understand that we must, at all costs, remain with each other. Even unto death. That it is our being together that makes the pain, even our dying, human.

Loving in the war years.[1]

I read these words sometime before I would be intimately affected by rape and AIDS and prostitution. I read these words sometime after my introduction to violence, police, parents, poverty, death, hunger, and faggotry. This summer, when writing a lover, these words again resurface into my thoughts, bubbling up like bile, reminding me of the taste of the poisons I have ingested.

I was born into this country with all the pomp and circumstance of any other military child. A number. A cheap hospital. A last excuse to remain in the Army. My father, a white man from Ohio, has returned to Vietnam a second time and, like the other times, it is through penetration and someone else's labor. A foreign wife and two children. He tells me later he had wanted a daughter, not another son. The *Leave it to Beaver* show has been off the air awhile. A new age of consumerism and "good homes" beckons. It is the '70s. The Brady and Partridge families and budding feminist movement have reshaped the U.S. popular view of a proper family. Daughters on TV. *Should have been a daughter.* My mother has little to add. Vietnamese is not yet legal tender in my family.

I have to look at the moment of birth. I am a child of an unnamed war. So much of the secrecy and lies and murder and life and poison rule me and mine. Twenty-three years later and still no one speaks. On penalty of death or slow torture. I search so as to create whole a place a home a family a movement I never knew. I write to remake the world. I write to preserve the unremembered.

Doing the Work/Speaking Scabs

We constitute the invisible brothers in our communities, those of us who live "in the life", the choir boys harboring secrets, the uncle living in an impeccable flat with a roommate who sleeps down the hall when family visits; men of power and humble peasantry, reduced to silence and invisibility for the safety they procure from these constructions. Men emasculated in the complicity of not speaking out, rendered mute by the middle-class aspirations of a people trying hard to forget the shame and cruelties of slavery and ghettos.[2]

UC Berkeley was a name on a sheet of paper. An invitation to an uncertain world. A lucky chance brought on by a well-meaning and impressed white man. I assumed even then my high school counselor to be a gay man. But not like me. Where I could flaunt my fag, uninhibited, he could not. He chose to fill out my applications and fee waivers, and make interview times. He chose to do what I had no time nor interest in. I had a full-time job, my own apartment, and a lifestyle custom-made like a leather phallus for a young city-fag. Mr. Biondi pursued a possibility never seen in my family. War and poverty shape my concept of survival and life.

But UC Berkeley changed that. I had never encountered that strange breed called college student. People with so much time and so little material need, they could go on extended trips into academia. As if it mattered. Post-modern this, Lacanian that. Deconstruction and restructuring. And more white people than I had ever dealt with.

It was my first meeting with a racial bourgeoisie. Folks who needed a voice bold and loud and rageful. Folks too ashamed of nice homes and clean suburbs to tap into their own flesh wounds. So caught up in skin, they fail to recognize that with our skin comes our sex and how we choose to use it. At a meeting for an Asian political organization, I hear a self-proclaimed progressive Asian American woman call an Asian social event "so gay." Her boyfriend wonders aloud why Asian gays and women feel excluded from this group, as we all "have the same struggle."

We are bodies, scarred and still bleeding and under fire. My friend and sister poetwarrior Ricardo asks me in a post-midnight discussion, "Do you think we have bodies as men of color or are we just territories of wounds?" I grimace, too aware of his truth, suddenly wondering how I look when I talk. Another hole opens. More pus escapes. The concept of community ruptures. I have little in common with college activists who are enraged by their own inactivity and ignorance. Instead of acting, they agonize. And for we who have been named other in this country, there is much pain. But to create a world we must do the work.

Audre Lorde asks,

What are the words you do not yet have? What do you need to say? What are the tyrannies you swallow day by day and attempt to make your own, until you will sicken and die of them, still in

silence? Perhaps for some of you here today, I am the face of one of your fears . . . a Black woman
warrior poet doing my work—come to ask you, are you doing yours?[3]

It's Not Black or White

Birth of a Nation was a technical miracle. The first full-length U.S. movie. An audience captivated by images calling out from screens. An experiment in reality. A techno-visual wonder.

I suppose I should be grateful. With the advent of film, I do not have to imagine the sexiness of Denzel Washington or Russell Wong, the diva of Jodie Foster. With this visual tool, I see people and places and things I might never otherwise. But the images that stick! White men painted in black. A white woman jumping off cliffs to escape coal-smeared savages. A legend of race and patriarchy. An assault on minds and history.

I look at this birthed nation. A Black and White film. A film with whites in blackface. Racial drag. A chase. A capture. A suicide. Smiling darkies sex-starved and sinister. We live in the legacy of this image. A worldview composed in Black or White. Seen as two extremes where death is preferable to interaction. Where to be black means to want white. A nation of limits and violence and lies. A nation at war.

A close friend tells me about *M. Butterfly*. An Asian man in gender drag seducing the poor unsuspecting white man. A groundbreaking musical. An introduction of Asian men in leading roles. A recognition of Asian in the body of these United States. It is decades after the explosion of *Birth of a Nation* and still we as people of color have such little control over how our bodies are depicted. We are images—larger than life with no substance. A mirage. We might evaporate into reality if touched.

We live a lie, even to each other. Our own realness terrorizes us. What if we spoke? The earth might not even notice but our comfortable untruths might shrivel. As people of color, it is our very real and multiple differences which make us stronger, our unity which makes us fearsome. And we are fearsome. We can struggle to create a new legacy of technicolor sound explosion. One where we do not sacrifice ourselves, our self, to win the race.

Essex Hemphill, Black gay cultural activist, states:

> *It is not enough to tell us that one was a brilliant poet, scientist, educator, or rebel. Whom did he love?*
> *It makes a difference. I can't become a whole man simply on what is fed to me: watered down versions of*
> *Black life in America. I need the ass-splitting truth to be told, so I will have something pure to emulate,*
> *a reason to remain loyal.*[4]

The March on Washington, 1993. I'm excited—a paid trip to be part of a historical event. Look at all of us. An older friend had told me the last March was snow white. And now look—a sea of shade at the point of so much white. African Americans, other peoples of African descent, Latinos, Chicanos, Native Americans, Asian Americans, and Pacific Islanders. Hundreds of us, marching proudly, carrying with us the absent living and the dead. We're ready. The people of African descent are leading the chants. I brought the stereo and mixed tapes. Too few Native Americans and Latinos have made it to the March. (Grimly, I note this is the first multi-people of color event I have attended where Asian Americans and Pacific Islanders outnumber Latinos.) The beat takes us as we mill about on the street. Then we realize that, as we stand alongside our brothers and sisters, others amongst our Asian and Black communities have chosen to include their (white) lovers in our contingents. The difficult discussion involves keeping both groups' decisions intact, as the interracialists do not understand our choice to gather as people of color. Hastily, a method is devised to honor all of us—the people of African descent went between the Asian Pacific Islander group and the API interracialists. The Black interracialists followed the API interracialists. Due to the peculiar and particular nature of racial difference/s, we knew that one would not cross the other.

The realities of class, race, and patriarchy have limited our numbers as usual. There are at least several hundred thousand gays, lesbians, and other people in support of our struggle present in D.C. In that staggering number, maybe a couple thousand could be people of color. So by including a significant amount of white people amongst our contingents, we are rendered invisible yet again. Gay and lesbian people of color who had chosen to walk without the intrusion of whiteness had to come together, we could not be torn apart again. And we're not. Our numbers and refusal to compromise win out. We march *en masse*, dancing, chanting, and looking too too good. D.C. streets become our club, the rhythm and the shade are keys to liberation.

Back to Back to Back

I walk with people who travel similar paths. The awareness of land mines and liberation. What can kill and what will make us stronger. Sometimes they are the same. I need to be with people who know the tastes of anger and shame. And can still spit joy.

> im so tired of my flesh
> i feel so dirty sometimes
> i want to shed myself
> i try each day i struggle
> with a new birth[5]

So another sister writes and this I know to be true. We have lived, eaten, danced, written, and cried together. My homegirl and me. Hatching worlds with the power of words and the fear of what could happen if we stayed silent. Our pens must labor an afterbirth.

Our means of finding one another was, as it so often is, in reaction to an offense. At another meeting to plan a protest, a rally, some kind of political event or other, we grew annoyed by the gay white men who were dominating, talking way too much and wasting all our time with repetition and cruising. Frustrated and impolite, I suggested that the white men stop repeating everyone else, and that the facilitator to the meeting, a young Black lesbian, could call on people on her own. After a white man excitedly blurted out, "Hey, maybe we are saying what other people say. Maybe we should stop," my sister turned and proposed loudly, but much more sweetly than me, that the white men leave the room. The white people were shocked, enraged, and sputtering. The other people of color were smiling or stunned, but quiet. Our refusal to take in the bullshit joined us. We stood strong together. My sister and me make a we.

I stand with those willing for a short time anyway to offer and receive a hand, a laugh, a look that is its own conversation. We who cannot ignore the ongoing battle around and within and between us.

When we stand face to face, I want us to be able to cross chasms placed between us. I want you to listen, to converse with the realness of bone. I am learning to put down my weapons, to come to the table unarmed, so that I can hear your voice split the space between us. I want us to fight, to spit up the bile we've swallowed. I want us to fight like we need to fight, there's too much pain otherwise. I'll take the room I need, talk loud and lengthy like I've learned. So come to the table, the bar, the corner, the bus, the hair salon, the laundry room ready to stand face to face and cross chasms of difference.

Tomas Almaguer, a Chicano gay sociologist, writes:

> It's not easy being an intermediary between two cultural worlds—or, as it were, two nations. So they
> can wallow in their identity angst all they want as long as the issues closest to my heart and my cul-

tural sensibilities aren't abused or ignored. Like I've said before, my work . . . is primarily a matter of coalition politics.[6]

His frustration a resonance inside me. I cannot be the bridge everyone expects of me. It is a trap. The easiest way to divide and conquer, from the inside. Sometimes I don't want to talk with white people or straight people. It's too much, struggling to translate culture and experience from sites of past pain and current bleeding. Still I know it will take all of us to transform the world. I want us to have each other's back, to be able to work knowing we won't stab each other through.

We are our strongest allies and most hated foes. Another gay man of color can look through and stab at the core of my holes. Fuck me like I was nothing. A straight woman of color can know the indifference and distaste of men of color and use every open sore against me. A lesbian of color can make me face the monster inside me. None of it is pleasant, all of it forged in the furnace of racism and capitalist patriarchy.

> *hide me*
> *i feel too exposed*
> *give me long skirts*
> *take me to where i am whipped*
> *for showing my ankles*
> *take me to where my clit*
> *is sli/ced*
> *i don't want to feel this dirty passion*[7]

Broken Glass

It comes back to men. The connections of culture and cock. The miracle of the dance and the culmination of the game. Where speech is only one way to communicate and meaning is conveyed through rituals. It comes back to the men who have gone through my life and still I do not want to face it. When I first sat to write this I had planned to focus on a lover or two and my true true sisters. Those other colored girls like me. Then I realized the community I have so deliberately built consists of far more than a bunch of gay men of color. So I chose to explore the connections of who they are, how we found each other, and what I do to make that bond solid. A stained glass portrait more formidable than any previous depiction of war and warriors. And now it comes back to men.

As I look into the eyes of a lover, I know him to be man like me, with skin that has marked him other like me, and a desire named abomination like mine. Like glass, we can reflect similar scars. Like glass, we can crack into a multitude of jagged slivers.

A love letter.

> *I'm writing this letter to keep in contact with you. To maintain the tenuous link between us. To say what I need to say outside of telephone wires and machines. A missive to include with your birthday present. A greeting, A smile. This letter is a smile, a wish I could kiss you.*

I wrote this at the start of the summer to a man I had not seen for far too long and at a time when his absence was the hunger pang I could not stifle. Now I'm not sure where we are and what could happen. We have seen each other once since then. Gay Pride 1993, San Francisco, for about ten minutes. We accidentally passed each other on the street.

> *It's hard. I want to see you, hold onto you. Kiss and hold tight. Laugh and speak and listen and play. And hold tight, hold tight gently. I want to be with you and it's hard to pass through/over to you.*

And still the words do not come as simple as they have. If I was speaking about comic books or the latest novel read or even how so and so missy thing tried me or her at the club, the words would ride freestyle off my tongue. But in facing the manlover in my head, on paper, face to face somehow the words shrivel in possibility.

> *I dare us to dream that we are worth wanting each other.*[8]
> *This life is hard though. The life you want from me. The monogamous one. I think about you almost all the time but I cannot afford to call daily anymore. I think about you all the time and your nearness/distance drives me crazy. Drives me to new lengths of masturbation and fairy god-mothers. Maybe if I had one we would have the time. I miss you and monogamy is difficult for me to puzzle through alone.*

Yet even in this letter I do not say what kind of life I need from him. Nor do we speak of the life we already experience. These are the words I need to say, the words I do not yet have. I have never learned a language that could bridge the spaces between men. There have been many such tongues though, of this I am hopeful. A language killed or subdued or strangled or kidnapped or kept as treasure to a secret society. But in this new era, this new nation, we must birth a new such speech. One which revisions this place this past this people we call our own. One which recognizes we must pick sides, we are at war. "And as long as injustice prevails, we do not have the luxury of calling ourselves either."[9]

I need to find these names, these sweet nothings, this permutation of talking before I am consumed by the battle I wage. I can write about the schisms between us as men, but I cringe, frightened of the poem the prayer the song the declaration that will bring us together. To another lover, I write,

> *i want you to eat me*
> *devour me now*
> *savor each bite on your tongue*
> *tear into my skin*
> *like i was your first meal in 3 days*
> *chew muscle into taffy*
> *swallow me for strength*
> *suck my marrow*
> *to quench your thirst*
>
> *i want to stay with you*
> *even after the storm*[10]

There are more storms on the horizon and some of them must be weathered alone. But part of suicide is to try it without another, a tribe to keep well. There are people—good friends, some blood relatives—the reconstructed family in this new life, that can hold and succor and will stand back to back to back. But there are places only a lover can soothe, caress, and kiss whole.

I write to remake the world. To utter the intimacy rendered mute. To preserve the unremembered. To birth a nation.

Notes

The title of this paper came out of a conversation with Ricardo Bracho. The paper was first presented, in slightly different form, at Earlham College for Peace & Justice Week, 1993.

1   Cherríe Moraga.1983. *Loving in the War Years*. Boston, Mass.: South End Press. p.i.

2   Essex Hemphill. 1992. "Loyalty." in *Ceremonies*, New York: Plume. p.64.

3   Audre Lorde. 1984. "The Transformation of Silence into Language and Action." *Sister Outsider*. Freedom, Calif.: Crossing Press. pp.41–42.

4   Essex Hemphill. 1992. "Loyalty." in *Ceremonies*, New York: Plume. p.64.

5   Natashia Lopez. 1991. "The Flesh." *Chicana Lesbians The Girls Our Mothers Warned Us About*, edited by Carla. Trujillo. Berkeley, Calif.: Third Woman Press. p.141.

6   Tomas Almaguer. 1991. "Editor's Welcome." *Out/Look*, vol.3, no.3, Spring p.5.

7   Lopez, p. 142.

8   Joseph Beam. 1986. "Brother to Brother : Words from the Heart." *In The Life*, Joseph Beam, ed. Boston, Mass.: Alyson . p.239.

9   Cherríe Moraga, this volume.

10 Andrew Spieldenner. 1992. "Wrath." unpublished.

17

Tippin' the Furniture
An Interview with Angela Maria Giudice
Elly Bulkin

The following is an edited transcript of an interview with Angela Maria Giudice conducted by Elly Bulkin in October, 1994.

Elly Bulkin: *What were your earliest memories about racial identity?*

Angela Giudice: When I was growing up, my paternal grandfather, my Nonno, my Italian grandfather, was very prominent in the Italian community. He figures very strongly in my life. He was a dark-skinned man. I was very aware that the men in my extended Italian family and community were dark-skinned. When I was growing up, I went to a Catholic school with two Black kids—Joey Miller and Tommy Banks. The Banks family was very light-skinned. They straightened their hair and were culturally assimilated and middle-class. The Miller family was very dark-skinned and working-class. When I was in the third or fourth grade, my grandparents moved to Fort Lauderdale during the winter and spring, and we visited at Easter. I tan very darkly, and when I would come back from Florida, I was much more the color of Joey Miller, who was in my class, and much darker than Tommy Banks. And I got called "nigger" a lot during those springs and summers. It made me just hate whatever was making that happen. I knew the problem was *them*—the other white kids—and not me, although no one ever explained that to me. But I knew the name-calling had much more to do with society than with the color of my skin, or Joey's or Tommy's. I imagine this racism had some impact on Joey and Tommy, but we never talked about it.

Looking back on it, I think the white kids were afraid of me. I was very passionate already, in terms of how I expressed myself. I was one of the smartest kids in my class and very articulate. I was also the tallest kid in my class, even of the boys, and the biggest, in terms of weight. I had breasts. By the time I was in the fifth grade, I wore a 34B size bra. I got called a "whore" a couple of times because my breasts were developed. So calling me a "nigger" because of my tan and skin color was another way for these kids to tell me they found me "disgusting" or "repellent."

I had a white, middle-class kid's kind of curiosity about the Millers and the Banks family. I interacted with them over the years, but it wasn't based on a sense that we were social equals. This name-calling experience made me curious about them in a different way—about who they were and what happened to them day-to-day. So, two things happened simultaneously for me: both the ostracism because of my weight and an experience about skin color that also made me disdainful to other white people. Although I doubt that Joey or Tommy felt connected to me, I felt connected to them in a way that also sensitized me to know, somehow, that Black people had a real life. That they weren't just part of a ghettoized picture. I knew, somehow, that they had real lives I didn't know about, but I valued.

A similar thing happened when I was in Florida. The development my grandparents lived in was surrounded by a community of Cuban refugees, including some migrant farmworkers. I developed a friendship with one girl and a boy, who were brother and sister. I loved being with them and hanging out, partly because I felt some kindred spirit. Their way of expressing themselves and way of being in the world slapped so in the face the conformity I was supposed to accept. My grandparents prohibited me from playing with them. My grandfather's only explanation was that they were "dark," although ironically, they were no darker than he was. Many years later, when I was talking to my Nonna, my grandmother, and I said something about his being from Florence, she laughed this laugh that I'd never heard from her before, and said, "Oh, Nonno wasn't from Florence, he was from Calabria!" Calabria's in Southern Italy, and it's seen as "less than" in terms of Italians—kind of like "country bumpkins" here. There's a lot of North African influence and poverty. But he'd tried to make like he was so sophisticated, a cosmopolitan man from Firenze, born from aristocracy. So by fifth or sixth grade, I was very aware of the contradictions and the absurdity of race in terms of skin color. I understood that this whole thing was ridiculous. I also was very curious about the implications of it all—although I didn't have the words for it. Mostly, I took it as a reflection of all the pressure put on me and other Italians to assimilate, both culturally and class-wise.

That pressure was related to my being fat, my passion, my soul, my sexuality, and how I expressed myself. I felt so different from all the white people I knew. The brief, at least superficial, glimpses that I got into the Black community, or the even smaller looks I had into the Latino community in Florida, always felt much more like what and who I was. I knew that part of that assimilation pressure was to not act like *that*. And I got the message over and over again from my peer group that I was too intense, that I really needed to cool it out. Fit in. I was *too* much. I didn't conform to Anglo cultural standards in terms of looks. I did look Italian in terms of my coloring, my nose, and having dark, facial hair on my upper lip. But those characteristics got complicated because I was big. As an adult, I have realized that many Italian women are big, but growing up I felt like being big was one way I didn't fit in culturally.

While growing up I also was struggling unconsciously with sexual abuse that had happened early in my life. I definitely felt that something was wrong with me. I was in a lot of pain . . . about the abuse, my sexual identity and other things as well. At the same time, this huge pressure to assimilate into mainstream culture supported the notion of "just don't talk about it." Even though I was hanging out with a very definite ethnic enclave of Italian Americans, I wasn't aware of any other Italian kids who were questioning or challenging this pressure to assimilate.

Then in the seventh grade we moved to a much more middle-class, WASP-y area called Sherwood Forest. I started to go to public schools in the tenth grade. I started hanging around a new peer group, and they were heavy into conformity. Charleston, West Virginia—at least the sections that I was part of and exposed to—was totally about conformity. That's a key to another relevant story. In Sherwood Forest there were ranch houses with plots of land that were almost all the same size. The houses weren't exactly all the same, like Malvina Reynolds' song about ticky-tacky little houses, but they were close. After you got to the top of the hill and drove down the road to my house, there was this perfect house, with this perfectly manicured lawn. We're talking about nail clippers to trim this lawn. Out in the front yard, they had white wrought iron furniture—two identical chairs and a table. Perfectly placed, right in the middle of the lawn. Totally ornamental. No one *ever* sat there or used the furniture.

When I was in high school, I used to stay up a lot all through the night, and I would go walking through the neighborhood. Every couple of nights, I would very precisely tip each piece of furniture over. Very carefully and very exactly. Every morning, on my way to school I'd see that the furniture was still tipped over. When I got home that afternoon, it would be set back up straight again, perfectly in place. Every couple of nights, I would go tip the furniture back over. That became symbolic for me about the kind of conformity and superficiality I grew up with. And the facade of it all.

This all had to do with the messages I got about being white and middle-class below the Mason-Dixon Line, though I guess this socialization happens in Yankee culture as well. The ideal was to aspire to a middle-class way, to try to make it look like you came from the upper class, and had inherited wealth. But to me, this perfect manicured lawn with this white, wrought-iron furniture sang of "Dixie and the verandah." It was so much about that kind of illusion or delusion.

EB: *Were there any Black people in Sherwood Forest and was it a mostly Christian community?*

AG: There was one Black family. I babysat for them, but I didn't know about the Black community in any kind of way. The much more working-class neighborhood where I first lived was mostly Catholic and Protestant. When I moved to Sherwood Forest, it was definitely predominantly Christian—mostly Presbyterian and a few Catholics. There were quite a few Jewish families in Sherwood Forest. You know how some teenagers search for another family and are informally taken in by it. Well, I was kind of adopted by a Jewish family, the Cohens, whom I babysat for. They were a middle-class family, professionals who were assimilating into dominant culture. I wouldn't call it passing. That would be going too far because they were very clear about their Jewish identity, and certainly observed several of the traditions and the holidays. But in terms of their way of being in the world and the community, there was a lot of that same kind of peer pressure and the desire to conform and to be included.

By the time I got to high school I stopped trying to fit in for the most part. Thank god, by then I had the option of being a hippie. We heard about how you became a hippie through TV and *Time* magazine. We're talking about Charleston, West Virginia, mind you, in the late 1960s. But Randie Glassman and her sister, who were hippies, moved in right next door to the Cohens when I was in the tenth grade. I was very aware of her being Jewish and that her family was very Jewish-identified. I became good friends with Randie, although we never found a way to talk about how our differences bonded us.

EB: *What made them seem more Jewish-identified than the Cohens?*

AG: I don't have a specific memory about that. But I think that they spoke Yiddish or at least interspersed it through their talking. The way they looked, their physical features, made them look distinctly different from the blonde blue-eyed WASPs in my neighborhood and school. Probably where their ancestors were from—I don't really know if they were Sephardic, but they certainly were darker. I remember Randie's sister as having very large lips and darker features and at that time that really stood out. It was their urban style too, a real different style. And the way that they talked—not just Yiddish, but they talked much faster, and they didn't have Southern or Appalachian accents. Regardless of whether it was specifically Jewish or cultural in that sense, they seemed different from other Jewish families.

EB: *So how did being fat play into your racial identity?*

AG: I was a competitive swimmer—and it was very formative for me—from the time I was five until I was sixteen or seventeen. The winter swim team practiced in two different places when I was growing up—at West Virginia State College and at the YWCA in downtown Charleston. Both of those places, I realize now, were Black institutions. West Virginia State was a traditionally Black college. Although I don't know how the YWCA in Charleston, West

Virginia evolved in terms of being interracial, my recollection was that it was predominantly African American girls and women who went there. Black kids in Charleston held a lot of their dances there.

When I looked at those folks, I just saw physical differences to be so much a part of who they were. I've definitely heard Black women talk about the ostracism they've felt because of their size. But to me, this ostracism just didn't seem to be happening on the same level as it was among white people. I could clearly see that some of the popular girls were big—as big as I was, and *out there*. I can almost feel myself in this constraint—trying to fit in and getting glimpses that it didn't have to be that way.

Yet seeing them, or even looking at pictures of myself during these times, I was not exceptionally big by any means. I have no pictures which I can now look at as a child, adolescent, or teen in which I would say that I was "fat." So when I think back about the Black girls whom I saw as my size I now know they were developed, substantial sized girls. My recollection has a lot to do with my frame of reference then about the "right" size—white, WASP girls who were, for the most part, petite, or thin. I had muscles and breasts. That was considered fat and I was taunted and ostracized because of it. When I think about my few images of young Black girls from that time in my life, they certainly ranged from petite to quite large. They differed physically from the white girls I knew in terms of size and body shapes, as well as their dark skin and their hair and their facial features. I confused seeing all that as "different" with seeing them as "big."

I remember two important stories related to the YWCA. I wore a 34B bra in the 5th grade, so by the time I was in the sixth or seventh grade I was fully developed physically. The people on the swim team were all WASPs, mostly upper-middle-class and upper-class WASPs. They had straight blond hair, straight, pert noses; they had cute little bodies that fit like a stick into these tank suits. They were everything I wasn't. One day, we'd just finished a Saturday afternoon swim practice, and, when I walked into the shower, there was a bra hanging from the shower curtain rod, all wet, and dripping off the pole. Everyone started laughing at it, and they were saying, "Oh my god, whoever wears that is *huge!* Get a load of the size of that bra." And I was participating in it too. And the bra was just this huge thing. Then I went to get dressed and I realized that it was *my* bra. Some of the girls had gotten it and done that as a joke on me, and they were all laughing at me. The humiliation was unbelievable. I can't even let myself remember now how much pain I felt.

I got dressed and out of there as quickly as I could. I hid in an activity room behind some screens or partitions. All the Black girls were down there. When I looked at them, their bodies were a lot more like mine. And I just *knew* they wouldn't have done that. Maybe they would have. But to me, right then, it *felt* like they wouldn't have done that. I wanted to talk to them so much. I was already aware of racial barriers and starting to learn how different we were. But somehow I *knew* that they would talk about this kind of thing: that because of the experience of racism, they talked about being oppressed, or they talked about ways of supporting each other or coping with that kind of ostracism. They didn't assume that they would fit into the world. They had a pact that they would hang with each other and that they would hang in there. It was one of those pivotal moments for me around racial identity. At that point, I was struck with the polarity of these pert little blond WASPs, with their facades of niceness, and these alive, expressive, real—I mean they felt *real* to me—Black girls. But I had absolutely *no* bridge to them. Nothing.

I vaguely recall, at that particular time or another time, being in their space and knowing that I was not welcomed. That was ok for me too. I didn't take that personally. I never experienced that kind of "pro-one's own group" as being against me. I just knew that I didn't belong there, and that there was no bridge. Just absolutely no possibility for connection. At least in that context. I later constructed some bridges for myself in high school, but this was in junior high.

The second thing that happened was also connected to the Y. We had had a swim meet over the weekend that started on a Friday night. There was a dance this night that the Black kids were having and I snuck in. I remember being so aware of this being a taboo. I had the kind of experience that many white folks have their first time in an all Black space, a kind of "oh my gawd" kind of mouth-dropping look. I danced a little bit, sort of by myself. I actually ended up seeing a couple of girls whom I knew from basketball games who all said "Girl, whatcha doin' *here?!*" I'm sure I didn't stay very long, probably because of the logistics of the swim meet—I had to get picked up. I do remember that later, in high school, I sometimes tried to figure out how I could get to their parties. Because what was happening there felt so "real" to me, contrasted with all the facade and illusion that was created all around me in my own white, middle-class community. I also had a sense that their space could be safe.

These early imprints are still relevant for me now, living here in Roxbury, which is one of Boston's traditionally Black communities. Many white people would consider my decision to live here in Roxbury as not a "safe choice." I had to fight like hell to get Dydee Diaper to drop off diapers here in Roxbury—they "don't deliver to this area code." All of the white people I spoke with, including the president of the company, said it was not "safe" for their drivers to deliver to Roxbury. I've never felt unsafe in this community. I feel safer living in this neighborhood than I have living in most other parts of Boston. I've always felt as if there is a place for me here. I'm very conscious of not imposing myself as a white person. For example, in neighborhood or community meetings, I'm much less assertive or vocal than I would be in a group that's either white or more mixed racially. But I can have my life here and I feel safe as a white person.

EB: *How did the connections between being fat and your racial identity continue to play out?*

AG: I made many connections during the ten years I lived in Northampton in the 1970s. It was a politically intense time in terms of women's studies and racism. I wasn't a student, but many of the women I knew were active in the lesbian community and the women's movement and were part of the Women's Studies Department at UMass Amherst, at Hampshire College, and at Smith College. So, I had a chance to work with some dynamite Black women—Gloria Joseph, Johnnetta Cole, Mary Ruth Warner—who were very instrumental in the changes going on. Mary Ruth was very highly regarded as an activist academic. She also was a very big woman, and we developed a friendship. One day we had a really intense conversation about size and our experiences as big women. She talked about exactly what I had fantasized it would be like in the Black community. Certainly, she had experienced pain. But she never felt like she didn't *belong*. She never felt like she should be anything other than what she was. She was just Mary Ruth. And Mary Ruth was a big Black girl. And she became a big Black woman. And that became part of her status and stature.

I was in awe of what it could mean to have lived my life then, and now as an adult, where my size was part of my *worth*. At that time, Sweet Honey in the Rock was becoming more well known, and I saw them many times. To see Bernice Johnson Reagon out on the stage, shaking and shimmying and just being there—I imagine she's had lots of pain associated with her size as well, but she was no less of a human being because of her size. Audre Lorde was a big woman too. I was also starting to see more in the Puerto Rican community, where in many ways, size was just part of who you were. I had the grief of not having had that experience, but I also saw this incredible possibility of another way of being in the world.

At that time I learned two key lessons about racism. One involved the concept of solidarity. I learned pretty quickly that I had to be doing this *for me*. I had to understand that doing antiracism work was going to be about my *own* liberation, whether on a personal, political, or cultural level. One way antiracism related to my own liberation had to do with size. Racism has stopped me from seeing how being my size didn't have to mean feeling humiliated and "less than." The other lesson was one I learned through discussions about family. In Northampton, during the mid to late '70s, many white lesbians were talking—both rhetorically and in real-life—about making new families. I don't mean children necessarily, but more about lovers and ex-lovers and friends. Making family from friends. There were no models around that I was aware of. I realized then that racism was keeping me from being able to see models of being in extended families, or created and constructed families. This is about racism on a cultural level especially: if I could really *get* this lesson, that would open up a whole other world of seeing the value of being able to understand and appreciate what Black people had done to create these families.

Yet when I look back on these perceptions, I realize that I was starting from a romanticized and depoliticized notion of how and why Black families came to live in extended families. Even now, as I'm looking at this experience as a way to challenge my own racism, I'm aware that I didn't include class or historical factors in my frame of reference either. I was using white, middle-class lesbians as my frame of reference for talking about building new kinds of family relationships, and we were, in many ways, looking at that challenge from a privileged point of view. At the same time, I still value the search to try to make new and different families. And it enriches my search to become more aware of the class and economic implications of the ways in which I saw extended Black families as positive role models.

EB: *But extended families occur in white working-class families, not just in Black families, or other families of color.*

AG: It's not even just about working-class families. My whole frame of reference, as an Italian, is that you live in an extended family. So part of the question then is: Where do we look for models? And how do we value them? In that picture, I wasn't even valuing my own cultural and familial experience of having grown up in an extended family situation—not only in terms of my Italian heritage, but also my mother grew up in a very poor Scots-Irish extended family in Appalachia. She was raised by her grandmother, with all these older uncles around in the house. They were very poor. That was always presented to me negatively, even though *I* was growing up in an extended family. So the economics really came to bear there as well. I remember the positive things I was told about my mother's family much less clearly than the several alcoholics in the family, illegitimate children, incest, living in trailers. And, of course, the general society has totally reinforced this negative picture of poor, white, Appalachian families. I couldn't bring *that* experience to the white, middle-class lesbian community as an example of how to live in extended families.

EB: *Even though there is probably a similar incidence of incest and alcoholism in Black extended families—and in all families.*

AG: *Now*, I see the image I had of the Black extended family as indicating how racism limited how I saw the world. But, at the time, I became really angry at the white lesbian community. We couldn't get it that if we dealt with our racism, we could have other options as models. Then, trying to speak about how I was seeing things felt like speaking to the wind.

I remember going into this racism workshop in 1979 or 1980 at Hampshire with Michelle Russell, an African American woman organizing in Detroit. All these white women from Hampshire were doing this workshop. They were all cool and hip—and now that I think about it, they were all upper-class and very WASP. They all just seemed so sure of themselves. I remember Michelle was talking honestly about something really deep while everyone was acting as if they knew what she was talking about. I realized that we didn't *really* know what she was talking about at all. So I said, "You know, I have this feeling that we're all sitting here acting like we know what you're talking about, but we really don't know at all." These white women jumped on my ass. It was just so clear to me that we were operating on a very different plane. Michelle started to have a much more connected conversation with me about the day-to-day life of Black folks and about white folks trying to "rescue" the "disadvantaged."

Through our conversations, I learned that the central question for me as a white woman was "*Why* am I doing this? *Why* am I dedicating myself to antiracism work?" So I said that out loud, and the white women started yelling at me, "What do you mean? Isn't it pretty obvious, the injustice of racism? You mean you still haven't even answered that question? It's so obvious." These women were incensed that I was asking this question. But I asked again. None of them could answer, except to say that it was the "right" thing to do, or to offer a political explanation that was devoid of anything about their own part in it. It was all about "them"—meaning people of color. It was just another more sophisticated way of talking about "saving the poor starving children in China"—which was just what Michelle had been criticizing. I felt myself fighting this sense of humiliation and feeling that, once again, I didn't fit in with the group. But Michelle validated me and helped me to move beyond their judgments of me.

This all comes back to size. And I wish I could get a good image of what I felt, because I had such a visceral feeling at the time. Size became the anchor that allowed me to start developing a political and personal analysis of myself as a white woman doing antiracism work and what was in it, or about it, for me. This understanding has continued to be my access—my door in—with people of color, especially within the African American and Latino communities. It became the access and the anchor.

EB: *How has size been an important way for you to make connections across racial lines? And what does that also mean about size in relation to other white women?*

AG: Well neither of those are very easy questions to wrap my mind around. A couple of weeks ago, we went to an event sponsored by a group that we do a lot of things with, MOCAA, Men of Color Against AIDS. They were doing their annual, end-of-summer boat trip. I was getting dressed in a way that I thought was really about me. But I also was aware that I never would have worn that outfit to a predominantly white event.

The pants themselves weren't anything. But the top was a black lacy little thing that you could see right through, a tank top over a black lacy bra. Because of my size, I typically will wear clothes that tunic me, or cover me, or A-line me. Even before the fifth or sixth grade, my Nonna—my Italian grandmother—had taught me to dress like that; she was hyper-conscious about size and how you look, and my mother reinforced these strong messages through her own struggles with body image and weight and eating problems.

Well, on this boat trip, all of me showed through. And I knew that was OK and safe. There would be lots of women there who would look like me in terms of size. Women who, to some degree, even with all the pain, revel in their size. The women of color on the boat trip were mostly dressed very fancy, very stylish, and in some instances, very revealingly, in terms of the femmes wearing low-cut blouses or short skirts. I grew up with the notion that if you were big, you *never* wore short skirts. I never see big white women in short skirts. But I see big Black women and Latina women walking around in short skirts. So what were the different messages that we got? I can't believe that it's simply a matter of defying all the pressures to not do that. This goes back to the acceptance that I fantasized Black girls got, but that wasn't given to me as a white, Italian girl. At some point, I think there has to be someone who gives you permission—whether it's verbal or non-verbal, explicit or not—to wear whatever you want to wear. And watching the African American and Latina women in my life doing that has really helped me to know that I can too. I had a sense of "I am OK." And that feeling, which has come out of the political and personal development that I've undergone in relation to my antiracism work then starts to circle back. So that the more OK I feel about me, the more able I am to be in mutual relationships with women of color and be real.

I think that somehow I'm able to communicate to African American friends and colleagues that I understand racism as best as I can. I don't pretend to understand any more than that, while I'm always trying to understand more and better. It's a paradox. The more that I accept myself, the easier it is. Being OK about my size is part of that acceptance. At the same time I'm saying this, I realize that you've repeatedly asked me how my experience of my size and my racial identity were connected, and I kept on not being able to directly answer your question. Because issues of race and racism are such an integral part of my life, I have a certain amount of practice talking about them. But to connect physical size with racial identity is to break another taboo. I imagine I felt I was breaking taboos ten or twelve years ago by speaking frankly about white privilege and white racism. I get really sad, because, although I have grown to truly accept and respect and love myself as a white woman challenging racism, I don't yet fully accept and respect and love myself as a big woman. So it's been much easier to veer to a place where I have self-respect, but much harder to go to a place where there's still a lot of pain and self-denial.

I would like to find some way of naming the personal and political work that I do around my size, my ethnicity, and related issues, such as being a lesbian, so I can more accurately describe how I see them as all connected. I'm not trying to equate oppressions. Quite the contrary. I would maintain that you can't equate them because they're different. The healing that I have done about my weight, about sexual abuse, or any other way that I have been oppressed or excluded in my life has been directly proportionate to my ability to understand how having privilege and entitlement perpetuates racism. So understanding and dealing with my own oppression becomes a wedge into challenging my racism and vice versa.

There is a tremendous frustration on the part of some African American women who work with white women about how we often refer to our experiences of sexual abuse in ways that assume that we know about their oppression. VISIONS, the organization I work with, which does antioppression training, was founded and has evolved very much from the energy of African American heterosexual women. Sometimes at VISIONS meetings someone comments about my feeling like I have a right to claim a time and space to do my healing around my own experiences of oppression. It's a struggle for me. Because first of all, the organization has a culture which upholds the importance of emotional healing and structures itself to make that happen in trainings and internally. All its language and process facilitate personal growth and institutional change.

At the same time, my own privilege and entitlement as a white woman enables me to believe that I have the right to take advantage of those personal and organizational resources. Even though they built and structured the organization for themselves, many of the Black women in it often don't seem to feel like they have the right to take advantage of what they've developed. I try to stay pretty aware of how often I just "take" the time to do my personal work. I never just take that space without at some point needing and wanting to go face-to-face with some of the Black women about how they feel about me, as a white woman, taking advantage of that privilege. Even if and when they are able to let themselves take the same advantages—which is much harder for them in many ways—it brings up lots of issues for them.

Issues of privilege and entitlement come up when white women talk about sexual abuse in racially mixed groups. I've heard repeatedly from Black women about how upset and angry they get when white women start crying about being survivors of sexual abuse when issues of racism start getting hard and direct. In the process the white women get all the attention while racism goes unaddressed. I'm not saying that crying is bad—it's an important part of healing—as long as it goes along with an awareness of the political and emotional significance of white women crying about racism and our own pain in a racially-mixed group.

EB: *Do you think the women of color who are survivors and have taken some space for healing have a different experience?*

AG: I think some women of color who have used more traditionally-white modes of exploring their traumas—individual therapy, self-help groups, 12 Step programs—have feelings similar to some white women about their right to bring up these issues in group settings. It would be very interesting to hear what Nia, my partner, would say about this, since she is trained as a therapist and she also has done a lot of personal healing work around her own abuse and trauma. In the next several years I think we're going to hear a lot more from women of color about their experiences of surviving abuse and trauma and how they're making their way in the world of healing and recovery. A lot of times, when white women talk about incest and abuse, class and race and culture are not essential pieces of our stories. My guess is that, for women of color, those issues are going to be integral to their stories.

EB: *But I think that for white women who identify as working-class, those issues are part of their stories. Or for Jewish women, that gets brought in.*

AG: I think that's very true. Middle-class women have exercised a lot of privilege and entitlement in how we talk and think about abuse and trauma.

EB: *How does class affect the way you live?*

AG: If my partner Nia were from a more working-class or poor family, our relationship probably wouldn't have worked. Nia would describe herself as Black middle-class without any money. Her father worked in the shipyard as a painter and her mother had different things like a flower shop, a wallpaper business, a thrift shop, and various other entrepreneurial ventures that never brought in much money. At the same time, both of her families aren't first-generation Black middle class. Nia often talks about what it's meant for her to have this legacy—she has her own way of describing it that goes back to slavery and her ancestors working in the "big house." She's very aware of what that's meant for her family over the generations.

Her middle-class identification is related to her educational opportunities and the positioning of her family within the African American community as one with some status. They probably did have some money at one time—and by money, of course, we're talking relative here. Nia often describes her family and herself as Black bourgeoisie. We go to a funeral and you just see it—all the women in furs, just a whole look and feel.

It's also about skin color and hair. Some of the advantages that Nia has appreciated stem from the fact that her family has been mixed racially—African American, Cherokee and white—for several generations. So they range all the way from having very dark skin and curly, kinky hair to being very light skinned with blond, straight hair. She's somewhere in the middle. So, as I understand it, skin color and hair plays a large part in terms of who defined themselves, and how they define themselves, as middle-class.

Nia has lots of memories of struggles with money. Her mother prioritized Nia's education and was determined to give her only child the "best." Nia went to private schools. She was one of the first, and, in many instances, the first, Black child to go to several of the private schools around Boston. She has memories of going to a school for a year or so and then the school authorities would figure out she was Black, or they would be confronted by other white families, and then, mysteriously, she wouldn't return to that school the next year. Finally, by high school, she stayed in one school until she graduated. A few years ago, we went to her 25th high school reunion, and someone told her that, before she came to school for the first day of classes, they had a special assembly to tell all the children that a Negro child would be coming. This was back in the mid-'60s.

Because she went to private schools, she was exposed to a kind of life which I never had any exposure to at all. I certainly had much more financial security, but, culturally and educationally speaking, I wasn't exposed to nearly as much as she was while growing up. Our struggles in our relationship have often revolved around this key difference between us.

I think my whiteness and being middle-class has a lot to do with this struggle. I thought that if I worked hard I could come to expect certain things, including an easier life and security. My struggle with confronting this illusion or entitled way of looking at life has somewhat polarized us. As an African American and Cherokee woman who grew up struggling financially, Nia never assumed that life, at any point, would get easier—struggling and overcoming obstacles were just the daily menu. And that's not how I saw the world, and I'm not sure that I *want* to see the world that way either. So we are really having to dig deep to reconcile these very different class- and race-bound world views.

EB: *What makes it possible for you to live so much of your life among people of color?*

AG: I don't have a lot of words to explain it. This is scary to try to talk about. The story that comes to mind is from three winters ago when some people were at our house to play cards. Mostly Black folks, but not all. We were playing bid whist. In terms of relationships, especially with Black lesbians whom I'm close to, there's this whole thing about me being able to "hang" and play bid whist with the best of them. I know what it means for me, as a white woman, to be doing that.

We had been hanging out, and this interracial lesbian couple was there. They hadn't hung out with us much before that. But the white woman was coming to our house in her own car, separately from the Black woman. You could tell that the white woman wasn't very comfortable. She didn't know a lot of these women and maybe she felt a little out of place. She had to go home earlier than the rest and without her lover. Three people tried to give her directions to her home. About twenty minutes later she was back at the house and she was undone. She'd gotten lost and she'd freaked herself out about being lost in the middle of Roxbury, although nothing had happened. Everyone rallied around and re-directed her again.

Well, hours later, after most of the folks had left, just a core group of us were left who hung out a lot. A couple of people started recapping what had happened and they were doing this whole rag on her about getting lost. The group of African American lesbians and gay men were having fun talking about this white woman. Personally, I don't feel put down by that kind of talk. I'll say something if I feel it's getting too mean-spirited. But I was aware that they were raggin' on her and this one gay man was going on about white people. Then he takes in that I'm sitting there— the only white woman—and he says, "Oh, but you're different, we don't really mean *you*, you're not really white." I let it go, because it was 3 or 4 in the morning.

But I thought about that comment for weeks. I've had that kind of comment made to me a lot by Black folks. Sometimes I luxuriate in it in a way that I'm very suspicious of in terms of what it means for me as a white woman to get that kind of validation. The subtle racism that I watch myself work through now includes the ways in which I don't want to be seen as "one of them."

But I also let myself begin to wonder what it was about me that allowed them to see me as different. In some ways, I've been able to be real with folks and not pretend that I'm anybody or anything that I'm not. I'm comfortable, and I think that comes across. In those kinds of situations I've been somewhat nonassuming and not felt the need to assert myself past the point of keeping my own integrity.

EB: *How do issues of race affect your relationships with other white women?*

AG: I feel tremendous grief and anger that I can't connect with white women that much. It's not that I don't have good, real, lasting, loving relationships with white women. In fact, some of my best friends are. . . . I need to understand more about my anger towards other white women, which relates to the experiences that I had both around my size and my inability to assimilate. For instance, in my high school, sororities were the whole world. For three years, I thought I was going to get "rushed" and for three years I didn't. For two of those three years, my best friend was the president of the most popular sorority and I was her best friend too. It became so clear to me, in retrospect, that there was no way in hell that any of those girls were going to let me into that sorority. I think that was about size, and being Italian. The exclusion also related to my being a lesbian, even though I didn't know that then. So I felt a deep level of betrayal—a feeling of both a desperate need to be a part of them and disgust and repulsion at who they were.

Today, there's some degree to which my white friends, most of whom are lesbians, don't "get" what my life is about. Or they don't go there with me. Or maybe they see me as "betraying" them. An example of this occurred when a friend of mine didn't come to Nia's and my son Mario's naming ceremony. Sandy, who was my best friend for many years, has been scared about coming into Boston, and especially into Roxbury. Largely, I think her fears are because of her lack of contact with people of color and lack of experience being in the city. She lives in an extremely white middle-class environment out in Northampton. When I pressed her about not coming to Mario's African Naming Ceremony and Welcoming—which was being held in Franklin Park, in the heart of Boston's Black community—and told her I *wanted* her there because this was such an important moment in my life, she was able to talk more openly about how different my life seems from hers. In some ways, she doesn't know how she fits into that any more.

When I'm in a situation like that, especially with someone whom I'm so close to, I can't help but feel betrayed myself. But then, I imagine she might feel that I'm betraying her too. Even though I wouldn't use the term "race traitor" in my everyday vocabulary, I think it's a very potent image of how some of my white friends or family might feel subconsciously about me.

I also relate this dynamic to organizing. I think, for example, about some of the important organizations and institutions in the white middle-class gay and lesbian community here. Yet, constantly, I feel like they're turning their backs on anyone who has a progressive vision about oppression beyond white, middle-class, gay, lesbian, and bisexual issues. Several times, when I've tried to raise issues about racism and classism at their events or meetings I've gotten a very distinct sense that many white people from these groups think my doing this involves trying to bring "our community" down, or betraying people on a personal and organizational level. I wonder who they see as "our" community, since they still are not inclusive of people from different racial and class groups. If I as a white person keep trying to talk about racism, other white people's guilt and fear about their own choices make them feel as if I'm exposing or betraying them. Their limitations and resistance make me sad and angry.

E B: *This makes me think about how dealing with racism means we gain a tremendous amount, but sometimes we also lose people.*

AG: I learned pretty early on in my own antiracism development that there were going to be losses, even on the level of family. It's even harder to accept that people I'm close to do not understand the significance of racism in our day-to-day lives and the importance of changing our everyday lives. Especially with someone that I've gone a long way with in terms of developing a relationship, I feel like, "What do you mean you can't go there with me? All you have to do is do it!"

E B: *I wonder how this makes you feel about being white.*

AG: Fortunately, I'm not one of those people who hates that I'm white. If I wasn't Italian, that might be different. There's always a way that I can still disconnect myself from being white and I work hard at not doing that.

E B: *I think I know what you mean, because I feel like if I wasn't Jewish, I might have a whole different feeling about being white.*

AG: I'm part of a very definite ethnic and cultural group that still has present-day relevance. When you hear some people try to talk about their ethnicity, they say, "Well, I'm just American." So it's been very helpful for me to be able to claim my Italian heritage—and also to strongly identify as Appalachian. Consequently, I'm not as threatened when I hear people of color claim their racial and ethnic identities. Maybe being Italian-American has allowed me a little more distance from some of the self-hate I hear some other white folks talk about in terms of their racial and ethnic identities.

I also value the experience of being an outsider that comes from being Italian and Appalachian. Even though there's not the same kind of historical and present-day experience of oppression and the legacy of struggle and resistance that many Jewish people feel, there *is* a heritage of Italians standing up for themselves. Sacco and Vanzetti immediately pop into my mind, and the continual struggles of West Virginians against outside coal and land interests. So I can find pockets of my people who have stood up for social justice.

The passion of Italian culture was also connected for a long time to a passion for justice. The roots (though exaggerated through stereotypes) of the Mafia—the Cosa Nostra—is that whole notion of justice, though in most ways gone awry. But there's a strong passion for what is felt to be right that I think, unfortunately, has gotten really lost as generation after generation has struggled to assimilate. Now you wouldn't hear it as "justice" in the way that we're talking about it, but rather, you'd hear it as a fierce defense of "saving our community" and not having to go to school out of our neighborhoods, or not having "outsiders" move in.

In terms of how I feel about being white, I get a certain kind of status or validity in some circles of people that comes from being in an interracial relationship and doing the kind of work that I do, having the kinds of relationships I have with people of color, living in Roxbury. I would never pretend that I don't get some needed validation in relation to being white. In my more vain and insecure moments I have used that to help me feel "better than" some other white people. I'm by no means beyond having those feelings. But I have done a lot of healing concerning my rage about being white and the legacy of racism I have inherited because I am white. That's partially been because of the kind of person I am. It's also connected to my healing from sexual abuse.

Also, I've made some very significant relationships with some African American and Latino people who have been willing to acknowledge my whiteness and not, on some level, hate it or me. I've experienced their rage about racism and even their very deep anger at me sometimes about my whiteness and the ways I might be using my privilege. I make mistakes all the time, or my arrogance seeps out, or my "Euro" way of seeing things comes through. But the relationships have developed in such a way that I can tolerate their getting angry with me. Through that process, I have been able to heal about being white, which has been important to me.

Now, I want to locate some of those feelings about being white with other white women. That's the missing piece for me. I need to talk much more with and hear about what we do with our fear, our shame, our guilt, our feelings of political impotence, our contradictions, our cop-outs. The thinking I've done can only be strengthened by working with other white women. And I love my biological family—white people—even though how they relate to racism varies from person to person. My immediate family is doing unbelievable work on racism as our family is becoming more and more biracial. My sister Gina also has a daughter who is biracial, so my family now includes three people who are Black. On the other side of the continuum are right-wing Republicans—my cousins whom I grew up living next door to. We run the whole gamut, including my grandfather who was dark-skinned, but was prejudiced against Cubans because *they* were dark-skinned and a cousin-in-law who wouldn't let his white children play with my Black niece. I claim them all—even though they have a hard time claiming me.

EB: *What I heard you describe early on was a pull towards people of color and a negative force away from white people. How does that affect your relationships with white women?*

AG: Both forces have been real strong for me. Do you think that my life reflects some very sophisticated, highly refined "wannabe" kind of thing? Maybe this is my fear—and I'm constantly challenging myself about it. I'm pretty aware of that. In fact, if I had another life of organizing, I'd like to work with the white young people who are heavily into this "wannabe" stuff. There's a whole movement and it really deeply disturbs me.

I understand the wannabe stuff as being about a dual force: one being disdain, the guilt and shame of being white, and the fear, anger and grief that comes with not accounting for what being white means in this world; and the other reflecting ostracism or not fitting into—or enjoying—mainstream white culture, and then wanting something else out there that is often exoticized and made appealing in terms of being "forbidden" or "other." For adults, it's been about having played while growing up with "talkin' cool" or hip, or "bein' down," or knowing more about Black history than many Black folks themselves. Or being more antiracist than any other white person could ever be.

For young white people today, this phenomenon is much more insidious—and frightening. There is a whole movement of white, middle-class, mostly suburban young people—mostly boys and young men—who say they are not white. A lot of the white rap artists are so "down" they are more hip-hop than the hippest hop. *VIBE*, a great hip hop magazine published by Quincy Jones, has run some fascinating articles about young white kids who are claiming they are not white. It's very ahistorical. It's very apolitical and out of cultural context. I find only very thin lines between how they express themselves and what I've heard of and seen from young, white skinheads. The skinheads profess a different line, but their personas, the way that they see the world and express themselves, are very close to some of what I hear from young, white wannabes.

EB: *When I asked about the pull away from white people and toward people of color, I was thinking partly about your stories about high school, and partly about the story about playing cards. What does it mean to you that you were practically the only white woman there? Something about that looks very isolating, although I hear you talking about it only in terms of connectedness and comfort.*

AG: When you used the word "isolated," that helped, because I *do* feel isolated a lot. The isolation, however—well, partly my fear—is that somehow I'm going to find out that all the good work I've done has been based on a bad motivation. There's been a long history of white people—and I'm including myself very much in this—who have, for ulterior emotional reasons, placed themselves in situations where we are one of a few white people. That has happened historically, and it's happening right now too. I've been really curious about what kind of emotional needs are being met through being "one of the only." I was trying to start talking with some of the people in my life who are Black about what their perceptions of me are. I've asked, "How do you see me?" or how could someone say, "Oh, Angela really doesn't count as white."

Several years ago, I was at a Kwanzaa celebration where I was the only white woman in a group of 12 or 13 African American and Latina women. The day was "Kujichagulia" and we were talking about self-determination. The host of the Kwanzaa party referred to how the women of color in the room just knew instinctively about the importance of self-determination. As she said it, she saw me, and she said, "Well, Angela too, because she's Jewish." I got such a good clue then about how some Black women have explained or rationalized my being who I am, because they assumed that, since I was Jewish and had experienced anti-Semitism personally, politically, and historically I had a greater potential to understand racism. But at the time I just said, "Thank you very much for acknowledging that I also would have some understanding of self-determination. However, I'm not Jewish. I was raised Catholic and I'm Italian, and self-determination does mean something very real to me." Everybody was cracking up. Most of the women in the room knew that I wasn't Jewish, and they wondered how I was going to handle the situation.

Even if part of what originally motivated me forward into this life is related to my feeling ostracized from my own peer group and community, and then romanticizing or fantasizing about this connection to Black folks that didn't really exist, that's OK. I'm willing to keep working that out. Yet I feel vulnerable about people's judgments—that they might discount what I have actually come to learn, or what I have come to *make* of my life, because of my original motivations or the emotional benefit that I get today.

EB: *I wasn't making a negative judgment. I was asking, What does it* mean? *I'm still back at the question of What does it mean to not have had other white women to hang out with?*

AG: It's very lonely. My reaction certainly communicates how vulnerable I feel about being judged. On a gut-level, it makes perfect sense that I would hear the question as a judgment. The history of white women being part of a Black community has, in large part, been in relation to Black men. Most white lesbians also derive our deepest connection to the Black community primarily through intimate relationships.

Because I'm aware of this history, I feel very vulnerable about judgments or projections about who I am and why I've made the choices I've made. I'm becoming acutely aware of this on a new level—as I go out into the world as the mother of Mario, a biracial child—just going down to the grocery store. So I'm feeling defensive as I'm working through it. At the same time, it reminds me of the incredible lack of role models that we've had as white women challenging racism, politically and in our personal lives. The only woman who even comes near for me as a role model in this sense is Lillian Smith, who, god bless her, lived with thousands of contradictions too. She had lots of money and an ability, or need, to distance herself while also being midst of it all—in a way which I don't aspire to at all. But her descriptions of the emotional costs of growing up as a white child in a racist society and then the impact of that on her as an adult are the closest I've ever come to reading on an emotional or personal level something that describes my experiences. I'm being very careful about how I'm talking about this and I'm wondering where that's coming from. I'm aware of how often I feel different. It's almost like recreating a whole other construct of feeling different and apart from the white community.

I'm working on a project which is a professional high point for me with the North End Union down in the Italian community of Boston. In fact, it's been a little hard for me professionally because I feel so personally involved. I'm anxious for the contract to be finished so I can re-enter as a human being and not as a consultant and continue the work I'm doing on a level of political organizing. That's the only way that I could continue that work—I couldn't do it as a paid consultant.

I intend to follow through with it, as maddening as I'm sure it's going to be at times. Italian folks in Boston are notorious for their prejudices. It's a racism that, in some ways, is portrayed differently from what happens, let's say, among the Irish in South Boston. But certainly, the impact is no less. It goes back to some of the contradictions that I was talking about earlier about my Nonno. How could those people even begin to think that these folks from Algeria or Morocco or Eritrea are less than them based on skin color? Half the time, they're the same color. The cultures are so inter-dependent and connected. It's an absurdity that I don't get—and that I *do* get, too. I don't think I have many illusions about how hard the work will be. I'm sure I'll be disappointed many times and meet tremendous resistance and denial and bigotry.

But I *do* long for being part of that community. I'm always looking for ways to construct community with people who are like me. I think of Patti DeRosa—another white woman, an Italian woman. Patti and I have been very deeply connected. We have similar politics. We lead somewhat parallel lives, even though she's more connected to the Black Caribbean community and she's heterosexual.

There is one piece about Mario that's very connected to my own identity as a white Italian woman. When Nia and I were getting closer to actually meeting Mario's birth mother, I admitted to Nia that even though I honored our decision to have or adopt a biracial child whose identity would be African American, I also felt a tremendous loss. We knew then that Mario was biracial, but we didn't know the particular ethnic mix. And I wanted this little *bambino*. To Italians, family and blood are everything. I feel no shame in admitting that that was real important to me.

So I cried my heart out. Fortunately, Nia could hear it and understand. Then, we went to meet Mario's birth mother, and the first thing out of her mouth, when she said something about herself, was, "I was born in Palermo, Sicily." And I cry now thinking about how when you let go, it comes.

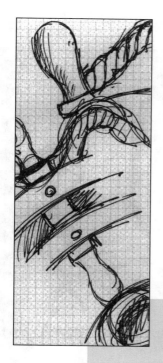

Part IV

"ACTS OF CREATION:
Sweat, Blood, Bone"

18

The Breakdown of the Bicultural Mind

Cherríe Moraga

Like many other prophetic leaders of nativistic movements, be they Moses ... or Malcolm X, the intensity of the vision seems to be fired by the internal conflict coming from a culturally mixed parentage.

—William Irwin Thompson, Blue Jade from the Morning Star

I read all I can for a clue. Looking to Moses and Malcolm to come up with some thread of connection, some sense of how my mixed-blood identity has driven me to politics, protest, and poetry, of why I awaken at three o'clock in the morning, a heaviness over my heart. *Who is sitting on my chest?*

I read of Quetzalcóatl—the story of the man, not the god, destined to relive, as Thompson writes, "the primal act of rape which brought his soul into the world." He compulsively re-enacts that history through sexual indulgences, subsequent penance, and submersion into the fire of transformation. And like the phoenix rising, Quetzalcóatl is reborn into the morning star.

I read and I remember. At nineteen, I first heard the story of the "mulatto," as my friend called him. A musician she knew who was born a black smudge into an otherwise lily-white family. No one ever spoke about it. He was never told he was Black, but figured it out in a life in and out of prison, drugs, and jazz clubs. And then one night, alone in his apartment and thrashing so bad inside, he went, without thinking, into the bathroom and filled the tub with scalding hot water. At the moment he submerged his body, long legs and back, then face into the water, he remembered. He remembered being no bigger than the length of his mother's arm as she dropped him suffocating into the liquid flame. So the story goes, the next day the man sold all that he owned, including his precious saxophone, but kept his car to live and sleep in, never moving it. One morning they found him in it, gassed to death. *Sometimes one lifetime is not enough to repair the damage. That is what we fear, isn't it?*

The story stuck. Twenty years later and I'm still thinking about it. This mixed-blood scenario that ends in suicide, that ends in rebirth. What fiery pit awaits us, we new breed of 21st-century mestizo? Into what shapes shall we be transformed?

I re-read my own writings of a decade ago and see the same struggles. Then I was no less the mixed-blood Mexican, *la mestiza's mestiza*. The difference now is that I understand that my writer's journey is not strictly wedded to my individual story—the marriage of my U.S.-born Mexican mother of Sonora roots to my San Francisco-born French and British-Canadian father. That story alone does not explain my dreams, my nightmares, my insistent cultural nationalism. There is something older, something I remember and live out again and again in the women I love, the family I make, the poems and characters I create. Thompson goes on to write, "we are more than we know," and there is consolation in this, that there may be a more powerful impetus than my mere forty-year-old biography to explain this unyielding need to re-live the rape, understand the rape, the loss . . . the truth.

We are no Moses, no Malcolm, no Queztalcóatl, but we are all our own gods. And our liberation won't happen by some man leading the way and parting the Red Sea for us. We are the Red Sea, we women.

We Invent Ourselves

10 noviembre 1992

Lifting off home turf I don't really feel I am leaving home until I spy the moon, a San Francisco dawn's full moon, descending into the skyline. She speaks to me of longevity, a sisterguide in an otherwise lonesome horizon. But I recognize that horizon, know the geography of peninsula and bay and eastside hills, northside bridge (not gold, but orange) buried beneath fog caps. I know dotted islands of empty prison cells, processing camps, cruel welcomings, and land grabs.

My Spanish surname is chiseled into a tombstone on the breastbone of mission tiles and Indian dirt. There are whole city blocks with his name attached to them and we—whoever we I am with—invariably fantasize about coming in the middle of the night, stealing the signs and leaving the streets nameless and unoccupied. It is a lesbian dream, like the moon, grander than city planners' visions, than blueprints, than conquistador maps.

But what I really wanted to write about was that rising sun spilling out of the Oakland Hills, that moon resting on a cushion of coastal fog. You are not asleep yet, but will be soon, driving the little blue Toyota, gas tank near empty, back to our sleeping home.

I have loved all kinds of women in all kinds of towns. Last night an old writer friend, a Southern woman, tells me over a meal of fried okra and chicken and polenta, *polenta's no more than grits, just a fancy name for grits*. But this is San Francisco (what-used-to-be-Black) upper Filmore, so polenta it is. I tell her, spooning the last of that upscale yellow mush into my mouth, *we've known a lot of women. Why is it so hard to write of what we know about women?* And much of what I know, I admit, is about race.

In love, color blurs but never wholly disappears. I have had only one great fear as a lesbian lover—that my eye would turn on my beloved, that I would see her through the stranger's eye, that what I fear in my own desire, its naked hunger, I would recoil from in her open-faced body.

And my eyes have turned over and over again.

I have never had a race-less relationship. Somehow I have always attributed this to being mixed-blood, but I wonder if anyone has. Maybe white people are the only ones in this country to enjoy the luxury of being "colorblind" with one another, white people in all the glory of their centrality. Not I. As deeply as I have feared the power of my infinite female darkness, feared my Mexican muteness, feared my bottomless rage in my brown-skinned lovers, I have feared the mirror of my passivity, my orphanhood, my arrogance and ignorance in the white women I have loved. It is not a pretty picture. I have at times seen Black women as cold as any white woman in their "gringa" chauvinism, and I have seen Latinas as spineless as any man in their disloyalty to women. I have been both *agringada* and spineless and this is not a confession, but an unholy testament to my unwavering faith in lesbians to name from the bed those battles being waged on the street.

We light-skinned breeds are like chameleons, those *lagartijas* with the capacity to change the color of their skins. We change not for lack of conviction, but lack of definitive shade and shape.

My lovers have always been the environment that defined my color. With a Black lover in apartheid Boston I was seen as a whitegirl. When we moved to Brooklyn, we were both Ricans. In Harlem I became "Spanish." In México, we were both Cubans. With my brown girlfriends we be brown girls sitting on brownstones. We be family. Among Indians in the States I'm a half-breed who looks like every other breed, colored mixed with cowboy. Among Indians in México I am *güera, ladina, extranjera,* and not to be trusted. Among Chicanas, I am everybody's cousin Carmen. Whitegirls change my shade to a paler version. People think I'm Italian, Jewish. In bed, I sizzle brown indifference, brown in difference. On downtown streets, I disappear grey into the color of sidewalk. No body notices me. For that reason, I got to be choosy 'bout who I hang with. Everybody so contagious, I pick up their gesture, their joke, their jive. We invent ourselves. A mixed-blood Hawaiian friend tells me, "I create whole biographies of the black childhood I never had. Give me enough time with you, I'll invent a Mexican one, too."

"The dark woman looking in through the glass is as frightened as I am. She is weeping. I will not let her in."

I remember Pacific Ocean Park in the fifties. She was a girl my age, my size. We stood in line for the "Wild Car" ride. I remember her darkness, her difference, her nappy hair corralled into three perfectly plaited pigtails. I didn't understand the third one. Why was it there? My mother always twisted my busterbrown straightness into two limp fountains spilling out from behind each ear, temples stretched to breaking point. So tight a hairdo, it could last for weeks. I didn't know about little black girls' hair and how their mothers sat them between their knees, greasing and separating and combing each section into that exact symmetry. So tight a hairdo, it could last for weeks. I didn't know how thick hair could be until I grew up and felt its soft density supporting my chin as we two slept.

I wanted to see her as different, that little girl. I remember her wearing pink and suddenly throwing up all of Pacific Ocean Park out of her roller-coastered gut, the puddle of stink and sickness one person away from me. That wasn't me. That was someone else's guts lying in a lumpy grey puddle in the line to the "Wild Ride." An hour later, getting off the same roller coaster, I fought desperately to keep down the cheap spaghetti dinner rolling around in my stomach, rising in my throat. I didn't want to be that human, that exposed, that dark.

There was a time when I truly believed I could never live without Black women in my life. And then I learned how—how to forget uptown city buses, her fedora-feathered dreads, her femme fatality sliding up next to me. We peer out onto street-soaked Harlem. She, small-town-colored-girl-import; me, "Spanish." But somehow we managed to make home in Harlem, her talking the talk, in girlsclubsboysclubs, with girls&boys always eyeing us, envying. Or so we imagined.

I imagined I could never live without that. That her. That life. But then I did learn to live without and then Audre died and I remembered that biography denied me. I dial New York, hear my name echoed back to me familiar. "We were so young," my sister says. And Black, a decade ago blackfamilia. Audre was our dark womanhood wrapped around dark womanhood in subways and on street corners, kissing under rain-soaked umbrellas, in the basement of a mid-town church where we plotted coloredgirl revolution. I had a Black family once and what happened to that? Like my Mexican childhood, my Puerto Rican dreams, my white forgetfulness. What happened to all those women I laid and made history with?

You Wanted a Real Mexican, You Got It

I can't write of pink-nippled breasts
how I've looked so harshly at my own,
how I grow in the delight of their darkening
how once a black-nippled Mexican lover
threw up my shirt exposed
my nipples and they all laughed

> *at their pathetic rose-colored softness*
> *they all laughed and I grew*
> *dark in my anger and resolve*

The first colored woman I slept with wasn't colored at all but darker than me in *her* anger, in *her* resolve. And I tasted on her immigrant tongue resting speechless upon mine a sister of tragic dimension. How she envied me my education, my seamless face, my freedom. The taste was bitter and mother-Mexican familiar. I wanted more. . . .

My first Chicana lover was the smoothness of the clay pots she dragged from home to home, making home out of anything, stolen milk crates, heavy tamales of woolen Indian blankets. She was a childless woman like me, a woman, as Don Juan describes it, "without holes in her body." Still, like those Mexican pots, she had a wide open mouth, ready to devour everything surrounding her. This was lesbian, I discovered. And I had never been so in love. . .

I thought I met a lesbian once, an Indian woman from the south of Oaxaca who sat three tables away from us at a club in the capital city. As the salsa band plays, I watch the woman in a short mannish haircut watch us, a table of U.S. Latinas, as Sabrina takes her girlfriend out to dance. When they return to the table, the waiter brings us another round, courtesy of the woman three tables away. We invite her to join us. She is already drunk and her tears well up and flow down effortlessly as she recounts to my *comadre*, Myrtha, the story of her passage here to this city of *ricos* and government officials and poverty. She speaks of a recent death, the murder of a family member. And with the same despair, she speaks of the sudden cutting of her *trenza*. A government program had brought her here, hundreds of miles away from her village, and filled her pockets with *pesos* and her belly with *mescal*. She cries, and eyeing Sabrina's Indian *trenza* and Mixteca features, keeps wanting to understand who we all were. We try to explain, but she only cries all the more as the full moon passes into view through the *zócalo* window. She tells us that at that very moment she is missing her village's *ceremonia* to the moon. I mention the moon's Indian name "Coyolxauhqui." She stares at me. It is the first time she has looked at me all evening. "How do you know that?" she asks. "You are white." And I look over to Myrtha whose watery eyes have held the woman's for over an hour. We smile, sadly. "She's right," I say later. "In her world, I'm just white."

It was Myrtha who told me on a particularly gloomy Berkeley afternoon, "You don't know what it feels like to always be perceived as 'Third World,' to see in everybody's eyes that disdain, that *desprecio*." And yet, we move around these ancient Mexican sites from Palenque to Monte Albán like long lost sister-companions. *Una puertorriqueña y una chicana*, we speak in a wordless code to each other. We are without nationality in the deepest sense, even though they only ask me and the Germans for passports on this bus full of Mexicanos and Myrtha. She doesn't mention it, her hand resting on mine. Neither do I.

And suddenly I remember the lover I had left, weeks earlier, on the sandy streets of a Mexican beach town, and the one distinct time I made love with her and shook. Shook from the tequila still poisoning my veins, shook from how boldly her americaneyes stripped me of my Chicana cultural bravado, shook from how naked I felt. And I remember vaguely, because I was so drunk, the trip across to the island, her holding my back as I threw up in a bag. I remember her getting us to the hotel in a cab. I remember her hand always guiding my back, and I remember again throwing up all that bitterness, all that self-hatred, all that disgust at my whiteness, my hunger to be part of that memory, that México. And I called her "sister," too. With a voice I use only for my own blood-sister's name, as I worked my hand and tongue inside of her, trying to find a place to rest all that homesickness.

In 1986, I wrote a play in which a Mexican woman says of her young Chicana lover, "*Sometimes I think with me that she only wanted to feel herself so much a woman that she would no longer be hungry for one.*" Today in my own voice I would add, "I only wanted to feel myself so much a Mexican . . ." But I am always hungry and always shamed by my hunger for the Mexican woman I miss in myself.

I would have left sooner if it hadn't been for the smell of albóndigas *in her kitchen, the sticky desert taste of* nopalito *behind her ears, the texture of that thick rope of hemp hair I twisted into my fist, holding her* hamaca *and swaying beneath me. I would have left her if her Spanish had been less than perfectly provincial, her repertoire of* rancheras *lacking, her knowledge of* brujería *anything but respectfully restrained. I would have left her for a woman less Mexican if México had not been so forgotten in me. Instead I stayed and stayed and stayed until México no longer mattered so much, became an island thoroughly remote and unreachable, grew dim in my explorer's imagination.*

I write the word "explorer" and shudder at the image it evokes, of some sixteenth-century iron-clad conquistador or beaver-capped Northwest trapper. I am both the "explorer" and the "*Indígena.*" Most Mexicans can claim the same, but my claim is more "explorer" than not. And yes, most days I am deathly ashamed. But of what, exactly? My white family was kept distant from me, not because of its conquests, but because of its failures.

She Won't Let Go

I grew up judging the white side of my family very cruelly. Our one family of white cousins were abandoned children, fed from giant-sized peanut butter jars, while we Mexican cousins ate homemade warm tortillas with a clean embroidered tablecloth under our elbows. There was the story one of those white cousins told of how her mother—my aunt, my father's only sister—would punish her by locking her in a room where she had to piss and shit in coffee cans. And I remember my sister at five, after a week's stay at my aunt's house, never wanting to return; she became frightened of the dark, of closed closet doors.

Many years later, after having not seen my aunt for nearly twenty years, we meet at a Chinese restaurant. She has just received word that she may have cancer. She fears she is dying and wants to repair any damages done. We are not her children. We have nothing to forgive in her, except her twenty-year absence. I am the last to arrive at the restaurant. My mother, father, sister, and she have already ordered drinks and appetizers. As I enter, I spot her first. She looks as I remembered her, only a little older, thicker, tougher. But she was always tough, tougher than her brother, the protected one. She reminds me of a dyke. She is not a dyke, but sees something queer in me as I approach the table smiling. "You're your grandma Hallie," she says to me after the second drink. "You've got her spirit. Did you know that?" No, I didn't know that, any more than I knew the woman herself. But I am hungry to know, as my sister is. So, the stories begin . . . stories that had been censored by my father. Stories of my French grandma's wild ways, her five marriages, the last to a homosexual, her adopted daughter never to be heard from again. My grandma was a wild woman in a white Cadillac with white skin and white bleached hair. But to my five-year-old mind, she was merely a strange wrinkled lady with long red painted fingernails that she used like a tortilla to push her food onto her fork. She was white, and therefore foreign. And now, over a generation later, her daughter tells me I was made in her likeness. Later, I learn of the WPA and my grandmother's vaudeville days; I learn to put the pieces together. She was an independent woman, my white grandma, a woman with an artist's hunger for love and limelight.

Once my aunt appeared to me in a dream. I cannot see her face, because she stands behind me, holding me, her arms around me like a straightjacket. I panic. She won't let go. I wake up, heart pounding. In another dream, my aunt is a waitress slapping hash onto a grill and plates onto customers' tables. My Mexican aunts and my mother are nearby. They sit hunched around a low table. They are whispering secrets. They appear very dark, like *brujas.* This gathering is a holy coven. I stand between this circle of witches and my working-class aunt. She throws a hand on her hip, wipes her brow with the back of the other. "These Mexicans," she says, "are so damn crazy!" My cousin David appears. He is brown and beautiful, indifferent to the world of women

around him. He does not have to choose. He remains aloof and elegant in his Mexican masculinity. He does not sweat. I envy him.

She will not let go. My aunt died this year, not of the cancer she had feared ten years ago, but of
a stroke. She died quietly and tragically a few months after she had retired from forty-plus years
working as a nurse and supporting seven children who have known drugs and alcoholism and
gun-shot wounds more intimately than any of us Mexicans. My girl-cousin, the one who suffered
those early "lock-ups" was the one who was at her side, holding her mother's square freckled hand
(my father's hand) until the moment of her passing.

"What's a 'Betty'?" I ask. We are coming out of the theatre, out from the world of Spike Lee's *X*.
The images still reel inside me: 1940s Black Boston strutting zoot suits and conks; Harlem in the
hopping fifties and heady sixties; a beautiful Denzel Washington, with smoked red hair, speaking revolution, "By any means necessary." In the congregation hall of Black Muslims, the women
are draped nun-like in white; the men are a stolid block of dark suits. A banner waves above their
heads: "Our women are our most valuable property." I cringe at the word, "property," as I do at
the blue-black prison scene where Malcolm Little swears off the "white man's swine" and the
"white man's women" in the same breath.

And the word "Betty" comes to mind, I don't know why. My companion answers, "She's a
'bimbo,' a Black man's white woman. She's considered 'trash' by everyone—Black *and* white—cuz,
this thinking goes, why would a woman who really had somethin' going for herself 'slum it' with
a Black man." "That's pretty ugly on all counts," I say. Still, I push her away from me that night,
that white away from me. *But she will not let go.*

My white aunt comes to visit me as all the women in my family have, uninvited through my
bedroom door. She will stay until she is given the respect due her. She will stay until she has
changed from a faceless entity straightjacketing my every movement into a woman of real flesh
and bones and name. My aunt's name is Barbara, and I am here to make peace with her in the
white women I love, in the white woman I am. All those "Bettys," that "trash," that working-class
whitegirl I learned to fear on the "other" side of the family, on the "other" side of me.

Talkin' Breed Talk

Some of my mixed-blood friends have had "Bettys" for mothers. Their task is a harder one, I
think—to carve out an identity as a "colored" woman without a colored woman to look to. I wrote
in 1983, "My brother's sex was white, mine brown." I still believe that to my core. But regardless
of how the dice were tossed and what series of accidents put our two parents—one white and one
colored—together, we, their offspring, have had to choose who we are in racist Amerika.

> *"It is best for them (Anglos) when we (Chicano/as) are light-skinned, but better still when Chicano/as
> are half-white and half-Chicano/a. That places half-breeds closer to Anglo language and culture. But
> these false privileges many recognize for what they are, a token, a maldición."*
> —Emma Pérez, "Sexuality and Discourse: Notes from a Chicana Survivor"

Emma's got it right. In the "choice" resides the curse, the "maldición." There is no denying that
this *güera*-face has often secured my safe passage through the minefields of Amerikan racism. *If
my thoughts could color my flesh, how dark I would turn.* But people can't read your mind, they read
your color, they read your womanhood, they read the women you're with. They read your walk
and talk. And then the privileges begin to wane and the choices become more limited, more
evident. I think that is why I have always hated the terms "biracial" and "bisexual." They are
passive terms, without political bite. They don't choose. They don't make a decision. They are
a declaration not of identity, but of biology, of sexual practice. They say nothing about where

one really stands. And as long as injustice prevails, we do not have the luxury of calling ourselves either.

Call me breed. Call me trash. Call me spic greaser beaner dyke jota bulldagger. Call me something meant to set me apart from you and I will know who I am. Do not call me "sister." I am not yours.

Do I write this to my brother who has chosen, against me, who he will be in this lifetime? He does not perceive his white manhood as a choice. To him it is the natural evolution of a light-skinned mixed-blood son of a white man. But Jacobo doesn't feel this way, Tim doesn't feel this way, Mekaya doesn't feel this way—all these breed-boys ever loyal to the dark side of their *mestizaje.* The blondest of the bunch writes it blue-veined into his skin: *¡Viva la Raza!* A lifelong mark of identity, of loyalty to his mother's and to his own people.

Only my sister understands. She tells me, "nobody I know talks about this, Ceci, about being mixed." Nobody else has to—prove who they are, prove who they aren't. Of our 100-plus cousins, she and I are the only ones working with *la Raza,* working to maintain that *conexión* under the constant threat of denial. I know full well that my *mestizaje*—my breed blood—is the catalyst of my activism and my art. I have tasted assimilation and it is bitter on my tongue. Had I been born a full-blood Mexican, I sometimes wonder whether I would have struggled so hard to stay a part of *la Raza.*

18 February 1990: Sueño

I see in the distance, a herd of calf-children traveling in packs with their white lesbian mothers. They are half-animal, half-human. They are goat-people, young calves with the expressions of injured children. One has the buttocks of a human, but it is fur-covered like an animal. They are me.

After they pass, I approach a table where one of the mothers is selling wares. I am eating cheese and she tells me I must stand away from the table, something about the mixing of elements (the cheese I am eating with what she is selling). I inquire about the half-breed children. She informs me that there is one father for all of them and they have turned out this way due to a mixing of bloods—too many with one father.

I want to chastise the women for their irresponsibility, but the thought passes through my mind that possibly there is another meaning here, inside the bodies of these deformed ones. The creation of a new species (half-human/half-animal). Maybe they are the hope of the future, these mixed beings who will bridge a world of opposition, re-unite the human with the natural world.

And I am not alone in this dreaming. Recently, a mixed-blood Indian sister told me of her dream like mine. In it she is raped by a lion and becomes pregnant. She is outraged until she realizes that she is the one named to bear the new species—half-beast half-she. She tells me how much the dream disturbed her. "I don't want to be the fuckin' Virgin Mary of the next generation." "Me neither," I say. "Me neither."

As mixed-blood women, we are the hybrid seed she carried in the dream and the mothers of a new generation. We are the products of rape and the creators of a new breed. We are Malinche's children and the new Malinches of the 21st century. We are talkin' breed talk when the whole world's turning breed at unprecedented rates,[1] when Third and Fourth and First Worlds are collapsing into one another. But make no mistake, there still is the Rapist Father and he is white and the Violated Mother and she is not. In spite of the personal stories to the contrary, the political conditions of miscegenation, to this day, occur within the larger framework of a white supremacist society. And miscegenation's children wrestle, in one way or another, with the consequences.

I am not that rare breed of mixed-blood person, a Jean Toomer, who writes, as Alice Walker said of *Cane,* "to memorialize a culture he thought was dying." I am that raging breed of mixed-blood person who writes to defend a culture that I know is being killed. I am of that endangered culture and of that murderous race, but I am loyal only to one. My mother culture, my mother land, my mother tongue, further back than even she can remember.

My father said it himself, speaking of the whiteman, "We are our own worst enemies." I don't betray my whitefather, that gentle man, in writing this. I live up to the mixed-raced legacy his people have betrothed to me.

Remembering Navajo Nation

July 22, 1992

I have witnessed speechless beauty, this nation of Diné. My insignificance enters me amid the antiquity of these red rock canyons. I have no desire to return or go forward. There is nowhere to arrive, only this journeying . . . .

I remember Phoenix. My cousin, Rudy, and my Tía Lupe: that dying breed of Mexican cowboy and his mother. My aunt of 83 years is speechless like me. She can't recall English *or* Spanish words, just can't seem to bring them to the surface of her tongue. The facts: dates, names, places. She falters. . . . *"Desde que murió mi viejo . . . ,"* forgetting who *is* her *"viejo."* At times her son, forty years younger, takes on that old indio's shape and voice. She looks to him to finish her lines. He waits. She suffers. Rainclouds form over Navajo Nation. The sky darkens. We wait. *The sun will break through these clouds.*

My companion mistakenly keeps calling Rudy my "brother," although he is a brother of sorts. More than my own. The queer son, like me, desperately clinging to history. The family anthropologist searching out *raíces* from the bowels of Mission churches in a Sonora that once hardly knew the word *"gringo."*

We are the childless ones, he and I. I find a brother in the *pasión* he exudes when pulling out death certificates and reproduced photos of what could be Indian, could be Arabe, could be "old country" great-great-grandmothers. He names them: Refugia, Paula, Victoria, braids stretched across seamless foreheads, skin stretched across chiseled cheekbones, hazel eyes buried into them. Conversing with my cousin, I search his words, his excited moving mouth. The Spanish surnames spill from his tongue . . . Figueroa, Mendibles, Rodríguez, . . . I swallow, hesitate. I ask, "And the Indians? . . . Did you find out anything about our Indian blood?" "Oh there must have been some," he says. But no mention, no unnamed *bisabuelo.* Still, the dark faces appear and disappear in photographs with no native claim, no name.

The road is red in Arizona. A river of red clay. I am surrounded by red and spin it green in poetic imagination. What are the names of these trees that hover like sentinels by the river's weed banks? This is Chimayó clay water that flows all the way from Nuevo México, Guatemala. This is Quiché clay. I remember Elena's words, "You have so much air, Ceci. Walk the earth with bare feet. Feel the ground."

I remove my shoes. I walk. I want this mud to stain me red from the soles up. My toes turn purple with the chill of the creek, bleed rose red into the clay.

> *No wonder you became a potter, a worker of clay,*
> *a sculptor.*
> *No wonder you studied how to shape your hands*
> *into forms these canón walls etch*
> *into the raingodskies.*
> *Half-breed sister, half-sister, no wonder.*

We are a mongrel nation, and yet this ground is testimony to the purity of the sacred. Water and earth blend, turn the river mud red, and it refreshes no less through the open pores of flesh and palm. Open palm.

When did our real ancestors arrive here?
Before Olmec heads and Mayan gods?
Before gods?

I am a trespasser. I do not need signs to remind me. My immigrant blood is a stain I carry in the fading of my flesh each winter. But I am made of clay. All our ancestors know this. It is no myth, but wholly evident in the slow dissolving of my skin into the red road of this river. *Where will you take me, immigrant and orphaned?*

All is *familia:* ancestor and future generations. The tree branches out, bears fruit. The *cañón* grows dark and I dream of dying. Not violence, but a slow and peaceful return to the river.

For my sister, Jo Ann.

Note

1   Although this essay concerns my personal experience of mixed parentage—one white and one of color—the "21st century mestizo" is increasingly born of two parents of color of different races and/or ethnicities.

19

Eating Salt

Lisa Kahaleole Chang Hall

"Are you sure, sweetheart, that you want to be well? . . . Just so's you're sure, sweetheart and ready to be healed, cause wholeness is no trifling matter."

—Toni Cade Bambara, *The Salt Eaters*

II

A re you sure, sweetheart, that you want to be well?" is the question that Toni has asked us, and some days I am not so sure. How do we become ready to be well; what in our histories has ever prepared us? We follow the hint of wholeness down its faint echoing paths, double back lost and confused, trying to keep moving. I never understood how others seemed to think the ground beneath their feet was so solid, how casually they assumed their connection to an origin.

I am a woman on the edge, dancing with a blade of knife-edged anger—a woman who is afraid to tell the truth, whose stomach hurts, whose nerves are shot. Tears crawl up the back of my throat. I am a woman who wants to go home but never figured out where it is or why to go there.

> *I've lost the words to chant my bloodline.*
> *My blood speaks me in tongues of fire, memory muttering*
> *just outside what I can hear, the history of unrecorded choices,*
> *unremembered fear.*

I have to go back to places I have never been because a song sings eerily in my bones, because the knot in my chest will never otherwise be eased, because I am coming closer, closer to my oldest truth, to the face of my great-grandmother holding me up in her arms against the Arizona sun, singing to me of the sea, imprinting the shame, the love, the homesick longing, changing the shape of my cells, my body, my bloodlines.

Writing these words I have intense bursts of insomnia, lie in bed, head aching, to watch the dawn come through the windows. My body buzzes with anxiety and I can't shake the feeling that something really bad is about to happen any minute. I was never supposed to tell. The generations sitting on my neck cover my ears, smother my voice—"Be quiet, you. No make shame."

I am irrevocably guilty of speaking what was never to be spoken and I am haunted by the fear that I will die for this transgression. Someone will kill me, someone will leave me. Dead, lost, forlorn.

In one session, I tell my therapist, "It feels so surreal, like I'm making all this up." She looks at me levelly, "Are you?" The speed and firmness of my response surprises me, "No."

My truths are always so much stranger than fiction.

Nommo

The power of the word. Words are nothing to play with; they are acts of creation. Storytelling is a responsibility, an art form, a legacy through which we honor our origins even as we fear betraying them in the act of revelation.

I am the only child of my generation who was not given a Hawai'ian middle name. When I was young, I took my great-grandmother's name from a faded xeroxed piece of family history, one of the few documents about her composed by one of her children, who as a child spoke Hawai'ian and could eavesdrop on her mother's conversations with friends. My great-grandmother would not speak of her own mother because she was ashamed of the many children her mother had with different men in the old style of Hawai'i. Raised by missionaries and given two alternative name possibilities, my great-grandmother chose to go by Kahaleole, with the literal meaning "without a house." When I saw this scrap of paper, I knew this was my name—homeless. Later I found out that one of her sons who died in infancy was also named Kahaleole.

Death, homelessness, silence.

Years later, the first Hawai'ian friend I ever had outside of Hawai'i was horrified by this story and worried about trying to find a new name to give me. Part of her distress was that I had unknowingly done the unthinkable—Hawai'ian names are given to you; you do not take them. But when she went home she consulted a *kupuna* about the name and he told her, "Oh, Kahaleole is a wonderful name. He was a poet and chanter and travelled around all the islands carrying stories."

Kahaleole—a double-edged sword. Homeless and without a single home. Homes are everywhere and the responsibility is to share their stories.

This Is Not My Land and This Is My Land

For a long time I thought I was essentially urban, could feel no real connection to the earth. Then I began to understand that this was not my land. It was alien corn, scenic vistas that held great beauty, but the distanced beauty of picture windows, murals and paintings.

I finally began to understand about trees, could stand next to them and feel their breathing, but it was not until I lay down on the solid ground at the stadium outside Honolulu that I felt the power of the land flowing up through the middle of my back, centered, spinning. On the stadium stage, the preschool children of Pūnana Leo, a Hawai'ian language immersion program, were reciting their genealogies to the wild applause of family members. Breathless strings of Hawai'ian were finally punctuated by their own names—"Misty," "Ledward." The loss of the land crashed through me like waves after that evening of sand and light. Tidal pulls from a center that's so very far away.

Here today I am a sometimes appreciative visitor in a country where the land breaks make no sense and the people so often look like cousins, uncles, aunts. Race becomes an absurdity; bloodline waves that flow across category and definition.

This is my land in that I am forcibly American, profoundly shaped by a worldview no other countries share. The dissenting fringe of a worldview is still a part of the scarf, bedraggled, dangling, flying out, woven into the fabric's whole.

The Source

During the memorial year of the hundredth-year anniversary of the illegal invasion and over-throw of the Kingdom of Hawai'i, the American Indian Contemporary Arts Gallery in San Francisco held several Hawai'ian cultural and arts events.

One night, the scheduled speaker ended up in New Zealand, and Auntie Raylene, an accomplished chanter and dancer, agreed to substitute for her. That evening she talked about the necessity of remembering and honoring where we come from. As she spoke, her dancer's hands traced out the umbilical path from piko to cosmic origin.

Later, during the question-and-answer session, a worried West African immigrant brother asked her, "But after colonization, what do we do? What if our parents and grandparents refuse to tell us anything? They don't want to talk about the old days. They are afraid. Or they don't remember."

She looked at him with great love and said, "Then you go back further, to the source," and her hand swept back with assurance to the beginning of time, to the birth of life.

The brother nodded, still confused, but comforted, and I was dazzled by the recognition that nothing is ever truly lost, just hidden. We are the sum of all our ancestors. Some speak louder than others but they all remain present, alive in our very blood and bone.

Later that same night I went over to speak to a young Hawai'ian woman who had asked respect-ful yet penetrating questions about the relationship between anger, politics and aloha. As we were talking, an older man came by and she introduced herself to him by her full name for the first time.

"Sproat!" I shrieked, "Are you related to David Sproat?"

"You know my dad?" she asked, equally excited, and I grabbed her. "You're my cousin! I'm Piki's daughter!"

She is almost in tears, "Aunty was just telling me over New Year's I should look you up but I never knew where to find you." We danced around the room in glee and as we tried to find a time to get together between her "Women of Color Coalition Meeting X" and "College Advisory Council Meeting Y" I knew she was my blood.

Genealogy

I'm going through old family photos with my friend on a kamikaze run of self-documenta-tion when it strikes me—I look at a photograph of my four immediate cousins and realize that I'm the only black person in my family. "Look," I tell her, "look. None of them could ever 'pass' as black." These cousins are as African and non-African derived as I am. We are a multiracial clan from way way back—our mixtures begin over a hundred years ago in Hawai'i alone. This is why "biracial" rhetoric has always left me cold. My father is white and I am not biracial.

In my family, racial features shift with age; two cousins began their lives as prototypes for Hawai'i Visitors Bureau hula dancers, became more Chinese as they grew older. One of their sis-ters is close to blond, fair-skinned with the slightest hint of Asian eyes. That's what that damned t-shirt emblazoned "No matter what color, you're still my sister" means to me. Not the white girls, but all the colored ones and the ones trapped in the genetic shuffle—blond Cherokees, blue-eyed Black girls, "exotic" Eurasians.

In my family, I'm the one that was raised on the continent bereft of a single recognizable identity. In Hawai'i the centuries of racial mixture are like the Caribbean, there is both lan-guage and a finely honed recognition of racial features. In the United States I am a con-stant question.

I wander the world incorrectly
I see family everywhere it's not supposed to be
intertribal pow-wows   16th and Mission queer bars
on the bus in downtown Oakland my cousins stare at me
Down the street at Lois the Pie Queen
my grandfather looks down from the wall
but the name beneath the poster reads Mandela.

I eavesdrop in Spanish i speak 14 different accents
at five spoke pidgin in Hawai'i complete with Texas flair
I have a repertoire of French with which to be pretentious.
Black English often comforts me
Sometimes I catch myself waving hands just like a drag queen.

Q & A

Q: *"Where were you born?"(What are you?)*
A: *Tempe, Arizona.*
Q: *"Oh, is that where you grew up?" (I still don't know what you are)*
A: *No. Alabama, Texas, Florida, Colorado and Virginia with a year in Hawai'i when my father was in Vietnam.*
Q: *"What's your nationality?" (What are you?)*
A: *American*

Black Q: *"Hey girl, you mixed?"*

Identify yourself:
I am a Native Hawaiian with a nationalist soul.
Identify yourself:
I am a lesbian of African descent.
Identify yourself:
I am the legacy of multiple diasporas.

Remembering to Forget

There are no stories in my family, nothing ever happened to anyone, and if anything ever did there would be no reason to discuss it.

My aunt is the only one who tells me stories; she's the one who told me about the cross country trip through the segregated South to my uncle's graduation from Annapolis. During World War II, a battalion from Texas was quartered in my grandparents' backyard on Kaua'i, and they developed family privileges, came in and out of the kitchen and played with the kids. It was these men who called ahead to neighbors to deliver an important message as my grandparents and their offspring crossed those small Southern towns—Don't mess with them, these are good colored people, from Hawai'i; they don't know our ways. As they crossed the Southland the question was always laid out for them in the literal form of which door to choose. "White" or "Colored." Every choice was questioned.

There are no stories in my family. Nothing ever happened, and if it did, there would be no reason to discuss it.

My grandmother comes in at the tail end of my aunt's story and begins fondly reminiscing about the Texans in a rare burst of loquacity. "Piki," she asks my mother, "Don't you remember how much those boys loved all of you and how they used to follow you around in the yard calling, 'Piki, Piki, pickaninny'?"

My grandmother is smiling, lost in memory, as I twist around in horror to see my mother's reaction. My mother's face is totally blank and empty. She doesn't say a word, just continues fixing dinner, and I remember how once, long ago, I asked her how she got her nickname and she said, "Oh I don't know, my hair used to stand up in peaks or something," and then she changed the subject.

They said they didn't know whether to shit or go blind, but they went blind and stayed that way. Behind them stands an endless line of people, ancestors with their eyes screwed tight shut, heads averted, waiting for the blow. The blindness becomes hereditary, passed down among the generations unable to see what is in front of or behind their faces.

You have to remember to forget. Remember terror remember running remember hiding remember the moment when the mask became the face and the original was imprisoned within the newly rigid shell of promised safety.

Be safe by not remembering.

Instead become the memory, let body act out the story it denies, let the children become the story till it repeats and repeats into an ugly patchwork quilt of tears.

Do not remember.

When the children wake in that space of empty safety, they pull the thread and everyone screams as the stories unravel, the stench is no longer described as perfume.

Everyone gathers and they all fall down.

Four Negroes Out on the Town

My first racial memory is of being chased by little white boys screaming, "Little nigger girl!" in Big Spring, Texas, but more often I was questioned about being everything else under the sun. Throughout my childhood anyone telling racial/ethnic jokes always questioned me first to make sure I wasn't one of the "them" they were about to degrade.

Depending on where we were stationed, I was offered many chances to be one of the good colored/(not Bad Black) people and sometimes I took them. Segregation was alive and well in the "ability tracking" of my Virginia high school with a few Black kids and some "honorary whites" in the top track. When those "other" Black girls used to confront and question me in the bathroom, I denied them. Not that. Never that. Instead I became white exotica.

At Yale I was often uncomfortable around groups of Black students—there seemed to be two major directions to go in: bourgeois assimilation or bourgeois nationalism. Assimilation has never been a realistic option for me and there are few things scarier than an Ivy League nationalist—we have entirely too much to prove.

My life became black people when I started graduate school at Berkeley. I studied African American literature and history; my adviser, my big-sister graduate student mentor, my lover, and the closest woman to me in my entering cohort were all Black. My big sister was straight; through her I met innumerable straight Black men at levels of intimacy I'd never had before. My Yale Women's Studies whitefeminist-derived ideas about "men" and "women" took a radical turn as I listened to their rage and grief-filled stories of living in a world of "purse-huggers" and white women who crossed the street upon seeing them.

I was comfortable in this world, but uneasy. I started to feel crazy every time my adviser looked straight at me and advise us all to go to the Black graduate student reception. On alternate days she would be convinced I was Asian and thus the Asian feminist professor was advising me, not her.

I felt subsumed and erased into the ethnocentric world of Blackness. (A Latina friend once told me, "I don't think Black people really truly believe that any other people of color exist.")

One day my lover, who had spent years stationed in Hawai'i in the military, another couple, and I were going out. On the way out the door, she announced, "Hey—it's just four Negroes out on the town!" and then, as my eyes widened, said, "Oh god, baby, I'm sorry. I forgot."

After struggling with my rage about appropriation and/or erasure by Black women for years, I went back to Hawai'i for the first time in a decade, to stay with an Irish great-aunt obsessed with genealogy. Among the many secrets she started spilling was the fact that the one marked on the chart as "E. Indian?" was in fact West Indian, the son of a plantation slave.

I lost my mind. Black. Not Black enough. Of African descent. Not African American. Black in the British sense. Not Black in the U.S. unless the Afrocentric worldview that encompasses Maori, Australian Aboriginal and Polynesian peoples is operating. (The Hawai'ian queen Ka'ahumanu is featured in *Black Women: For Beginners*.)

I began spinning and I have not yet stopped.

Last year I held my breath and attended Nia, a gathering for lesbians of African descent. I was terrified, wasn't even going to go until one night when helping the collective make banners for the gathering, they all demanded to know why not. When I finally told them, one said, "Oh no, girl, it's not like that. There's plenty of women as light as you or lighter, lots of high yellow."

"Yeah," another collective member agreed, "like 'x' " pointing to yet another, who, offended, demanded, "Who you callin' high yellow?" and I was torn between laughter and despair at this quintessentially mixed message.

She Wanted to Be Darker

The darker the berry, the sweeter the juice,
I am a sour berry, lemon yellow in winter's paleness.

In high school I was dark like my Puerto Rican best friend's big sister, the cheerleader who was only hit on by the Black boys from June to October—the season of color.

I almost cried with relief the first time I read mary hope lee's poem "On not bein'" in the newly published *This Bridge Called My Back*, with the lines, "she never wanted/no never once wanted/to be white/she wanted to be darker."

In one of the rare moments of honesty between me and a high yellow friend, we admitted to each other that we would go to tanning parlors on a regular basis if we were sure nobody would ever find out.

In my senior essay at Yale I included several pages of xeroxed color photos. On one, a series of school I.D.s traced my descent into paleness over a decade. Bleached and beached in the academy, I became lighter and lighter, though my eyes stayed dark with layers of pain.

For years after Yale I looked in the mirror and was constantly surprised by what I saw because in my mind I was so much darker. When I finally adjusted to what I saw, I started to get darker.

Last month I gave a friend a massage and looked down in fascination to see my brown hands against her stark white neck. It reminded me of the lesbian pornography that profoundly upsets me—the eroticization of the contrasting play of black and white skin.

It's usually the opposite problem for me—the color is leached from me by white people, not highlighted. Who I'm with so often determines who others decide I am and sometimes I become that person.

La güera. Pocha. High-yella dreamchild. The not-quite-white girl.

We're on a weekend mission—one butch, one femme and one declines-to-state—at the mall in Richmond, the city of poor colored people where the mall McDonald's has a Hamburglar jail for the multicolored children to happily practice playing.

Keisha, the butch, is lounging, bored like a husband, as Loretta, who declines to state, tries on an endless succession of bathing suits. I am over the top and evil, running on the edgy adrenaline that rules my relationship with Keisha. She's been dogging me all day, so I start fucking with her. I reach out my hand to her hair that she's been complaining about needing to get cut all day, and ask her, "What's up with this? How come it's going all sideways and shit?"

She comes back at me hard, grabs my hair and smacks me. Loretta emerges from the dressing room and I complain to her like a bratty child, "She hit me." Then Keisha plays the race card, "You know she better not come up to a black person and start fucking with their hair." Loretta says to me, "I'm sorry, I'd have to go with Keisha on that" and I am stung, marked off to an alien status that I resent, with no appeal. What can I say—the truth? It ain't that it's a black thing, I wouldn't understand; I am fucking with you with purpose. I am not culturally incompetent; I am rude.

I have my own history of hair, my own bruises. In the mall store I remember the black lesbian at the Russian River Women's Weekend who looked me up and down as I waited for her friend to come back to my motel with me for the night. "Mm," she finally said without smiling, "I saw you out on the dance floor earlier. You and your pretty hair," and then she smiled, her bared teeth as sharp and white as ice. I looked down, was surprised to see no blood.

she had wild hair, her hair was wild, she had a wild hair.
her mother looked at her with mouth askew,
dragged her off to base beauticians for a $5 cut and style
because she had wild hair.

It wouldn't lay down, wouldn't obey. It was too big too much
she had a wild hair.

her mother forced relaxers on her hair, cut it short,
cut her down and they called it the American dream.
her skin got lighter; her English got whiter—
it was a long dream that she twisted in uneasily, sweating.

her forehead hurt from the chemical burns.
she had a wild hair
so she got burned.

she started to go black from the outside in
something started to happen
in another new world her hair became "good" she became
light-skinned

who what where when the litany had always followed her
what nationality? American

she went black not back
her hair went back to its natural state, its national state
sin fronteras

Later, after the mall, we're all at home with the newspaper and clippers as Loretta makes her maiden voyage as a barber trying to shave Keisha's sides as Keisha holds up a big pink plastic mirror to monitor her. Loretta doesn't have the guard on the clippers, however, and her first stroke cuts down to the scalp, close to bald. I fall out laughing as Keisha yelps, "You don't have the guard on!"

Loretta is mortified, saying, "This is why I don't cut people's hair. You tell them you've never done it before and they say okay, but friendships end over this kind of stuff." Loretta's own hair has been through a number of processes, but shaving isn't one of them, and Keisha and I are rolling on the floor as she waves the clippers indignantly. Keisha checks herself and looks over to me to make sure I get it about the guard and once again I am alien and annoyed for no rational reason.

Why should she think I understand the maintenance of her hair, though it is as familiar to me as my own? The dreadlocks, naps and shaved sides of my lovers a living memory on my fingertips. I smell coconut pomade in my dreams.

Later I take advantage of the still spread-out newspapers and begin twisting my hair to cut the split and shattered ends with silver scissors. Loretta looks at me in astonishment and asks, "What are you doing?"

The One You Call Sister

What does it mean that there are more men that call me sister than women who claim kin?

"Sister, can you help me out?" Old black men, young black men with old faces. Sister, ma'am, bitch you think you too good, beautiful lady, sister, sister.

I have visceral revulsion for the "sister" claims of white feminists, am uneasily proud within the variously colored sistas, waiting for the promised offer to be revoked.

"Oh, you have some black in you?" she asks me and when I say yes, laughs and pokes me— "Where?"

I am the secret sister, the illegitimate child that no one speaks of. I am the one that everyone questions, not sure if they will claim me, not sure if I claim them.

I have been the light-bright-and-damn-near-white sister, the dark sister, the sister who builds bridges, the sister who reveals the family secrets, sister, sister.

I have been the good sister, the bad sister, the one who turned her back. Loyalties are treacherous in the human family.

I am walking down Grand Avenue in Oakland on the way to the ATM, feeling fine on a Saturday night when brotherman with a pail full of car cleaning supplies steps in front of me to demand, "Excuse me. Do you hate black people?"

"What?" I ask him, not sure if I am hallucinating.

"Do you hate black people?" he asks again, and I stare at him in disbelief—"Excuse me?"

He looks into my face for the first time and then says, "Oh I'm sorry, you're black," and I watch him trying to shift strategy,"—listen, I got a kid with Down's syndrome, you know what that is, and I'm tryin' to do this so I don't hafta steal . . . "

"I'm sorry, brother, I don't have anything for you." But maybe I lied. Maybe I did.

My Life with the Four Food Groups

The first time I got a glimpse of what my adult life as an ambiguous colored girl was going to be like was at "Minority Pre-Freshmen Weekend" at Wesleyan University in Connecticut. The cultural houses had gotten together for the first time ever and combined forces to bring all the prospective multicolored students to visit. It was the first time that many of the older Wesleyan students had even talked to each other, much less taken collective "people of color" action.

I had a blast, took the train up from Virginia to hang out with everyone—Puerto Ricans and black kids from ABC (A Better Chance) programs in New York, Asians from suburban Maryland. I got to run with everyone because nobody was sure what I was. I was only lonely when we periodically broke up to separate into "our own" groups. There are almost never any Pacific Islanders in "Asian/Pacific" groups and this was no exception. I sat on the floor with the Japanese and Chinese students feeling like a peculiar too-tall, lumpy, big-haired, dark-skinned monster and waited to go to "Malcolm X" House and feel normal.

Latina is the category in which I am most often misfiled, the only one of the Four Food Groups with which I have no blood connection. Parking lot attendants, *taqueria* waitresses and the home health care workers at my ex-lover's apartment building constantly talk to or around me in Spanish.

The shame that I carry about my inadequate Spanish does not belong to me, but I feel it deeply. My history is branded with too many looks of dismissal and scorn from Latinos who have leapt at my ambiguous face with the language of belonging only to meet my embarrassed half-shrug—*no sé*. Worse is when they take my shamed paralysis for complete ignorance and begin explaining the most elementary things to me and I am trapped once again in the familiar gap of knowing too much and never enough, always too little.

sometimes there are unexpected connections

The first Latina lover I ever had spoke five languages; I was always fascinated and saddened by the knowledge of just how much of her I had no access to, all the thoughts and feelings lost in multiple translation. But I reached hard for her, entering into the intimacy of Spanish, the language of our lovemaking and my third-grade attempts to tell her about my day in response to her patient inquiries—"¿Y que más?"

> *Now Spanish remains her tongue on my body*
> *words loving ears as her lips loved me*
> *An entire language retains an overtone of*
> *intimate familiarity and loss*
> *A piece of my voice is lost to me along with*
> *her piece of my heart*
> *Some things are not returned*
> *at the final accounting at love's end*
> *Objects change hands, but hands remain changed*
> *indelibly marked with memories of skin.*

Thinking About "Us"

"Asian/Pacific Islander" is the census category that drives me into a rage, a nonsensical statistical convenience that conveniently both erases my presence and joins me to the group with which I feel the least affinity. The "pure" Chinese in my family occurred three generations back and mixed with plenty else in the meantime.

So when I got the call from one of the organizers of the "Asian Pacific Lesbian Network" retreat requesting my presence as a plenary speaker on the topic "APLs: Moving Beyond Visibility," my response was relatively curt and disinterested.

"I don't think so," I said, "It doesn't really have much to do with what I'm working on."

But then I reconsidered, since I'm always complaining about the lack of coalition-building in the world, and the bargain was struck. In exchange for the plenary speech, I got free conference admission for me and another Hawai'ian activist friend and a slot to do a workshop on Hawai'ian sovereignty. And off we both went with major attitude born of years of Asian appropriation and erasure of us.

January of 1993 was the hundredth year anniversary of the illegal invasion and overthrow of the Kingdom of Hawai'i and the incarceration of Queen Lili'uokalani. Thousands of Hawai'ians marched on Iolani Palace in one of the largest demonstrations ever occurring in Hawai'i. An explosion of videos, articles and debates on sovereignty followed.

We did our workshop for a small but attentive audience, laid out the issues and then showed a video of recent land eviction struggles. On screen women were being dragged out of makeshift buildings by the state police while children were screaming. One girl wailed, "We no mo' house," while next to her a little boy stood with a cardboard sign around his neck that read, "My house is a box."

By the end of the video, the women at the workshop were stone silent and weeping. "Why didn't we know?" one asked, "Why isn't this being shown to the entire conference?"

"I don't know," I responded, "Why isn't it?"

But what happened next surprised me. From grief and guilt, these Asian women got up and kicked ass, interrupted the full group plenary session the next day to show the video, and started a full-scale debate on Pacific Islander representation in the APLN. After the conference was over, they contacted the editor of a new "API" lesbian/bisexual anthology and offered her concrete help in getting Pacific Islander representation, formed a working committee, solicited pieces from around the country, put together a Hawai'ian women's roundtable and transcribed it.

I was in shock, deeply moved and astonished at the self-revelation of just how cynical I had been. In that moment I recognized once again how closed hearts breed closed hearts, and I began to truly see the faces of the women I was looking at, began to think about an "us."

As an Ethnic Studies graduate student, I know a lot about immigration issues on an intellectual basis. Now I heard illegal immigration and refugee horror stories that raised the hair on the back of my neck because finally the barrier of distance had been shattered from the other side. These women finally became real to me and I was horrified to realize they never really had been before this moment.

I was so ashamed of my arrogant dismissal, felt such grief at recognizing that the ability to stretch to others' issues that I am so proud of had only gone so far and no further.

It is only when we find a moment of safety that the full weight of old betrayals given and received falls on us.

there are always moments of connection

At the annual hula festival in Hayward, California several years ago I wandered the craft booths and stopped short at the display of red, yellow, and green t-shirts with the Lion of Judah and the state motto of Hawai'i, "the life of the land is perpetuated in righteousness," emblazoned on them.

Later I asked a friend what was going on and she said, "Haven't you heard; it's the whole new thing—it's 'Jawaiian'." In the '80s there was an explosion of reggae music in Hawai'i and t-shirts, baseball caps, and other marketing paraphernalia marked "Island Revolution" are everywhere. Young local kids have become convinced that reggae is an indigenous Hawai'ian art form.

Once again reality had proved itself to be stranger than anything I could make up and I was left to ponder the multiple ironies of coalition and appropriation, ignorance and remembrance, mixing and melding—the deeply complex interpenetrations of our lives.

Some days I want to believe that the P-Funk Mothership will arrive and we will indeed become one nation under a groove—the rhythm nation.

Sisters: Doing It for Ourselves

It is New Year's Eve at El Rio in the Mission, the bar with the apt slogan "It's Your Dive." "Azúcar y Crema," a women's salsa band, is playing and the night is live. I'm with the homegirls and the bar is packed with dykes of color. In between trips to the party, Winnebago parked outside, we are inside seriously styling. Late in the evening a carload of drunken white frat boys with blond girlfriends blow in and begin crashing around, running into people and accidentally stepping on toes. The girlfriends smirk nervously and roll their eyes at us as femmes calm butches down who have grown dangerously quiet.

Twenty minutes later, the dangerous quiet has spread as one frat boy steps on one dyke too many. The band stops and the entire bar becomes still before an eerie spontaneous chant erupts from the floor. "Go! Go! Go!" we chant with one voice until a wall of sound pushes them out the door and into the night, whereupon the bandleader, who has been standing onstage in silence, arms crossed over her tough red-sequined bustier, raises one diva arm and snaps into the silence.

"Can't stop this party!" she announces; the band blasts into action, and the scream becomes a song.

We are sisters and doing it for ourselves.

For the Seventh Generation

I pace the floor searching for the messages of the women who have come before me, mark poems, underline books and remember that the issue is to leave a record, a trail for the seventh generation to follow, a clue that will suddenly reveal the crucial fact of our connection, invisible like heat lightning—crackles and changes in the most unexpected places when the singing is a scream, when the screaming is a song.

When I listen to my sisters' stories of how they have
resisted death, destruction,
wounded limping we are still singing that survival song—
I say, thank you for continuing to live that I might also.

Without your words I am deaf to all sound,
a girl in a plastic bubble, an isolation tank of empty dead,
echoing whiteness, no borders, without end,
where sound fades without definition and has no origin,
no history of desire, no record of stubborn existence.

Sing to me, to call me home in languages I do not yet
understand, to childhoods I have not yet experienced,
to loves that have not yet touched me.
Fill me with the details of our lives. Filling up, emptying out
and diving in.
It is the holy spirit of existence, the flesh, the blood,
the naked truth that will not be covered.

Tell me everything, all the details—sweat, blood, bone.

para Cherríe
and all my relations

20

Turning the Myths of
Black Masculinity Inside/Out

Herb Green

There have been a lot of changes in the academy that have called into question the entire system of knowledge. Consequently, issues such as sexuality, race, and gender are no longer thought of as irrelevant and unworthy of critical investigation, but are accepted as legitimate fields of study. Although this is a vitally important step in the right direction, the problem remains that they are all too often discussed in isolation—as mutually exclusive concepts that exist in a vacuum. As a gay Black academic, I have been struggling with the ways in which the academy undermines the value of my personal experience, the Black community chooses to ignore the relevance of my sexuality, and the gay community fails to acknowledge the struggles I face as a Black man. Although I know that the oppositional ideas of the various communities of which I am a part are often difficult to avoid, I still feel that I am a part of these communities simultaneously.

Instead of simply refocusing the eyes of others to see the "I" that I *truly* represent, I think we need to deconstruct and problematize predetermined identities. In order to begin to live life as a whole instead of performing it in parts, we must undiscipline ourselves and step out of the predetermined ideas about who we are becoming, and who we are supposed to be. We must also acknowledge the fact that we live in multiple realities that cannot always conform to the efficient compartmentalized identities that are forced upon us as seemingly efficient systems of categorizing who we are.

I wish that more people would realize that being Black does not negate my sexual desires, that those sexual desires are not the defining characteristic of my identity and that being an academic does not mean that I yearn to produce work that is unintelligible to my family. The parameters of my identity are not constrained by a single static border—my identity is fluid and flexible. In fact, sometimes the very essentialistic and reductive nationalistic ideas that are supposed to unite us and make us identifiable to ourselves and others often render us silent about significant realities about ourselves and our individual desires. In my opinion, identities are far too complex to be reduced to pure essence.

I often feel like I am trapped in a cell block of racial stereotypes, and I struggle to find some way to escape the racial difference that eroticizes and exoticizes my body. When I think about the images of Black men that I grew up watching at the movies, I recall how my siblings and I used to wonder how anyone in his right mind could not question how glaringly contrived and one dimensional these images were. Although we felt a certain pride in simply seeing Black actors in films, we were always disappointed by the roles that most Black people portrayed. Black men were always drug dealers and pimps—they were dangerous; Black women were always domestic and/or sexual providers; and Black children were always tragically struggling against the odds stacked up against them.

My siblings and I knew that these caricatures of Blackness were profoundly detrimental to the image that other people had about us. When we watched films, we asked ourselves why the Black fathers were always absent? We wondered why Black women were always single and struggling to make ends meet while Carol Brady spent her day baking cookies. We also wanted to understand why Raquel Welch was a sex symbol and Pam Grier was exotic and primitive. We wanted to understand why we were always presented as a problem, something that good-natured and well meaning white people had to control, solve, or eliminate. We knew that since most people believe that a picture never lies, they would reasonably assume that the slick, life-like images of Black people on the big screen must be recorded fragments of reality.

Our daily experience of dealing with what James Baldwin calls "America's pathological racial dynamics," while simultaneously struggling to find a way to articulate our pain, gave us the insight to recognize that Hollywood and most white people in general had a specific idea of our 'place,' a location that was impoverished, crime-ridden, and undesirable. Today, I continue my struggle to comprehend and articulate the same questions about Black identity that I battled with as a child.

My most vivid memories are of the two Black male movie characters Shaft and Superfly. Superfly was a ghetto smart drug dealer who wore fancy clothes and was ultra smooth with the ladies. When I was about seven or eight his name was synonymous with style. If you were Superfly, you were ultra hip; you knew the world was a runway and you intended to walk it; you had a look and knew how to work it. Everything was hip, in place —you were Superfly.

Although many of the details of my childhood experiences escape my memory, I can still hear the rhythm and lyrics of one of Curtis Mayfield's theme songs for the movie *Superfly*. The song begins with the pulsating beat of drums, followed by the funky twang of the electric guitars that my older sister used to like so much. Then came the slick rhythmic voice of Mayfield that fixed an image of Superfly forever in mind:

> *I'm your mama, I'm our daddy,*
> *I'm that nigger in the alley*
> *I'm your doctor, when you need.*
> *Want some coke? Have some weed.*
> *You know me, I'm your friend,*
> *Your main boy, thick and thin,*
> *I'm your pusherman...* [1]

When the image of *Shaft* hit the big screen several years later, Isaac Hayes depicted an even more graphic image of straight Black male sexuality in his soundtrack for the film. The song begins with the rich voice of Hayes asking, "Who is the Black private Dick, the sex machine with all the chicks,"[2] which is followed by a chorus of female singers who seductively slide the response "Shaft" off their lips.

These lyrics take me back in time, as I was bombarded by imagery that constantly reduced me to a black body.

I'm your pusherman
Your sex machine
The Black private dick
Superfly
A long weapon
A Black Spear, A Black Lance
A Black Shaft

I thought that the academy would be a good place to investigate why people gave credence to the idea that these one dimensional characterizations were totalizing realities. The academy was also important for me because it gave me a sense of hope, for I internalized the myth that I truly would end up like one of the tragic characterizations of Black masculinity that I consistently viewed in the popular media if I did not do 'the right thing.' Education, in my mind, became a tool I could use to imagine, theorize, and ultimately practice new and different ways of living.

While thinking more and more about what I hoped to achieve via the academy, I constantly examined how the multiple and ostensibly conflicting identities that I occupy informed and helped shape the kinds of academic writing that I produced or desired to produce. I make a distinction between what I "produce" and what I "desire to produce" because of the academy's false distinction between subjectivity and critical analysis. For instance, when I try to talk about my interpretation of post-colonial theory and literature in relation to my experience growing-up for the first thirteen years of my life in the Bahamas, I have been told that I am being "anti-intellectual," that I am "privileging my nativism," and that I need to stick to the assigned text. Somehow, the assumption is that I just don't get it. Again, I am the problem.

My years of experience as a Black male trying to gain an education in American public and private schools have taught me that academic protocol necessitates disengagement with the personal, an epistemological splitting of the mind from the body. In other words, I know that despite the fact that I constantly feel different and outside the modes of academic discourse, it is my responsibility to blend in and mimic the status quo; this is what is known as 'academic responsibility.' The act of silencing the multiple-realities that I experience as a gay man and an African American in order to stay in line with the prescribed rules of academic training/reasoning/disciplining has had a profound effect on the way in which I write, giving me the sense that I am not writing in dialogue but in response to what is deemed rational, meaningful, and worth critical examination. Experience has also taught me that if I do not play by the rules of the academy there is a big price to pay. I know that the fellowship office staff is not concerned with what radical changes I have attempted to make in the academy (no matter how important I think these changes are). In direct contrast, they want to know my grades, what professional conferences I attended, what courses I took, what classes I taught, what *academic* publications I was published in, and how I am progressing towards my 'professionalization' as an academic. Sometimes I seriously wonder if the real question isn't 'Do you have what it takes to uphold the ideologies and aims of Western Civilization?'

Reflecting upon the painful experience of being constrained by academic protocol has empowered me to realize that the stories, feelings, and emotions that I repressed were not only a primary source of originality and creativity in my work, but were also what made it possible for me to analyze and theorize my thoughts in the first place. I wonder what kind of theorization of sexuality and race I could produce, if a distinction is not made between what constitutes the academic and the personal? What happens to my writing and thinking when I attempt to weave different voices, genres, and subject locations together? What happens to my writing and thinking when I allow myself the opportunity to openly theorize the personal? Most importantly, what happens when academic discourse is not viewed as a privileged form of critical investigation and knowledge?

In *The Alchemy of Race and Rights*, Patricia Williams encourages us to "acknowledge the extent to which denial of one's authority in authorship is not the same as elimination of oneself; it is ruse, not reality."[3] The blending of personal fragments and experiences of my life in this essay is a refusal to deny my authority in authorship; it is a refusal to compartmentalize myself, or to deny personal feelings, emotions, and desires that others have deemed tangential, insignificant, and wrong. My unwillingness to deny my authority represents my persistent yearning to carve a space for myself in a Eurocentric, homophobic, and racist world that still believes to a large degree that I am inappropriate or insignificant. My refusal to eliminate myself in my writing is a matter of survival.

I also believe firmly that it is in my best interest to undiscipline myself —to write myself Out of compartmentalized notions of who I am and what I am supposed to represent. For instance, when I am teaching a Lesbian and Gay Studies course, most students expect sexuality to be the only focal point. Similarly, when I teach an African American Studies course, my students expect the course to focus on race. An attempt to discuss how sexuality is racialized or how race and sexuality are intricately linked is not usually well received.

In an African American Studies literature course that I taught recently, I assigned Nella Larsen's *Passing*, and I asked my students to think about the possibility that there are other forms of 'passing' that occur in the novel besides racial passing. In response to my request, a young woman boldly informed me that 'Race is the main theme of the novel, and it should be our *only* focus because the course is not supposed to be a Gay Studies course.' What I found particularly interesting when I talked to the student more about her perspective of what is appropriate to deal with in African American Studies, it became clear that she was not interested in issues of sexuality simply because the course was in the African American Studies Department; somehow there is the idea that the location of the course places a limitation on the line of inquiry that we are 'allowed' to pursue. The young woman's comment is not just homophobic; it is also an indication that she found it impossible to undiscipline herself—to go beyond what she has been told that the department is supposed to deal with.

While my teachers concentrate on my personal motivation and my commitment to academic work, my family views my education as a communal achievement that has been gained against the great odds American racism forces a Black child to face every single day of his life. From my earliest recollections, my parents impressed upon me the importance of education not simply as a regurgitation of facts and statistics or a source of financial security, but also as a powerful political tool that would enable me to critically reflect upon the past and radically revise the future. In fact, my degrees are not viewed solely as personal achievements; they are considered something which my entire family has supported me through and can take pride in. This difference in interpretation manifests itself most strikingly in the language I use to communicate the knowledge I acquire.

Recently, for example, during a study break prior to the day of my exam—the academic rite of passage—my mother asked me what I was required to know for the exam. As she put it, "Tell me what you have been doing." To answer her question, I decided to read to her from a note card that I had written concerning the linkage between race and sexuality, and how dissemination of knowledge produces performative identities. The card contained three quotations from Judith Butler's *Bodies That Matter: On the Discursive Limits of "Sex."*

> *What would it mean to "cite" the law to produce it differently, to "cite" the law in order to reiterate and coopt its power, to expose the heterosexual matrix and to displace the effect of its necessity?*[4]

How, then can one think through the matter of bodies as a kind of materialization governed by regulatory norms in order to ascertain the workings of heterosexual hegemony in the formation of what qualifies as a viable body?[5]

. . . what qualifies as bodies that matter, ways of living that count as "life," lives worth protecting, lives worth saving, lives worth grieving?[6]

After I read the quotations, my mother's response went something like this:

Is this what you are worried about? Is this what you have spent years trying to master? Did you have to leave New Jersey to come all the way to California to learn what I thought I taught you? Every Black person in his right mind knows that you have to speak against the powers that be. The law is the power that be. What is so profound about these statements? Shit, I could have told you that idea and saved you and myself a hell of a lot of money. I'm proud of you but sometimes I think you lose sight of the common sense that I tried to teach you. Remember you are a Black man and you do not need to be told that you need to work against the powers that be.

Of all the comments that my mother made in reference to Butler's text, the one that still echoes vividly in my mind was her declaration that: "Instead of driving yourself crazy going over these big words again and again, why don't you think about how all these ideas about power and oppression relate to your personal knowledge and experience of what it means to deal with racism?" Suddenly and without warning, she leaned over my computer and began removing the dead leaves from the ficus tree by my desk. She ended the conversation by telling me, "you need to learn how to take better care of yourself and your plants."

My mother helped me understand that I probably would fail my exam if I did not have what she called "the common sense" to realize that a lot of the theories about multiculturalism, cultural hybridity, epistemic violence, and hegemony were not totally alien concepts to me. It was just that encoding my personal experience and desires in this highly academic language had rendered the words lifeless, abstract and seemingly irrelevant.

Stories have always played an important role in my family. I remember hearing my mother's horror stories about what it was like for her when, after spending the first twelve years of her life on the island of Nassau, she moved from the Bahamas, to live in up-state New York. A lot of her stories concentrated on how she learned to deal with American racism, and what dreams and visions she had for our family. She talked about segregation and the countless times she was attacked because she is Black and "happened to be in the wrong place at the wrong time." Although my mother's stories were full of pain and suffering, I cherished them, for no matter what seemingly inescapable predicament she was in, her stories always ended with her sisters and brothers, or some other Black person she may not have even known personally, coming to her defense; her community gave her pride, strength, and hope. As a result of listening to her stories, I learned that I came from a strong group of people who would support me no matter how difficult times may become. Early on, I learned to be conscious of the ways in which racial and gender differences confined me within stereotypical images, and my mother had special advice as to how to survive its consequences. Every now and then, before I left home to go to school or before I went to bed at night, she would hold me in her arms and tell me things she knew I needed to hear. The knowledge that she wanted to pass on to me was never disciplined into a linear narrative that went from point to point. Instead, her advice flowed in one direction and then would suddenly bend back on itself and expose some hidden point that I had failed to observe on my own.

One of the most powerful stories that my mother ever told me concerned the reason why she and my father decided to move back to her homeland when I was only six months old. This particular story always began with questions she thought I should think about:

Why would any Black child in his right mind want to grow up in Lockport, New York, when there were smiling Black faces back home that were waiting to accept and love him? Why would any Black child want to grow up in a country that hates high yella and blue Black niggas?

My parents immigrated to the Bahamas during the turbulent race riots of the 1960s, and they constantly remind me of this fact. Having spent a good portion of her life in the Bahamas, my mother said she did not want to raise her kids in the United States. "Your father and I saw all the killing that was going on in the South, and all the riots in the North, and the potential earthquakes in the West, and we decided to just leave the country altogether." She shared things with me that she knew from experience as an African American that I, in time, would experience as well.

Your whole life will be wrapped up in what other people think they know about you. A lot of white people seriously believe that they have something to teach you, to tell you about being Black. They think they have seen you before. They honestly think they know you. Your biggest struggle will not be attempting to destroy these images altogether. You could not do that in a lifetime. Believe me, I know. Experience. Your biggest goal is to make sure you don't accept these images.

I know through personal experience how the overwhelming feeling of being consumed by race has a way of teaching a child not to speak about parts of his identity that he does not have the language to articulate yet.

My family generally assumed that I would be too preoccupied dealing with racism to consider marginalizing myself even more. Consequently, homosexuality never seemed like a viable option for me. I was continually reminded of what the Black community considered to be acceptable and appropriate behavior. For example, when I was ten years old, my mother and I were in New York City and a very effeminate Black man walked by us. She looked at the man, shook her head and said that "faggots are a disgrace, homosexuality is a white disease. It's just not natural. Has he no pride?" She also warned me that she would die of shame if I were to become a "sissy." I would be a disgrace to our race. She reinforced this with a lot of neck movements, the rolling of her eyes, and the repetition of the words, "I tell you."

I learned my lessons early; I learned them well. By the highly impressionable age of ten, I knew that one of the worst things I could ever do was to bring disgrace to my race by expressing the wrong sexual feelings and desires; consequently, I was terrified of the possibility of being found Out; I did not want to be even more different in a world that I knew was not very interested in loving, protecting, and caring for little Black boys in the first place. My fear of being rejected from the only community that I had ever known compelled me to make my mother and the entire Black community proud. I acted as if I too believed that only white people were gay. Confusion silenced me when I could not find the courage within myself to question the bigoted ideas and mobbish attitudes that the Black community often has about gays and lesbians.

I tried to be the best possible child any mother could hope for, whether in the classroom, on the sports field, or at home. I wanted to excel, to be the exceptional Black child. I felt that if I were exceedingly good in every other way, then perhaps if my family and community ever "found me Out" they might overlook my sexual flaw. I became an "A" student. I won the most prestigious scholarships and fellowships. I always had a well paying job. My bills were paid on time. I went to the gym. In other words, I tried to achieve and do everything that would make me seem more "masculine," "natural," and "acceptable."

I became an obedient creation, and in the process I unwittingly pushed myself deeper into the closet. My aunts, uncles, and grandparents always used to comment on how successfully my parents had raised me. But, they were praising the representation of *myself* that I performed for their benefit. Why, then, if I am so worth praising, does one aspect of my identity outweigh all the positive attributes that I contribute to our community? Like Joseph Beam, I understand the torment of being "perceived as a threat to the family," being "tolerated if I am silent and inconspicuous," and "most often rendered invisible."[7]

Years later, when I began to accept the fact that I am attracted to men, I was terrified of rejection. I began to realize how important and empowering it was for me to be around other African Americans who would love, support, and accept me (even if only in part). I always knew that after a difficult day at school my mother would be there for me. I always knew that if I talked to my African American peers, they would understand the pain of sitting through an all white history class and listening to the other students laugh when the teacher spoke about slavery. I had to ask myself over and over, where would I be without my community? Could I risk exposing and exploring my sexual desires? What kinds of repercussions would I create for others if I *selfishly* pursued my own desires?

I was so conscious of the danger of being rejected by my racial community that my fear overwhelmed me into silence and denial. For instance, when I was an undergraduate at U.C. Berkeley, I wrote an entire honors thesis on James Baldwin in which I did not include the issue of his sexuality in the final version of my paper. Secretly, when I was by myself, I would write down fragments of my ideas that I thought I could not share. Alone, I tried to assimilate what it meant to read Baldwin's text with the knowledge that he was a Black gay male. I tried to think about the ways in which I could discuss *Go Tell It On The Mountain* as a homotextual novel because of the subtle homoerotic attraction between the main character, John, and his friend, Elisha. Every time I met my thesis advisors, I secretly hoped that one of them would find it peculiar that I had not shown them any indication that I intended to deal with the question of sexuality, despite the fact that the subject of my thesis was James Baldwin's critique of the "American dream." When my thesis was finally completed, I turned in fifty pages of my seventy-page text. The other twenty pages remained stored on my computer, waiting in memory under the heading "Baldwin: Gay Related Themes."

I did not share my ideas about Baldwin's gay related themes because I feared the possible repercussions. I recall being the only Black person in the English Department's honors thesis course. Over five hundred students were going to graduate from the department, fifty or sixty with honors, and I was the Black one. I felt I could not take any chances. I felt very alone and scared because I knew that a lot was at stake. My family and my community were depending on me. I had to be *safe*; discipline was needed in order for me to prove that "I" am a *worthy* representative; reason was also needed to make sure that I did not selfishly risk the distinction of graduating with honors for my race. My fear was real at the time because I did not know how to deal with it. As a result, I stored my emotions, my thoughts, and my feelings deep within my consciousness until, after many years of silence, I began to run out of space in which to store them all. I wanted Out.

* * * * * *

Contrary to popular belief, racial myths and stereotypes are not left outside the gates of the academy, nor is what Frantz Fanon call "the fact of Blackness" renounced in the *real* world by fancy degrees from prestigious universities or expensive material items that mark me as being middle-class and educated. I am still "given no chance. I am overdetermined from without. I am the slave not of the 'idea' that others have of me but of my own appearance."[8] I cannot escape this reality; I continue to represent the Native Other. A casual glance transforms me from a young academic into a potential disturbance, a violent rapist, a deadly threat — a Black man, a walking manifestation of all of society's fears. Again, I hear the lyrical representations of "myself". . .

I'm your pusherman
Your sex machine
The Black private dick
Superfly
A long weapon
A Black Spear, A Black Lance
A Black Shaft

Ironically, sometimes the material and educational accessories that are supposed to mark me as cultured and respectable exaggerate my "fact of Blackness" to my detriment. For instance, I can vividly recall driving my father's shiny new Volvo two years ago in an exclusive neighborhood in Philadelphia, "the city of brotherly love," when a police officer who was traveling in the opposite direction made a sudden U-turn, put on his high beams, and signaled for me to pull over to the side of the road. The first thing the officer said to me was, "What are you doing in this neighborhood and where did you get this car?" When I answered that the car was my father's, the police officer, the supposed neutral and objective hand of the law, looked at me with a very condescending grin and proceeded to explain that there had been many thefts in the area lately. The assumption was that I was naturally supposed to understand why he had stopped me, a young Black male between the age of twenty and twenty-five—everybody knows that you are supposed to watch out for them.

When I attempted to get my license out of my wallet to identify myself, the officer unfastened the safety latch on his gun and told me to sit back and "be careful" because he had a gun and "was not afraid to use it." On the back window of the car, my father had placed a sticker from each of the various schools my siblings and I attended, and I watched as the officer read them. As I looked up and gazed into the policeman's pale gray eyes, I knew that he was looking for an excuse to make trouble; I knew that when he looked at me all the degrees in the world could not negate my "fact of Blackness"—I was still a Black man, a repulsive object, a threat to all those law abiding white people in this exclusive neighborhood.

In the end, the officer never asked for my identification or to see the car registration and insurance papers. Instead, he pointed to the rear window and asked me to identify in what state and city the various universities were located. The implication of the question was that if I knew where these prestigious schools were located, that it would somehow mean that I was not some ordinary uneducated Negro, that I was somehow more valid. When he asked me to locate the schools, I knew that he no longer assumed that I was a thief, or a murderer, or a rapist, but nonetheless, he still wanted to remind me of my place, to make sure I knew that he (the law) was watching me, and that he would and could 'discipline' me if he wanted to because he was the embodiment of 'the powers that be.' I became more and more conscious of being in an all-white neighborhood on a very dark street in the middle of the night without anyone else around to witness what was happening; I was aware that I was *out of place*. I simply did all that I could do given the situation; I swallowed my pride and remained silent until the officer was done using my body as a toy, a 'Black thing.'

Having to deal with the pathological racial dynamics of American society has armed me with a clear understanding of the officer's line of reasoning. It probably went something like this: 'young Black man in an expensive foreign car must be dealing drugs. But drug dealers usually tint their windows instead of putting university emblems on them—he must have stolen it. I better take *reasonable* action and investigate the suspect.' Sadly, many people might argue that this line of reasoning and the actions that followed from it were justified; recall how during the Rodney King trial the defense lawyers argued successfully that the officers who brutally clubbed King had simply used reasonable force. Undeniably, the bizarre notion of reasonable force has everything to do with racial myths about Black identity, especially Black masculinity. Incidents such as this compromise my objectivity because my survival is largely dependent upon my ability to remember the past and to be conscious of who I am as opposed to what others think I represent.

* * * * * *

During the past seven months I have struggled to commit some of my innermost thoughts to paper, to express feelings and beliefs that I often feared to share. I have also wondered whether, like me, my mother (and the Black community at large) would understand the profound effect that Butler's words—"what qualifies as bodies that matter, ways of living that count as 'life,' lives worth protecting, lives worth saving, lives worth grieving [over],"[9]—have had on me if she knew what it was like to hold a lover in your arms and have him tell you that he is HIV-positive. Or perhaps she/they might comprehend what it is like to have a friend bashed on the streets by other African Americans not because she is Black but because she is an out-of-the-closet Black dyke—an anomaly, a freak accident, a tragedy, a disgrace to the race. I am a young gay Black male who is painfully aware that sometimes home—that space that is so nurturing and loving—can be one of the loneliest places to exist, especially in the closet.

When I first thought about venturing out of the closet, I fantasized about a supportive and nurturing gay community that would accept my sexuality, and encourage me to believe that loving or having sex with another man was indeed a "natural" thing, an alternative way of existing in the world. I did find the fulfillment of these needs. But then there was the matter of race.

While the academy is interested in race as a depersonalized subject matter, the gay community has a tendency to look at race as a purely sexual issue. The white gay community's tendency to define itself primarily in terms of sex is a significant problem because it follows naturally, therefore, that Black gay men are going to be defined only in terms of sex. The urban gay subculture represents Black men according to stereotypical images. When I read gay papers, magazines, and promotional flyers Black men are frequently portrayed as sexually insatiable and untameable studs—men who cannot be controlled. In direct contrast, however, homoerotic mass media images of white men do not confine the sexual appeal of white men to their race; it is as if white men have the option to conveniently accessorize their sexuality to meet their needs. Whereas the performance of white macho styles (cowboy, officer, biker, leather, etc.) can be viewed as "costume drama," the *bare* fact that Black gay men are Black limits them "to 'being' purely sexual and nothing but sexual."[10] The gay community often fails to realize that racial difference is made "legible as a sexual practice rather than as a social, economic and cultural difference with a history of great cost for those marked by it as Other."[11] It is this short sightedness that perpetuates the fallacies concerning Black masculinity.

Most of the time, when I try to make critical interventions about the silence that surrounds the issue of race in the gay community, I am told that I am 'policing desires' or that I cannot ask for sexual liberation and simultaneously critique how others opt to liberate themselves even if their emancipation uses and exploits my body in the process. When I go to bars and clubs, I understand that it is my responsibility as a modernized, urban, gay man never to question the man next to me who superficially resembles a skinhead or a Nazi. I am supposed to allow the racist and fascist connotations of these 'macho' styles to escape criticism.[12] I am told not to question the ways in which the urban gay scene eroticizes masculinity because 'gay men who dress like skinheads are just doing their own thing,' and 'white men in Gestapo regalia are only playing; they do not mean anything personal by it.' When I refuse to be silent about the "ambivalent meanings and messages" apparent in the gay community's fascination with racist and fascist imaginaries, white gay men gaze at me as if I am being selfish, prudish, and irrational.[13]

They fail to realize that the ways in which they choose to present their sexual preferences legitimize one particular system of oppression and that by expressing their liberation from the accepted norms of society at large, they undermine the struggle for a much more comprehensive freedom. I saw this need to consider the effect of the specific on the general in terms of oppression best illustrated at the Fifth Annual Lesbian and Gay Studies Conference at Rutgers University which I attended in November 1991.

During one of the panel sessions entitled, "Race, Ethnicity, Sexuality," a young Black woman in the audience made the point that the gay community needs to be more attentive to how systems of oppression overlap, and how her struggle to deal with sexism and racism should not be viewed as tangential or insignificant. Even before the woman was finished making her points, a middle-aged white man angrily asked the woman, "How are we supposed to deal with racism when so many of us are dying of AIDS? Sometimes, I do not even have the energy to take care of myself."

While listening to the rather heated exchange that developed between the man and the woman, I thought about how many white gay men and women often have a difficult time understanding that my inescapable reality as a racial minority tells me that being Black is perhaps just as—if not sometimes even more—influential to the form of oppression that I encounter as a sexual minority.[14] As James Baldwin succinctly explains it, "A Black gay person who is a sexual conundrum to society is already, long before the question of sexuality comes into it, menaced and marked because he's Black or she's Black. The sexual question comes after the question of color."[15]

* * * * * *

In my struggle to communicate and interact with the diverse communities that I am a part of, I have found allies and new possibilities for living in the most unlikely places. My introduction to feminist theory, particularly by women of color, gave me an insight into the language necessary to begin to (re)construct my notions about how sexuality and race are inextricably linked. In many respects, this relates to going to college during the 1980s, a period when feminism played a dramatic and powerful role in the re-shaping of what constitutes academic writing. I particularly admired the work of Black feminist writers such as Audre Lorde, Angela Davis, Cheryl Clarke, Barbara Christian, and bell hooks because they dealt with issues of gender and sexuality while simultaneously theorizing ways to dismantle racism. bell hooks', *Feminist Theory: From Margin To Center*, for instance, taught me that "most people are socialized to think in terms of opposition rather than compatibility. Rather than see antiracist work as totally compatible with working to end sexist oppression, they are often seen as two movements competing for first place."[16] bell hooks's theory encouraged me to deal with the notion of multiple-subjectivity. Instead of thinking in terms of racism versus homophobia, I began to think about how racism operates within the gay community as well as society at large. Rather than thinking oppositionally, I decided that my race and sexuality are equally important and compatible parts of identity, and that I should not have to choose one over the other. Part of my being silenced at home, in the academy, and within the gay community over the years has been related to the fact that I have been trying to decide which part of my marginalized self to prioritize; it often feels like trying to select between forfeiting my vocal cords or my tongue—without either of which I am silent and incomplete.

Notes

I would like to acknowledge the help and support that I received from the editors, Becky Thompson and Sangeeta Tyagi, as well as from Amalia Cabezas, Yvette Gullatt, Michael Simmons, Joe Nickerson, Nancy Ordorver, Kim Savo, Caroline Streeter and especially Duncan Thomas. Without their encouragement and constructive criticism, this essay would not have been possible.

1   Curtis Mayfield. Pusherman. Curton Records of Atlanta, Inc. 1988.

2   Isaac Hayes. Theme From Shaft. Stax Records, ENS-2-5002. 1978.

3   Patricia Williams, *The Alchemy of Race and Rights*, (Cambridge: Harvard University Press, 1991) 92.

4   Judith Butler, *Bodies That Matter: On The Discursive Limits of "Sex"*, (New York: Routledge, 1993) 15.

5   Ibid. 16.

6   Ibid. 16.

7   Joseph Beam, "Brother to Brother: Words from the Heart," *In the Life: A Black Gay Anthology*, ed. Joseph Beam (Boston: Alyson Publications, 1986) 231.

8   Frantz Fanon, *Black Skin, White Masks*, (New York: Grove Press, 1967) 116.

9   Butler 16.

10   Kobena Mercer, "Looking For Trouble," *Transition* 51 (1991) 187.

11   Thomas Yingling, "How the Eye Is Caste: Robert Mapplethorpe and the Limits of Controversy," *Discourse* 12.2 (Spring-Summer 1990): 10.

12   Isaac Julien and Kobena Mercer, *Ten 8*, no 22 (Summer 1986) 131.

13   Ibid. 132.

14   Gay Black Group, *Gay News* no. 251, London: October 1982. This article is also published in *Male Order: Unwrapping Masculinity*, ed. Rowena Chapman and Jonathan Rutherford (London: Lawrence & Wishart Limited, 1988) 104-110.

15   Richard Goldstein, "'Go the Way Your Blood Beats': An Interview with James Baldwin (1984)," *James Baldwin The Legacy*, ed. Quincy Troupe (New York: Simon & Schuster) 180.

16   bell hooks.1984. *Feminist Theory: From Margin To Center* Boston: South End Press. 29.

21

"Wandering between Two Worlds, One Dead, the Other Powerless to Be Born"

Ramon S. Torrecilha

They tell me I am an American, but who indeed am I?[1] There is a sense of urgency that drives me to search for an answer to this question. The search leads me to painfully confront and define who I am. My identity is constructed, inherited, chosen, assigned, and some times distorted by those who, for whatever reason, insist on granting me less than full membership in this society.

I have several identities. They are neither fixed nor unambiguous. I am the product of two cultures, yet I feel marginal to both. I was born in Casa Branca, Brazil, the second child of a Brazilian woman and a Puerto Rican man. The story goes that my father came to Casa Branca to work in the local sugar cane refinery where he met and married my mother after a short courtship. Casa Branca is a sleepy little town in the southwest of the state of São Paulo. The city's economy is underdeveloped and opportunities are few. Life was difficult, but my parents made ends meet until my father lost his job at the sugar refinery. With no prospect for employment, the family decided to move to San Juan, Puerto Rico. I was three years old then, and my memories of these events are sketchy at best. The move was hard on my mother.

All she knew during her whole life was that sleepy town and the surrounding area where everything was familiar and almost everyone was related to each other. In San Juan, she became consumed by loneliness and sunk into a depression which lasted until after the birth of her third child, my youngest sister. The migration North did not change the family's fortune and after three years in Puerto Rico my mother, together with her kids, returned to Brazil. I did not realize then that I wasn't going to see my father ever again.

Back in Brazil, the family moved again, this time to São José do Rio Pardo where we lived with my grandmother. São José do Rio Pardo sits in a valley surrounded by evenly arranged mountains which are covered by coffee trees and topped by crisp blue skies. From the hill where my grandmother's house stood, the city's narrow streets resemble a carefully designed mosaic divided exactly into two even parts by the Rio Pardo. I felt safe and on top of the world.

The familiarity of São José soon gave way to the unfamiliar halls of the state's boarding school. I was eight years old when, on a bright Sunday morning, my mother left me on the front steps of the boarding school. I don't remember feeling upset by her departure, but leaving my grandmother behind was difficult. She represented stability in a life which had been very unstable, and besides we had become very good friends.

The decision to send me to the boarding school resulted from my mother's financial inability to care for me and my siblings. There were just too many demands on her and, despite my grandmother's generosity, my mother was constantly being reminded by my uncles about the extra burden we represented. My brother was old enough to help around the house, and my sister too young to be sent away. That meant that my absence was the only contribution I could make to the household. I did not question my mother's decision, but remember making a mental note about how my fate was being determined by my size. The boarding school was far from a place with manicured gardens where well-behaved young men are sent to be groomed for positions of power. In fact, most students attending the school came from families like mine: poverty put us there, not wealth. The school year was long, but the summer never failed to arrive on time. At the boarding school, I roomed with a neighbor from São José whose friendship made all the difference in buffering my loneliness.

For the next few years I managed a happy, predictable routine. The predictability of my days in the boarding school was interrupted when I learned that the school counselor had recommended me for the technical track instead of the academic one. I was outraged by the fact that my family's economic background, and not my scholastic ability, was the decisive factor in my placement.

The opportunities denied to me because of my family's social class were not the only source of my discontent. As a male, I was trusted with a privileged place in Brazilian society. I was given the right to celebrate the subjugation of women, including my own mother and sister. The disparities between the sexes loomed too large to be ignored. Through my mother's own struggle, I learned about the ways in which men and women occupy unequal positions in society, and how cultural symbols, in turn, validate such positions. In a community where women are seen as extensions of their men, my mother's freedom was too daring for some and the subject of intrigue for others. My father was never blamed for having abandoned his family, neither was his integrity ever questioned. I took comfort in the fact that my mother was able to maintain her posture in the midst of so much ridicule, never bowing her head in apology.

At times, my empathy towards her plight did not prevent me from being critical of her apathy. I remember feeling ill at ease when she told me about painful experiences with men, including my father, and I found myself caught in two polarized positions: the rapist and the rape victim. I will never forget the morning when I found my mother crying at the foot of her bed. My grandmother was standing by her side, holding her hand. She told me to go back to bed, but I refused, knowing well that the pain on my mother's face would follow me. Instead, I stood by her side, not sure about the reason for so many tears. My grandmother went into the kitchen. From a distance, I saw her resting her head against the wall as she waited for the water to fill in the saucepan for some coffee. I moved closer towards my mother, trying to comfort her with my hands. She took my hand and shook her head, almost in shame. I realized that she did not want to be touched. I finally mustered the courage to ask what happened. She dried her eyes with the hem of her camisole and told me that my uncle tried to get into her bed. I wanted to tell her to stop talking, but instead I just stood there motionless. She described being wakened by the touch of his sweaty hands. When she looked up, half awake and afraid, she saw his naked body standing by her bed. She screamed and he left. I felt the burden of her rescue, but how could I? Suddenly love had melted into pain, leaving an ugly memory behind which neither time nor love itself has been able to remove. As soon as I heard my grandmother's footsteps against the cracking wood floor I left the room consumed by an indescribable feeling of failure.

My mother's pain led me to confront my own existence as a young man. It was ironic that as a male I was expected to mold myself after those whose abusive behavior had a direct effect on my being. And if I refused to mold myself after the men in my family, could I still be a boy? Were abuse, anger, and power central to masculinity? I have often wondered how I came to confront these questions when others who shared similar circumstances did not, and, would I have done so if my father had been around? Probably not. I now realize that my assessment of my mother's life was defined from a vantage point of privilege which I reluctantly occupied.

Feeling out of place in my family, I began to entertain the idea of migrating North. My inquietude was fueled by stories I heard about some distant relatives who lived in a place called "Bruklin." I remember the day when my mother sent my brother and me to the bus station to pick up a box that my father's sister had sent. Back at home, the whole family sat anxiously around the kitchen table as mother sorted the gifts. I appreciated the gifts very much, but the importance of that box rested on the fact that "Bruklin" was no longer an imaginary place. Suddenly, the world had grown bigger before my very eyes, as did the possibilities of finding my own place in that world. And while the poverty around me created some formidable obstacles, I was not about to let my fate go unchallenged. I did not realize that my search was going to take me to blind alleys. However, my yearning did increase my chances to make a number of rewarding discoveries.

The death of my grandmother in 1976 convinced me that there was little reason for me to remain in Brazil. Acting on this realization was not easy however. For one thing, the migration North was expensive, and familial relations with my father and his family had been severed for a good many years. I thought, nevertheless, that as a son of a Puerto Rican I could gain entrance into the United States with little problem. I was wrong. I tried in vain to persuade the officials at the American Consulate of my legitimate status and of my right to enter the U.S.

This encounter revealed the fragility of my rights, but it also taught me how to negotiate such rights even though I was being told that I had none. My disillusionment served to reduce the universe. I did not realize it immediately, but my respect for authority had suffered a considerable diminution. I understood that my survival depended, partly, on my ability to channel my discontent, to read the situation and negotiate the rules of the system even though that meant breaking them. I felt no obligation to abide by social norms which negated my rights.

Back at the boarding school, my desire to migrate North persisted. I remember feeling consumed by an inexplicable need to leave: I was not searching for the promise of riches, but for a safe space where I could be myself. It took a long time before I realized that when you are a nobody you are someone. As a "nobody," I had only my silence to shield me from others. Through my silence however, I was my own master and lived my inner life as I saw fit. There was never any question about whether my thoughts belonged to me. I owned my own thoughts and that was enough. Yet, I longed for a space where I could make my feelings and thoughts public. It was not that I feared sharing my world with others; I just refused to play the parts expected of me for the amusement of others. That for me was dreary.

The boarding school was located near a large agribusiness development. The area has been a point of destination for Japanese immigrants since the Second World War; the majority work in the fields. The integration of Japanese immigrants and Japanese-Brazilians into the local community was marginal, except during the annual agricultural festival when everyone came together to celebrate the harvest. It was during one of these events that I learned about an exchange agricultural program. To be sure, information about the program was sketchy and misleading, a fact that I later came to regret. Nevertheless, it was hard to escape the enthusiasm of the recruiter, who promised food and shelter, a salary of $260 dollars per month, and the opportunity to live and work on a U.S. farm. The prospects caught my attention, and in less than six months I was on my way to an apple farm, Mount Adams Orchard, in White Salmon, Washington State.

I never really liked agriculture. I never really intended to pursue a career in that field, but the agricultural exchange program was my only way out of the country. My inability to read English made it impossible for me to understand the fine print in the contract. The recruiter marketed the program as an educational exchange experience which included instruction in English as a second language and U.S. agriculture. Once in the U.S., however, it did not take very long for me to realize that the program was nothing more than a way to provide cheap labor for American farmers. No language instruction was given. As for a course on U.S. agriculture, we were told that we would learn all about it at our work sites.

After a few days in Sacramento, California, I was given a one-way bus ticket to Hood River, Oregon, and dropped at the bus station. There I waited patiently, trying to understand the announcer over the loud speaker—not an easy task for someone who spoke no English. Somehow I managed to find my way to the right boarding gate. A rotten smell of urine permeated the Greyhound bus, but I was too tired to care about what to me seemed like a minor detail and before long I fell asleep.

Over twenty hours had passed when the squeaky bus finally arrived in Hood River, a small town on the foot of Mount Adams. An employee from Mount Adams Orchard, Mr. John—whose last name I never learned—was waiting for me at the station, holding a sign with my name on it. It did not take long for Mr. John to realize that I could not speak English. As he drove, he tried to communicate in broken Spanish, but I shook my head signaling that I didn't understand what he was saying. I was determined to learn English.

At Mount Adams Orchard I shared a small house with twelve Mexican migrant workers. The house was sparsely furnished and dirty. The air was so thick and musty that a cloud of smoke could not dance around the light bulb hanging from the kitchen ceiling. There were bunk beds in every room, except the kitchen and bathroom. Mr. John introduced me to my housemates, left my suitcases near an empty bed in the living room, told me to report to work on Monday morning, and left in a hurry.

My days at the farm were long and the work was harsh. I remember driving a John Deere tractor up and down the fields from sunrise to sundown. My work assignments consisted of either plowing the semi-frozen ground or spraying old tired apple trees with a sticky white solution. I was given no protective gear and the bitter taste of the pesticide remained in my mouth for hours. At night, exhausted, I would sit in front of a black and white television screen, even though I didn't understand a word of what was being said. It was important, however, to train my ear to the sounds of the new language and to learn how to decode facial and body expressions which at first communicated nothing. It didn't take very long for isolation to replace the novelty of the new surroundings. I felt lonely; my thoughts were my only companion.

White Salmon, the nearest city, was a good ten miles away and there was no transportation except on Saturdays when Mr. John would take me and my housemates to the supermarket so that we could buy the groceries for the week. On a crisp Sunday morning, I decided to go to town. As I was walking towards the road, I thought of São José where Sundays were almost like a holiday. On Sundays, the city's tranquil streets would be filled with people dressed in their Sunday best for the ten o'clock mass. The church bells would start ringing half an hour before the mass, and the crowd, in a procession-like march, would find their way into the church, ready to repent their sins and eager to commit new ones. The church was the city's prize possession. It stood right in the middle of the dusty unpaved plaza where its majestic tower almost touched the heaven.

I stood on the side of the road for nearly one hour, somewhat amused by the parade of cars that would not stop. The cold wind, cutting through my flannel shirt, convinced me to return to Mount Adams when a couple in a station wagon made a sudden U-turn and picked me up. Somehow I managed to communicate to them that I wanted to go to Mass. They however were on their way to Sunday school at the local Southern Baptist church, which is where I ended up too.

At the church, my eyes were fixed on the man behind the pulpit whose light blue robe would wave like a flag every time he lifted his arms and shouted "praise the lord, alleluia, alleluia." After the service, Mr. and Mrs. Hart, the couple who picked me up, invited me to join them for lunch. On our way back from the church, we drove past Mount Adams and onto Glenwood where they lived. I was as curious about them as they were about me, but my broken English made it difficult to communicate. From then on the Harts took me to church every Sunday morning. I was glad to see them, since going to church meant breaking away from the isolation that haunted me still. My motives for befriending the Harts had less to do with my desire to be saved, however. Rather, I was determined to locate my father's family in New York and I soon thought that the Harts would help me.

It took me a whole year before I found my aunts and cousins in New York. By the time the search ended I was emotionally drained. The uncertainty of our reunion and the possibility of another rejection consumed every little bit of hope I had. Yet, I was happy that I had persisted. Our first encounter was filled with both joy and disappointment. I realized that it would take a long time before we could bridge the distance which kept us apart; we were very much strangers to one another. My aunt María Silvia told me where to find my father, but advised me to wait for a while before seeking him out. Later on, I learned that he was not interested in revisiting the past, of which I was very much a part. His rejection reopened a deep wound which I worked hard to heal. I felt betrayed by my own vulnerability, for allowing myself to believe that he was going to prove otherwise the stories my mother told me about him.

I was paralyzed by my father's rejection. I remember standing by the bedroom window of my aunt's apartment in Spanish Harlem and letting the salsa beat, coming from the streets, take me back to São José, to a day when my grandmother sent me to the panadaria for some coffee and bread. A man, sipping a bitter sweet cup of coffee, looked at me and smiled. I thought about my father's smile and wished that one day I could look him in the eye and smile, something I could not bring myself to do with that stranger sitting on the edge of the bakery counter. As I relived this memory, a drop rolled down my cheek, but before it got very far the wind blew it away as if nothing had happened. My aunt María Silvia walked into the room. We stood by the window, side by side, motionless, gazing at nowhere. She saw the pain on my face, but knew no words to comfort me. Gently, she reached for my shoulders, moving her hand from side to side as if trying to spread a potion into my porous skin and heal my open wound.

It took more than a few days before I shook off the hangover left by this disappointment. I remember trying to label what I was feeling. In the process I discovered that the universality of feeling rejected adds a public dimension to this very private emotion. While I alone felt the sting of my father's rejection, others around me knew what it felt like to be rejected. My aunt's support was not enough to keep me in New York; the city no longer excited me. Instead, I decided to head back to the West Coast and start all over again. I got a hold of some acquaintances in

Portland, Oregon, a family of missionaries whom I had met through the Harts, and asked if I could stay with them for a while. Mr. and Mrs. Linden were not overwhelmed with joy by the prospect of having yet another mouth to feed, but they took me in anyway. Room and board at the Linden's was not exactly free. In exchange for living there, I agreed to cook for the family: two meals a day, five days a week. Things began to go sour when Mrs. Linden told me that I had to wait until everyone had eaten before I could make myself a plate. Her comment was enough to drive me away. From then on, I spent as little time in the house as possible, preferring instead to wander in the streets of Portland.

I would leave the house shortly after breakfast, and come back just in time to fix supper. The donut shop at the corner of Sandy Boulevard and Union Avenue was my first stop. There, for less than a dollar, I could order a hot cup of coffee and a Boston cream. The donut shop was not a very inviting place; nevertheless it sheltered me from the cold rain that continued to drip off my raincoat as I carried my coffee and donut into the back of the sitting area. I would glance at the other customers, mostly urban transients, but our eyes would rarely meet. I learned, almost instinctively, that one was permitted to strike a conversation only if seated at the counter. I, however, preferred to sit by the window, quietly. A thick film of vapor covered the dirty glass like a shower curtain, making it difficult to see outside. Sitting there, the memories of a place that no longer existed would crash with the noise coming from the streets like a fire alarm, reminding me that it was time to go.

It didn't take me long to cross the Burnside bridge. The water below moved like a gushing sewer, without grace. Waiting for me, on the other side of the bridge, were countless beggars too drunk to beg, too ashamed to look me in the eye. I too avoided their company and was happy to leave them behind. Standing on the corner of Burnside and 11th Avenue was Powell's Books, the city's largest second-hand bookstore. From afar, I would marvel at the books, but when I looked inside I saw no one of color caressing the books with their eyes. It took a while before I began to patronize such places.

My daily excursions often ended at Washington Park in the northwest part of town where Mount Hood stood majestically in the background like a picture perfect postcard. There, in a flowerless garden, I sat for hours, plotting my next move. Having found my father's family in New York meant that I could, once and for all, resolve my predicament with the U.S. Immigration and Naturalization Service. Before that, however, I had to find another place to live. I remember roaming through the streets one day when I ran across a St. Vincent de Paul's store which was bustling with people whose land is not this land. On my way out, I stopped to check the bulletin board by the door. There, I found a poster advertising a room for rent, and in less than a week I was out of the Linden's residence.

Settled into my new room, I decided to pay a visit to the U.S. Immigration and Naturalization Service. I gathered my ammunition and marched into the immigration office not knowing what to expect. I took a number from the red tag dispenser and waited patiently for my number to be called. There was something very dehumanizing about that place. The room was crowded with people whose faces were sanitized by the bright fluorescent light and transfigured into pale figurines. Also, the manner in which people were processed accentuated the impersonality of the scene: I felt reduced to a number. It took a good forty minutes before a white, middle-aged women called my number. She went through my documents methodically, wetting her index finger every so often so that the pages would not stick. She asked me to raise my right hand and repeat after her a string of words that I could hardly pronounce. I did it anyway, since those words meant nothing to me. It was apparent that she was oblivious to my language and culture and that she refused to assume any penalty for such oblivion. I was then sent to the room next door where another clerk reached for my hand and began painting my fingers with a soft sponge-like roller. The black, viscous ink filled the skin-deep rings on the tip of my fingers.

Slowly, the clerk lifted each finger, pressing it against a white sheet of paper and rolling it from side to side before releasing it. I felt branded, like a cow: the ink on my fingers was easily removed with a dab of borax, but the mark remained. I left in silence. At last, I had claimed my right to be here. The excitement I felt was both real and tenuous. Not even during that moment could I afford to lose sight of the fact that the right to be here did not include privileges which others around me took for granted.

My room was in the basement of a seven story building near Portland State University, on Park Avenue. The room was small, but so was my need for space. It faced a courtyard in the center of the building and its proximity to the ground made the room dark and humid. A bed sheet covered the small window facing the patio and uncovered pipes carrying water and waste criss-crossed the ceiling. Lying on the hardwood floor was my sleeping bag and an empty apple crate, which I used as a nightstand. At the end of the hallway, on the left-hand side, was the community bathroom. The bathroom's sour smell was so penetrating that I preferred to use a public restroom whenever possible. The tiles in the shower room were covered with a thick layer of black mildew, but as soon as the water started to pour through the shower-head, I would forget about the foul smell and the slippery floor, letting the warm stream wash the transparent oil off my sweaty body. I shared a kitchen with other residents of my floor. Roaches, mice, and other friendly bugs visited the kitchen with an assiduous punctuality, always feasting on the yellow, aged grease on the stove. The refrigerator was so old that its delirious motor would grind in protest, supplicating to be disconnected. But I was so happy about having my own room that none of these inconveniences seemed to bother me. It is only in retrospect that I see how inhospitable that place was and how intransigent I have since become regarding my own space.

It had taken me a whole year to save $2,000 from my wages at Mount Adams. I managed the money carefully, yet each day my reserves diminished. Other than selling plasma, I had no steady employment despite numerous attempts to find a job. Neither discouragement nor rejection kept me from looking, however. I remember walking one afternoon and seeing a help wanted sign hanging on the door of a Seven Eleven convenience store. I walked into the store and inquired about the position. The unkempt man behind the counter ripped a yellow page from a pad and handed it to me. He was very tall and massively built, and in his broad face his thick lips seemed to have difficulty smiling. I glanced at the application and asked if I could bring it back by the following day, knowing that I did not understand half of what was being asked. I took the application to the St. Vincent de Paul's store hoping to find someone who could help me fill it out. Once in the store, I heard two women speaking Spanish, one of whom patiently helped me fill out my application. The next day, I went back to the store and gave the application to the same man. He took the application, put it on the side, and asked me if I had any experience. I tried to explain to him that my eagerness to work compensated for the lack of experience, and that he did not have to pay me if I had not learned the job in three days. He was very noncommittal, telling me instead that he would get hold of me if anything came up. His arrogance was so real that I could almost touch it. As I was getting ready to leave, I noticed that he wrote a big M on the right hand corner of the application. Curiously, I asked what that letter meant, and without hesitation he replied, "Ah, it is just to remind me that you are a Mexican." Hope turned into a sizzling rage: my ethnicity did not lend any credibility for securing that position. As I walked down the streets, I searched for an explanation and dreaded the thought that this was not going to be the only time I was going to face such a blunt display of racism.

Eventually, I landed a job in a restaurant. At the Ship-A-Shore I worked mostly in the kitchen, washing dishes and doing prep work for the line cook. After a short time on the job, the manager asked if I wanted to bus tables. I was happy to do so, especially after learning that bus persons usually received a cut of the waiter's tip at the end of the shift. I remember being nervous during my first weeks on the floor. I feared not the work, but my inability to understand the customers. My recourse was to observe every move the waiters made and to memorize the sequence they followed from greeting the customers to refilling their last cup of coffee just before handing them the bill. On one occasion, a customer asked me for a bottle of ketchup. I heard the customer's request, but could not understand what he wanted. My face turned red, like a hot copper skillet, making it impossible for me to hide my embarrassment. I left quickly, unable to utter an answer. I passed by his table for a second time, hoping that somebody else had delivered the condiment. I was wrong. He asked again for the undelivered good, and I again ignored his request. Annoyed by the lack of response, he asked Luis, the other bus person working that shift, for the ketchup and complained about my aloofness and unprofessional behavior. Luis, knowing perfectly well that my lack of response was not intentional but probably due to my inability to understand his request, scolded the man, telling him that I was hard of hearing. The customer, feeling guilty, retracted his judgment, and proceeded to inhale his open-face sandwich. Luis went straight to the kitchen to tell me what had just taken place. We laughed, snapped our fingers, and were back on the floor in no time.

The routine of my days kept me content for a while. From time to time, I would retrace the now familiar steps to Washington Park for a moment of solitude. To my surprise, the city below looked and felt different, however. The smell of wet grass replaced the crisp, delicate scent of the dogwood tree next to my favorite bench. Rattling leaves muted the birds and butterflies. The clouds were so close that I almost touched them. Magically, their wings moved back and forth, spreading a fine mist against the dark, gray skies. I was so taken by how nature had transformed itself that I could hardly recognize that place. But then again, I sometimes could hardly recognize myself. The changes had been so many that I wondered what aspect of myself had not changed. I felt hardened by my experiences and puzzled by the realization that there was no turning back. And when sadness, loneliness, and disdain came knocking, I reminded myself that survival is the greatest revenge.

With my eyes closed, I felt a drop of rain bounce against my forehead. The skies had turned even darker, and the gentle mist which a few minutes ago caressed the falling leaves now pierced the earth with purpose and intensity. Before leaving the park, I took a second look at the city below: I knew exactly where I was going. I had been touched by my own vigilance and realized that I had lost myself in a solitude so deep that I felt like a stranger to this world. I did not forget my past, but my behavior defied the ideals of a life that no longer existed.

I have become my own creation. I am the product of different cultures, but I resemble none in its entirety. I experience life differently according to the cultures that define who I am. As an American, I appreciate the beauty of life from a distance, never touching it; as a Brazilian and Puerto Rican I live that beauty.

I have used my time in the United States to create a space where I can confront and reshape my own being. Racism has kept me from embracing American culture. Privileged people around me have been quite at home in their roles: they have not been aware of their own racism, ignorance, selfishness, and greed. The difficulty has been to deal with the ugliness of racism without stepping on myself.

My reluctance to embrace life in America gave me the freedom to probe into anxieties hidden where others could not see. This freedom allowed me to remake myself—as a Latino and as a man. As I began to face my own identities, I discovered a seductive desire for dominance and power which I shared with other men, here and elsewhere. This dominance was both passive and active, loving and brutal, obvious and sometimes carefully disguised under the mantle of tradition. At first, I was afraid to question it, since that meant questioning my own masculinity. I understood however that one's integrity is no greater than the number of compromises one makes with one's self. Over the years I have begun to realize that neither power nor masculinity is a precondition for self-actualization. I felt intensely elated by this realization. I wanted life, a whole life. I was first a boy, then a man, anchored to Latino culture who was not self-reflexive. Now I am a Latino man willing to take it all apart. I have come full circle and found myself at home again.

Note

1   The quote in the chapter title is from *Poetic Works*, 1907, by Matthew Arnold. London: Macmillan.

22

Playing the Devil's Advocate
Defending a Multiracial Identity in Fractured Community

Sarah Willie

Conundrum

Neither the life of an individual nor the history of a society can be understood without understanding both.

C.Wright Mills, *The Sociological Imagination*

As a multiracial person with Black African ancestry, I spend a great deal of time and energy either defending my right to identify with the category Black or my right not to identify with the category Black.[1] I often feel like I'm playing the devil's advocate, making one argument in one setting and another argument in another setting. Playing the devil's advocate, though, usually suggests a certain detachment from or disinterestedness in either side of any argument. To the contrary, my interests are vested and I often feel as if I am participating in some bizarre courtroom scene in which at any moment either the prosecutor or the defense attorney might call out "Objection!" to my very existence and the jury will find me "Guilty."

This is no paranoiac fantasy, as Lise Funderburg, author of *Black, White, Other* (1994), explains: "One way people of mixed race have been pathologized is by looking at this shifting of identity as an inability to adjust, to reconcile." Her interviewer agrees: "[T]his is a group seen as aberrant—aberrant psychologically, aberrant legally."[2]

For me, this shifting of identity has been most obvious during three moments in my own life that have informed my thinking on what it means to be a multiracial person in the United States. They are moments that have challenged me to be more conscious about learning from, living in, and creating community. They are moments that have made me aware that we live in an embarrassed and embarrassingly racialized country, a country sorely in need of communal fellowship.

Longing

[E]very Black person with White ancestry should, no matter how they came by it, own it. That is not a rejection of African American identity, but an affirmation of the complex ancestry that defines us as an ethnic group. It will normalize what is erroneously treated as . . . exotic and, consequently, divisive. . . .

Itabari Njeri, *Lure and Loathing*

My good friend and colleague, philosopher Darrell Moore, began an Afro-roundtable while we were in graduate school at Northwestern. Black graduate students from Northwestern and occasionally from Loyola, Illinois Circle, DePaul, and the University of Chicago met once every week or two at a café or someone's home to read and discuss Black scholarship that pertained to the lives of African Americans. I feel like I fought in that group for my right to embrace my multicultural heritage. At the Afro-roundtable I wanted to be a biracial person who identified as Black; I wanted to suggest that I could raise my children as Black *regardless* of their color or the color of their father. I wanted to insist on an understanding of Black as a political identity.[3] And when a couple of my colleagues in that group were willing to concede that there were some hip enough white people who it would be okay to spend our lives with, I found myself wanting to scream "It's not a question of being 'hip enough'! Black is a legacy that we *all* share in this country. No one in such a racialized society is exempt." Instead, I ended up tearfully invoking the successful interracial marriage of my parents who, I insisted, were not "hip," according to my friends' definition.

What I was unable to articulate then was that some questions cannot be resolved simply by analyzing our racial categories, although that is a terribly important aspect of the process. Some questions are only answerable and some relationships are only possible by working long and hard at them—whether the relationships or the questions are between friends or lovers, between co-workers, students, or teachers. Against the backdrop and within the context of a deeply troubled history, I see no other alternative.

I am descended from Black people, I care about Black people, I identify with Black people. I choose to acknowledge my European heritage (which is as close as my mother, my grandmother, my aunt, uncle, and my cousins). I fantasized about standing up in one of those Chicago coffee houses and warning my Black comrades in the Afro-Roundtable: "Do not condescend to me. Do not donate your acceptance." But next to this fantasy in which I "taught" my friends what I thought Black should mean, I also wanted to be fully accepted as an authentic Black person by them.

The fact that I look colored and get treated correspondingly is a status that I did not choose. That is the sense in which I have been chosen, against my will. But I also choose Black people—choose to stand on behalf of Black people, with Black people, as a Black person, not half a Black person—and that decision, I want to argue, has less to do with my color than with my politics.

I believe that anyone (even if you think you're White) can choose to stand on behalf of Black people, with Black people, as a Black person. This is not encouragement to go out and misrepresent oneself or to dis-acknowledge the privilege that one's society or school or company of friends affords one. The good news, however, is that anyone can choose to suffer the consequences and partake of the joys of identifying with Black people or other misrepresented, marginalized, and disenfranchised people.

Oxymoron

When the census taker, a woman of African descent, skin the color of coffee-no-cream, came to my door with twelve-inch extensions in her hair and glow-in-the-dark blue contact lenses, I looked into the face of my sister.

"I sent it in," I said, referring to the census form.

She didn't believe me. She did not ask me my racial background but checked off the box next to Black American/African American/Afro-Caribbean/Black African. Having checked that same box myself when I mailed my census form in, this time I hesitated.

"Will this invalidate my previous form?" I asked.

Her mouth said it would. But my powers of telepathy heard her mind ask, "What does this annoying girlfriend do for a living?"

I agreed to satisfy her request and answered, for the second time, the census questions. Having checked the box marked Black American/African American/Afro-Caribbean/Black African when I mailed my census form in, this time I met her eyes and said, "I'm not Black; I'm Other, Mixed, Black and White." Her pupils, fixed by the contact lenses, neither expanded nor contracted, she did not smile, smirk, or frown, but checked the box marked "Other," and lifted her eyes quickly to mine again. I wanted to see her erase "Black." She did not do so in my presence. Pre-occupied with self, my telepathic ability had instantly evaporated and I could not read her. She thanked me. But the price of my self-definition had been the wall I felt I'd built between us before I ever closed the door.

I had been focused on my personal freedom, on my right to define who I am, on my responsibility to my sense of self. The dignity of the census taker was not a part of my mental equation. "But the census isn't about the census takers," a friend said to me. Oh, but it is. And what we do with that knowledge requires vigilant thoughtfulness.

Dehydration

To acknowledge our dreams is to sometimes acknowledge the distance between those dreams and our present situation.

Audre Lorde, *Sister Outsider*

I moved to Chicago for graduate school. "University of . . . ?" my East Coast acquaintances often asked. I did not tell them that I had turned down "University of" for Northwestern. It was hard enough to explain why I'd forfeited authentic Ivies. My reasons did not fit neatly into popular categories like "fear of success" or "fear of failure." I don't know if they would have understood what was for me a choice of a better fit over the status of the Midwest's most prestigious institution of higher education.

I do know that I never felt at home in Chicago. It lacked aspects of what I had come to define as East Coast culture that I identified as nutritional to my emotional health. The city lacked a pace and style that I wanted from a place of its size. When I went downtown, I longed to see high fashion and perversity—women in high-heeled shoes or bizarre hats, men in double-breasted suits or dredlocks, teenagers with black lipstick and safety pins through their noses. What I saw were lots of regular working people who dressed conservatively and looked tired.

But I think what bothered me most about Chicago was the severe segregation of the city— the almost all-Black South Side and the nearly all-White North Side. Relatives of mine lived in one of the northern suburbs. I always used to feel like I needed to show my identification papers when I entered my aunt's favorite supermarket in Wilmette, invariably the only non-white shopper.

For three of my five years in the area I lived in Evanston, a heterogeneous suburb that lay between Chicago and some of the wealthiest suburban towns in the country. Black, White, a few Chicano and Asian American families lived in Evanston. Granted, most of the white kids had parents who taught at the university and most of the Black kids had parents who cleaned it up. But I remember feeling right at home with my could-be-Chicana-could-be-Black looks in the Evanston supermarkets: none of the hypervisibility I experienced in the supermarket just twenty minutes north.

I don't know why the apartheid nature of most of American society hadn't seemed as apparent to me before I moved to Chicago. Maybe I was reaching new consciousness as I came out of adolescence. Maybe it was living in a city for the first time. Maybe it was this particular phase in my life that I now refer to as "the wilderness years." Maybe it was the fact that Chicago continues to be one of the most segregated cities in the country.

In any case, I found myself in one of Evanston's what-a-relief-to-be-anonymous grocery stores one day, not thinking about much, as the cashier was checking out my groceries. I was wearing my college sweatshirt. I had worried over its purchase. I wondered at my own motivations for wanting one, especially since I had left college ambivalent about the place. Was wanting to wear the name of my college a simple desire to show institutional affiliation or was it answering some deeper insecurity about my own worth by proclaiming to others where I'd gone to college, indeed, simply, *that* I'd gone to college? I had not come up with an answer, but I had bought the sweatshirt.

The bag boy, perhaps fifteen or sixteen, smiled at me sheepishly. He was dark brown skinned, coffee bean brown. His packing of my paper grocery bag slowed as he sounded out the letters across my chest. With a mix of incredulity and admiration, he stuttered, "D-d-d-you r-r-really g-g-go to H-h-harvard?" In that moment, I wished with everything inside me—with every choice I'd ever made for me and not The Race, that I had gone to Harvard. That I could say to that boy, "sister done made good." That I could say, with assurance for the possibility, the probability that WE WILL ALL OVERCOME TOGETHER: "I'm proof of that beginning!" That he should be proud of himself. That he could be proud of me. That the world was getting fairer. In that naked, bloated moment, filled with grandiosity and self-loathing, I wanted to be she who would wipe out any doubt in his mind that people like us are not on the move. I wanted to have gone to Harvard for him.

"No," I said. "Haverford; it's a different college." And then and there in the anguish of my answer, I began to drown. I wanted to drop my groceries, find out how he was doing in school, make sure that he went on to college. I was ready to make promises I couldn't keep, and I knew I wanted to dis-acknowledge all the privilege that had brought me to that place. I wanted the hard work alone to have made my life what it was, and I wanted to have chosen differently than I did.

He nodded. I don't know what was going on behind those dark eyes. But I do know that, paying for my groceries, I was going under.

"Shields Up, Mr. Worf"

I am not african. Africa is in me, but I cannot return. . . . I am not european. Europe lives in me, but I have no home there. I am new. History made me. . . . I was born at the crossroads and I am whole.
Rosario Morales, *This Bridge Called My Back*

A defense of a multiracial identity is complicated because it entails simultaneously embracing community and individuality in a society where people tend to see that goal as two discrete goals, oppositional and conflictual. While I affirm that piece of myself and my heritage that has been devalued and degraded as well as the foremothers and forefathers who persevered and triumphed, I also acknowledge and celebrate the heritage of the European American foremothers and forefathers who persevered and triumphed in sometimes similar and sometimes different ways. And I celebrate the particularity of my explicitly multiracial experience.

That is not easy to do without appearing to many people as if I am at odds with my own identity, unable to celebrate fully the uniqueness of my particularity. While I celebrate that uniqueness, I live and write in a time when racism against people of color continues. While this reality affects the quality and purpose of all of our lives, it affects our lives differently; it has different implications for the choices we will make and how those choices will be received. My brothers and sisters who do not identify as multiracial can, as Funderburg argues, "always retreat to, or perhaps take comfort in, their monoracial identity."[4] They need not confront the assumptions of racial separateness that are so taken for granted in order simply to affirm their sense of self.

One of my choices is to embrace the label that I cannot escape. That might seem to be an obvious and inescapable choice; it is not. The pathos-evoking and confused works of scholars of color like Shelby Steele, Stephen Carter, Glenn Loury, and Dinesh D'Souza are testaments to the range of responses, including self-hatred, that we can make in defining ourselves and others in a racist society.

Relationship and Ideology

The reason that each of the autobiographical moments I told above is important to me is that, with each of them, I gained a new knowledge, sometimes about the larger world, sometimes about my own situation, sometimes about my scholarship. The kind of thinking that I was forced to do in confronting the implications that race has for me and those around me *could not be done in isolation.* The step of admitting and seeking to understand the ways in which we are shaped by and shape others is crucial. If it is skipped, we remain unable to be in healthy relationships with others, unable to be clear with ourselves, unable to change, and are trapped by a false sense of history, of present, and of possibility that will not cease to haunt us.

Relationship is, at the same time, not exempt from ideological distortion. Racial ideologies can be mutual and complementary, affecting our lives so completely that we are virtually unaware of them. I want to demonstrate one of the frustrating ways in which I am constantly reminded of my relationship to others within the context of a racial ideology. It is an ideology based on assumptions that I may not be able to escape but also one I choose not to embrace.

In college and graduate school, several of my professors and classmates reminded me that I had been dependent on others for admission to school, for the receipt of fellowships and research assistantships, and even dependent upon others for friendship. They were not in error, but neither was their characterization complete. Now that I have a job, many of my students and colleagues continue to remind me of my utter dependence on them even as they construct situations in which I am apt to show approval and acceptance of them for my own political survival.

The fact that I am reminded of my "dependence" has everything to do with my being African American and female. I cannot get into school, get a job, or win a friend on my own. I must be donated one, allowed one, pitied one. In fact, finding a lover has for too long been one of the only areas of personal agency that Black women have been given 'credit' for and that is largely because of the myths of our insatiable and animalistic lust. Those are the messages all around all of us, directed at some of us. There is a profound and nearly unshakable belief in this country that Black people, especially Black women, cannot do it on our own. I refer to this belief as ideology.

This belief has convinced many people that I am unable to exist without the will of the government. It will be supporting me in some capacity, whether by "giving" me welfare, forcing schools to admit me, or threatening organizations into hiring me. And the ideology that explains the "generosity," for which I am supposed to be grateful and somewhat ashamed, is the same ideology that explains my "neediness" and "dependence." And all of this rests on the categorical assumption of Black female inferiority.

In this society, if I am, on the other hand, white and male, and especially if I am also straight, Protestant, and affluent, the message, of which I am constantly reminded, is that I am dependent on no one. I am admitted to school because I am smart; I am hired for a job because of my skill; I am paid my salary because I have earned it. I am responsible for everyone else. And the ideology that explains both my self-sufficiency and my decision to be either charitable or miserly rests on the categorical assumption of white male superiority.

What is so dangerous about this particular ideology of dependence and independence is that it denies the complexity of reality for each of us. If I am the Black woman, it steals from me the ownership that I would claim over my own life, decisions, ideas, and skills. My accomplishments might include feeding my family, deciding to take back the options in my life by having an abortion, supporting my parents while attending community college, prostituting myself in order to pay for my mother's medication, enforcing an unpopular law from my seat on the bench as a Superior Court judge, working hard on a paper for my high school English class, advising the President on health care policy, or adopting a child. However, this particular race/sex ideology of dependence encourages all of us to see those accomplishments as always and only dependent on the generosity or pity of others. And that interpretation is an affront to my personal dignity, destructive to community, and terribly inaccurate.

If I am a white man, the ideology requires from me a level of ownership that gives me a false sense of my own power and sets me up for failure. My accomplishments might also include feeding my family, deciding to take back the options in my life by taking a G.E.D. course, supporting my parents while attending community college, enforcing an unpopular law from my seat on the Circuit Court, working hard on a paper for my English class, advising the President on health care policy, or adopting a child. However, this particular race/sex ideology of independence encourages all of us to see those accomplishments as always and only the result of self-discipline, individual merit, and natural stamina. Such an interpretation misrepresents my need for community, undermines my personal ability to cope, and constructs ideals that are painfully unattainable and can lead to self-destruction, abuse of others, and general arrogance.

Faith

> [T]ruth-telling . . . requires us to relinquish our habitual, patterned modes of reaction and thought, so that we can move toward an expanded vision of reality that is multilayered, complex, inclusive, and accurate. . . . [It] requires us to be in conversation with other[s] . . . similar to and radically different from ourselves.
>
> Harriet Goldhor Lerner, *The Dance of Deception*

In searching to define and identify ourselves and tell our truths, we must embrace the complexity of our selves and our lives. One of the ways to do that is to face the complexity *outside* of ourselves. As we look into the mirror that our fellow travellers provide with their very difference, I believe we can begin to accept the complexity in our own lives by accepting the differences in others. Funderburg reminds me that I do not have to defend my role as devil's advocate, that identity with multiple bases is not the same as multiple personality disorder:

> . . . [H]aving to choose between black and white is like asking you to choose between being African-American and being a woman. They're not mutually exclusive. People's shifting identity can be a very healthy response. . . [5]

Embracing complexity is part of the process. In addition, being responsible world citizens includes taking responsibility for our decisions, well made and poorly made. When they are poorly made, taking responsibility means apologizing, asking forgiveness, making reparation, starting over, moving on, and being open to different ways of doing things. When they are well made, taking responsibility includes wearing those well-made choices and well-thought-out ideas with dignity, style, humility, and grace, especially if the category of people to which we belong has been systematically humiliated. Taking responsibility also includes claiming our continual need for relation with others, especially if the category of people to which we belong has been systematically expected to shun intimacy and prioritize independence. These are difficult things to do alone. That's why we need to seek out those people who give the concepts of dignity, style, humility, and grace meaning for us by their presence in our lives, by the way they take responsibility for us, the way they boost us up, or calm us down, by the way they listen to our fears, bring us cookies, celebrate our triumphs, and hold us through the darkness.

Notes

1   I also recognize my right to identify with the category White. I have not, however, expended much energy defending that right. That such an argument would seem absurd to many is a testament that ours is not yet so post-modern a society that any one of us can choose our racial or ethnic labels. Rather we continue to struggle in the transition between the now and the yet-to-come with color still very much on the collective mind and choice allowed to those with lighter rather than darker skin.

2   Margo Jefferson. "A Spy in the House of Race: Interview with Lise Funderburg," author of *Black, White, Other: Biracial Americans Talk About Race*, in *Glamour Magazine*, May: 1994, pp. 74, 76.

3   Avtar Brah. "Difference, diversity and differentiation," in James Donald and Ali Rattansi, eds. *'Race', Culture and Difference*, (Newbury Park, Calif.: Sage, 1992), pp. 126-148.

4   Jefferson. "A Spy in the House of Race," p. 78.

5   Ibid., p. 74.

23

Black Women and the Wilderness

Evelyn C. White

I wanted to sit outside and listen to the roar of the ocean, but I was afraid.
I wanted to walk through the redwoods, but I was afraid.
I wanted to glide in a kayak and feel the cool water splash in my face, but I was afraid.

For me, the fear is like a heartbeat, always present, while at the same time intangible, elusive, and difficult to define. So pervasive, so much a part of me, that I hardly knew it was there.

In fact, I wasn't fully aware of my troubled feelings about nature until I was invited to teach at a women's writing workshop held each summer on the McKenzie River in the foothills of Oregon's Cascade Mountains. I was invited to "Flight of the Mind" by a Seattle writer and her friend, a poet who had moved from her native England to Oregon many years before. Both committed feminists, they asked me to teach because they believe as I do, that language and literature transcend the man-made boundaries that are too often placed upon them. I welcomed and appreciated their interest in me and my work.

Once I got there, I did not welcome the steady stream of invitations to explore the great outdoors. It seemed as though the minute I finished my teaching duties, I'd be faced with a student or fellow faculty member clamoring for me to trek to the lava beds, soak in the hotsprings, or hike into the mountains that loomed over the site like white-capped security guards. I claimed fatigue, a backlog of class work, concern about "proper" student/teacher relations; whatever the excuse, I always declined to join the expeditions into the woods. When I wasn't teaching, eating in the dining hall, or attending our evening readings, I stayed holed up in my riverfront cabin with all doors locked and window shades drawn. While the river's roar gave me a certain comfort and my heart warmed when I gazed at the sun-dappled trees out of a classroom window, I didn't want to get closer. I was certain that if I ventured outside to admire a meadow or to feel the cool ripples in a stream, I'd be taunted, attacked, raped, maybe even murdered because of the color of my skin.

I believe the fear I experience in the outdoors is shared by many African-American women and that it limits the way we move through the world and colors the decisions we make about our lives. For instance, for several years now I have been thinking about moving out of the city to a wooded, vineyard-laden area in Northern California. It is there, among the birds, creeks, and trees that I long to settle down and make a home. Each house-hunting trip I have made to the countryside has been fraught with emotions: elation at the prospect of living closer to nature and a sense of absolute doom about what might befall me in the backwoods. My genetic memory of ancestors hunted down and preyed upon in rural settings counters my fervent hopes of finding peace in the wilderness. Instead of the solace and comfort I seek, I imagine myself in the country as my forbears were—exposed, vulnerable, and unprotected—a target of cruelty and hate.

I am certain that the terror I felt in my Oregon cabin is directly linked to my memory of September 15, 1963. On that day, Denise McNair, Addie Mae Collins, Cynthia Wesley, and Carol Robertson were sitting in their Sunday school class at the Sixteenth Street Church in Birmingham, Alabama. Before the bright-eyed Black girls could deliver the speeches they had prepared for the church's annual Youth Day program, a bomb planted by racists flattened the building, killing them all. In Black households throughout the nation, families grieved for the martyred children and expressed their outrage at whites who seemed to have no limits on the depths they would sink to in their ultimately futile effort to curtail the Civil Rights Movement.

To protest the Birmingham bombing and to show solidarity with the struggles in the South, my mother bought a spool of black cotton ribbon which she fashioned into armbands for me and my siblings to wear to school the next day. Nine-years-old at the time, I remember standing in my house in Gary, Indiana and watching in horror as my mother ironed the black fabric that, in my mind, would align me with the bloody dresses, limbless bodies, and dust-covered patent leather shoes that had been entombed in the blast.

The next morning, I put on my favorite school dress—a V-necked cranberry jumper with a matching cranberry-and-white pin-striped shirt. Motionless, I stared stoically straight ahead as my mother leaned down and pinned the black ribbon around my right sleeve shortly before I left the house.

As soon as I rounded the corner at the end of our street I ripped the ribbon off my arm, looking nervously up into the sky for the "evil white people" I'd heard my parents talk about in the aftermath of the bombing. I feared that if I wore the armband I'd be blown to bits like the Black girls who were at that moment rotting under the rubble. Thirty years later, I know that another part of my "defense strategy" that day was to wear the outfit that had always garnered me compliments from teachers and friends. "Don't drop a bomb on me," was the message I was desperately trying to convey through my cranberry jumper. "I'm a pretty Black girl. Not like the ones at the church."

The sense of vulnerability and exposure that I felt in the wake of the Birmingham bombing was compounded by feelings that I already had about Emmett Till. Emmett was a rambunctious, fourteen-year-old Black boy from Chicago, who in 1955 was sent to rural Mississippi to enjoy the pleasures of summer with relatives. Emmett was delivered home in a pine box long before season's end, bloated and battered beyond recognition. He had been lynched and dumped in the Tallahatchie River, with the rope still dangling around his neck, for allegedly whistling at a white woman at a country store.

During those summers in Oregon when I walked past the country store where thick-necked loggers drank beer while leaning on their big-rig trucks, it seemed like Emmett's fate had been a part of my identity from birth. Averting my eyes from those of the loggers. I'd remember the ghoulish photos of Emmett I had seen in *JET* magazine with my childhood friends Tyrone and Lynette Henry. The Henrys subscribed to *JET*, an inexpensive magazine for Blacks, and kept each issue neatly filed on the top shelf of a bookcase in their living room. Among Black parents, the *JET* with Emmett's story was always carefully handled and treated like one of the most valuable treasures on earth. For within its page rested an important lesson they felt duty-bound to teach their children: how little white society valued our lives.

Mesmerized by Emmett's monstrous face, Lynette, Tyrone, and I would drag a flower-patterned vinyl chair from the kitchen, take the Emmett *JET* from the bookcase and spirit to a back bedroom where we played. Heads together, bellies on the floor as if we were shooting marbles or scribbling in our coloring books, we'd silently gaze at Emmett's photo for what seemed like hours before returning it to its sacred place. As with thousands of Black children from that era, Emmett's murder cast a nightmarish pall over my youth. In his pummeled and contorted face I saw a reflection of myself and the blood-chilling violence that would greet me if I ever dared to venture into the wilderness.

I grew up. I went to college. I traveled abroad. Still, thoughts of Emmett Till could leave me speechless and paralyzed with the heart-stopping fear that swept over me when I crossed paths with loggers near the McKenzie River or whenever I visited the outdoors. His death seemed to be summed up in the prophetic warning of writer Alice Walker, herself a native of rural Georgia: "Never be the only one, except, possibly, in your own house."

For several Oregon summers, I concealed my pained feelings about the outdoors until I could no longer reconcile my silence with my mandate to my students to face their fears. They found the courage to write openly about incest, poverty, and other ills that had constricted their lives: how could I turn away from my fears about being in nature?

But the one time I had attempted to be as bold as my students, I had been faced with an unsettling incident. Legend had it that the source of the McKenzie was a tiny trickle of water that bubbled up from a pocket in a nearby lake. Intrigued by the local lore, two other Flight teachers and a staffperson, all white women, invited me to join them on an excursion to the lake. The plan was to rent rowboats and paddle around the lake Sacajawea-style, until we, brave and undaunted women, "discovered the source" of the mighty river. As we approached the lake, we could see dozens of rowboats tied to the dock. We had barely begun our inquiry about renting one when the boathouse man interrupted and tersely announced: "No boats."

We stood shocked and surprised on a sun drenched dock with a vista of rowboats before us. No matter how much we insisted that our eyes belied his words, the man held fast to his two-note response: "No boats."

Distressed but determined to complete our mission, we set out on foot. As we trampled along the trail that circled the lake we tried to make sense of our "Twilight Zone" encounter. We laughed and joked about the incident and it ultimately drifted out of our thoughts in our jubilation at finding the gurgling bubble that gave birth to the McKenzie. Yet I always felt that our triumph was undermined by a searing question that went unvoiced that day: Had we been denied the boat because our group included a Black?

In an effort to contain my fears, I forced myself to revisit the encounter and to re-examine my childhood wounds from the Birmingham bombing and the lynching of Emmett Till. I touched the terror of my Ibo and Ashanti ancestors as they were dragged from Africa and enslaved on southern plantations. I conjured bloodhounds, burning crosses and white-robed Klansmen hunting down people who looked just like me. I imagined myself being captured in a swampy backwater, my back ripped open and bloodied by the whip's lash. I cradled an ancestral mother, broken and keening, as her baby was snatched from her arms and sold down the river.

Every year, the "Flight of the Mind" workshop offers a rafting trip on the McKenzie River. Each day we'd watch as flotillas of rafters, shrieking excitedly and with their oars held aloft rumbled by the deck where students and teachers routinely gathered. While I always cheered their adventuresome spirit, I never joined the group of Flight women who took the trip. I was always mindful that I had never seen one Black person in any of those boats.

Determined to reconnect myself to the comfort my African ancestors felt in the rift valleys of Kenya and on the shores of Sierra Leone, I eventually decided to go on a rafting trip. Familiar with my feelings about nature, Judith, a dear friend and workshop founder, offered to be one of my raftmates. With her sturdy, gentle, and wise body as my anchor, I lowered myself into a raft at the bank of the river. As we pushed off into the current, I felt myself make an unsure but authentic shift from my painful past.

At first the water was calm—nearly hypnotic in its pristine tranquillity. Then we met the rapids, sometimes swirling, other times jolting us forward like a runaway roller coaster. The guide roared out commands, "Highside! All forward! All back!" To my amazement, I responded. Periodically, my brown eyes would meet Judith's steady aquamarine gaze and we'd smile at each other as the cool water splashed in our faces and shimmered like diamonds in our hair.

Charging over the river, orange life vest firmly secured, my breathing relaxed and I allowed myself to drink in the stately rocks, soaring birds, towering trees, and affirming anglers who waved their rods as we rushed by in our raft. About an hour into the trip, in a magnificently still moment, I looked up into the heavens and heard the voice of Black poet Langston Hughes:

> I've known rivers ancient as the world and older than the flow of human blood in human veins. . . .
> My soul has grown deep like the rivers.[1]

Soaking wet and shivering with emotion, I felt tears welling in my eyes as I stepped out of the raft onto solid ground. Like my African forbears who survived the Middle Passage, I was stronger at journey's end.

Since that voyage, I have stayed at country farms, napped on secluded beaches, and taken wilderness treks, all in an effort to find peace in the outdoors. No matter where I travel, I will always carry Emmett Till and the four Black girls whose death affected me so. But comforted by our tribal ancestors—herders, gatherers, and fishers all—I am less fearful, ready to come home.

Note

1   Langston Hughes. 1959. *Selected Poems of Langston Hughes*. NY: Knopf. p.4.

24

Toward the Light

Vickie Sears

L ife is a circle—a harmony. Sometimes we grow out of balance within that circle. My task is always to move back toward balance—to go toward the light, to be whole and in harmony. I begin this essay by describing what has disrupted harmony in my life and then I work my way toward how my life is now, within a circle of light.

One of my first memories is of my white/pink mother leaning over the crib and saying to my brother, "You'll be all right. You're only half Indian." It was not her words as much as their desperate sound that let me know that "Indian" was "bad." I shared my crib with my brother, who was ten months younger than I. Until my mother's statement, it had not been a "truth" to me that "Indians" were "bad brown." "Brown and bad" became a phrase my half-Spanish half-English mother spoke often during my earliest years.

While I was growing up, my mother frequently explained that her Spanish heritage was Castilian rather than the "wetback trash" of the people down the road. I had seen my father, a full blood Tsalagi (Cherokee), laugh with flat eyes or look to the ground when fellow soldiers called him "chief." I knew that he had never seen a horse before joining the Army and that he did not like the soldiers' notion that the cavalry was the proper place for Indians. I was also very aware that my mother preferred my chubby, rose-cheeked brother over me. She had very little patience with my hazel-colored, eye-floating self. Today I can only speculate that her feelings reflected a combination of racism and sexism that had lasting effects.

My father taught my brother and me that we were equal to every plant, rock, animal, or human being. We all had spirits to which we should listen. Everything was important and interwoven. My mother praised individuality based on the idea that people must forge ahead to gain wealth and value. Value was not intrinsic in my mother's worldview as it was in my father's. My father's hands turned over rocks to show us new life, tickled us, and played his bugle. His hands pointed to things as he talked about their spirits. Our mother's hands disciplined, did not hug, or play.

She taught me to read, sang me "Chattanooga choo-choo," and read me books. Dad told us stories constantly that he mixed into everyday conversation. He sang songs that made my thoughts float away. Often, his stories had to do with his large extended family. My mother's family was smaller and included her grandmother, mother and father, a brother, and an Italian woman who had cared for my mother when she was growing up.

When I was four, my parents took me and my brother to a party which was loud and fun until I heard someone reciting the poem, "If you are white, you're right. If you're black, stay back. If you're red, you're dead." I took my brother from the room thinking I could protect him. Older children always help care for smaller ones in Native homes since this teaches responsibility and interdependence. I explained the poem to him in Spanish rather than in English or Cherokee, all of which we spoke. In my mind, Spanish was the right language for the moment since the poem had included nothing about killing Mexicans. We crept to our car to wait for our parents to return to the trailer we lived in along the California/Mexican border where my father rode patrol duty for the government. In my mind, I had done what I was supposed to do—I had taken care of my brother.

Our parents eventually came back to the car and everything seemed fine again. Life was in order. My brother and I were alive and in familiar hands. I watched the stars as we rode home, thinking about how the runaway dog spilling his stolen milk bowl had made the milky way. My grandmother, Elisi, had told me this story once when I had taken a penny from my mother's purse. It was an important story about how people's behavior has consequences. My brother slept with his head on my lap. On the car ride home I dreamt about being in safe hands, not knowing that the hands of my two totally opposite parents were about to drop us children.

When World War II ended and my father was discharged from the army, we moved to the Pacific Northwest where my mother had lived prior to her marriage. My father transplanted his family—his twenty-six relations—to live by my mother's family. All of his family eventually settled within a four block area of each other. The crucial extended family structure was reshaped as it had been when I was younger. During those years, I knew that willing hands were just a walk up the hill from my house. My maternal grandfather lived with his new wife, a Suguamish woman, on a nearby reservation. My mother's family were blue collar workers, lived apart from each other, and spent little time together. My mother's family read but only my mother had gone to high school. My father's family was also working-class but they did not read and none of them had gone past junior high school. When my maternal relatives read, they did so silently. My father's folks talked stories, constantly. Between my mother's family and my father's extended family, I grew up amid people of thirty-four different racial and ethnic identities who spoke Cherokee, English, Spanish, or a combination of these languages. I learned early about classism and the difficulties brown people face as they look for work and places to live. That's another reason the safe hands began to slip open.

As time went on, our parents fought with greater frequency. My father drank more and stayed with his family more often. My mother began to go out dancing at night alone. At this point, my paternal grandmother, Elisi, became the cornerstone of my life. She had recently moved close to our home so we got to see her much more often than before. Her English consisted of "no," "maybe," and "outside" but she was an encyclopedia of smiles and stories. She taught my brother and me how to make baskets and pottery and took us on long walks. It was a total joy to live close to her. She was more huggable than my dad and warmer than my mother—a reality that was at the root of my mother's jealousy and racism. Soon, I began to hear my mother pepper our home with words like "heathen," "lazy," "savage squaw," and "camp follower." What had been a home started to feel like a house.

When my parents separated, white court workers came to the house and took me and my brother away to different locations. I had never been apart from my brother, had not gone off on my own before, and was not used to being with white people. Although my mother's family was white, I hadn't thought of them in that way. To me, they were just family. When I was taken away, the phrases "brown brat" and "red you're dead" kept scurrying through my mind. While my brother and I were still separated they asked us similar questions: "What do you think of your cousins having to share beds?" "What do you think about your daddy's drinking and your mother's dancing?" "Which church do you like best, the Catholic church or your father's superstitions?" And finally, "Which parent would you prefer to live with?"

Racism, classism, and Christian "righteousness" prevailed during the divorce proceedings. Both parents were declared unfit—our mother because of "moral turpitude," my father for being an alcoholic. Both of my parents were excoriated for being poorly educated, thus unable to adequately provide for our well-being. While our mother's fractured family had no one willing to take us into their homes, my father's extended family wanted to but were not allowed to do so. Government and academic records are filled with statements about Indians' poor child-rearing techniques. While I was not able to label the "isms" when I was five years old, I now know that classism and anti-Indian discrimination robbed my brother and me of a home.

I had already begun to learn how to armor myself in response to racial slurs that children threw in my direction and school policy that forced Indian and white children to play on separate playgrounds. But armoring became an entrenched and normal part of my life when the pain of the divorce and my separation from the family began. The courts made it clear how "horrid" Indians were but it was also clear that white folks didn't fare well either if they were poor or uneducated. In my child's mind my mother was "unfit" because she liked to dance, which I translated to mean that having any kind of fun was wicked. To me, social workers and judges did whatever they wanted with children and granted them no rights. The court decision called for immediate placement in the Juvenile Receiving Center followed by long term placement at the Washington Children's Home Society.

In front of the court house, I said goodbye to my father and Elisi. She said, "A nv da di s di" (remember). That word would wrap itself around me during many upheavals in the coming years. "A nv da di s di" became a prayer that floated in my heart. It would be five and a half years before I would see Elisi or my father's extended family again. As an adult I would come to learn that the destruction of our extended family, our main resource, was part of a widespread attack on Indian families by the United States government. Destroying the Indian family destroys the culture. In that way, my story is not unique. During the twenty-six years I have been a social worker, I have heard many stories, especially from First Americans, about individuals who were separated from their families. In my situation, however, the court's attempt to separate me from my family and culture did not work because, although my identity was fractured, the foundation of my identity had already been laid.

At the orphanage, the first loss was the falling of "heathen" hair to the swift shredding of shears. It was an uneven cut and a violation of my spirit. I had learned that one only cuts one's hair as a sign of a great change or grief. In my mind, this time away from my family was an aberration— an obvious error that I thought would soon end. Next, they put all of my clothing in a common cupboard. Then, the authorities paraded me around to the other children while saying, "This is the new 'brown brat' who has come to stay with us." I was viewed as different from the other children and a pariah. I felt like a failure because I hadn't been able to protect my brother from the same shaming treatment. The rest of our first day at the orphanage we huddled behind a tree and prayed that Elisi would find us to take us home. That night I was introduced to sex at the hands of the house matron. This violation led me to distrust women, especially authority figures, and I would have to work hard to overcome my fears as an adult. After the matron's violation, I had great difficulty being able to go to sleep at night. For years, the night was my friend only when I was awake.

Both my brother and I were abused sexually and spiritually. When we were caught speaking Cherokee our ears were boxed. We spoke in secret. I told him stories. I sang silent songs to myself. Within a year my brother had lost most of our language. By the end of the next year, I could remember only "A nv da di s di," a few stories, and some prayers. I'd tell myself a story or sing a prayer every day as a way to find beauty and harmony. In the field behind the buildings I tried to remember the use of plants, but soon instead of "a tsi na," I would say the name "Cedar" which is not nearly as musical a sound. I became a failure to myself because I could not "remember," yet I kept singing even as the pain of the initial losses joined with shame. Internalized oppression became my reality—first came pain, then an injured perception of myself.

By this time in my life, I had already developed several "inner children"—other selves who dealt with the difficult experiences I faced. In retrospect, developing multiple selves, or dissociative identities, is quite an amazing coping technique and a way to stay within a growing circle of caring. It is almost like creating an extended family. Since my earliest ethnic identity was most strongly formed by my father and paternal grandmother, the early "inner children" retained their stories and identities. As is true about the extended family of my early years, my "inner children" saved my ethnic/cultural identity and became the weave in my circle.

At the orphanage, I began to hide in the library by sliding down into the "L" where two couches met. Snug in the silence of the seldom-used room, I stumbled onto the works of E. Pauline Johnson and Charles Eastman, First American writers, and the poems of the Bronte children. The first two writers let me know that there was goodness in being "Indian." The Bronte's work taught me that others knew about isolation. Those books were lights for me. Word magic became beauty and continuity for me. Books became my solace—another heart bloom to grow with the word "remember." I wanted to write—to be a storyteller—to shine Elisi's joy and share her practical wonderment about living in the world in union with all things. The land had become a constancy for me that always had magic and beauty to keep me moving forward. Writing became a way for me to describe it.

When I came across the work of Laura Ingalls Wilder, a Western Anglo-American writer, I felt conflicted about reading and books for the first time. In her writing about the prairie winds she referred to the same intimacy with the land that my father had spoken about. But her racism clouded her writing. Up to this point, I seldom believed people who talked to me but, in my mind, books had been sacred. After reading Wilder I never quite read books with the same fascination and abandonment I had before. I still read voraciously, but I was less trusting.

Every week we were taken to a different church for an eclectic spiritual experience. Mass was familiar but there were no corn songs anywhere. I felt I was a failure at religion. I thought something was wrong with me since I didn't feel satisfied at any of the churches. I waited for the wind to echo Elisi's corn songs. My brother ran with no old songs inside. I stopped wanting to talk. By the time I was seven years old, I had begun to steal the house matron's alcohol. It was gut-wrenching to know that I was too old to be adopted but strong enough to be sent to large homes of wealthy white people for spring or fall cleaning or to farms during planting and harvesting seasons. I grew to believe that wealthy people only took us "in" when they had a need and then sent us back when their need was gone. Farm life was just plain cruel and hard. With the exception of one Native foster home, each placement made an enormous issue of taking my brother and I—those "dark children," the "special needs cases." The pride of the Indian writers and the recollection of Elisi's fast-moving basket-weaving fingers were tarnished. Silence with alcohol became my spiritual masseuse. I lost the ability to see the faces of my parents, and, eventually, I could not see Elisi's face either.

My brother and I traversed the state from foster home to foster home. The homes were almost always of a different ethnic/cultural group than our own. Some were African American, one was

Japanese, one was German, and many were white. Finally, we were placed in a First American family in Walla Walla. Their home was ordinary and magical and reminded me in some ways of my father's family. We were never spanked or sexually abused. Living there was a blessing that cradled me for several years. We were returned to the orphanage after the man died and the authorities thought the woman was too old to care for us alone. But the similarities between that home and the gentleness of Elisi's loving added a layer of continuity to "remember" and they reminded me to follow the "good way" of my father and his family. The foster mother's name was Grace and she was that. I remember one early morning she showed me the sun's brightness on a wheat kernel and told me that it would change in the afternoon light. She said I was a part of that light and the wheat and that I must always let myself shine. I tucked her words away as protection against darkness and depression.

Right after returning to the orphanage, my brother disappeared without explanation. I did not see him again for two years, as he continued to go in and out of foster homes. When I was ten and a half, my dying father requested that I live with him. I was taken to his eldest sister's home not yet knowing that my father lived there, or that my brother had been placed in her guardianship two years before, or that Elisi lived next door. It was traumatic for me— a self-hating, scrawny, moody, distrustful and inordinately cautious child—to learn that my brother had been called home much earlier than I had. I became defiant, holding so much at arm's length that it is amazing that any of the caring that came my direction ever found a way inside.

My father was very ill with diabetes, which is still an epidemic among First Americans. But he was sober. He taught us again to listen to the spirits of all living things. Grandmother retaught me plants as I wrote down everything I could, which went against the long tradition of simply memorizing information. I did not trust that I would not lose her and the knowledge again.

Even though all of the learning and reconnection was amazing, another inner child or dissociative identity evolved who was revulsed by some of what was happening in my father's family—my two aunts' many marriages, the family's poor grammar and illiteracy, and even Elisi's burlap black medicine bags that she hung on nails on her walls. Not everything was magical anymore. Things seemed painfully real. I was expecting abandonment. My family saw me as very different from them, as a kid with my "head stuck in them books." I no longer knew how to have "fun" as it was "sinful" to me. I was reclusive and individualistic. As my conflicts grew so did the quantity of alcohol I consumed. One of my inner children, or alter identities as psychiatrists call them, hated me and began to gouge at cuts, fall from trees, and despise my father for being Native. One child could only soothe with alcohol. One child became very tough, stuffing every pain and tear inside. One wanted to be next to Elisi all of the time, folded into the safety of her consistency and warm body. Another punched my brother, jealous that he had gotten so much more than I had during the two years he had lived with our father. Reality, to me, was that I damned well didn't fit anywhere.

Within a year, my father became increasingly ill and I was returned to the orphanage. I accepted the fact that a child's lot was up to the whim of adults. To me, children were on hold until adulthood. Besides, what else would they have done, I reasoned, with a child who did not belong anywhere? I returned to the orphanage to sit up in the trees whenever I could. The trees loved me, rocked me, and sang to me.

After being at the orphanage for some time, I remember waiting on the steps of the front entrance with my suitcase. I had been told I was going to another home. A pregnant white woman passed me without speaking. Shortly, she emerged from the building and said, "let's go." I picked up the suitcase to follow her into a green car. I made no comments. I asked no questions. Fatalism had become a way of life.

When I began to unpack my suitcase at her home, she exploded about what she called my "heathen paraphernalia." Out went the rocks, feathers and plants. She shredded my notebook. I snuck everything away that I could. I refused to cry. I was forbidden to visit my father's family. Two months later, my father died. The woman I was staying with took out a photo album to show me right before the funeral. In it were pictures of my great-grandmother, my brother until age four, my father, and other family members, some of whom I knew and some whom I didn't. Among the photos was a picture of the woman I was staying with. It dawned on me that she might be my mother and so I asked her. Upon hearing my question, she slapped me in the face, which set the tone for our relationship.

I was allowed to attend my father's funeral but I did not see my brother again until his sixteenth birthday, four years later. He did not want to see me because he thought I had gotten a better deal by living with our mother. I wanted to say, "What I got was a home with no love, a babysitter for whom I am the primary caretaker." But I remembered my earlier jealousy about his being able to live with my father. I feel a great sadness that my brother and I have had minimal contact as adults. We both became alcoholics and are in recovery, but we have never been able to mend the rift that occurred between us. The governmental policies that separated us succeeded in destroying the richness of an extended family for my brother. I have used a piece of cultural goodness in myself to create a large chosen extended family. Friends are more than that—they are family.

Within my biological mother's and step-father's family, I learned another set of racist phrases and class attitudes. There were "rich assholes," "educated eggheads," "scabs," and a host of racial derogatives. There was an angry atmosphere of "us against them." People of color and anti-union "scum" were all out to "screw" or steal from the "working stiff." "Injuns" were "lazy dummies" who were too drunk and stupid to understand that they didn't own America "no more." The rest of "them" people "should have never come here no how." Amid these confusing messages evolved an inner child who believed that "everyone is out to get me." My coping tool was to leave the room to do some homework or write. Writing calmed me, although I constantly heard that I would not be able to live on "castles in the air."

I was beaten at school for being too dark. I faced conflicts as I was drawn toward girls rather than boys and was taunted about my visual disability. And there was a war inside me as all my "children" pushed to be their own people. Each wanted to see the world with individual eyes. I never talked about any of the conflicts. They all created shame inside me, and self-hatred. My effort to be in harmony then was to hide what I saw as deficiencies or abnormalities. I knew I could overcome everything if no one knew. I would smile through to the brightness of the world by writing, sitting in trees, listening to the wind, and watching birds.

During high school I began to sneak to the Indian Center. While the tribal influences were mostly from the Northwest, the Center felt familiar to me. It allowed me to listen quietly as my A da to da (father) had taught. I began to understand that my father and Elisi were the earliest and most important influences on my identities (my inner children) and how I felt in the world. The ways my mother influenced me while I was living with her during adolescence—including the humorless brittle anger that was part of her world view—were overlays on the softly spoken practical, less judgmental ways of my father. Even if things were difficult in my father's life, there was a sense of a delicate balance in the world and humor made all things more bearable. Humor is a major coping tool in First American cultures to deal with the violence and hostility in life. And humor provided continuity in my extended family, including my relationship with and responsibility to all fellow beings, two-legged and otherwise. Experiencing humor and gentleness did not squelch the conflicting voices inside of me; it was just the closest thing I knew to loving.

By the time I began attending college, I had become a paint-smeared, cut-off-at-the-arms-sweatshirt wearer who declared herself an artist, a supporter of civil rights, an antiwar demonstrator, and a socialist activist. I could talk street jive, spell the blue-collar union rap, and be a brilliant reclusive writer. All of it was me. None of it was me. It was my armoring and my struggle to find my true identity. I was also that "crazy Indian" with all the voices in my head that I could tell no one about because I knew I'd be hauled away to a "nut house." I looked and sounded like all the "flower children" of the 1960s. For me, though, it all seemed like "returning to the earth." "Flower power" was just doing things the "Indian" way. Earth communion was my cultural norm, so I was finally fitting into the Anglo and Indian world. I did belong. I was part of the circle, as I used my father's and Elisi's words and what I had learned at the Indian Center while in high school. And I thought I was being the self-actualizing individual my mother declared we needed to be. My cultural/ethnic, Indian/White selves were finally in union, living life as one person. I thought I had straddled the line.

It was the 1960s. Siddhartha, Mohammed, Nehru, Kennedy, Martin Luther King, and God were all alive and, as Leonard Cohen wrote, "magic was afoot." I led as monkish a life as possible while going to school, working, and trying out bold forms of self-expression through acting, painting, and writing. I added sweat lodges and other drugs to my drinking. But it all seemed to start to unravel one night when my poetry teacher said, "You'll never be a writer. Indians have no natural rhythm for poetry." I grew angry and sad. I had not straddled the cultural/ethnic line after all. I grew afraid of my dissociated selves with their claims that each had a distinct personality with separate traits and capabilities. Before, I had hidden the voices, and even, from time to time, denied them. So . . . what to do?

I began a long, healing journey in therapy. I studied with traditional teachers and learned everything I could about racism. I worked hard to "remember" the prayers, stories, and songs I had been taught. I struggled to leave behind all that did not feel like a good fit in my body, mind, or spirit. I retrieved a commitment to spiritual practice every day.

The internalized racism with a multiple personality is incredibly powerful. This became very clear to me as I learned about each of my characters. As they told me about themselves, I began to understand how their identities evolved, racially and culturally. When each split occurred, if the child identified with the father, the Native American identity was preserved and dominated. Of my three inner children who identify with my mother, two believe they are mixed-blood and one, a sixteen year old boy, believes he is totally white, has no Native parent, and never experienced an extended family.

According to a patriarchal worldview, there is only one acceptable personality structure—that of a monolithic, hierarchical system. A feminist view allows for many more diverse pieces, all relating to each other, all containing each one as a whole—a hologram. So, the early love I received continued to provide light for me to go toward, even though there was pain along the way.

I moved from teaching to working with runaway youth with drug and alcohol problems. My life seemed different from the "norm." Others around me verified that children are given no rights. I began to understand how armoring and dissociating evolved as defense mechanisms. I accepted even more that there are many parts on a continuum of myself. I believe there is a spectrum of "other selves" in all people, but not everyone develops dissociative identities. I have very distinct personalities. Some I like. Some I do not. I am still learning about them and I am developing what is called co-consciousness—the ability for all of us to be aware of each other. With this co-consciousness, it is possible to call on each other as a built-in extended family. This recognition was another moving toward the light—an affirmation and a sign of trusting myself.

Over the years, I have taught courses and workshops on racism, feminism, child abuse/domestic violence, women's literature, and history from a Native American perspective. I am consistently amazed by what people either do not know or refuse to hear, especially with regard to racism or violence. I once took a job in a new alcoholism program in Virginia. Newspaper writers interviewed all of the staff and profiled the program. On the first working day, I received a telephone call from a stranger—a woman who invited me over to Sunday supper. She explained that if I came, I would be her "only Indian friend there." While I declined politely, the woman was highly offended that I would not accept such a generous invitation. That was in 1971.

In 1978, when I was teaching at a university in a small Washington town, I was the first Native American teacher in a school of blond-haired blue-eyed young people. I was also teaching the first course on racism at the school as well as a history course from a Native perspective. The course evaluations were filled with comments such as "a challenging course but couldn't a white teacher teach it." I framed one of the evaluations as a way to remind myself to move away from darkness and toward the light.

Given my roots and selves, who am I now? I am someone who knows that love is stronger than hate. I see myself as a Cherokee/Spanish/English two-spirited woman who is a writer and a feminist social worker/teacher. I have been clean and sober for almost twenty-three years after being an alcoholic and amphetamine addict. I am also a woman with hidden disabilities due to poor eyesight and diabetes. I do not consider being a multiple personality a disability. Rather, it provides a series of funny life gifts and challenges through which I am allowed to move. What has having multiple personalities really meant? Whoever I was at the time of pain and trauma realized that "this is too big and I can't handle it alone."

All of these parts of myself inform me. They have determined how I have armored myself, how I have moved forward in life, how I view the world and how and why I write. So much of what has happened to me has seemed like an accident. But it is the Creator's path for me to move toward my balance and harmony in the world—a healing path toward brightness.

Eight years ago, I began a relationship with my partner, who is Jewish, and is decidedly an "egghead." It has been a joyful challenge. We bump into class and cultural values all the time. I talk a tribal "we" and she states an individualistic "I." A piece of ease we have is that I too am an "egghead." Our ethnic and cultural identities are different, sometimes conflictual. But we talk about the differences. We cry, then we laugh, and we both can see the shine of a dew-colored spiderweb wrapped over a flower.

It would be wonderful to end this piece by saying that all is "perfection" in the world. But I cannot. We know there is too much racism and little appreciation of diversities of all kinds in our world. On occasion, when I feel armor surround me, I am quicker than I used to be about letting light come instead—trying to be open. I still feel impatient about the "isms" in the world, including the internal oppressions within myself. All but three of my known twenty-two selves are fine with being a "breed." Some are not comfortable with being two-spirited and some are angry with having a disability or dealing with ableistic attitudes. It is a movement toward self-love and acceptance for me to acknowledge all of my roots. I continue to learn to deal with all of myself as I am in the world and how the world will or will not deal with me. I examine myself. I listen for answers in the light of a slight brushing wind or the dance of a tree or the slow weave of river water in its winter heaviness. I speak out when I think it is needed. I change the things I can and accept what I cannot. That is always going toward self-harmony—the light.

One of Elisi's stories that always held me was that of a Meadowlark. A long time ago, as the Old Ones would say, the Owl and the Meadowlark were discussing how ugly the Meadowlark felt she was. She insisted that her long legs were useless and awkward. Owl insisted that they were a gift of the Creator even if she didn't think they were good for anything. The Meadowlark would fly into the tree and only sing sad songs of no real beauty. Then, one day, Duck came streaking to the Owl in a great rainstorm. She cried that she needed help as her eggs were floating away and would soon be lost. Owl told Duck to ask the Meadowlark for help. So Duck flew to Meadowlark, frantically telling her story. Meadowlark said there was nothing she could do, but Duck insisted that Owl had said she could. So Meadowlark followed Duck to the river's edge where her eggs were. Three were already floating away, as the nest had broken. Meadowlark flew over the eggs, scooped them up with her big feet, and placed them on higher ground. She returned for the second bunch and saved all the eggs. Duck was enormously grateful and thanked Meadowlark profusely. Meadowlark flew back to her own nest feeling rather good. She preened herself and sat high in the tree and suddenly gave forth a great long song. And that is why the Meadowlark still has such a lovely song today.

So I say to all of those of us who are different, in any kind of way—and is that not all of us?—that "you'll be alright."

A prayer: to all of my relations.

25

Waiting for a Taxi

June Jordan

We weren't doing anything. We hadn't hurt anybody, and we didn't want to. We were on holiday. We had studied maps of the city and taken hundreds of photographs. We had walked ourselves dizzy and stared at the other visitors and stammered out our barely Berlitz versions of a beautiful language. We had marveled at the convenient frequency of the Metro and devoured vegetarian crêpes from a sidewalk concession. Among ourselves, we extolled the seductive intelligence and sensual style of this Paris, this magical place to celebrate the two-hundredth anniversary of the French Revolution, this obvious place to sit back with a good glass of wine and think about a world lit by longings for *Liberté, Egalité, Fraternité.*

It was raining. It was dark. It was late. We hurried along, punch-drunk with happiness and fatigue. Behind us, the Cathedral of the Sacred Heart glowed ivory and gorgeous in a flattering wash of artificial, mellow light.

These last hours of our last full day in Paris seemed to roll and slide into pleasure and surprise. I was happy. I was thinking that, as a matter of fact, the more things change, the more things change.

I was thinking that if we—all of us Black, all of us women, all of us deriving from connected varieties of peasant/immigrant/persecuted histories of struggle and significant triumph—if we could find and trust each other enough to travel together into a land where none of us belonged, nothing on earth was impossible anymore.

But then we tried to get a cab to stop for us, and we failed. We tried again, and then again. One driver actually stopped and then, suddenly, he sped away almost taking with him the arm of one of my companions who had been about to open the door to his taxi.

This was a miserable conclusion to a day of so much tourist privilege and delight, a day of feeling powerful because to be a sightseer is to be completely welcome among strangers. And that's the trick of it: No one will say "no" to freely given admiration and respect. But now we had asked for something in return—a taxi. And with that single ordinary request, the problems of our identity, our problems of power, reappeared and trashed our holiday confidence and joy.

I am looking for a way to catch a taxi. I am looking for an umbrella big enough to overcome the tactical and moral limitations of "identity politics"—politics based on gender, class, or race. I am searching for the language of a new political consciousness of identity.

Many of us function on the basis of habits of thought that automatically concede paramount importance to race or class. These habits may, for example, correlate race with class in monolithic, absolute ways: for instance, white people have, Black people have not, or, poor people equals Black people. Although understandable, these dominating habits of thought tend to deny the full functions of race and class, both.

If we defer mainly to race, then what about realities of class that point to huge numbers of poor white people or severe differences of many kinds among various, sometimes conflicting classes of Black people?

Or, if we attend primarily to factors of class, then we may mislead ourselves significantly by ignoring privileges inherent to white identity, per se, or the socially contemptible status of minority-group members regardless of class.

Both forms of analysis encourage exaggerated—or plainly mistaken—suppositions about racial or class grounds for political solidarity. Equally important, any exclusive mode of analysis will overlook, or obviate, the genuine potential for political unity across class and race boundaries.

Habits of racial and class analyses also deny universal functions of gender which determine at least as much, if not more, about any citizen's psychological, economic, and physical life-force and well-being. Focusing on racial *or* class *or* gender attributes will yield only distorted and deeply inadequate images of ourselves.

Traditional calls to "unity" on the basis of only one of these factors—race or class or gender—will fail, finally, and again and again, I believe, because no single one of these components provides for a valid fathoming of the complete individual.

And yet, many of us persist in our race/class habits of thought. And why is that? We know the negative, the evil origins, the evil circumstances that have demanded our development of race and class analyses. For those of us born into an historically scorned and jeopardized status, our bodily survival testifies to the defensively positive meanings of race and class identity because we have created these positive implications as a source of self-defense.

We have wrested, we have invented positive consequences from facts of unequal conflict, facts of oppression. Facts such as I am Black, or I do not have much money, or I am Lithuanian, or I am Senegalese, or I am a girl, or my father mends shoes, become necessary and crucial facts of race and class and gender inside the negative contexts of unequal conflict and the oppression of one group by another, the oppression of somebody weak by somebody more powerful.

Race and *class*, then, are not the same kinds of words as *grass* and *stars*. *Gender* is not the same kind of noun as *sunlight*. *Grass, stars,* and *sunlight* all enjoy self-evident, positive connotations, everywhere on the planet. They are physical phenomena unencumbered by our knowledge or our experience of slavery, discrimination, rape, and murder. They do not presuppose an evil any one of us must seek to extirpate.

I am wondering if those of us who began our lives in difficult conditions defined by our race or our class or our gender identities—I am wondering if we can become more carefully aware of the limitations of race and class and gender analyses, for these yield only distorted and deeply inadequate images of ourselves.

There is another realm of possibility, political unity and human community based upon concepts that underlie or supersede relatively immutable factors of race, class, and gender: the concept of justice, the concept of equality, the concept of tenderness.

I rejoice to see that, last year, more than eight million American voters—Black and white and Latino and Asian and Native American and straight and gay and lesbian and working-class and Ivy League—voted for Jesse Jackson.

I rejoice to see that 300,000 people demonstrated for pro-choice rights in Washington, D.C. on April 9, 1989. Of that 300,000, an estimated 100,000 who stood up for women's rights were men.

I rejoice at this good news, this happy evidence of moral and tactical outreach and response beyond identity politics. This is getting us where all of us need to go.

On the other hand, the hideous despoiling of Prince William Sound in Alaska, the Exxon spill of ten million gallons of oil contaminating 3,000 square miles of those previously clear and lovely waters, makes plain the total irrelevance—the dismal inadequacy—of identity politics, or even national politics. From the torn sky of Antarctica to the Port of Valdez in Alaska, we need vigilant, international agencies empowered to assure the survival of our life-supporting environments.

But we are creatures of habit. I consider myself fortunate, therefore, to keep coming upon immediate, personal events that challenge my inclinations toward a politics as preoccupied with the known old enemies as it is alert to the potential for new allies.

Less than a month ago, I traveled to Liverpool, England, for the first time. I brought with me a selection of my poetry that includes poems written during the 1960s, during the Civil Rights Revolution. I had heard about the poverty characteristic of much of Liverpool, but I was not ready for what I encountered face to face.

One of my hosts was Ruth Grosvenor, a young Black woman who described herself, at lunch, as a half-caste Irish-Caribbean. I asked her for more detail about her family background, and she told me about her mother, who had grown up in Ireland so poor she regularly used to dig in the pig bins, searching for scraps of edible garbage. And for additional pennies, her mother was given soiled sanitary napkins to launder by hand.

Ruth's mother, of course, is white. I had lost my appetite, by now, completely, and I could not comprehend the evident cheeriness of Ruth, who had moved on in conversation to describe the building success of the Africa Art Collective in Liverpool that she codirects.

"But," I interrupted, "what about your mother? What has happened to her?"

"Oh," Ruth told me, instantly switching subjects but not altering her bright and proselytizing tone, "my mother is very happy. She remarried, and she has her own little flat, at last. And she has a telephone!"

I felt mortified by the contrast between what would allow me, a Black woman from America, to feel happy and the late and minimal amenities that could ease the daily experience of a white woman living in England. To speak with Ruth's mother, to speak for Ruth's mother, I would certainly have to eschew facile notions of race and class correlation. On the basis of class alone, Ruth's mother might very well distrust or resent me. On the basis of race alone, I might very well be inclined to distrust or resent Ruth's mother.

And yet, identity politics aside, we both had infinitely more to gain as possible comrades joined against socioeconomic inequities than we could conceivably benefit from hostilities exchanged in serious ignorance of each other.

After our lunch, we drove to the Liverpool public library, where I was scheduled to read. By then we were forty-five minutes late, and on arrival we saw five middle-aged white women heading away towards an old car across the street. When they recognized me, the women came over and apologized: they were really sorry, they said, but they had to leave or they'd get in trouble on the job. I looked at them. Every one of them was wearing an inexpensive faded housedress and, over that, a cheap and shapeless cardigan sweater. I felt honored by their open-mindedness in having wanted to come and listen to my poetry. I thought and I said that it was I who should apologize: I was late. It was I who felt, moreover, unprepared: what in my work, to date, deserves the open-minded attention of blue-collar white women terrified by the prospect of overstaying a union-guaranteed hour for lunch?

Two and a half weeks after Liverpool, I sat sorting through my messages and mail at the university where I teach. One message kept recurring: A young Black man—the son, in fact, of a colleague—had been accused of raping a young white woman. The message, as delivered by my secretary, was this: call So-and-So at once about the young Black man who supposedly raped some white woman.

I was appalled by the accusation leveled against the son of my colleague. I was stunned to learn that yet another female student, of whatever color, had been raped. I felt a kind of nausea overtaking me as I reread the phone messages. They seemed to assume I would commit myself to one side or the other, automatically. The sides, apparently, were Young Black Man versus Young White Woman.

I got up from my desk and snatched the nearest newspaper I could find. I needed to know more. As best I could tell, the young Black student could not have raped anybody; he had several witnesses who established him as being off campus throughout the evening of the alleged assault. As far as I could tell, the young white woman had been raped and she was certain, if mistaken, about the face and the voice of her assailant.

I declined to make any public comment: I do not yet know what the truth of this terrible matter may be. I believe there is a likelihood of mistaken identification on the part of the victim. And I believe that such a mistake, if that is the case, will have created a second victim, the wrongly accused Black student. But these are my opinions merely. And I cannot comprehend why or how anyone would expect me to choose between my gender and racial identities.

I do not agree that rape is less serious than any other heinous felony. I do not agree that the skin color of a female victim shall alienate me from a gender sense of unity and peril. I do not agree that the mistaken accusation of a Black man is less than a very serious crime. I do not agree that the genuine gender concerns that I embody shall alienate me from a racial sense of unity and peril.

But there is a route out of the paralysis of identity politics, even here, in this ugly heartbreaking crisis. There is available to me a moral attachment to a concept beyond gender and race. I am referring to the concept of justice, which I am prepared to embrace and monitor so that justice shall equally serve the young Black man and the young white woman. It is that concept and it is on behalf of both the primary and the possible second victim of yet another on-campus rape that I am willing to commit my energies and my trust.

Returning to the recent rainy evening in Paris, I am still looking for an umbrella big enough to overcome the tactical and moral limitations of identity politics.

Yes, I am exhilarated by the holiday I enjoyed with my friends, and I am proud of the intimate camaraderie we shared. But somebody, pretty soon, needs to be talking, sisterly and brotherly, with the taxi drivers of the world, as well.

Contributors

Faith Adiele, an administrator at Radcliffe College, Harvard University, is writing a memoir about growing up biracial among a family of Scandinavian immigrants in the rural Northwest and then traveling to Africa to meet her father as an adult. Her recent work appears in *Ms.*, *Ploughshares*, Patricia Bell-Scott's *Life Notes: Personal Writings by Contemporary Black Women* (Norton, 1994), and *SAGE: A Scholarly Journal on Black Women and Testimony* (Beacon Press, 1995).

Beth Brant is a Bay of Quinte Mohawk from Tyendinaga Mohawk Territory in Ontario. She is the editor of *A Gathering of Spirit*, a groundbreaking collection of writing and art by Native women (Firebrand Books, USA and the Women's Press, Canada, 1988). She is the author of *Mohawk Trail*, prose and poetry (Firebrand Books and the Women's Press, 1985) and *Food and Spirits*, short fiction (Firebrand Books and Press Gang, 1991).

Beth Brant is currently working on a book of essays entitled *Testimony From the Faithful*. A collection of her speeches and talks, *Good Red Roads*, will soon be published by Women's Press in Canada. She divides her time between living in Michigan and Canada. She is a mother and grandmother and lives with her partner of seventeen years, Denise Dorsz. She has been writing since the age of forty and considers it a gift for her community.

Elly Bulkin is a middle-class Jewish lesbian who was born in the Bronx in 1944. She is coauthor (with Minnie Bruce Pratt and Barbara Smith) of *Yours in Struggle: Three Feminist Perspectives on Anti-Semitism and Racism* (Firebrand Books, 1984). She edited *Lesbian Fiction: An Anthology* (Persephone Press, 1981), and coedited (with Joan Larkin) *Amazon Poetry* (Out & Out Books, 1975) and *Lesbian Poetry: An Anthology* (Persephone Press, 1981). She was a founding editor (1975–1984) of *Conditions: A Magazine of Writing by Women with an Emphasis on Writing by Lesbians*; and of *Bridges: A Journal for Jewish Feminists and Our Friends* (1989–1993). Among the groups she has been politically active in over the past twenty years are: DARE (Dykes Against Racism Everywhere); New Jewish

Agenda; and Women Free Women in Prison (New York City); Feminist Action Network (Albany); and White Women Challenging Racism (Boston). She earns her living as a grants writer, and is the mother of a grown daughter.

Angela Y. Davis is Professor of History of Consciousness at the University of California, Santa Cruz. She is the author of five books, including *Angela Davis: An Autobiography; Women, Race & Class;* and the forthcoming *Ma Rainey, Bessie Smith and Billie Holiday: Black Women's Music and Social Consciousness.* She is currently conducting research on incarcerated women, racism in the U.S. criminal justice system, and alternatives to jails and prisons.

Ruth Frankenberg is an Associate Professor of American Studies at the University of California, Davis. She is the author of the critically acclaimed *White Women, Race Matters: The Social Construction of Whiteness* (University of Minnesota, 1993 and Routledge UK, 1993). She has been active against racism in the classroom and elsewhere since the late 1970s. She is the editor of *Local Whitenesses/Localizing Whiteness,* a collection of examinations of whiteness both international and multiethnic in scope (forthcoming, Duke University Press).

Angela Maria Giudice is an educator, community activist, and training consultant whose work has focused on issues of racism and social justice for the past twwenty-three years. Formerly the executive director of The Multicultural Project, Inc., Angela now works with VISIONS, Inc., a multiracial organization that provides a range of services to support individuals and organizations as they address issues of diversity and oppression and implement personal and institutional changes. In 1995, she was awarded a Drylongo Award for her contribution in the struggle against racism.

Herb Green grew up in the Bahamas and is currently a Ph.D. student in Ethnic Studies at the University of California at Berkeley. In addition to co-teaching a course on comparative lesbian and gay ethnic identities in the United States at the University of California at Berkeley, he also teaches at the Early Academic Outreach Program in San Francisco for underrepresented minority junior high and high school students.

Donald Andrew Grinde, Jr. is Professor of History at the University of Vermont. Some of his books and anthologies include *The Ecocide of American Indian Lands,* with Bruce Johansen (Santa Fe: Clear Light Publishers, 1994); *The Unheard Voices: American Indian Responses to the Columbian Quincentenary,* Carole Gentry and Donald Grinde, eds. (Los Angeles: UC Regents and UCLA American Indian Studies Center, 1994); *Exiles in the Land of the Free: Democracy, the Iroquois Nation and the U.S. Constitution,* Oren Lyons, John Mohawk, and Donald Grinde, Jr. eds. (Santa Fe: Clear Light Publishers, 1992); *The Iroquois and the Founding of the American Indian* (Indian Historian Press, 1977); *Exemplar of History: Native Americans and the Evolution of American Democracy,* with Bruce Johansen (UCLA Indian Studies, 1991).

He is currently completing work on *The Encyclopedia of American Indian Biography,* with Bruce Johansen (New York: Holt, 1995) and another manuscript titled *Human Rights and Home Rule: The Mission Indian Federation of Southern California.* He is a Yamasee Indian who was born in Savannah, Georgia and spends his time away from work at his home on the Navajo reservation in Arizona.

Lisa Kahaleole Chang Hall is a writer, activist, and doctoral candidate in Ethnic Studies at the University of California at Berkeley. She coordinated the first two years of Out/Write, the national lesbian and gay writers conference. Her latest essays appear in *Sisters, Sexperts, Queers: Beyond the Lesbian Nation,* Arlene Stein,ed. (Plume,1993); and *Beyond A Dream Deferred: Multicultural*

Education and the Politics of Excellence, Becky Thompson and Sangeeta Tyagi, eds. (University of Minnesota Press, 1993).

Calvin Hernton is a poet, novelist, writer, social scientist, and Professor of African American Studies and teaches African, West Indian, and African American Literature at Oberlin College. He is the author of *Medicine Man* (1976), *Sex and Racism in America* (1988), *The Sexual Mountain and Black Women Writers* and *Adventure in Sex, Literature and Real Life* (1987), among other books.

Earl Jackson, Jr. is an Associate Professor of Literature at the University of California, Santa Cruz and the author of *Strategies of Deviance: Studies in Gay Male Representation* (1995, Indiana University Press) and *Fantastic Living: The Speculative Autobiographies of Samuel R. Delany* (forthcoming, Oxford University Press). "Oxydol Poisoning" is the first of a series of meta-memoirs of his sexual life that Jackson is writing under the collective title *Breathless Cadenzas*.

June Jordan is Professor of African American Studies at the University of California at Berkeley. She is also a poet, activist, political analyst, and author of *Technical Difficulties: African-American Notes on the State of the Union* (1992), *On Call: Political Essays* (1985), *Civil Wars* (1981), and many other books.

Melanie Kaye/Kantrowitz is the author of *My Jewish Face & Other Stories* and *The Issue Is Power: Essays on Women, Jews, Violence and Resistance* (1992). She is co-editor of *The Tribe of Dina: A Jewish Women's Anthology*, and former editor of *Sinister Wisdom*, one of the nation's oldest lesbian/feminist journals. She earned a Ph.D. in Comparative Literature from the University of California at-Berkeley, where she was an early teacher of women studies. She works as Executive Director of Jews for Racial and Economic Justice in New York City.

Harry Kitano was born and raised as a person of Japanese ancestry in San Francisco's Chinatown, is Professor of Social Welfare and Sociology, and holder of the first Endowed Chair of Japanese American Studies at the University of California at Los Angeles. He has served as a visiting professor at the International Christian University in Tokyo and was the Director of the University of California Tokyo Study Center. He has also held Visiting Professorships at the Hilo and Manoa Campus' of the University of Hawai'i, the University of Bristol in England, and Yamaguchi University in Japan.

Pam Mitchell has written extensively in the queer and feminist press about a variety of issues including class, race, Jewish identity, fat liberation, and sexual abuse. She is a former associate editor of *Sojourner* and former staffwriter and typesetter for *Gay Community News*, editor of the anthology *Pink Triangles: Radical Perspectives in Gay Liberation* (Alyson Publications, 1980), and co-editor of "Call It Class," *Gay Community News's* three-part supplement on class politics in the queer liberation movement (1989–90). She has been organizing workshops and political actions around violence against women and children since 1983, and is currently active in resisting the "false memory" backlash against incest survivors as media coordinator for the Courage to Heal Legal Defense Committee. She is also a member of the collective that runs Inkworks, a worker-owned printshop serving movements for social change in the San Francisco Bay Area.

Cherríe Moraga is a California-based Chicana poet, playwright, and essayist who is the author of *The Last Generation: Poetry and Prose* (1993), *Loving in the War Years: Lo Que Nunca Pasó Por Sus Labios*, (1983) and co-editor, with Gloria Anzaldúa, of the award winning, *This Bridge Called My Back: Writings By Radical Women of Color* (1981, 1983).

Gayle Pemberton is the author of a book of essays, *The Hottest Water in Chicago: Notes of a Native Daughter* (1992). She is currently Chair of African American Studies and the William R. Kenan Professor of the Humanities in the English Department at Wesleyan University in Connecticut.

Her work has been most recently anthologized in *Hiding in Plain Sight*, Wendy Lesser, ed. (Mercury House, 1993) and *The Art of the Personal Essay*, Phillip Lopate, ed. (Anchor, 1994). Her play "And I Am Not Resigned" was produced by the McCarter Theater in 1994. She is a former W.E.B. Du Bois Foundation Fellow and a recent John Simon Guggenheim Memorial Foundation Fellow. She is currently completing a book of essays on Black women in American cinema, *And the Colored Girls Go . . . : Meditations on Black Women in the Movies*, (W.W. Norton).

Gloria Johnson-Powell, M.D., a child psychiatrist, formerly a Professor of Child Psychiatry at the Neuropsychiatric Institute at the University of California at Los Angeles, is currently Professor of Child Psychiatry at Harvard Medical School and the first African American in the 200-year history of the institution to achieve this distinction. Notable among her publications are *The Psychosocial Development of Minority Group Children* (in conjunction with Joe Yamamoto, Armando Morales and Anneliese Romero), *Black Monday's Children: A Study of the Effects of School Desegregation on the Self-Concepts of Southern Children*, *The Afro-American Family: Evaluation and Treatment* (with Barbara Bass and Gail Wyatt), *The Lasting Effects of Child Sexual Abuse* (with Gail Wyatt), and numerous articles and chapters. Dr. Johnson-Powell has traveled, worked and taught at universities in Ethiopia, Uganda, Tanzania, Nigeria, South Africa, and Brazil. She is Director of the Ambulatory Care Center at the Judge Baker Children's Center in Boston. At the present time, she is most excited about coauthoring a book with her daughter, April Powell Willingham, entitled, *The House on Elbert Street: The Psycho-History of the Welfare System and a Welfare Mother*. In 1989, she received the Rosa Parks Award from the Martin Luther King, Jr. Legacy Foundation and the Southern Christian Leadership Conference, and in 1992, the American Psychiatric Association awarded her the Dr. Solomon Carter Fuller Award.

Kate Rushin is an African American poet and teacher. Her book of poems, *The Black Back-Ups*, published in 1993 by Firebrand Books, Ithaca NY, was chosen by the New York Public Library as a "Books for the Teen Age, 1994" selection and was nominated for a Lambda Book Award. Her poems have appeared in *The Black Woman's Health Book*, *Double Stitch*, *This Bridge Called My Back: Writings By Radical Women of Color*, *Home Girls: A Black Feminist Anthology*, *An Ear to the Ground: An Anthology of Contemporary American Poetry*, *New Worlds of Literature*, *Ms.* Magazine, *The English Teaching Forum*, and *Callaloo*. From 1982–1992, she was a member of the New Words Book Store Collective in Cambridge, MA. Currently, she is Director of The Center for African American Studies and Visiting Writer at Wesleyan University in Connecticut.

Vickie Sears is a Cherokee writer and social worker who lives in Seattle, Washington. Her primary practice is with children and adults who have been sexually abused. Her work has been published in *Icon*, *Backbone*, *Feminist Ethics in Psychotherapy*, *A Gathering of Spirit*, *Talking Leaves*, *Spider Grandmother's Daugher*, and *Literature and Language*, a textbook for children. Her book, *Simple Songs* was nominated for a Lambda Award.

Andrew Spieldenner received his A.B. in Ethnic Studies from the University of California, Berkeley in 1995. He teaches, writes, hangs out in bars with friends, and works in the HIV field. His writing appears in a few magazines, including the Vietnamese gay/lesbian magazine *Doi Dien*.

Becky Thompson teaches African American Studies and American Studies at Wesleyan University in Connecticut, is the author of *A Hunger So Wide and So Deep: American Women Speak*

Out on Eating Problems (University of Minnesota Press, 1994) and coeditor of *Beyond a Dream Deferred: Multicultural Education and the Politics of Excellence.* (University of Minnesota Press, 1993). She is a member of White Women Challenging Racism, a Boston-based antiracist organization.

Ramon S. Torrecilha is Director for Public Policy Research on Contemporary Hispanic Issues at the Social Science Research Council.

Sangeeta Tyagi grew up in India and has been living in the United States since 1985. She is coeditor of *Beyond a Dream Deferred: Multicultural Education and the Politics of Excellence* and is completing a book on counter-narrative strategies in Indian women's folk songs. She is Visiting Assistant Professor of Sociology at Boston College, where she teaches comparative race and ethnic relations and Third World feminist theory, and Director of "Exploration," a summer educational program for high school students at Wellesley College.

David Wellman was born in New York City, educated on the northwest side of Detroit, Michigan and in the Civil Rights Movement. He is currently Professor of Community Studies at the University of California, Santa Cruz and Research Sociologist at the Institute for the Study of Social Change, the University of California at Berkeley. He is author of *The Union Makes Us Strong: Radical Unionism on the San Francisco Waterfront* (Cambridge University Press, 1995), *Portraits of White Racism*, 2nd ed. (Cambridge University Press, 1993), and is a contributing author to the *Diversity Project* (Institute for the Study of Social Change, 1992).

Evelyn C. White is author of *Chain Chain Change: For Black Women in Abusive Relationships* (Seal Press, 1995), editor of *The Black Women's Health Book* (Seal Press, 1994), and coauthor of the photography book *The African Americans* (Viking, 1993). A Visiting Scholar in Women's Studies at Mills College, she is the official biographer of Alice Walker. Recent essays appear in *Afrekete: An Anthology of Black Lesbian Writing* (Anchor, 1995) and *The Stories That Shape Us: Contemporary Women Write About The West* (Norton, 1995). She teaches at the "Flight of the Mind" summer writing workshop for women in Oregon.

Sarah Willie teaches Sociology at Bard College. She uses poetry, fiction, and essay to search for truths and to build community.

Photo Credits